A Different Death

Euthanasia & the Christian Tradition

EDWARD J. LARSON & DARREL W. AMUNDSEN

InterVarsity Press
Downers Grove, Illinois

179.7
Lar

InterVarsity Press
P.O. Box 1400, Downers Grove, IL 60515
World Wide Web: www.ivpress.com
E-mail: mail@ivpress.com

InterVarsity Press® is the book-publishing division of InterVarsity Christian Fellowship/USA®, a student movement active on campus at hundreds of universities, colleges and schools of nursing in the United States of America, and a member movement of the International Fellowship of Evangelical Students. For information about local and regional activities, write Public Relations Dept., InterVarsity Christian Fellowship/USA, 6400 Schroeder Rd., P.O. Box 7895, Madison, WI 53707-7895.

Scripture taken from the New American Standard Bible, *©1960, 1962, 1963, 1968, 1971, 1972, 1973, 1975, 1977 by the Lockman Foundation. Used by permission.*

ISBN 0-8308-1518-X

Printed in the United States of America ♻

Library of Congress Cataloging-in-Publication Data

Larson, Edward J. (Edward John)
  A different death : euthanasia in the Christian tradition / by
Edward J. Larson and Darrel W. Amundsen.
      p.   cm.
  Includes bibliographical references and index.
  ISBN 0-8308-1518-X (pbk. : alk. paper)
  1. Euthanasia—Religious aspects—Christianity.   I. Amundsen,
Darrel W.   II. Title.
R726.L369   1998
179.7—dc21   *98-9544*
                                                                                          CIP

| 23 | 22 | 21 | 20 | 19 | 18 | 17 | 16 | 15 | 14 | 13 | 12 | 11 | 10 | 9 | 8 | 7 | 6 | 5 | 4 | 3 | 2 | 1 |

| 18 | 17 | 16 | 15 | 14 | 13 | 12 | 11 | 10 | 09 | 08 | 07 | 06 | 05 | 04 | 03 | 02 | 01 | 00 | 99 | 98 |

In memory of a strong mother,

Jean Uncapher Larson,

who nobly suffered grave physical afflictions

and died with dignity in the natural course;

and

in memory of a loving father,

George Amundsen, a devoted servant of the Lord,

who was spared end-of-life decisions,

for God took him suddenly.

Preface

Facing a New Age of Death

Amid picturesque sea stacks at Cannon Beach on the Oregon coast, residents daily view some of the most spectacular sunsets in the world. Due to the shape of the North American continent, it is one of the last sunsets of the day in the contiguous forty-eight states. On November 4, 1997, that sunset marked the end of a momentous election day. By the initiative and referendum process, Oregon voters had legalized physician-assisted suicide in their state. "Suicide Law Stands," read the banner headline in the next morning's edition of the *Portland Oregonian.*

The *New York Times* headline put the news in context for all Americans: "In Oregon, Opening a New Front in the World of Medicine." By a margin that the *Times* described as "surprising," a state founded by evangelical Presbyterian and Methodist missionaries lured to the fertile Willamette Valley during the 1840s (the prettiest place in God's green earth, they called it) voted to become the first jurisdiction in the Western world since the rise of Christianity to enact a valid statute authorizing physician-assisted suicide or euthanasia.[1] Many residents of the still-largely Christian Cannon Beach resort and retirement community prayed for a different election result that day, but it came just as surely as the sunset.

The vote represented the culmination of a six-year-long legal battle over physician-assisted suicide in Oregon. Advocates of legalized euthanasia had targeted the state for nearly a decade. The nation's leading euthanasia advocacy group, the Hemlock Society, established its headquarters in Oregon during the early 1990s, and its founder and president, bestselling pro-euthanasia author Derek Humphry, moved to the Eugene area. With an electorate split between an anything-goes left wing and a libertarian right wing, both open to radical ideas, and the lowest church-attendance rate in the country, Oregon presented a promising target for the growing euthanasia movement. Yet bills to legalize euthanasia and physician-assisted suicide died in the state senate during the 1991 and 1993 legislative sessions. In 1994 proponents put the issue directly to the voters in a ballot measure limited to physician-assisted suicide. Under the measure any state resident diagnosed by two doctors as having fewer than six months to live could request lethal drugs, which a physician could then legally prescribe unless the patient had psychological disorders or depression causing impaired judgment. In an election dominated by national issues and in which many voters apparently did not understand this complex proposal, the measure narrowly passed with 51 percent of the vote.

Passage of the 1994 ballot measure settled little. Opponents claimed that by allowing physician-assisted suicide, the new law went too far in threatening the lives of the elderly and infirm. Led by Indiana prolife attorney James Bopp, they promptly obtained a federal court order staying implementation of the law. Supporters countered that by not including physician-administered euthanasia, the law did not go far enough in giving options to the terminally ill. "Evidence I have accumulated shows that about 25 percent of assisted suicides fail, which casts doubts on the effectiveness of the new Oregon law," Humphry soon wrote in a letter to the *New York Times*. "The new Oregon way to die will only work if in every instance a doctor is standing by to administer the coup de grace if necessary."[2] Some people from both sides went to the state legislature to alter the law in their favor before it went into effect. After much pushing and pulling, state legislators in 1997 sent the measure back to the voters without change. Either repeal the law or retain it as originally drafted: a high-stakes gamble for opponents, who hoped that voters would not approve the obviously flawed measure a second time. Meanwhile a federal appellate court lifted the stay against the earlier law, and the U.S. Supreme Court refused to hear further challenges against it. Supporters rallied around the original measure as their best hope, and the campaign took off.

Oregon voters could no longer plausibly claim that they did not understand the issue. With only a few local races to distract voters, the "Suicide Measure," as the press dubbed it, dominated the 1997 election in Oregon. The media throughout the state presented stories on the topic almost daily; many of these stories addressed issues of accuracy in diagnosing terminal illness and identifying depression in dying patients. Each side poured millions of dollars into the campaign, a record for any such election in Oregon. Much of this money went to buy television ads, which typically featured doctors or patients pleading for or against the measure. Underscoring the national implications of the vote, most of the funds on both sides came from out-of-state sources, with various Roman Catholic groups contributing over a million dollars to repeal the law while New York billionaire George Soros kicked in $250,000 to retain it. The prestigious American Medical Association and such national evangelical organizations as Focus on the Family tried to rally the antisuicide forces from outside with mailings and pronouncements. "Oregon really is the fire wall on this issue," one Focus on the Family speaker warned. "If the fire wall is breached, it's more likely we'll see it spread across the country." The Hemlock Society and various individual physicians stepped forward to counter these arguments. "Ten years ago, this was just seen as crazy, cuckoo, left-wing stuff," a Hemlock Society board member declared, but now "the establishment . . . takes it seriously."[3]

A record number of Oregonians turned out for an off-year election, and they voted by a three-to-two margin to retain their physician-assisted suicide law. National television networks, joined by media crews from Europe and Asia, broadcast the results live from Portland. Some local election experts attributed the magnitude of the victory to voter frustration at legislators for forcing a second vote on an issue, but most conceded that it also reflected growing public acceptance of physician-assisted suicide. "There was an appeal to libertarian, Republican types and an appeal to Democrats who favor choice," a Portland political scientist reported. Asked about the results, bioethicist Arthur Caplan commented, "You think this is the end? Ha, ha. This is just the beginning." Harvard Medical School professor Ezekiel J. Emanuel, an opponent of euthanasia, added, "It's not just an Oregon issue. What Oregon does is precedent-setting for everyone else."[4]

Americans can no longer afford to ignore the twin issues of physician-assisted suicide and euthanasia or think about them in abstract terms. Oregonians will die by these methods by 1998, and people elsewhere who favor this method of death already talk about joining them. "This will never happen in Pennsylvania," commented one Philadelphia-area contributor to Oregon's prosuicide campaign. "We may have to move to Oregon."[5] But it might happen in Pennsylvania, and it could easily happen for these resourceful Pennsylvanians.

Christians and others who traditionally rejected suicide and euthanasia must reexamine their positions in light of new realities and consider their alternatives. This will be especially pressing for those in Oregon. Within days after the vote, hospitals and health-care providers throughout the state began announcing whether they would participate in the new practice. The state's largest health insurer, Blue Cross Blue Shield of Oregon, stated that it would begin paying for lethal prescriptions. The Roman Catholic-affiliated Providence Health System, however, adopted rules against assisting suicides in its Oregon hospitals and hospices.[6] Oregonians must consider choosing their health-care providers in light of how those providers might handle terminal illnesses. Others need to consider how they should now live and die within the bounds of their beliefs. Awareness of individual values becomes more important than ever when those values are not shared by society or public institutions. Christians could once assume that they would receive treatment that comported with their values from any physician or at any hospital. The euthanasia movement erodes this assurance in the United States and elsewhere.

Through this book the authors seek to assist readers to reexamine the issues of euthanasia and suicide in light of the historic Christian faith. Each of us has attempted to bring his special expertise to bear on these issues. Darrel Amundsen is a professor of classics with training in medieval, Renaissance and medical history. Edward Larson is a professor of history and law. Both of us teach, write and speak about the history of medicine, with Amundsen focusing on matters of medical practice and ethics in ancient and medieval times and Larson specializing in health-care theory and law during the modern period. We have divided the task at hand in accordance with our respective expertise and apologize for the resulting changes in voice.

We recognize that this is a long book, but Christianity has a long history. Although we seek to be comprehensive in our analysis of the subject, we recognize that many readers have special interests. Therefore we organized this book so that its various parts can stand alone.

There are several distinct parts to this book. In the introduction we present an overview of the academic literature on the subject at hand: medical suicide and euthanasia in the Christian tradition. In our first chapter we review the Greek, Roman and Jewish backgrounds from which the distinctively Christian approach to these issues emerged. The next three chapters closely examine the attitudes of the early Christian church on matters that relate to treatment of the terminally ill. These matters include medical practice and ethics, death and dying, suicide and euthanasia. Chapters five and six carry the story through the Catholic Middle Ages and the Protestant Reformation to the advent of modern medicine.

The current generation has experienced both the introduction of powerful, new life-sustaining medical therapies and the spread of secular pluralism. These developments transformed the way that many people in the United States think about matters of death and dying, which in turn influenced our public laws and private ethics. "As recently as 15 years ago, doctors were prosecuted for withdrawing life-support systems from dying patients, even at the behest of a family," The *New York Times* noted in its report on the November 4, 1997, election. "Today in Oregon, after a surprisingly strong vote that takes one state to the frontier of medical ethics, doctors can begin helping terminally ill patients kill themselves. The vote reflects how far and how fast public opinion, at least in this state, has moved on an issue once considered taboo."[7] We examine this recent history in chapters seven through ten, which are followed by a brief conclusion discussing practical alternatives to euthanasia and physician-assisted suicide.

In closing this preface, we wish to thank those who helped to make this book possible. Larson began thinking about legal issues relating to terminal health care while working on the Older Americans Act as staff counsel for the U.S. House of Representatives Committee on Education and Labor during the early 1980s and by then writing a cover article on those issues for *Christianity Today.* That article led to a 1988 book, *Euthanasia: Medical, Spiritual and Legal Issues in Terminal Health Care* (Multnomah), written with *Christianity Today* Washington editor Beth Spring. Since that time, as a professor of history and law at the University of Georgia, Larson continued to ponder those issues and while doing so benefited from meeting with and studying the writings of other scholars working in the field, especially Yale Kamisar, Cicely Saunders, Alexander Morton Capron, David Rothman, Leon Cass, Mark Siegler, Albert Jonsen, John Robertson, George Annas, Thomas Eaton and Rebecca Dresser. Larson also confronted these issues as counsel for Crista Senior Community, which includes an exemplary Christian nursing home. In 1994, in response to a lawsuit in his home state of Washington challenging the state's authority to outlaw physician-assisted suicide, Larson resumed writing and speaking on this topic, including the publication of two law-review articles, participation in various public lectures and debates and the submission of a legal brief to the U.S. Supreme Court in defense of the Washington law. These activities (and his collaboration in them with Kim Colby, Bruce Chapman, John West, and various editors at *DePaul Law Review* and *Seattle University Law Review*) helped to shape the arguments that appear in the later chapters of this book. And he would be remiss in not acknowledging his ongoing conversation about this topic with Patrick Clark, a faithful family doctor with an extensive practice among the elderly and infirm.

Amundsen began thinking about this issue earlier than did Larson, as a professor of classics at Western Washington University with a research specialty in the relationship of medicine with law, ethics and religion in classical antiquity and the Middle Ages. Various publications resulted in an invitation to join the Hastings Center's Death and Dying Research Group, soon renamed the Death, Suffering, and Well-Being Research Group. Stimulating discussions with and presentations to that disparate group of scholars extended over several years. As adjunct professor of interdisciplinary studies at Regent College, he helped to develop and teach a course in the theology of suffering. From these and related ventures, publications ensued in such journals as the *Hastings Center Report, Crux, Christian Bioethics* and *Christian Research Journal,* and in a book of essays, *Medicine, Society and Faith in the Ancient and Medieval Worlds* (Johns Hopkins University Press).

Drawing on our different backgrounds, we joined forces to write this book and have since profited immensely from the editorial assistance of Rodney Clapp, a distinguished author in his own right. We thank all those who inspired and influenced our thinking on this topic, and our families for their patience with this project, all the while acknowledging that we alone are responsible for the failings of this book.

Introduction

Euthanasia & Christianity—
The Nature of the Controversies

Term-paper assignment for Sociology 302: Research and write a well-documented paper on the position of Christianity on active, voluntary euthanasia. In preparing your paper, first summarize the extreme anti-euthanasia position of modern Protestant prolife advocacy groups and the Roman Catholic hierarchy. Then research the history of Christian attitudes in order to determine whether the positions articulated by contemporary Christians accurately reflect the values of earlier generations of Christians. Note: you will have to investigate the history of suicide to discover earlier Christian position(s) on active, voluntary euthanasia. You may wish to start with a seminal work that has had a greater impact on modern conceptualization of suicide than any other. It is by the founder of French sociology, Émile Durkheim: *Le suicide: Étude sociologique.* Although it was published in 1897, it was not translated into English until 1951. Copies of the English translation are on reserve in the library.

What will the typical student find?

First, she will see that Durkheim created three categories of suicide that he explained with reference to social structures: egoistic, resulting from a lack of social integration; anomic, precipitated by the destabilizing effects of sudden negative or positive social change; and altruistic, resulting from overintegration, especially when the individual is completely controlled by religious or political groups.

Second, she will adopt Durkheim's definition of suicide: "All cases of death resulting directly or indirectly from a positive or negative act of the victim himself, which he knows will produce this result."[1]

Third, she will learn that Durkheim was determined to avoid the question of motivation or even whether the individual desired to die. It is suicide if one believes that one's actions or passivity will eventuate in one's own death. Hence Durkheim classified the death of Christian martyrs as altruistic suicide, since

> though they did not kill themselves, they sought death with all their power and behaved so as to make it inevitable. To be suicide, the act from which death must necessarily result need only have been performed by the victim with full knowledge of the facts. Besides, the passionate enthusiasm with which the believers in the new religion faced final torture shows that at this moment they had completely discarded their personalities for the idea of which they had become the servants.[2]

According to Durkheim, dying for one's beliefs is suicide. Since those who thus committed "suicide" were, in Durkheim's construct, victims of pathological social phenomena, martyrs were victims not of the people who killed them but of their own religious group's demand for excessive integration, control and regimentation.

So to Durkheim martyrs were suicides. But weren't the Christians who were martyred by the Romans heroes to the early Christians? The student next scans the electronic library information system for works on suicide that may possibly include references to early Christianity. One sounds especially intriguing: *The Savage God: A Study of Suicide* by Alfred Alvarez. Several copies of this popular and influential book prove to reside in the stacks. Although he is writing on a historical topic, Alvarez is not a historian. He is a poet and a literary critic, but the student does not know this. To her the first chapter, "The Background," looks pertinent. Skimming it, she finds that the very semantic ambiguity of "suicide" and synonymous expressions such as "self-murder" and "self-destruction,"

> all expressions reflecting the associations with murder . . . also reflect the difficulty the Church had in rationalizing its ban on suicide, since neither the Old nor the New Testament directly prohibits it. There are four suicides recorded in the Old Testament—Samson, Saul, Abimelech and Achitephel—and none of them earns adverse comment. In fact, they are scarcely commented on at all. In the New Testament, the suicide of even the greatest criminal, Judas Iscariot, is recorded as perfunctorily; instead of being added to his crimes, it seems a measure of his repentance. Only much later did the theologians reverse the implicit judgment of St. Matthew and suggest that Judas was more

damned by his suicide than by his betrayal of Christ. In the first years of the Church, suicide was such a neutral subject that even the death of Jesus was regarded by Tertullian, one of the most fiery of early Fathers, as a kind of suicide. . . . The idea of suicide as a crime comes late in Christian doctrine, and as an afterthought. It was not until the sixth century that the Church finally legislated against it, and then the only Biblical authority was a special interpretation of the Sixth Commandment: "Thou shalt not kill." The bishops were urged into action by St. Augustine; but he, as Rousseau remarked, took his arguments from Plato's *Phaedo,* not from the Bible. Augustine's arguments were sharpened by the suicide mania which was, above all, the distinguishing mark of the early Christians. . . .[3]

Viewed from the Christian Heaven, life itself was at best unimportant; at worst, evil: the fuller the life, the greater the temptation to sin. Death, therefore, was a release awaited or sought out with impatience. In other words, the more powerfully the Church instilled in believers the idea that this world was a vale of tears and sin and temptation, where they waited uneasily until death released them into eternal glory, the more irresistible the temptation to suicide became. Even the most stoical Romans committed suicide only as a last resort; they at least waited until their lives had become intolerable. But for the primitive Church, life was intolerable whatever its conditions. Why, then, live unredeemed when heavenly bliss is only a knife stroke away? Christian teaching was at first a powerful incitement to suicide.[4]

[Suicide was] an act which during the flowering of Western civilization had been tolerated, later admired, and later still sought as a supreme mark of zealotry, became finally the object of intense moral revulsion.[5]

According to Alvarez, Augustine was primarily responsible for this dramatic change.

Wanting more than just two authorities to cite in her bibliography, the student picks another promising book off the shelf. This one, obviously written by a philosopher, is entitled *Ethical Issues in Suicide.* In it the author, Margaret Pabst Battin, provides further support for Durkheim's and Alvarez's interpretation of early Christianity's changing attitude to suicide:

Christianity *invites* suicide in a way in which other major religions do not. . . . The lure exerted by the promise of reunion with the deceased, release of the soul, the rewards of martyrdom, and the attainment of the highest spiritual states, including union with God, all occur in Christianity. . . . Thus the question of the permissibility of suicide arises, though often only inchoately, for any sincere believer in a religious

tradition of this sort, whether that individual's present life is a happy
one or filled with suffering. Religious suicide is not always a matter of
despair; it is often a matter of zeal. The general problem presented by
the promise of a better afterlife may be strongest in Christianity, since
the afterlife of spiritual bliss depicted by Christianity is a particularly
powerful attraction. . . . The early Christian community appeared to
be on the verge of complete self-decimation in voluntary martyrdom
and suicide until Augustine took a firm position against such practices.
. . . Although there is little reason to think that Augustine's position is
authentically Christian . . . it nevertheless rapidly took hold and within
an extremely short time had become universally accepted as fundamental Christian law.[6]

An endnote sends the student to *The Sanctity of Life and the Criminal Law* by
the noted philosopher and legal theorist Glanville Williams. Yet one more
citation may mean a better grade. This book lends even further weight to
what the student is now convinced is the record of a religious tradition that
essentially had done an about-face on the morality of suicide:

There is no condemnation of suicide in the New Testament, and little
to be found among the early Christians, who were, indeed, morbidly
obsessed with death. . . . The Christian belief was that life on earth was
important only as a preparation for the hereafter; the supreme duty
was to avoid sin, which would result in perpetual punishment. Since
all natural desires tended toward sin, the risk of failure was great. Many
Christians, therefore, committed suicide for fear of falling before
temptation. It was especially good if the believer could commit suicide
by provoking infidels to martyr him, or by austerities so severe that
they undermined the constitution, but in the last resort he might do
away with himself directly.[7]

Now having more than enough authorities to cite in her paper, the student
prepares to leave the library. Departing from the stacks, she remembers
that she needs to check a source for another project. While browsing in
the reference section of the library, she notices a large set entitled *The
Anchor Bible Dictionary*. If there is an article here about suicide it would be
interesting to see if it parrots what the religious right says. There is indeed
an article on suicide. Much to the student's surprise it begins, "The idea
that suicide is both a sin and a crime is a relatively late Christian invention,
taking its impetus from Augustine's polemics against the 'suicidal mania'
of the Donatists in the late 4th and early 5th centuries. . . ."[8]

So it is not just sociologists and philosophers who are aware that
Christians had diametrically changed their attitude toward suicide within
the first few centuries of Christianity's existence. The author of this article

in a Bible dictionary must be a theologian. Get his name—Arthur J. Droge—and check the computer to see if he has written more extensively on this subject. A combined subject/name search identifies Droge as the author of an intriguing article, "Did Paul Commit Suicide?" In the periodical room she locates the article, which begins,

> The question this article will explore may appear disturbing at first sight, and for good reason. Since Augustine's time, the church has condemned suicide as a sin—a sin beyond redemption, just like apostasy and adultery. How then could Paul, the premier apostle of early Christianity, even have contemplated suicide, much less gone through with it?[9]

After describing the openness of the Old and New Testaments to suicide, Droge returns to the question of whether Paul may have committed suicide with the caution that his readers must consider the question "in the context in which suicide was regarded in Paul's time, not from our own perspective and not from the perspective of the post-Augustinian period."[10] After discussing several passages in letters written by or attributed to Paul, Droge concludes that although Paul had suppressed the urge to kill himself that he expressed in Philippians 1:23, later

> what if Paul believed that his missionary work was finished, that the divine necessity that had been placed upon him had been finally removed? What if he became convinced that "he had fought the good fight and finished the race," that the time of his departure had come? What if Paul reached the position of failing health or old age, so that he could no longer carry out his divine commission? Then I think it equally possible that Paul would have committed suicide and done so with a clear conscience and with the expectation that he would pass into immortality, united with Christ.[11]

Paul may have committed suicide? Wouldn't that throw the religious right into disarray! Curious to find out whether Droge wrote anything more on suicide in early Christianity, the student makes another trip to the electronic card catalog. He had collaborated with James D. Tabor in writing *A Noble Death: Suicide and Martyrdom Among Christians and Jews in Antiquity.*[12] This book, devoted to a study of suicide in antiquity, mostly in early Christianity, warrants more than providing some hastily scribbled quotations. So, with Droge and Tabor checked out and in her backpack, she heads for the dorm. Reading the book intermittently over the next two days she finds that, rejecting for their purposes the word *suicide* as "a recent innovation and pejorative term," Droge and Tabor prefer the designation "voluntary death." "By this term we mean to describe the act resulting from an individual's intentional decision to die, either by his own agency, by another's, or by contriving the circumstances in which death is the known, ineluctable result." The authors concede that their definition of voluntary death is similar to Durkheim's definition of suicide and assert that theirs is "intended to be morally neutral, since our enterprise is not one of moral (or clinical) judgment but an attempt to understand the ways in which voluntary death was evaluated in antiquity."[13]

Emphasizing that both "suicide" and "martyrdom" are semantically and conceptually ambiguous, Droge and Tabor argue that they have reduced the ambiguity and confusion by providing the concept of "voluntary death" as a much more objective grid for the historian. They dislike the word *suicide* especially because of its typically pejorative connotations. They convey a positive view of voluntary death; a voluntary death is a noble death, as the title of their book declares. And they acknowledge in their conclusion that their purpose had been "to deconstruct the 'linguistics of suicide' by examining the precise terms and formulations employed in antiquity to denote the act of voluntary death."[14]

"It is a profound irony of Western history," Droge and Tabor maintain, that Christian theologians, beginning with Augustine, "condemned the act of voluntary death as a sin for which Christ's similar act could not atone."[15] "Despite the claim of Augustine and later theologians, the New Testament expresses no condemnation of voluntary death. . . . Yet, to say only that the writers of the New Testament did not condemn voluntary death is to miss the positive significance they attached to the act. The authors of the Gospel created a Jesus who died by his own choice, if not by his own hand."[16] They ask regarding Jesus' death, "Was it the legal execution of a criminal, an example of heroic martyrdom, or a case of suicide?"[17] Judas's death was similar to Jesus' in that both were voluntary: "In the *Umwelt* of early Christianity the act of taking one's life was judged to be acceptable and, in certain circumstances, noble. This was Matthew's implicit judgment on Judas' death. Judas was condemned for betraying the Messiah, not for killing himself. According to Matthew, Judas' act of self-destruction was the measure of his remorse and repentance."[18]

Droge and Tabor are especially interested in the apostle Paul's supposed "fascination with death and his desire to escape from life"[19] and suggest that "for Paul, an individual could kill himself and be 'glorifying God with his body' by doing so. . . . In a world-negating system like the apostle Paul's, the question became how to justify continued existence in the world rather than voluntary death."[20] "Voluntary death," as they conclude their book, "was one of the ideals on which the church was founded."[21] So persuasive is their argument that Hemlock Society founder Derek Humphry enthusiastically exclaims on their book's dust jacket, "This book will upset traditional Christian views about the right to choose to die."

The student is now well equipped to write a well-documented paper that will greatly impress her professor. The substance of her argument will be that the position from which Protestant prolife activists and the Roman Catholic hierarchy argue against active, voluntary euthanasia, including physician-assisted suicide, would be substantially weakened if they were aware of the history of their own tradition. The essence of her historicotheological section will be as follows:

1. Not only does the Old Testament nowhere condemn suicide, but it records several suicides without any hint of disapproval.

2. The New Testament nowhere forbids suicide. The one suicide that it relates, that of Judas, is presented as a mark of his repentance rather than as a further sin. Even Jesus' death was in a sense suicide. And there is a real possibility that the apostle Paul committed suicide.

3. So eager were many early Christians to realize their fullness of joy in heaven that they committed suicide if they were unable to provoke pagans to put them to death as martyrs.

4. So depressing was the burden of sin and guilt of many early Christians that they killed themselves in despair.

5. So intensely did many early Christians despise their sinful flesh that they killed themselves, often through severe asceticism.

6. So low a regard did early Christians have for their lives that they were willing to die for their faith, some even volunteering for or provoking martyrdom. And martyrdom is suicide.

7. Augustine was the first Christian to denounce suicide as a sin. His negative influence has subsequently tempered the Christian attitude to suicide, including both active and passive euthanasia.

Historicism in the Courts

Working in a secular academic environment, students not well grounded in both Christian history and theology will more than likely arrive at these same conclusions, relying on sources such as those that we have quoted. Adult church members grappling with the issue for themselves or family members may well reach similar conclusions. What is even more worrisome for public policy, these students and adults will find themselves in the company of two judges who have recently ruled on the constitutionality of physician-assisted suicide, Michigan appellate-court judge Andrew Kaufman and Stephen Reinhardt of the Ninth Circuit U.S. Court of Appeals in California.

Kaufman was particularly impressed by the U.S. Supreme Court's landmark 1973 abortion-rights opinion, *Roe* v. *Wade*. In that opinion Justice Harry Blackmun, writing for the majority, had assured his audience that the court had investigated both the medical-legal history of abortion and the history of attitudes toward abortion generally, beginning with antiquity.[22] In dissent even Justice William Rehnquist compliments the majority for having brought "to the decision of this troubling question both extensive historical fact and a wealth of legal scholarship."[23] Two decades later, in his "Opinion and Order Concerning the Constitutionality of the Michigan Statute Proscribing Assisted Suicide" in one of several prosecutions of retired pathologist Jack Kevorkian for assisting the suicide of chronically ill patients, Kaufman wrote, "Most strikingly, in *Roe* v. *Wade* . . . the Court justified its result, in part, by an appeal to history."[24] Kevorkian had insisted that a right to commit suicide is fundamental to those liberty interests protected by the Fourteenth Amendment. Kaufman related that "the prosecutor argues that a right cannot be deemed fundamental, and thus entitled to protection through the 'liberty' provision of the Fourteenth Amendment, unless it is based upon our Nation's history and tradition. In contrast, the defendant insists that history and tradition can be completely ignored in distilling the existence of a fundamental liberty interest. This Court rejects both approaches."[25]

In order to arrive at this decision, Kaufman felt it incumbent "to analyze whether the claimed right is 'deeply rooted in this Nation's history and traditions.'"[26] After mentioning that "many commentators . . . have disputed the Roe Court's historical analysis," he asseverated: "To the extent that Roe's historical analysis is not totally accurate, the decision is grounded more in a contemporary view of what is 'implicit in the concept of ordered liberty.'"[27] Hence it is reasonable to assume that in formulating his own legal opinion Kaufman would be cautious in accepting as "totally accurate" the Roe court's historical analysis and be thorough in his own historical research so as to ensure that his own historical analysis be "totally accurate." At the conclusion of his historical analysis he exclaimed, "It is striking that so much of the historical analysis of the Roe Court with respect to abortion mirrors historical traditions with respect to suicide."[28]

Kaufman wrote, "Just as the Roe Court found some support for abortion being freely practiced in Greek and Roman times, there is significant support that historical attitudes toward suicide were not in line with a blanket proscription. The idea that one's honor or one's quality of life would allow society to recognize the act of suicide as not contrary to societal norms has great historical support."[29] The "great historical support," which Kaufman marshals in reference to ancient attitudes toward suicide, is the popularized account written by Alvarez.[30]

Kaufman asserted, "Much of what we know about Greek society supports the conclusion that suicide in many circumstances was acceptable." In support of this statement he quoted Alvarez:

> Plato . . . suggested that if life itself became immoderate, then suicide became a rational, justifiable act. Painful disease or intolerable constraint were sufficient reasons to depart. . . . Within a hundred years of Socrates' death, the Stoics had made suicide into the most reasonable and desirable of all ways out.[31]

"These attitudes toward suicide," Kaufman wrote, "continued during Roman times." He again quoted Alvarez:

> The evidence is, then, that the Romans looked on suicide with neither fear nor revulsion, but as a carefully considered and chosen validation of the way they had lived and the principles they had lived by. . . . According to Justinian's *Digest*, suicide of a private citizen was not punishable[32] if it was caused by "impatience of pain or sickness, or by another cause," or by "weariness of life . . . lunacy, or fear of dishonor." Since this covered every rational cause, all that was left was the utterly irrational suicide "without cause," and that was punishable.[33]

After summarizing and quoting from Alvarez's assessment of Christianity's effect on Western attitudes toward suicide, Kaufman quoted from the Supreme Court's *Roe* v. *Wade* opinion regarding abortion that during classical antiquity "only the Pythagorean school of philosophers frowned upon the related act of suicide." Depending on the works of the late classicist Ludwig Edelstein, the court attributed the Hippocratic Oath to this school. Kaufman explained,

> The Roe Court goes on to determine that the Pythagorean school was a minority view, and "'in no other stratum of Greek opinion were such views held or proposed in the same spirit of uncompromising austerity.'[34] . . . Edelstein then concludes that the Oath originated in a group representing only a small segment of Greek opinion and that it certainly was not accepted by all ancient physicians. He points out that medical writings down to Galen (A.D. 130-200) 'give evidence of the violation of almost every one of its injunctions.' But with the end of antiquity a decided change took place. Resistance against suicide and against abortion became common. The Oath came to be popular. The emerging teachings of Christianity were in agreement with the Pythagorean ethic. The Oath 'became the nucleus of all medical ethics' and 'was applauded as the embodiment of truth.' Thus, suggests Dr. Edelstein, it is 'a Pythagorean manifesto and not the expression of an absolute standard of medical conduct.'"[35]

The Roe court's dependence on Edelstein was unfortunate, for Edelstein was somewhat of an iconoclast. While his analysis of the Hippocratic Oath was the fruit of exquisitely competent classical scholarship, his support of his thesis of the Pythagorean authorship of the oath,[36] which is now accepted by few if any specialists in ancient medical history, suffers from the inevitably debilitating effects of special pleading. Alvarez's amateurish survey is rife with minor errors of fact. Nevertheless, what Kaufman provided from Alvarez and from Blackmun's opinion in *Roe* v. *Wade* is accurate insofar as it conveys the fact that throughout classical antiquity there was no blanket prohibition of either abortion or suicide. It should be stressed, however, that in classical antiquity there also was a strong though minority view that would sanction abortion and suicide only under the most circumscribed conditions. Evidence for that position can be found outside the oath, as will be seen in chapter one.

While Blackmun's and Kaufman's assessments of suicide in classical antiquity are simplistic, the latter's analysis of suicide in early Christianity is blatantly inaccurate.

As we have seen, Kaufman adopted without reservations Blackmun's acceptance in *Roe* v. *Wade* of Edelstein's thesis that the Hippocratic Oath was a Pythagorean manifesto and that its condemnation of abortion therefore represented a minority view. "But with the end of antiquity," Kaufman quoted from Blackmun, "a decided change took place. Resistance against suicide and against abortion became common. The Oath came to be popular. The emerging teachings of Christianity were in agreement with the Pythagorean ethic."[37]

An adequate discussion of the variety of possible alternative interpretations of these four sentences would take several pages. By "the end of antiquity" did Blackmun mean the period that began with the legalization of Christianity (313) and closed with the fall of the western Roman Empire (476)? The "decided change" that he maintained took place then is that "resistance against suicide and against abortion became common." Blackmun appears to have been saying that there were two related causes for this change: "the Oath came to be popular," and "the emerging teachings of Christianity were in agreement with the Pythagorean ethic." Who were then resisting suicide and abortion? Apparently Christians. With whom did the oath come to be popular? Apparently Christians. Just when were the teachings of Christianity, which ostensibly were consonant with the ethics of the oath (i.e., for Blackmun, "with the Pythagorean ethic"), emerging? Is Blackmun's suggestion that Christian teachings did not "emerge" until the "end of antiquity" an indication that he accepted the contention of some historians and theologians that it is inaccurate to speak of an orthodox or even a normative Christianity before late antiquity? Or is he saying that the Christian teachings did not emerge as dominant until late antiquity?

In either event Blackmun does not give the slightest intimation that he questioned the very well-known and easily demonstrable fact that even the earliest post-New Testament Christian literature fervently and uncompromisingly condemned abortion. Yet Kaufman does just this when he asserts, "It is striking that so much of the historical analysis of the Roe Court with respect to abortion mirrors historical traditions with respect to suicide" and his unquestioning endorsement of Alvarez's thesis that suicide was both approved and widely practiced by Christians before the "end of antiquity" (the time of the Augustinian "reversal").

Although he may well be a competent legal scholar, Kaufman has proven careless in his historical analysis. In great part his dismissing of "history and tradition" as irrelevant to the case[38] appears to have stemmed from his misunderstanding of history. This raises an obvious question. If Kaufman's understanding of the history of the issue had not been distorted by the glaring inaccuracies of his primary authority, Alvarez, would he have been more inclined to see greater merit in the prosecutor's argument regarding the relevance of "history and tradition"? Yet so long as history appeared inconclusive with respect to the church's position on suicide, it could provide scant guidance to the court.

We have already seen the extent to which Kaufman depended on Alvarez for his understanding of the place of suicide in the Old Testament and in early Christianity. Judge Reinhardt of the Ninth Circuit Court also relied in great part upon Alvarez and adopted four assumptions regarding suicide in early Christianity, all of which are mistaken or misleading.[39]

First, Reinhardt asserts that because the church promoted such a bleak view of life and such a glorious view of heaven, suicide became an increasingly strong temptation for early Christians. Yet there is, as we shall argue, no evidence of any Christian, during the early centuries of Christianity, committing suicide in order to accelerate his entering heaven.

Second, Reinhardt described the type of suicide in question as martyrdom. Yet martyrdom was, as we shall see, a special situation involving, prior to the legalization of Christianity, state persecution of a specific religion. Martyrdom was not indicative of a general desire for death per se but only for death at the hands of another for the sake of Christ, an imitation of Christ's death. It was that which was "tempting." Death as a release from physical or mental suffering was not at issue. Hence Christianity did not teach that one had a general right to control the end of one's own life but that one was not permitted to do so.

Third, Reinhardt suggests that the martyrdoms, which were predominantly of Donatists (a splinter group that arose nearly simultaneously with the legalization of Christianity), so threatened to deplete the ranks of Christendom that Augustine condemned suicide in general as a damnable sin. But if the church were to have adopted an antisuicide stance because of utilitarian concerns, it surely would have done so earlier when Christians were a small minority, rather than during Augustine's lifetime when the church was being flooded with converts whose attraction to Christianity was the social and political advantages legally available to Christians. Further, if Augustine's concern was that the ranks of Christendom were being depleted by martyrdom and if these martyrs were Donatists (i.e., members of a heretical sect), then allowing the practice to continue would have reduced the ranks of the very people who were the church's greatest religious competition at that time. And finally to regard the antics of the Donatists (primarily those of the Circumcellions, an extremist group of Donatists) as normative for the Christian community of late antiquity is tantamount to portraying cult leaders such as Jim Jones and David Koresh as typical of late-twentieth-century American Christianity. Hence Reinhardt's argument is not only historically inaccurate but also illogical.

Fourth, Reinhardt adds that before Augustine's time there was considerable confusion between suicide and martyrdom within the Christian community. Yet there is still considerable confusion and disagreement regarding the precise nuances and application of the word *suicide*. An entirely objective and consistent definition of suicide will never be made to everyone's satisfaction. The differences are so significant between, for instance, hanging oneself after being jilted by one's lover, burning oneself to death as a public protest against a government's policies, sacrificing one's life to save others' lives, and being executed for refusing to renounce one's most deeply held convictions that to label them all as "suicide" and then insist that anyone who approves of any of them approves of all forms of suicide flies in the face of even the most basic logic and common sense. Reinhardt's analogy to martyrdom sheds little light on the particular issue of physician-assisted suicide, which even he distinguishes from other types of suicide,[40] just as he should have distinguished martyrdom.

Suicidal Complexity

As we have seen, Droge and Tabor contributed to this confusion in *A Noble Death*, which seeks to provide a noble Christian pedigree for physician-assisted suicide. While insisting that "when the conventional distinction between 'suicide' and 'martyrdom' is read back into antiquity, it conceals rather than reveals the issues,"[41] their labeling as "voluntary death" everything that Durkheim calls "suicide" proves nothing other than that it is as meaningless or as misleading a grid to apply to any period of history as is Durkheim's. At least one reviewer of Droge and Tabor's book understands this. William Birmingham observes in *Cross Currents: The Journal of the Association for Religion and Intellectual Life,* of which he is an editor:

> The authors' perhaps unconscious tendency to legitimate one form of voluntary death, suicide, by too closely associating it with others—death for the sake of honor, martyrdom for the sake of faith—blurs ethical lines and vitiates readers' confidence in their handling of evidence that neither the ancient Jews nor the pre-Augustinian Christians proscribed suicide with the virulence that characterized the attitudes of later centuries.[42]

The first paragraph of Droge and Tabor's "Conclusion" reads,

> Why did the Augustinian condemnation of voluntary death succeed in reversing the perspective of an entire period of history, a period that Augustine himself is often thought to have brought to a close? We confess not to have a satisfying answer to that question, save for the obvious one of the enormous influence of Augustine's legacy in the West. But this does not explain why a similar attitude toward voluntary death came to be held in Eastern Christianity, where Augustine was little read. Have we then misinterpreted the evidence by making too much of the Augustinian "reversal"?[43]

The answer that they should have given to this last question is yes, and then they should have recognized both the church's clear historical repudiation of suicide and its consistent distinction between that act and martyrdom. What confused Droge and Tabor has not been confusing to Christians in the past.

Our book traces that historical Christian attitude toward euthanasia and physician-assisted suicide. We begin by describing the relevant features of the pluralistic milieu in which Christianity arose. What were the pertinent religious and ethical foundations of Gentile converts? And what would Jewish converts to Christianity have brought from their tradition that would have informed their understanding of the issues that we are considering? We devote a disproportionately large number of pages to early Christian attitudes toward suicide performed as a means to avoid suffering. The reason should be obvious: the most egregious misunderstandings and distortions that currently prevail regarding physician-assisted suicide come from that epoch. We demonstrate the historical constancy, from the first century to the present, of Christianity's rejection of suicide, particularly to escape the suffering that is the common liability of all humanity.

We also trace the gradual development of the physician's obligation to preserve life. We see how, in the era of modern medical technology, such a perceived obligation has led to the medical and moral horrors that precipitated the right-to-die movement as patients, in the name of personal autonomy, asserted their legal right to refuse life-sustaining treatments that merely prolonged the dying process. We then examine how this legitimate movement has led some people to make misguided calls for legalized euthanasia, a practice that finds no support in the Christian tradition and would inevitably result in less rather than more patient autonomy.

We are aware of how frightfully complex and bewilderingly subtle is the moral realm with which we are dealing. While few people would dispute that it is suicide for a terminally ill person to expedite his or her own death through, for example, taking a deadly drug, would many people label as suicide the decision by a terminally ill patient to refuse to be attached to life-support systems? We think not. Is it assisted suicide for a physician, at the request or with the consent of the patient who is on the threshold of death, to increase the level of morphine to a lethal dosage when anything short of that will not alleviate his or her unbearable pain? We see a distinction here. Once a Christian classifies any such category as suicide, are all those individuals thus labeled as suicides to be regarded as dying in sin? Surely not, we believe. We must employ great caution and Christian charity in examining individual cases. We do no service, however, to the cause of Christ and to truth if we insist that those Christians who flagrantly provoked pagans to martyr them and those ascetics who, through severe mortification and self-denial, killed themselves because of the supposedly expiatory spiritual rewards of severe asceticism must not be classified as suicides. And what of the eternal destiny of those who, suffering from the unfathomable misery that is the despair of severe depressive illness, take their own lives?

Joseph Bayly was a man of deep spirituality. *The Last Thing We Talk About* (originally entitled *The View from a Hearse*) is dedicated "to the memory of three sons Danny, John and Joe who introduced us to death—its tragedy, its glory." He writes,

> The Mosaic law commanded, "Thou shalt not kill." This includes killing oneself, although the Bible does not single suicide out for special discussion. There are five instances of suicide in the Bible. All were mature adults, most were outstanding leaders. The best known is Judas Iscariot, who hanged himself in remorse for betraying Jesus. The examples indicate that suicide is not the will of God. . . . At one time the church taught that suicide was the greatest sin, greater even than murder. The reason: there is no opportunity to repent afterward.

(But how long does it take to repent and ask for God's forgiveness?) The Bible does not contain a hierarchy of sins. And all sin, including suicide, is included in the forgiving work of Jesus Christ. Can a mind break under pressure, like an arm or leg? I believe it can, and I believe that God "knows our frame, remembers that we are dust." This does not condone suicide; it does commit the person who takes his own life to God rather than to man's judgment. And thank God, He knows all the factors in the total situation.[44]

The issues before us are not black and white. There are many shades of gray. But before we proceed, it is imperative that we provide you, the reader, with the definitions of the terms that we shall be using regularly — terms that, as the preceding introduction suggests, are inevitably imprecise around the edges and controversial to the core. A standard dictionary definition of *suicide* is "the act or an instance of intentionally killing oneself."[45] The term *physician-assisted suicide* adds that a doctor provided the means by which a patient commits suicide with the intention that the patient so use those means and typically is understood to involve situations in which the patient has severely diminished quality of life.

Euthanasia is derived from Greek words meaning "good death." According to Carlos F. Gomez, a University of Virginia Medical School professor who has studied the practice of euthanasia in the Netherlands, this term has "come to connote a shortening of the agonal stages before death and a relatively painless, easy passage into death. In modern Holland (and in most commentaries on the subject) it also implies that the agent or coagent in the act is a physician."[46] We accept and use these conventional definitions but recognize that in various individual cases the distinction between these terms is blurred or lost. Is it suicide or physician-assisted suicide if the doctor prescribes pain medication that the patient predictably hoards into a lethal dose? Is it physician-assisted suicide or euthanasia if the doctor puts a lethal dose of medication in the mouth of a patient who then willingly and knowingly swallows it? When we use the word *euthanasia* without a qualifying adjective, we mean an active medical intervention (whether requested by the patient or not) done with the intention of causing death. Sometimes, for the sake of clarity, we modify *euthanasia* with the adjective *voluntary* or *involuntary*. Also we occasionally use or quote others using, in place of *euthanasia*, such common expressions as *mercy killing* and *physician aid in dying*, although the latter also includes physician-assisted suicide. We shall try to use the most appropriate term in describing various situations but maintain that the precise term is not critical so long as readers understand the action being discussed.

A distinct line exists between forgoing life-sustaining medical treatment and actively intervening with the intent to cause death. Although we recognize both that patients die and doctors allow death to happen through withholding or withdrawing life-sustaining medical treatment and that some people refer to such acts as "passive euthanasia," we broadly distinguish them from suicide, physician-assisted suicide and euthanasia (or what those same people tend to call "active euthanasia"). Western legal and moral codes historically have recognized a sharp distinction between these two types of actions. Clinical medical practice supports this basic distinction as well, even though the line blurs in some individual cases.[47] For us the right to die implicit in acknowledging an individual's autonomy over receiving or rejecting medical treatment is fundamentally different from the duty to die and right to kill the dying that seem to follow from the social acceptance of physician-assisted suicide and euthanasia. As the following study will show, the former can affirm the sanctity of life within the Christian tradition, while the latter would inevitably deny it.

1

Suicide & Euthanasia
When Christianity Arose

"I think it a sign of human weakness to try to find out the shape and form of God. Whoever God is—provided he does exist—and in whatever region he is, God is the complete embodiment of sense, sight, hearing, soul, mind and of himself. . . . It is ridiculous to think that a supreme being—whatever it is—cares about human affairs,"[1] wrote Pliny (A.D. 23-79), an urbane and educated Roman military officer, magistrate, scientist, man of letters and intimate friend of the emperor Vespasian. A little later he mused, "The chief consolation for Nature's shortcomings in regard to man is that not even God can do all things. For he cannot, even if he should so wish, commit suicide, which is the greatest advantage he has given man among all the great drawbacks of life."[2]

There is little if anything in these quotations from Pliny with which his Jewish contemporaries could have agreed. And the idea that people have one advantage over God, namely, that they can kill themselves—would this not have been blasphemous to Pliny's Jewish contemporaries? The answer is yes. These quotations highlight the most fundamental differences between the ancient Jews and the pagan Greeks and Romans.

Suicide and Euthanasia in Classical Antiquity
Greek culture ranged from that described in the Homeric epics (the product of an oral tradition dating back to at least a millennium before

Christ) to the distinctly Byzantine ethos of late antiquity. Roman culture evolved from the early monarchy of the seventh century B.C. to the Latin ambience of the western Mediterranean of late antiquity. To describe any feature of two such diverse and evolving cultures over such a great sweep of time requires caution and circumspection.

The philosopher and classical scholar John M. Rist, in the introduction to his insightful monograph *Human Value: A Study in Ancient Philosophical Ethics,* asserted that the view that such rights as "the right to life, to have enough to eat, to live without fear of torture or degrading punishments, the right to work or to withhold one's labour," or any other rights, "are the universal property of men as such was virtually unknown in classical antiquity." The ancient Greeks and Romans, he maintained, had no theory "that all men are endowed at birth (or before) with a certain value . . . though some of its philosophers took certain steps toward such a theory."[3] We concur with Rist and assert categorically that in spite of some philosophical groping toward a theory of human value and, particularly during the late Hellenistic and early imperial eras, the emergence of an altruism predicated upon an ill-defined sense that people have a value to which compassion is owed, the pagan Greeks and Romans had no premise of inherent or intrinsic human value from which "respect for human life" could be derived.

We also believe that the principle of human autonomy that informed Pliny's statement about the boon that suicide is to humanity typifies most streams of ancient Greek and Roman cultures.

Suicide, whether assisted or not, is a complex issue in any society, more so in some cultures than in others. When we are dealing with the vast panorama of classical pagan cultures, we are faced with an enormously complex array of religious, philosophical and popular attitudes.[4] But despite this great diversity, three strong conclusions appear reasonably clear and certainly defensible:

1. There is no evidence of any train of ancient pagan thought and values that endorsed suicide as always appropriate and proper for anyone desiring to die under any and all circumstances with no qualifications, restrictions or limits.

2. It is highly questionable that any train of ancient pagan thought and values condemned all suicides irrespective of individual circumstances. Pythagoreanism and some strains of Platonism were possible exceptions.

3. There is scant evidence that any train of ancient pagan thought and values condemned suicide by the hopelessly ill. Again Pythagoreanism and some strains of Platonism were possible exceptions.

We should note that Pythagoreanism appears to have condemned suicide unequivocally. Platonism's stance is ambiguous since it teaches that suicide is permissible if one has received a divine command to quit this life. A crucial sentence in Plato's *Phaedo* (62b) says that people are in a kind of *phroura* from which they must neither release themselves nor flee. *Phroura* can mean either a post at which one is stationed or a prison in which one is incarcerated. Those who interpret it as the latter have justified suicide, as an escape of the soul from the prison of the flesh, under a wider variety of circumstances than have those who view the body as one's divinely appointed post.

In exploring the classical attitudes toward euthanasia, physician-assisted suicide and the treatment of dying patients, we shall focus primarily on classical medical ethics.

"To help or at least to do no harm" is a frequently quoted maxim that appears in one treatise in the Hippocratic Corpus (a collection of medical writings, some composed as early as the fifth century B.C. but most dating from the Hellenistic era).[5] Ancient physicians were not in a distinct philosophical, religious or ethical category unto themselves. Hence the answers that individual physicians would have given to the question, Is it helping or harming to assist a person who wished to end his or her life? would vary no less than attitudes toward suicide varied within and between the diverse strains of classical cultures. We shall present four categories of physicians:

1. Some physicians were so unscrupulous that they would have done anything for a fee, including killing a patient if bribed by someone who wanted that person dead. They also would not have hesitated to help a patient or a healthy person commit suicide. Some drew the line only between legal and illegal acts; others did not. For such, the question of whether assisting people in killing themselves or administering the coup de grace at their request was helping or harming them was of little significance. These physicians constituted an unsavory and notorious minority.

2. Likely the majority of physicians felt that under some circumstance it would be helping, under others harming to assist a person, whether ill or not, to commit suicide. The distinctions that they made depended on where they drew the line between licit and illicit, honorable and shameful, courageous and cowardly, necessary and unnecessary suicide. Some people who successfully sought physicians' help in ending their lives were in good health—hence not patients, strictly speaking—and others were in ill health, painfully or terminally ill—hence properly categorized as patients. Some authors composed lists of medical conditions that they felt justified suicide.[6] For example, Pliny considered pain due to bladder

stones, stomach disorders and headache valid reasons for suicide.[7] Whether or not to commit suicide was up to the individual; whether or not to assist in the act was up to the physician, if he was asked. The literature contains references to physicians cutting the veins of people, both ill and well, who asked for such a procedure. Poison was even more common, and various poisons were developed by physicians who were praised for employing their toxicological knowledge in the production of drugs for inducing a pleasant and painless death.[8]

3. Some physicians would under no circumstances have assisted a person in committing suicide or have killed him or her if asked. For such physicians the hypothetical question that we have been posing would have been irrelevant, if not at an ideological level at least at a functional one. These physicians, although they viewed suicide as morally permissible under some circumstances, were convinced that it was not the role of the physician to end patients' lives or assist them in doing so. Furthermore, some physicians may have preferred not to assist in suicide, for it could prove to be a messy business, at least from a legal perspective. Under Greek and Roman law, physicians could be charged with poisoning their patients. Physicians were sometimes charged with or at least frequently suspected of doing so.[9]

4. There may have been some, although undoubtedly only a very small minority of physicians, who viewed all suicide under all circumstances as morally wrong. Their answer to our question would have been an unequivocal "harming!"

Assisting in suicide and practicing voluntary euthanasia appear to have been quite common practices for Greek and Roman physicians, especially during the Hellenistic and early imperial eras. Examples abound. But to cull from classical sources evidence of physicians' refusing to assist in suicide or active voluntary euthanasia is a daunting task. The only unequivocally clear text is the Hippocratic Oath. Although scholarly opinion varies considerably as to how many (if any) of the treatises in the Hippocratic Corpus were written by Hippocrates, few if any scholars today hold that the oath that bears his name was written by the historically elusive father of medicine. Even the date of the composition of the oath is unknown. Some scholars place it as early as the fifth century B.C. and others as late as the first century A.D. It apparently did not excite a great deal of attention on the part of physicians or others earlier than the beginning of the Christian era. The first known reference to it was made by Scribonius Largus in the first century A.D.10

Some of the stipulations in the oath are not consistent either with ethical precepts prevalent elsewhere in the Hippocratic Corpus and in other classical literature or with the realities of medical practice as revealed in the sources. This has inspired a number of attempts to explain away those inconsistencies or to attribute the oath to an author or school whose views were in other respects as well discordant with those characteristic of the pagan classical ethos. Most influential has been the theory advanced by the classicist Ludwig Edelstein that the oath was a product of the Pythagorean school, whose tenets included belief in reincarnation, the practice of vegetarianism and sexual purity, and a condemnation of abortion, suicide and the shedding of blood.[11] Although his thesis had appealed to many scholars, few now accept it.[12] Parallels for even the most esoteric injunctions in the oath can be found outside Pythagoreanism. Furthermore, the Greek text offers many variant readings, some of which can be translated in significantly different ways. It is reasonable, however, to say that the oath in many of its particulars is often inconsonant with the larger picture of ancient Greek and Roman medical ethics.

Among the stipulations in the Hippocratic Oath are prohibitions of performing abortions and engaging in surgery, both of which were common practices of Greek and Roman physicians. Immediately before these two injunctions is the famous passage that reads, "I will neither give a deadly drug to anybody, not even if asked for it, nor will I make a suggestion to this effect."[13] These three prohibitions have at least this much in common: they are discordant with the values expressed by the majority of sources and atypical of the realities of ancient medical practice.

We shall not debate the various possible origins of this oath. We simply reiterate that it must be considered esoteric in many of its essentials. And one of these is the injunction against euthanasia and physician-assisted suicide. The other classical sources that suggest opposition to euthanasia within the Greek or Roman medical community are more problematic. All of these are inconclusive and sufficiently equivocal to be subject to differing interpretations.[14]

In sum, there is a plethora of evidence for the practice of euthanasia and physician-assisted suicide in the classical world. But evidence for those who held that a physician should not be involved in such activities is painfully scarce. The most that can be said with certainty is that in some quarters, particularly during the late Hellenistic and early imperial eras, a limited respect for life was articulated by a very small minority of the extant sources. Ironically, it is from these same eras that the preponderance of evidence for physician-assisted suicide and euthanasia dates.

Nor did ancient Greek and Roman physicians feel any sense of moral obligation to attempt to preserve the lives of patients who appeared to have little or no hope of recovery. One treatise in the Hippocratic Corpus defines medicine as having three roles: doing away with the sufferings of the sick, lessening the violence of their diseases and refusing to treat those overwhelmed by their diseases, realizing that in such cases medicine was powerless. [15] It was the physician's decision whether to take on a probably incurable case. The ancient medical texts were divided on the question of whether physicians should withdraw from cases once it had become clear that they would be unable to restore the patient to health. Some argued that they should withdraw if they had a respectable excuse, especially if continuing treatment might hasten the patient's death. Others recommended that physicians should not withdraw, even if they might incur blame for staying with the patient.

In recent times it has become almost dogma to assert that the Hippocratic physician would not take on hopeless cases, which is demonstrably false since there were many instances in which physicians did take on hopeless cases in order to learn from the experience what might prove useful in helping other patients and in advancing medical knowledge. [16] Nevertheless some laypeople in antiquity held that, as Cicero wrote to his friend Atticus, "Hippocrates too forbids employing medicine in hopeless [cases]." [17] On balance extant sources suggest that physicians who preserved or attempted to preserve the life of patients who could not ultimately recover their health were generally viewed as acting unethically. [18]

We quoted Rist to the effect that in classical philosophy and law there was no principle of inherent rights or of intrinsic human value, "though some . . . philosophers took certain steps toward such a theory." The evidence bears him out. One ancient people, however, did have a highly developed and cogently articulated belief in inherent, intrinsic, ontological human value. These were the Jews. Their belief depended less on what became in Christianity the foundational doctrine upon which a principle of human value was constructed, that is, that "God created man in His own image" (Gen 1:27), than it did upon God's having chosen the Jews as his special people, entrusting them with his sacred oracles, both written and oral. Hence in postscriptural Jewish literature of antiquity, there is little if any emphasis placed on the inherent value of human life per se but rather on the inherent value of the life of an Israelite.

Suicide and Euthanasia in Ancient Judaism

The Jewish Scriptures, which constitute the Christian Old Testament, unequivocally proclaim God's total and ultimate sovereignty over life and death. God the Creator "formed man of dust from the ground, and breathed into his nostrils the breath of life; and man became a living being"

(Gen 2:7). God imposed as a penalty for sin both spiritual death and physical death: "from the tree of the knowledge of good and evil you shall not eat, for in the day that you eat from it you shall surely die" (Gen 2:17) and "By the sweat of your face you shall eat bread, till you return to the ground, because from it you were taken; for you are dust, and to dust you shall return" (Gen 3:19). The first act of murder brought forth a curse on the murderer. After Cain had slain his brother, Abel, God said, "What have you done? The voice of your brother's blood is crying to Me from the ground. And now you are cursed from the ground, which has opened its mouth to receive your brother's blood from your hand" (Gen 4:10-11). The law given by God to Noah immediately after the flood addressed homicide: "Whoever sheds man's blood, by man his blood shall be shed, for in the image of God He made man" (Gen 9:6). And God commanded the Israelites: "you shall not pollute the land in which you are; for blood pollutes the land and no expiation can be made for the land for the blood that is shed on it, except by the blood of him who shed it" (Num 35:33).

The sovereignty of God over life and death is repeatedly emphasized in the Old Testament. "It is I who put to death and give life" (Deut 32:39). "The LORD kills and makes alive" (1 Sam 2:6). Job rhetorically asks, "In whose hand is the life of every living thing, and the breath of all mankind?" (Job 12:10). The context supplies the unequivocal answer: God. "Thou dost turn man back into dust" (Ps 90:3). "Thou dost take away their spirit, they expire, and return to their dust" (Ps 104:29). "There is an appointed time for everything. And there is a time for every event under heaven—a time to give birth, and a time to die" (Eccles 3:1-2). "No man has authority . . . over the day of death" (Eccles 8:8). "Then the dust will return to the earth as it was, and the spirit will return to God who gave it" (Eccles 12:7). "Behold, all souls are Mine; the soul of the father as well as the soul of the son is Mine" (Ezek 18:4).

Although God is equally sovereign over the deaths of all people, the deaths of his own touch him deeply: "Precious in the sight of the LORD is the death of His godly ones" (Ps 116:15). For God placed before his people two paths, life and death: "I have set before you life and death, the blessing and the curse. So choose life in order that you may live, you and your descendants, by loving the LORD your God, by obeying His voice, and by holding fast to Him; for this is your life and the length of your days" (Deut 30:19-20). And he made it clear that within the strictures of the Mosaic covenant, prosperity, military success, fertility, health and long life were rewards for his people's love, loyalty and obedience. The curses, diametrical opposites of these blessings, God would visit upon his people if they spurned his love and disobeyed his law. He continually wooed his people into fellowship with himself and urged them to choose life.

The Hebrew phrase *pikku'ah nefesh* means "regard for human life." It is used in rabbinical literature to express the duty to save human life (the life of a fellow Israelite)[19] when it is in peril, which is one of the most sacred obligations in Judaism. This obligation included the sacred duty to preserve one's own life under most circumstances. But sometimes a Jew had to die rather than violate the law. To die thus is *kiddush ha-Shem* ("sanctification of the [Divine] name"); the alternative is *hillul ha-Shem* ("defamation of the [Divine] name").

Martyrdom

In his apologia for Judaism, rebutting Apion's anti-Jewish writings, the Jewish general and historian Josephus (A.D. 37-c. 100) asseverated that he and his fellow Jews "regard as the most essential task in life the observance of our laws and of the pious practices, based thereupon, which we have inherited."[20] Earlier in the same work he had remarked about their Scriptures that "it is an instinct with every Jew, from the day of his birth, to regard them as the decrees of God, to abide by them, and, if need be, cheerfully to die for them. Time and again ere now the sight has been witnessed of prisoners enduring tortures and death in every form in the theatres, rather than utter a single word against the laws and the allied documents."[21]

The laws of martyrdom were formulated at a rabbinic council held in the early second century A.D. In the Babylonian Talmud we read, "R. [Rabbi] Johanan said in the name of R. Simeon b. Jehozadak: 'By a majority vote, it was resolved in the upper chambers of the house of Nithza in Lydda, that in every [other] law of the Torah, if a man is commanded: "Transgress and suffer not death" he may transgress and not suffer death, excepting idolatry, incest [which includes adultery], and murder.'" Later in the same text this qualification is made: "When R. Dimi came, he said: 'This was taught only if there is no royal decree [i.e., forbidding the practice of Judaism], but if there is a royal decree, one must incur martyrdom rather than transgress even a minor precept.' When Rabin came, he said in R. Johanan's name: 'Even without a royal decree, it was only permitted in private; but in public one must be martyred even for a minor precept rather than violate it.'"[22] Upon this text hang all subsequent halakic interpretations of the licitness and illicitness of martyrdom and suicide under the duress of persecution.

This qualification is further refined in other talmudic tractates. Commenting on the sentence "He shall live by them, but not die by them," Rabbi Ishmael observed, "This is only meant when in private, but not in public; for it has been taught. . . . Whence can we deduce that if they say to one, 'Worship the idol and thou wilt not be killed,' that he may worship it so as not to be killed? because Scripture says, 'He shall live by them,' but not die by them; you might take this to mean even in public, there Scripture says, 'And ye shall not profane my holy name' [Lev 22:32]."[23] And Rabbi Raba said about the same sentence, "It excludes the man who acts under pressure. After that, however, the All-merciful wrote, 'And ye shall not profane My holy name'—i.e., not even under compulsion! How is it, then?—The former refers to an act in private, the latter to an act in public."[24] In another tractate the same rabbi said, "If a Gentile said to a Jew, 'Cut grass on the Sabbath for the cattle, and if not I will slay thee,' he must rather be killed than cut it; 'Cut and throw it into the river,' he should rather be slain than cut it. Why so?—Because his intention is to force him to violate his religion."[25]

The Talmud sees in the story of Shadrach, Meshach and Abednego, related in Daniel 3, an Old Testament example of *kiddush ha-Shem*.[26] Their lives were preserved in the fiery furnace, as was Daniel's in the lions' den (Dan 6), though they were willing to die rather than violate the law. But were there any martyrs in the Old Testament other than prophets who had been killed by apostate Jews? We are aware of none, unless we thus categorize Jews killed by invading armies.

It is in the intertestamental literature that Jewish martyrdom truly came into its own. In 2 Maccabees the deaths of Eleazar and seven brothers along with their mother are the most spectacular martyrdoms recounted. The events leading up to the Jewish revolt against Antiochus IV Epiphanes provide the context. Eleazar, a ninety-year-old man, submitted to torture and death rather than eat pork publicly, "preferring an honourable death to an unclean life . . . and by his death he left a heroic example and a glorious memory, not only for the young but also for the great body of the nation."[27]

Immediately following Eleazar's martyrdom, the martyrdoms of seven brothers and their mother are related. All eight are put to death for refusing to violate the law, the test case again being the public eating of pork (2 Macc 7:1-42). The author of 2 Maccabees puts the following theological pronouncement in the mouth of the sixth brother: "It is our own fault that we suffer these things; we have sinned against our God and brought these appalling disasters upon ourselves" (2 Macc 7:18). The author had prefaced the story of Eleazar with a similar theological emphasis: "Now I beg my readers not to be disheartened by these calamities, but to reflect that such penalties were inflicted for the discipline of our race and not for its destruction. It is a sign of great kindness that acts of impiety should not be let alone for long but meet their due recompense at once. The Lord did not see fit to deal with us as he does with the other nations: with them he patiently holds his hand until they have reached the full extent of their sins, but upon us he inflicted retribution before our sins reached their height. So he never withdraws his mercy from us; though he disciplines his people by calamity, he never deserts them. Let it be enough for me to have recalled this truth" (2 Macc 6:12-17). This theological understanding, which is consistent with the provisions of the Mosaic covenant, will continue to condition Jewish theodicy.

The fourth book of Maccabees was written very early in the Christian era, possibly as early as the first half of the first century A.D.[28] H. Anderson observed, "Doctrinally, the most significant contribution of 4 Maccabees is the development of the notion that the suffering and death of the martyred righteous had redemptive efficacy for all Israel and secured God's grace and pardon for his people. Eleazar first expresses the idea in his prayer in 6:28f: 'Be merciful to your people and let our punishment be a satisfaction on their behalf. Make my blood their purification and take my life as a ransom for theirs.' Later, we find the same thought: 'The tyrant was punished and our land purified, since they [the martyrs] became, as it were, a ransom for the sin of our nation. Through the blood of these righteous ones and through the propitiation of their death the divine providence rescued Israel, which had been shamefully treated' (17:21f.)."[29]

The central theme of 4 Maccabees is martyrdom. Fourth Maccabees 5—7 recounts and expatiates on the martyrdom of Eleazar; the remainder of the book (4 Macc 8—18) is devoted to the martyrdoms of the seven brothers and their mother. Substantially longer than the account in 2 Maccabees, the version of the death of the seven brothers and their mother in 4 Maccabees is embellished with considerable gory detail, lengthier speeches by all eight martyrs and extensive panegyrics and theological commentary by the author. The story in 4 Maccabees also includes some differences in detail from that in 2 Maccabees. In the earlier account the mother and sons encourage each other to face death bravely, and all die courageously; in the later version they display a zealous eagerness to die. And in 4 Maccabees the seventh and youngest brother "threw himself into the braziers and so gave up his life" (4 Macc 12:19). Of the mother's death 4 Maccabees says, "Some of the guards declared that when she, too, was about to be seized and put to death, she threw herself into the fire so that no one would touch her body" (4 Macc 17:1). Anderson comments, "There is no hint of the mother's suicide in 2 Mac, and at this point our author himself is rather squeamish about it. . . . He attributes the report of it to the guards (Did he possess no tradition on this matter?) and refers to the matter in a strangely oblique and fleeting way."[30]

Suicide as Martyrdom

Was the author of 4 Maccabees uneasy about the suicide of the mother of the seven martyred youths? Rabbinic tradition certainly was not. In the Babylonian Talmud Rabbi Judah maintained that the text "Yea, for thy sake we are killed all the day long, we are counted as sheep for the slaughter" (Ps 44:23) "refers to the woman and her seven sons." Then the account, which is very brief, relates that the first six brothers were led away and killed and that the soldiers "were leading [the seventh brother] away to kill him when his mother said: 'Give him to me that I may kiss him a little.' She said to him: 'My son, go and say to your father Abraham, "Thou didst bind one [son to the] altar, but I have bound seven altars." ' Then she also went up on to a roof and threw herself down and was killed. A voice thereupon came forth from heaven saying, 'A joyful mother of children' [Ps 113:9]."[31] There is no reticence in this talmudic account. God himself commended her action. The Israeli judge H. H. Cohn has recently remarked, "The former source [4 Macc] implies that she killed herself in order to forestall being seized and killed by the guardsmen, while from the latter [the Talmud] it would appear that she committed suicide voluntarily, whether to identify with her children, or out of the agony of her heart at seeing them tortured and assassinated. Both versions carry the same undertone of approval and admiration."[32]

Whether, as Anderson contends, the author of 4 Maccabees was uneasy about the suicide of this mother or, as Cohn asserts, approved and admired her act, the account of the suicide of Razis in 2 Maccabees is unequivocally positive. Soldiers who had been sent to arrest him "were on the point of capturing the tower where Razis was, and were trying to force the outer door. Then an order was given to set the door on fire, and Razis, hemmed in on all sides, turned his sword on himself. He preferred to die nobly rather than fall into the hands of criminals and be subject to gross humiliation. In his haste and anxiety he misjudged the blow, and with the troops pouring through the doors he ran without hesitation on to the wall and heroically threw himself down into the crowd. The crowd hurriedly gave way and he fell in the space they left. He was still breathing, still on fire with courage; so, streaming with blood and severely wounded, he picked himself up and dashed through the crowd. Finally, standing on a sheer rock, and now completely drained of blood, he took his entrails in both hands and flung them at the crowd. And thus, invoking the Lord of life and breath to give these entrails back to him again, he died" (4 Macc 14:37-46).

The concluding sentence reflects the same hope of physical resurrection that the third martyred brother expressed (as recorded in 2 Macc) when he was asked whether he would publicly eat pork to escape death: "He at once showed his tongue, boldly held out his hands, and said courageously: 'The God of heaven gave me these. His laws mean far more to me than they do, and it is from him that I trust to receive them back'" (2 Macc 7:10-11). The two deaths, though, are significantly different: the youth was a passive martyr; Razis was an active suicide. Both, however, were regarded as worthy of praise. Both incidents occurred under conditions of severe persecution. So also the following recorded in the Babylonian Talmud: "On one occasion four hundred boys and girls were carried off for immoral purposes. They divined what they were wanted for and said to themselves, 'If we drown in the sea we shall attain the life of the future world.' The eldest among them expounded the verse, 'The Lord said, "I will bring again from Bashan, I will bring again from the depth of the sea" [Ps 68:23]. "I will bring again from Bashan," from between the lions' teeth. "I will bring again from the depths of the sea," those who drown in the sea.' When the girls heard this they all leaped into the sea. The boys then drew the moral for themselves, saying, 'If these, for whom this [i.e., the sexual activity for which they had been selected] is natural, act so, shall not we, for whom it [i.e., the male prostitution awaiting them] is unnatural?' They also leaped into the sea. Of them the text says, 'Yea, for thy sake we are killed all the day long, we are counted as sheep for the slaughter' [Ps 44:23]."[33]

All the suicides discussed thus far were regarded as honorable, indeed praiseworthy—suicide as martyrdom, consistent with talmudic casuistry. Many other suicides are recorded in Jewish literature from the Old Testament through the end of the talmudic period (c. A.D. 500). None of them, however, offers support for medical euthanasia or physician-assisted suicide, because they do not involve situations similar to those faced by terminally or seriously ill patients. Let us attempt to categorize them.

War-Related Suicide by Individuals
First chronologically in this category is Abimelech. After capturing the city of Thebez, he assaulted a fortified tower in the center of the city. The Old Testament account of his death reads, "So Abimelech came to the

tower and fought against it, and approached the entrance of the tower to burn it with fire. But a certain woman threw an upper millstone on Abimelech's head, crushing his skull. Then he called quickly to the young man, his armor bearer, and said to him, 'Draw your sword and kill me, lest it be said of me, "A woman slew him." ' So the young man pierced him through, and he died" (Judg 9:52-54). Although Scripture neither explicitly approves nor disapproves of this act of assisted suicide, it was a fitting end for an evil man: "Thus God repaid the wickedness of Abimelech, which he had done to his father, in killing his seventy brothers" (Judg 9:56). Josephus echoes Scripture's moral judgment.[34]

Samson's death is thus recorded in Judges:

It so happened when [the Philistines] were in high spirits, that they said, "Call for Samson, that he may amuse us." So they called for Samson from the prison, and he entertained them. And they made him stand between the pillars. . . . Now the house was full of men and women, and all the lords of the Philistines were there. And about 3,000 men and women were on the roof looking on while Samson was amusing them. Then Samson called to the LORD and said, "O LORD God, please remember me and please strengthen me just this time, O God, that I may at once be avenged of the Philistines for my two eyes." And Samson grasped the two middle pillars on which the house rested, and braced himself against them, the one with his right hand and the other with his left. And Samson said, "Let me die with the Philistines!" And he bent with all his might so that the house fell on the lords and all the people who were in it. So the dead whom he killed at his death were more than those whom he killed in his life. (Judg 16:25-30)

Scripture passed no judgment on the manner of Samson's death. It is probably reasonable to regard his death as incidental to the simultaneous destruction of a multitude of the enemies of Israel. Josephus wrote that Samson deemed as more severe than all his ills his inability to be avenged of the Philistines' mockery and insults. After describing Samson's death, Josephus observed, "Such was his end, after governing Israel for twenty years. And it is but right to admire the man for his valour, his strength, and the grandeur of his end, as also for the wrath which he cherished to the last against his enemies. That he let himself be ensnared by a woman must be imputed to human nature which succumbs to sins, but testimony is due to him for his surpassing excellence in all the rest."[35]

Saul's death has evoked considerable discussion. The accounts in 1 Samuel 31:1-6 and 1 Chronicles 10:1-6 are virtually identical. In the words of the former, "And the battle went heavily against Saul, and the archers hit him; and he was badly wounded by the archers. Then Saul said to his armor bearer, 'Draw your sword and pierce me through with it, lest these uncircumcised come and pierce me through and make sport of me.' But his armor bearer would not, for he was greatly afraid. So Saul took his sword and fell on it. And when his armor bearer saw that Saul was dead, he also fell on his sword and died with him."

In 2 Samuel 1 a variant is introduced. A young man approached David after the battle in which Saul died and said, "By chance I happened to be on Mount Gilboa, and behold, Saul was leaning on his spear. And behold, the chariots and the horsemen pursued him closely. And when he looked behind him, he saw me and called to me. And I said, 'Here I am.' And he said to me, 'Who are you?' And I answered him, 'I am an Amalekite.' Then he said to me, 'Please stand beside me and kill me; for agony has seized me because my life still lingers in me.' So I stood beside him and killed him, because I knew that he could not live after he had fallen. And I took the crown which was on his head and the bracelet which was on his arm, and I have brought them here to my lord." Instead of rewarding him, David asked him, "How is it you were not afraid to stretch out your hand to destroy the Lord's anointed?" David then ordered him to be put to death (2 Sam 1:6-16). Either the young Amalekite had fabricated his story in the hope of winning David's favor, in which case Saul's suicide attempt had been successful, or his account was factual, in which case Saul's suicide attempt had been unsuccessful and the young man had administered the coup de grace, just as Abimelech's armor bearer had done.

Josephus melded the two accounts into one: "He himself, after fighting magnificently and receiving numerous wounds, until he could no longer hold out nor endure under these blows, was too weak to kill himself and bade his armour-bearer draw his sword and thrust it through him before the enemy should take him alive. But, as the armour-bearer did not dare to slay his master, Saul drew his own sword himself and, fixing it with its point toward him, sought to fling himself upon it, but was unable either to push it in or, by leaning upon it, to drive the weapon home. Then he turned and, seeing a youth standing there, asked him who he was, and, on learning that he was an Amalekite, begged him to force the sword in, since he could not do this with his own hands, and so procure him such a death as he desired. This he did."[36]

Saul is condemned in both 1 Samuel and 1 Chronicles. In 1 Samuel 28:16-19, Samuel's spirit, conjured by the witch of Endor the previous night, rebuked Saul and told him that he would die the next day because of his disobedience to the Lord. In 1 Chronicles 10:13-14 we read, "So Saul died for his trespass which he committed against the LORD, because of the word of the LORD which he did not keep; and also because he asked counsel of a medium, making inquiry of it, and did not inquire of the LORD. Therefore He killed him, and turned the kingdom to David the son of Jesse." Hence, according to the chronicler, God himself killed Saul, either indirectly by Saul's own hand or by that of the Amalekite who killed Saul at the latter's request. Nevertheless, rabbinic tradition generally treats his death favorably, categorizing it as martyrdom.[37]

Both Scripture and Josephus report Saul's armor bearer's suicide laconically and without comment. His duress was twofold. Not only did he choose to die with his king (suicide by identification), but also his only alternative was death at the hands of the enemy.

Ahithophel (or Achitophel), who was King David's counselor, became Absalom's when the latter revolted against his father, David. David prayed that his advice would be made foolishness (2 Sam 15:31). "Now when Ahithophel saw that his counsel was not followed, he saddled his donkey and arose and went to his home, to his city, and set his house in order, and strangled himself; thus he died and was buried in the grave of his father" (2 Sam 17:23). Josephus wrote that when his proposal was not accepted he thought that he would soon perish. "Therefore, he said, it was better for him to remove himself from the world in a free and noble spirit than surrender himself to David to be punished for having in all ways helped Absalom against him. [So] he went into the innermost part of the house and hanged himself. Such was the death to which Achitophel, as his own judge, sentenced himself."[38] Josephus is hard to understand. He seems to have agreed that suicide in this case was preferable to dying at the hand of the king whom Ahithophel had betrayed, and he allowed Ahithophel's ostensibly classifying his suicide as "remov[ing] himself from the world in a free and noble spirit" to stand unchallenged. Yet Josephus appears to have regarded Ahithophel's self-inflicted death as an appropriate self-imposed penalty.

Zimri (or Zambrias) gained the throne of Israel by assassination. He lacked popular support and after a reign of only one week was attacked by a rival. "And it came about, when Zimri saw that the city was taken, that he went into the citadel of the king's house, and burned the king's house over him with fire, and died, because of his sins which he sinned, doing evil in the sight of the LORD, walking in the way of Jeroboam, and in his sin which he did, making Israel sin" (1 Kings 16:18-19). Scripture unequivocally maintained that Zimri's death was judgment for his sins. Josephus was equally forthright: "It came about that, because of his impiety, his house perished root and branch in the same way as the house of Jeroboam was destroyed."[39] A little later Josephus remarked, "From these events one may learn how close a watch the Deity keeps over human affairs and how He loves good men but hates the wicked, whom He destroys root and branch."[40]

War-Related Suicides by Groups

In the Talmud and Josephus's writings there are several accounts of suicide by civilians when the besieging army had successfully breached the walls of their city and destruction was imminent.[41] In Josephus's writings are also several accounts of suicide by soldiers or partisans when defeat was inevitable. The two most spectacular examples in the latter category are instructive.

Early in the revolt against Rome, Josephus and his men are hiding in a cave outside Jotapata. The Romans are preparing to smoke them out if they do not surrender. Josephus's men are appalled and outraged at his suggestion that they surrender. "Well may a cry go up to heaven from the laws of our fathers," they say, "ordained by God Himself, who endowed our race with spirits that despise death! Are you so in love with life, Josephus, that you can bear to live as a slave?. . . We will lend you a sword and a hand to wield it. If you die willingly, you will die as commander-in-chief of the Jews; if unwillingly, as a traitor."[42]

Josephus then delivers a closely argued case against the moral probity of suicide in their particular circumstances. While it is a glorious thing to die in war, it is a craven and cowardly act to take one's own life. God has placed in all creatures the instinct to survive. Hence suicide is an act of impiety toward God. It is to treat God's gift of life with contempt. "It is from Him we have received our being, and it is to Him we must leave the right to take it away." Our soul "is immortal for ever, a fragment of God dwelling in our bodies. If a man destroys something entrusted to him by another man or misuses it, he is judged a faithless rogue, is he not? Then if a man throws away what God has entrusted to his personal keeping, does he think the One he has wronged is unaware? To punish runaway slaves is considered right, even if the masters they are leaving are rogues; if we ourselves run away from the best of masters, God, shan't we be judged impious? Don't you know that those who depart this life according to the law of nature, and repay the loan they received from God at such time as the Lender chooses to claim it back, win everlasting glory?" Consequently, "It is our duty then, comrades, to choose the honourable course and not to add to our human sufferings impiety towards our Creator."[43]

Josephus's soldiers are not convinced; hence he must either die at their hands or join their suicide pact. Never without a clever plan, "putting his trust in divine protection he staked his life on one last throw. 'You have chosen to die,' he exclaimed; 'well then, let's draw lots and kill each other in turn. Whoever draws the first lot shall be dispatched by number two, and so on down the whole line as luck *[tychē]* decides. In this way no one will die by his own hand—it would be unfair when the rest were gone if one man changed his mind and saved his life.' The audience swallowed the bait, and getting his way Josephus drew lots with the rest. Without hesitation each man in turn offered his throat for the next man to cut." As it turned out, Josephus and one other man were left. The latter "did not relish the thought either of being condemned by the lot or, if he was left till last, of staining his hand with the blood of a fellow Jew. So he used persuasion, they made a pact, and both remained alive."

Josephus had always opposed the revolt of his countrymen against Rome. To put it bluntly, he was convinced that the Jewish rebels not only were acting against their own best interests but also were opposing God himself. In short, God was on the Romans' side. And God had destined the Roman commander-in-chief, Vespasian, for the purple. This was the prophecy that Josephus felt God had entrusted to him to deliver to Vespasian. Immediately before he suggests that he and his men surrender, he prays, "Inasmuch as it pleaseth Thee to visit Thy wrath on the Jewish people whom Thou didst create, and all prosperity hath passed to the Romans, and because Thou didst choose my spirit to make known the things to come, I yield myself willingly to the Romans that I may live, but I solemnly declare that I go, not as a traitor, but as Thy servant."[44]

After the fall of Jerusalem in A.D. 70, zealots remained atop Masada. After a long and arduous siege, the Romans took that mountain fortress in May 73, only to find everyone except two women and five children dead: 960 men, women and children. According to the survivors, who had hidden themselves but apparently were able to observe or at least to hear what had transpired, each man had slain his own wife and children. Next, ten men had been chosen by lot to kill the rest of the men, then one of the ten chosen by lot to kill the other nine and himself. According to Josephus, the zealots had been convinced to take this course of action by their leader, Eleazar. Josephus later constructed two speeches that he would have his readers believe represented the arguments Eleazar had employed.

Eleazar's first speech contains this sequence of arguments. He and his fellow zealots had determined from the beginning never to submit. At the present juncture they can neither escape from nor defeat the Romans. "But we are free to choose an honourable death with our loved ones." From the beginning, having "suffered such constant misery at each other's hands and worse at the enemy's, we ought perhaps to have read the mind of God and realized that His once beloved Jewish race had been sentenced to extinction. . . . God Himself without a doubt has taken away all hope of survival. . . . These things are God's vengeance for the many wrongs that in our madness we dared to do to our own countrymen. For those wrongs let us pay the penalty not to our bitterest enemies, the Romans, but to God—by our own hands."[45]

This short speech was greeted with mixed reactions, so Eleazer launched into a lengthier exhortation. After berating those of his fellow zealots "who fear death even when it means the end of utter misery," he asserts that "life is the calamity for man, not death. Death gives freedom to our souls and lets them depart to their own pure home where they will know nothing of any calamity; but while they are confined within a mortal body and share its miseries, in strict truth they are dead. For association of the divine with the mortal is most improper. Certainly the soul can do a great deal even when imprisoned in the body. . . . But when, freed from the weight that drags it down to earth and is hung about it, the soul returns to its own place, then in truth it partakes of a blessed power and utterly unfettered strength."

After making the commonplace analogy between death and sleep, Eleazar says, "It might be expected that we, so carefully taught at home, would be an example to others of readiness to die." He then gives the example of the Indians who "hasten to release their souls from their bodies . . . though no misfortune presses or drives them away. . . . Are we not ashamed to show a poorer spirit than Indians, and by our want of courage to bring the Law of our fathers, the envy of all the world, into utter contempt? Even if," he continues, "from the very first we had been taught the contrary belief, that life is indeed the greatest good of mankind and death a disaster, the situation is such that we should still be called upon to bear it with a stout heart, for God's will and sheer necessity doom us to death. Long ago, it seems, God issued this warning to the whole Jewish race together, that life would be taken from us if we misused it. . . . A mightier hand [than that of the Romans] has intervened to give them the outward shape of victory."

Eleazar next rehearses various cases of Jews being slaughtered by non-Roman Gentiles early in the revolt. Jerusalem has been destroyed, the countryside has been ravaged and the women ravished. The zealots, their wives and their children have unimaginable horrors awaiting them if the Romans take them alive. So, he concludes, "Let us die unenslaved by our enemies, and leave this world as free men in company with our wives and children. That is what the Law ordains, that is what our wives and children demand of us, the necessity God has laid on us, the opposite of what the Romans wish—they are anxious that none of us should die before the town is captured. So let us deny the enemy their hoped-for pleasure at our expense, and without more ado leave them to be dumbfounded by our death and awed by our courage."[46]

Josephus maintained that one of the women who had survived had provided the Romans "a lucid report of Eleazar's speech."[47] Regardless of whether Josephus had opportunity to interview this woman or any of the other survivors or had heard an account from the Romans, it is unlikely that a Jewish zealot would have constructed such arguments, based as they are so heavily on Greek philosophy. So why did Josephus formulate such arguments to attribute to the zealot chief? The question is complicated by Josephus's character and reputation and by the mythic aura that has come to surround the fall of Masada, of which, surprisingly, there is no reference in the Talmud. After all, it is at Masada that Israeli soldiers are sworn into military service. Josephus was and still is typically regarded by Jews as a traitor and the zealots as martyrs and heroes.

Most scholars regard Josephus's account of the death of the zealots on Masada as his acknowledgment that by their death they had proved themselves to be true heroes, thus vindicated of their earlier acts for which he had castigated them. Perhaps by thus vindicating them, Josephus, the traitor, was attempting to vindicate himself. But elsewhere in his writings Josephus had had nothing good to say about the zealots. For him they were the real traitors. Not only had they instigated suicidal revolt against Rome, but also during the course of the war they had killed many more of their fellow Jews than they had Romans. Furthermore, some modern translations distort the meaning of crucial vocabulary.[48] For example, Josephus consistently used the word *tolmēma* to convey the idea of boldness in the sense of audacity. Translators who thus render the word elsewhere in the *Jewish War* translate it as "fortitude" when Josephus applies it to the mass suicide at Masada.[49] It is as if they approach the narrative about Masada with the assumption that Josephus regarded the final events there as truly heroic and laudable and translate accordingly.

Since Josephus, however, had always and consistently opposed rebelling against Rome as rashly suicidal and had consistently portrayed the zealots negatively, David J. Ladouceur may be correct when he asserts that in his entire narrative of the fall of Masada, "Josephus is carefully controlling his presentation and thus manipulating his audience's response. The suicide he portrays is retributive, both atonement for and acknowledgment of crimes against the rebels' own countrymen. In Eleazar's *enumeratio malorum,* the suicide becomes a means of escaping brutal Roman punishment. The irony lies in the fact that the defenders display resolution not in fighting the Romans but in murder and suicide."[50]

Josephus's speech at Jotapata and Eleazar's speeches at Masada bear little resemblance to each other. The one most significant similarity is at the same time the most significant difference. Both indicate a familiarity with Plato's *Phaedo*. Each takes a different interpretation of a matter about which scholars are still uncertain: Is the soul entrusted to a person, like a loan or a deposit, perhaps like a sentinel assigned to a post, or is it a captive, imprisoned in the body? Josephus at Jotapata presents it favorably as the former. But he causes Eleazar to depict it negatively as the latter.[51]

Suicide as Salvation

We relate two examples of "suicide as salvation."[52] The story is told in the Babylonian Talmud of Rabbi Eleazar ben Dordia, who had a propensity to seek out and buy the services of any and every prostitute. Finally, stricken with deep remorse, he despaired of salvation. In the depths of gloom and hopelessness, "having placed his head between his knees, he wept aloud until his soul departed. Then a *bath-kol* [a voice from heaven] was heard proclaiming: 'Rabbi Eleazar b. Dordai is destined for the life of the world to come!'" A particular rabbi, on hearing of it, "wept and said: 'One may acquire eternal life after many years, another in one hour!'"[53]

The second account in this category, also from the Babylonian Talmud, involves martyrdom and provides some preliminary insights into active, voluntary euthanasia and assisted suicide. During the persecution of Jews under the emperor Hadrian, some Roman officials "found R. Hanina b. Teradion sitting and occupying himself with the Torah, publicly gathering assemblies, and keeping a scroll of the Law in his bosom. Straightaway they took hold of him, wrapt him in the Scroll of the Law, placed bundles of branches round him and set them on fire. They then brought tufts of wool, which they had soaked in water, and placed them over his heart, so that he should not expire quickly. His daughter exclaimed, 'Father, that I should see you in this state!' He replied, 'If it were I alone being burnt it would have been a thing hard to bear; but now that I am burning together with the Scroll of the Law, He who will have regard for the plight of the Torah will also have regard for my plight.' His disciples called out, 'Rabbi, what seest thou?' He answered them, 'The parchments are being burnt but the letters are soaring on high.' 'Open then thy mouth' [said they] 'so that the fire enter into thee.' He replied, 'Let Him who gave me [my soul] take it away, but no one should injure oneself.' The Executioner then said to him, 'Rabbi, if I raise the flame and take away the tufts of wool from over thy heart, will thou cause me to enter into the life to come?' 'Yes,' he replied. 'Then swear unto me' [he urged]. He swore unto him. He thereupon raised the flame and removed the tufts of wool from over his heart, and his soul departed speedily. The Executioner then jumped and threw himself into the fire. And a *bath-kol* exclaimed: 'R. Hanina b. Teradion and the Executioner have been assigned to the world to come.' When Rabbi heard it he wept and said: 'One may acquire eternal life in a single hour, another after many years.'"[54]

We should note that the first of these examples of suicide as salvation, if it can even be classified as suicide, involved the sinful but repentant rabbi who wept himself to death. The concluding talmudic comment was "One may acquire eternal life after many years, another in one hour!" Our second example involved the rabbi who was being slowly roasted to death. When his disciples pleaded with him to inhale the flames to expedite his death, he refused: "Let Him who gave me [my soul] take it away, but no one should injure oneself." Nevertheless, when the executioner volunteered to increase the intensity of the fire and take away the impediments that had been placed on his chest to prolong the dying process, if the rabbi would promise his admission to heaven, the rabbi agreed. As soon as the rabbi died, the executioner committed suicide by leaping into the fire. After a voice from heaven proclaimed that both the rabbi and the executioner had been "assigned to the world to come," the same concluding observation was made as in the first story: "One may acquire eternal life in a single hour, another after many years."

Given what we have seen thus far under the rubrics of martyrdom and suicide, it is no wonder that the ancient texts may cause some modern readers, including some scholars, to regard ancient Judaism as open and sympathetic to suicide generally. Nevertheless when one turns to authoritative modern Jewish sources (rabbinic responsa) that speak for any branch of Judaism (e.g., Orthodox, Conservative and Reform), one uniformly encounters such statements as the following, made in 1997 by a Responsa Committee of Reform rabbis: "Jewish tradition, as is well known, prohibits suicide, if by 'suicide' we mean a rational, premeditated act of self-killing."[55] A little later in the article the Responsa Committee added the qualification that "the prohibition against suicide is not absolute."[56] They then gave martyrdom on the principle of *kiddush ha-Shem* as the primary exception.

We have seen that Rabbi Hanina ben Teradion's reason for refusing to hasten his own death was twofold: it is for God, who had given life, to take it, and no one should injure oneself. The talmudic text typically cited as forbidding suicide deals inconclusively with the question of whether it is permitted to injure oneself.[57]

It was in the tractate *On Mourning (Semahot)* that Jewish law governing suicide was first formalized. The date of this tractate has been and still is much disputed. Some scholars place it as late as the eighth century and others as early as the third. We incline toward the earlier date on the basis of the arguments articulated by Dov Zlotnick in the introduction to his translation of *Semahot* that is part of the Yale Judaica Series.[58] The section on suicide reads as follows:

1. For a suicide, no rites whatsoever should be observed. Rabbi Ishmael said: "He may be lamented: 'Alas, misguided fool! Alas misguided fool!'" Whereupon Rabbi 'Akiba said to him: "Leave him to his oblivion: Neither bless him, nor curse him!" There may be no rending of clothes, no baring of shoulders, and no eulogizing for him. But people should line up for him and the mourners' blessing should be recited over him, out of respect for the living. The general rule is: The public should participate in whatsoever is done out of respect for the living; it should not participate in whatsoever is done out of respect for the dead.

2. Who is to be accounted a suicide? Not one who climbs to the top of a tree or to the top of a roof and falls to his death. Rather it is one who says "Behold, I am going to climb to the top of the tree," or "to the top of the roof, and then throw myself down to my death," and thereupon others see him climb to the top of the tree or to the top of the roof and fall to his death. Such a one is presumed to be a suicide, and for such a person no rites whatsoever should be observed.

The final two paragraphs of this section involve children committing suicide to escape paternal discipline. Last rites were not to be denied them.[59]

The Hebrew expression for suicide *(hame' abed atzmo leda 'at)* literally means "he who destroys himself knowingly." The primary concern with suicide in *Semahot* was with distinguishing those who had taken their own lives deliberately and willfully from those who had done so without premeditation, as the result of mental illness or being youths who should not be held responsible for such an act. The burden of proof rested on those who maintained that persons who had killed themselves had done so knowingly and with premeditation.

In antiquity Judaism appears to have striven to be compassionate and nonjudgmental by assigning moral and spiritual culpability for suicide only if the evidence for rational premeditation was unequivocal unless motivated by *kiddush ha-Shem* and in those rare instance of suicide as salvation.

Suicide by the Ill and Euthanasia

Of the three major branches of Judaism today, Reform Judaism is the most "liberal" and "progressive." The Reform rabbis who authored the Responsa Committee's statement on euthanasia, from which we have quoted, call themselves "liberal Jews who seek guidance from our tradition in facing the moral dilemmas of our age."[60] They acknowledge that some voices within Judaism use examples of martyrdom and King Saul's suicide "to argue that Judaism actually permits suicide and mercy killing for those who face the pain and agony of terminal illness."[61] The Responsa Committee's reaction to such an interpretation bears quoting extensively:

> On the one hand, it is certainly true that these stories might plausibly be read so as to support the option of active euthanasia. On the other hand, through the long history of the Jewish study of the Bible and the Talmud, the texts in question have not been understood in this way. This is a point of no little importance to our discussion. We wish to know, after all, whether the "Jewish tradition" offers evidence in support of active euthanasia. It is for this reason that advocates of mercy killing cite these stories in the first place. Yet we find that the very *tradition* of learning which created these passages and which has studied them for fifteen centuries and more as sources of moral meaning declares consistently and unequivocally *against* euthanasia. Indeed, the message that emerges from traditional halakhic thought on this subject is quite clear and uniform: we do almost anything to relieve the suffering of the terminally ill, but we do not kill them and we do not help them kill themselves. It is always possible to read these texts differently than they have ever been read by the Jewish religious community, to discover in them levels of meaning that generations of rabbis and *talmidey hakhamim* may have missed. Still, the unequivocal voice of the halakhic literature renders it most difficult to sustain an argument, based upon the citation of a few stories from the Bible and the Talmud, that the "Jewish tradition" permits euthanasia. As Reform Jews, of course, we consider ourselves free to ascribe "new" Jewish meanings to our texts, to depart from tradition when we think it necessary to secure an essential religious or moral value. In this case, though, we fail to see why we should do so.[62]

The Responsa Committee then gives three reasons for remaining faithful to the traditional Jewish understanding of the issues: "We see no good reason, first of all, to abandon the traditional Jewish teaching concerning the inestimable value of human life."[63] "Second, we do not believe that the existence of pain and suffering constitutes a sufficient Jewish justification for killing a human being in the name of compassion."[64] "Third, we are uncomfortable with arguments for assisted suicide that proceed from judgments concerning the 'quality of life.' "[65]

This Responsa Committee is stressing that there is no evidence that Jewish religious tradition has ever understood the pertinent issues in such a way as to approve either suicide by the ill or euthanasia. To interpret any of the texts of historic Judaism as supporting these acts requires a revisionism to which Reform Judaism is not ipso facto inimical. But so basic to historic Judaic values are the undergirding issues that even Reform Judaism cannot condone suicide by the ill and euthanasia as consistent with Jewish values. Hence the burden of proof rests upon those who would interpret the relevant texts as supporting these acts. Yet Jewish scholars, although not ahistorical in their approach, base much of their arguments against euthanasia and suicide of the ill on medieval, Renaissance, early modern and modern interpretations of ancient texts, interpretations that have often themselves become authoritative texts in their own right. One could argue that the cumulative and dynamic interpretations of these ancient texts have rendered these early texts themselves dynamic and evolving and that the original meanings of these texts have inevitably been altered. So it is our purpose to consider the relevant ancient texts without immediate reference to later Jewish halakic tradition.

Before looking at any of these texts, all of which are postbiblical, let us survey the background. In the Old Testament there are no cases of people committing suicide or having others assist them in doing so in order to put an end to suffering caused by illness. Two Old Testament figures, Abimelech and Saul, after having been severely wounded in battle, killed themselves or requested another to administer the coup de grace. We have discussed these. There are, however, in the Old Testament several examples of people who were severely despondent and prayed or at least wished for death.

Moses, crushed by the burden of leading an obstinate and rebellious people, pled with God, "Please kill me at once, if I have found favor in Thy sight" (Num 11:15). Elijah cried out in despair, "It is enough; now, O LORD, take my life" (1 Kings 19:4). Jeremiah cursed the day of his birth and wished that he had died in his mother's womb (Jer 15:10; 20:14-18). Jonah became despondent when God spared the repentant Ninevites and said, "Therefore now, O LORD, please take my life from me, for death is better to me than life" (Jon 4:3). Shortly thereafter Jonah was cheered by the shade of a plant that God had provided. When God caused the plant to die, "the sun beat down on Jonah's head so that he became faint and begged with all his soul to die, saying, 'Death is better to me than life'" (Jon 4:8).

And Job, that exemplar of tried faith, when, after the loss of his children and his estate, was urged by his wife to "curse God and die," reproved her and asked, "Shall we indeed accept good from God and not accept adversity?" (Job 2:9-11). Soon, however, when his body was sorely afflicted, he cursed the day on which he had been born and wished that he had died at birth (Job 3:1-19). He then identified himself with those "who long for death, but there is none, and dig for it more than for hidden treasures; who rejoice greatly, they exult when they find the grave" (Job 3:21-22). Later he cried out, "Oh that my request might come to pass, and that God would grant my longing! Would that God were willing to crush me; that He would loose His hand and cut me off!" (Job 6:8-9), and then he exclaimed, "My soul would choose suffocation, death rather than my pains" (Job 7:15). But regardless of how intensely these men yearned for an end to their suffering, indeed for death itself, there is not a scintilla of evidence that they for an instant seriously considered suicide as an option.

In the entirety of Jewish literature from the Old Testament through the fifth century A.D., we know of not one case of a Jew taking his own life or having someone kill him in order to escape from illness. There is only one instance of which we are aware of anyone in the sources attempting suicide when he was ill, and that was Herod. According to Josephus, when Herod the Great was nearing death, "he was so tormented by lack of food and a racking cough that his sufferings mastered him and he made an effort to anticipate his appointed end. He took an apple and asked for a knife, it being his habit to cut up apples when he ate them; then looking round to make sure there was no one to stop him he raised his hand to stab himself. But his cousin Achiab dashed up and stopped him by grasping his wrist."[66]

Why is this literature devoid of examples of Jews committing suicide, assisted or unassisted, when they were painfully or terminally ill? And why is the Talmud silent on this issue? It appears that suicide by the ill was so far from the Jewish experience that it did not present itself as a matter that the rabbis and interpreters of the law had occasion to address.

We should note that the Hebrew expression that can be translated as "euthanasia" (*mitah yafah*, "pleasant death") occurs in the Babylonian Talmud several times, but it is always with reference to the scriptural injunction "You shall love your neighbor as yourself" (Lev 19:18) as the basis for choosing the least painful execution for a condemned criminal.[67] But the Talmud and *Semahot* have much to say about death that was the result of natural processes, accident or violence other than that of war or persecution.

The opening sentence of *Semahot* is "A dying man is considered the same as a living man in every respect."[68] The Hebrew word translated "dying man" is *goses* (or *gosses*). It is important to distinguish this category of the dying from that of the *terefah* (or *tereifa*). We quote from Zlotnick's introduction to his translation of *Semahot*: "The term goses . . . must not be confused with *terefah*, a man who cannot possibly survive because of a fatal injury to a vital organ. Since the imminent death of the terefah is certain, he is called *gabra ketila*, 'a man slain,' and if one kills him, he cannot be tried, for in the eyes of the Sages he has killed a man already dead. Our text, however, is concerned only with the goses, a man who is dying but not necessarily of an obviously fatal organic injury. Although the Sages accept the rule that 'most gosesim die,' i.e. succumb to this illness, yet up to the moment of death the goses is legally alive, the rule itself conceding that some may live."[69]

There is a crucial text in the Babylonian Talmud on the distinctions between a *goses* and a *terefah*: "Our Rabbis taught: If ten men smote a man with ten staves, whether simultaneously or successively, and he died, they are exempt. R. Judah b. Bathyra said: 'If successively, the last is liable, because he struck the actual death blow.' R. Johanan said: 'Both derive [their rulings] from the same verse. "And he that killeth *kol nefesh* [lit. 'all life'] of man shall surely be put to death" ' (Lev. 24:17). The Rabbis maintain that *kol nefesh* implies the whole life; but R. Judah b. Bathyra holds that *kol nefesh* implies, whatever there is of life. Raba said: 'Both agree that if he killed a *terefah*, he is exempt; if he slew one who was dying through an act of God, he is liable; their dispute refers only to one who was dying through man's act; the one likens him to a *terefah*, the other to a person dying naturally. Now, he who likens him to a *terefah*, why does he not liken him to a person dying naturally? —Because no injury has been done to the latter; but an injury has been done to this one. Whilst he who likens him to a person dying naturally, why does he not liken him to a *terefah*? —A *terefah* has his vital organs affected, but this one has not.' "[70]

Baruch A. Brody, a philosopher and rabbi, comments: "This is a difficult text, one which has attracted considerable attention. The crucial point to keep in mind is that this is not a controversy about the licitness of the actions in question. Both parties agree, for example, that no one is punished if all ten beat the victim simultaneously, but obviously they all agree that doing that is illicit. So this text, as important as it is for understanding the full rabbinic attitude to the dying patient, is not relevant to the question of the moral licitness of killing a dying individual, even one whose vital organs have been fatally injured."[71] It is imperative to be aware that halakic discussions of the killing of a *terefah* focus entirely on the question of legal liability in a chain of causality, not moral culpability.

Semahot not only defined a *goses* as "the same as a living man in every respect" but also forbade anything to be done that would hasten his dying:

I.2. His jaws may not be bound, nor his orifices stopped, and no metal vessel or any other cooling object may be placed upon his belly until the moment he dies. . . .

I.3. He may not be stirred, nor may he be washed, and he should not be laid upon sand or salt, until the moment he dies.

I.4. His eyes may not be closed. Whosoever touches him or stirs him sheds blood. Rabbi Meir used to compare a dying man to a flickering lamp: the moment one touches it he puts it out. So, too, whosoever closes the eyes of a dying man is accounted as though he has snuffed out his life.

I.5. There may be no rending of clothes, nor baring of shoulders, nor eulogizing, and no coffin may be brought into the house, until the moment he dies.

I.6. There may be no heralding for him and no acclaiming of his works. Rabbi Judah said: "If the man was a scholar, his works may be acclaimed."

The purpose of these stipulations was to ensure that nothing be done that would hasten the death of the *goses*. As Zlotnick remarks, "All these are post-mortem practices, and are forbidden in the case of a goses because, being premature, they might hasten his death."[72] In I.2 those postmortem practices that would ostensibly retard the process of putrefaction are interdicted. The stipulations of I.3 involve the preparation of a corpse for burial. Placing the cadaver on sand or salt was also thought to retard putrefaction. Sections I.5 and I.6 deal with mourning for or eulogizing the dead. If a dying man, other than a scholar, heard his works acclaimed, he would regard such as probably the hyperbolic encomium for the deceased. Bringing in a coffin would obviously not encourage a dying person either.

In regard to I.4, we read in the Mishnah: "They do not close the eyes of a corpse on the Sabbath, nor on an ordinary day at the moment the soul goes forth. And he who closes the eyes of a corpse at the moment the soul goes forth, lo, this one sheds blood."[73] The Gemara on this mishnaic passage in the Babylonian Talmud begins, "He who closes [the eyes of a dying man] at the point of death is a murderer. This may be compared to a lamp that is going out: If a man places his finger upon it, it is immediately extinguished."[74]

The rabbinic literature of antiquity drew some lines, but not always precisely, between *pikku'ah nefesh,* the duty to preserve life, and the propriety of letting a *goses* die. *Pikku'ah nefesh* was the basis for the interdiction of any act that would hasten death. It was also the basis for not only permitting but also mandating that the sabbath be violated to care for the ill.[75] But there is a text in the Babylonian Talmud that is difficult to reconcile with the principle of *pikku'ah nefesh.* The passage in question is in the context of a sustained discussion of the propriety, indeed the licitness, of employing the services of the heathen (including Samaritans and Christians), especially those of midwives, wet nurses and physicians. In regard to the latter, "Said Raba in the name of R. Johanan: 'In the case where it is doubtful whether [the patient] will live or die, we must not allow them to heal; but if he will certainly die, we may allow them to heal.' 'Die [etc.]'! Surely there is still the life of the hour [to be considered]? The life of the hour is not to be considered. What authority have you for saying that the life of the hour is not to be considered? — The scriptural words, 'If we say: we will enter into the city, then the famine is in the city and we shall die there' [2 Kings 7:4]. Now there is the life of the hour [which they might forfeit]! This implies that the life of the hour is not to be considered. An objection was raised: 'No man should have any dealings with *Minim,* nor is it allowed to be healed by them even [in risking] an hour's life.' "[76]

Brody comments, "The rabbis prove that claim [that there is no necessity to be concerned about the loss of such a short period of life] by reference to the story in II Kings 7, of the four lepers who risked the short period of life they had left without food to enter a city in which they might be killed in the hope of finding food that would keep them alive. There is, despite this proof, an obvious difficulty with this text. . . . The Talmud specifically allows the violation of the Sabbath to save a person's life for a short period of time. Why then does this text say that we do not worry about short periods of remaining life?"[77] Brody answered his rhetorical question by quoting a text of *Tasafot,* a rabbinic work composed a millennium after the completion of the Talmud. It appears that ancient halakic authorities did not wrestle with the ambiguities of this talmudic text.

A question about which modern Jews continue to debate is whether it is licit to refrain from administering medical care that would only extend the dying process of the hopelessly ill or discontinue such treatment. There is a richly dynamic tradition of halakic considerations of this issue from antiquity to the present. We shall limit our discussion to the relevant talmudic texts. The central feature of these texts is prayer.

While there are several examples in the Old Testament of people praying for death—requests that God did not grant—in the Babylonian Talmud there is one instance in which God did answer the prayer in the affirmative. Honi the Circle-Drawer had slept for seventy years. When he awoke no one would believe that he was whom he claimed to be "nor did they give him the honour due to him. This hurt him greatly and he prayed [for death] and he died."[78]

Was it permissible to pray for the death of others to bring an end to their suffering? Rabbi Johanan "was plunged into deep grief" because of the death of a close friend. When some rabbis who had tried to comfort him found him to be inconsolable, they prayed for him, and he died.[79]

The only talmudic text that directly speaks to withdrawing "life-sustaining treatment" is the following: A famous rabbi was ill. His

handmaid ascended the roof and prayed: "The immortals desire Rabbi [to join them] and the mortals desire Rabbi [to remain with them]; may it be the will [of God] that the mortals may overpower the immortals." When, however, she saw how often he resorted to the privy, painfully taking off his *tefillin* and putting them on again, she prayed: "May it be the will [of the Almighty] that the immortals may overpower the mortals." As the Rabbis incessantly continued their prayers for [heavenly] mercy she took up a jar and threw it down from the roof to the ground. [For a moment] they ceased praying and the soul of Rabbi departed to its eternal rest.[80]

Jewish scholars refer frequently to this incident. It has been central to halakic discussions of preserving life from the close of the talmudic period until the present.

The evidence that we have surveyed suggests that in ancient Judaism the active hastening of the death of a *goses* was tantamount to homicide. While actively hastening the death of a *terefah* was not actionable as homicide (unless the *terefah* became a *goses*), nevertheless the killing of a *terefah* was condemned as morally reprehensible. While respect for life—specifically *pikku'ah nefesh*, the obligation to preserve life—was the moral imperative that condemned the active taking of the life of a dying person, it did not foster a sense of obligation to attempt to preserve at all costs the life of the dying or of the suffering. Not only is this the surface meaning of the texts, but also halakic tradition has thus interpreted these texts and has built upon them accordingly during the fifteen hundred years since the end of antiquity.

Cohn maintains that "Jewish law does not take formal cognizance of any 'rights.' . . . [It] is a system of duties: the service and worship of God is its general and overriding purpose, and as all law is God's law, it is self-evident that the duty to obey God is paramount. . . . The object of divine law can only be to establish divine rights and impose on human beings the corresponding duties. The conferment of rights by divine law can only be a consequence incidental to compliance with duties."[81] This is a vitally significant consideration. Add to it Rabbi Brody's observation that "one of the major [secular] arguments for the licitness of suicide is that one's life, like one's body and one's property, is one's own to control, to use, and to dispose of as one sees fit. . . . Judaism rejects that whole line of thought. One's life, as well as one's body and one's property, is not one's own to use and to dispose of as one sees fit."[82] Later he asserts, "The opposition to suicide is part of the general opposition to the view that human autonomy is *the* fundamental moral value."[83]

The same moral choices that informed suicide and euthanasia in the milieu in which Christianity arose are remarkably similar to those that prevail today. Many pagans today, although they would express it differently, would concur with the essence of the quotation from Pliny the Elder that we introduced early in this chapter: unlimited autonomy to take one's own life "rationally." Other pagans are uneasy with this nearly cavalier independence and in perhaps an ill-defined way emulate the Platonists' position that we do not have such unlimited authority. But there are both Jews and Christians who, regardless of the extent that they differ from each other and within their own diverse communities, share a sense of dependence upon their Creator who has endued human life with intrinsic and inherent value.

2

Why Early Christians Condemned Euthanasia & Suicide

Understanding suicide as a moral issue in early Christianity presents some interesting problems. In two respects it resembles the ethics of abortion: First, Scripture is silent about both.[1] Second, arguments against the moral permissibility of either, formulated inferentially from Scripture by the church fathers, are easily rejected as later moral developments read back into the Bible. Suicide, however, differs from abortion in that while even the earliest noncanonical Christian literature denounces abortion in unequivocal terms, condemnations of suicide by the early church fathers are relatively rare and hardly unequivocal.

There are at least three reasons for the comparative rarity and the equivocal nature of these condemnations. First, such condemnations of suicide by the church fathers as are extant were not part of the broad moral condemnation leveled by early Christian authors against what they regarded as the depravity of pagan society. The moral indignation of the early Christian community, particularly as it was directed against abortion and infanticide, received much of its vigor from the perceived helplessness of the victim, whether a fetus or an infant. Even the occasional condemnation of contraception was motivated in part by concern for the victim (in this case potential life); so also with gladiatorial combat and extremely cruel executions, in which the pagans needed victims to satisfy their lust for blood. Even acts of sexual immorality were often seen as involving victims, for the greatest indignation of Christians authors was reserved for the forced prostitution of both female and male slaves, helpless victims of pagan depravity. Even outside the brothel sexual immorality generally involved more than one individual in the act and hence the potential for there being unwilling victims of others' depravity. It is especially the helplessness of the victims of others' sins that increased the extent of moral indignation to the level so frequently encountered in Christian literature.

Second, the ethics of suicide in early Christianity is more ambiguous than are various other ethical issues such as infanticide or abortion. Condemnations of infanticide and abortion by early Christians were unequivocal: no exceptions were discussed. Furthermore, there was no ambiguity regarding what constituted infanticide or what constituted abortion.[2] Is severe asceticism that incidentally but not intentionally results in death suicide? And what of martyrdom? Discussions of what constitutes suicide flourish today. Such discussions often show a lack of precision in defining the English word *suicide* and in delineating the concept usually conveyed by that word. The situation in the ancient world permitted even more confusion since neither Greek nor Latin had a specific word for suicide.[3]

The third reason for the comparative rarity of condemnations of suicide by the early church fathers is that suicide does not appear to have been a sufficiently strong temptation for early Christians to be a problem for the early Christian community. We shall enlarge on this later in this and subsequent chapters.

The Yale historian George P. Fisher, in the second decade of the twentieth century, noted that for the Stoics, who justified suicide under many circumstances, "Life and Death are among the *adiaphora* — things indifferent, which may be chosen or rejected according to circumstances." He then remarked,

> How contrary is all this to the Christian feeling! The Christian believes in a Providence which makes all things work together for his good, and believes that there are no circumstances in which he is authorized to lay violent hands upon himself. There is no situation in which he cannot live with honor, and with advantage to himself as long as God chooses to continue him in being.[4]

Fisher perspicaciously grasped the most essential values of early Christianity and as a consequence concluded, "Hence, in the Scriptures there is no express prohibition of suicide, and no need of one."[5]

Fisher's assessment is also valid for the patristic ethos with one modification: toward the end of the patristic era some sources did approve of one form of suicide, and that is by women to preserve their chastity. Were it not for the fact that patristic literature does include prohibitions of suicide, his conclusion would be equally accurate for post-New Testament Christianity because the most basic Christian values expressed in the New Testament are the same values undergirding and elaborated in patristic literature.

Eternal Life, Physical Life—Eternal Death, Physical Death

The New Testament consistently juxtaposes for believers the certainty of physical death and the certainty of eternal life. Jesus promised his followers when "I go and prepare a place for you, I will come again, and receive you to Myself; that where I am, there you may be also" (Jn 14:3). This assurance of the promise of resurrection, Christ's return and impending heavenly glory[6] conditions the New Testament attitude toward physical life and physical death. Physical life at its best is acknowledged as brief and uncertain (e.g., Jas 4:13-16; 1 Pet 1:24), and spiritual life is regarded as being of inestimably greater value.

For Jesus' followers this mortal life was to be a pilgrimage (Eph 2:19; Phil 3:20; Heb 13:14; 1 Pet 2:11). Hence it is not surprising that Jesus told his disciples not to "fear those who kill the body, but are unable to kill the soul; but rather fear Him who is able to destroy both soul and body in hell" (Mt 10:28; Lk 12:4-5). He assured his disciples that no one could snatch them out of his hand (Jn 10:28). Since Christ's followers belong to him (e.g., Jn 10:27-30; Rom 6:1-10; Eph 2:6; Col 2:12; 3:1), they should not fear physical death. As Paul writes to the Romans, "If we live, we live for the Lord, or if we die, we die for the Lord; therefore whether we live or die, we are the Lord's. For to this end Christ died and lived again, that He might be Lord both of the dead and of the living" (Rom 14:8-9).

Earlier in the same epistle Paul had asked, "Who shall separate us from the love of Christ?" (Rom 8:35). His answer was that nothing can "separate us from the love of God, which is in Christ Jesus our Lord" (Rom 8:39), and the list of examples of realities that cannot separate the believer from Christ is headed by death (Rom 8:38). Hence Paul, when writing to the Corinthians, can quote Isaiah 25:8, "Death is swallowed up in victory," and Hosea 13:14, "O death, where is your victory? O death, where is your sting?" and then go on to say, "The sting of death is sin, and the power of sin is the law; but thanks be to God, who gives us the victory through our Lord Jesus Christ" (1 Cor 15:54-57).

The sting of death having been removed, the fear of death having been vitiated, Jesus' followers were to look to "an inheritance which is imperishable and undefiled and will not fade away, reserved in heaven" for them

(1 Pet 1:4), where their names are written (Lk 10:20; cf. Mt 13:43; Jn 14:3; Rom 8:17; 2 Cor 4:17). For the Christian death is also described as a state of being "at home with the Lord" (2 Cor 5:8; cf. Lk 23:43; Acts 7:59-60).

To the church fathers spiritual life was of infinitely greater value than physical life, and spiritual death was much more to be feared than physical death. They felt Christians should not fear physical death, for it would be the means whereby they would be brought to those ineffable delights that heaven had in store for them. Numerous examples could be given from patristic sources, but typical is a treatise written by Ambrose (c. 339-397) entitled *Death as a Good*. He begins by asserting, "Should death do injury to the soul, it can be considered an evil, but should it do the soul no harm, it cannot."[7] Only Christians have the correct perspective on life and death, and they have always "lamented the longevity of this pilgrimage, since they consider it more glorious 'to depart and to be with Christ'. . . ."[8] After an extensive discussion of a wide variety of related issues, he says, "To the just, death is a harbor of rest; to the guilty, it is reckoned a shipwreck."[9] Then after quoting Colossians 3:3-4, he begins his concluding paragraph with the exclamation "let us therefore hasten to life."[10]

Sentiments identical to those which Ambrose expressed can be found in virtually all the church fathers. Their attitude toward death is nicely described by Peter Brown when he observes that "the early church tended to leapfrog the grave. The long process of mourning and the slow adjustment to the great sadness of mortality tended to be repressed by a heady belief in the afterlife."[11] Hence with great frequency we encounter statements such as the following by John Chrysostom (349-407), "We should rejoice in the death of the righteous,"[12] and by Tertullian (c. 160-c. 220), "He who had gone ahead is not to be mourned, though certainly he will be missed." One's longing for the deceased was not to be a desire for the departed to be here but rather a desire to go and be with them. A few sentences later, Tertullian asserts that "if we bear it with impatience and grief that others have attained their goal, we ourselves do not want to attain our goal."[13] This was frequently given as the mark of the truly committed and serious follower of Christ: a desire to die and be with Christ, demonstrated by a genuine envy for those who have gone home already.

Doing God's Will

Whether one is reading the Gospel narratives or the epistles, the pattern that one sees for the Christian's life is to do God's will. Jesus said, "If you love Me, you will keep My commandments" (Jn 14:15; cf. Jn 14:21, 23;

15:10). His commandments are varied but are summed up in his exchange with a scribe who asked him, "Teacher, which is the great commandment in the Law?" Jesus replied: "'You shall love the Lord your God with all your heart, and with all your soul, and with all your mind.' This is the great and foremost commandment. And a second is like it, 'You shall love your neighbor as yourself.' On these two commandments depend the whole Law and the Prophets" (Mt 22:34-40; Mk 12:28-31; cf. Lk 10:25-37).

Potential applications of these two commandments are diverse, and specific injunctions contained in the New Testament are numerous; but all may be conveniently placed under two rubrics: service and holiness. Service to God and to humanity includes caring both for people's spiritual needs and for their material needs.[14] Caring for their spiritual needs requires evangelism, which is bearing witness to the truth of the gospel. Holiness involves a sustained warfare against sin, that is, against one's own sins or propensity to sin. These categories provide the framework for a consideration of various types of and motivations for suicide. If any form of martyrdom can reasonably be regarded as suicide, then the New Testament teaching most specifically applicable to the question is on bearing witness for Christ. Can suicide from despair over the struggle within, from a desire to preserve holiness in the face of assaults against it or death resulting from severe asceticism be vindicated by reference to the New Testament? If so, it could only be within the context of the New Testament's exhortations to holiness. So also would suicide to escape the afflictions of life, when seen in the context of New Testament teaching about the edificatory and sanctifying role of suffering in the Christian's life.

Persecution and Martyrdom

Jesus had assured his disciples that if people persecuted him, they would also persecute them.[15] It was to be regarded as a special sign of blessedness when Christians were persecuted for righteousness' sake, for "theirs is the kingdom of heaven." Christians were to rejoice when they were reviled and persecuted for Christ's sake. Paul writes to the Philippians that "to you it has been granted for Christ's sake, not only to believe in Him, but also to suffer for His sake" (Phil 1:29). The verb translated "granted" is a form of *charizomai*, a word that means "to bestow graciously." These sufferings were not the exclusive privilege of a select few but of anyone who followed Christ in the manner Paul described when he wrote to Timothy, "Indeed, all who desire to live godly in Christ Jesus will be persecuted" (2 Tim 3:12). Persecution in its most violent or extreme forms might result in martyrdom.

Does the New Testament provide any encouragement for courting martyrdom? In a sense, yes. Jesus taught that one should rejoice when persecuted. The apostles felt that it was an honor when they were counted worthy of suffering for Christ's sake, and Paul saw persecution as a gift graciously given by God. Furthermore in several passages the correspondence between the sufferings and the glory of Christ is stressed (e.g., Jn 17:4-5; Phil 2:8-9; Heb 2:9). In suffering the Christian was said to share or participate in Christ's sufferings. Sometimes this was linked with the idea of sharing in Christ's glory (e.g., Rom 8:17-18; 1 Pet 4:13).

These ideas, however, could not reasonably be taken as injunctions to seek martyrdom when they are tempered by the precepts and examples that the New Testament provided for those who would bear witness for Christ. Paul urged his readers, "If possible, so far as it depends on you, be at peace with all men" (Rom 12:18). Likewise Peter admonished his audience to be kind-hearted and humble in spirit (1 Pet 3:8). Just a few sentences later he urged his readers to always be "ready to make a defense to every one who asks you to give an account for the hope that is in you, yet with gentleness and reverence" (1 Pet 3:15). These epistolary injunctions correspond closely to the commands regarding conduct and the precepts of character that Jesus gave in his Sermon on the Mount (Mt 5—7).

Not only were Christians to refrain from giving offense by their response to affliction, but also they were to display a positive witness of love when they were persecuted. Christ said that although one commonly hears the adage "You shall love your neighbor, and hate your enemy," his teaching was "Love your enemies, and pray for those who persecute you" (Mt 5:43-44). Paul, in the same spirit, wrote to the Romans: "Bless those who persecute you; bless and curse not" (Rom 12:14). Specifically Christians were to follow Jesus as their example (Mt 11:29; 16:24; Phil 2:5-8; 1 Pet 2:21). The Gospel narratives show that Jesus often withdrew from his enemies. Nor did he give himself up to the authorities in Jerusalem. Rather he allowed himself to be arrested. Also he told his disciples that men would deliver them up (Mt 10:17), not that they should deliver themselves up. Paul fled from Damascus to avoid those who wanted to kill him, and his flight was ignominious and personally humbling: he allowed himself to be lowered over the walls of the city in a basket (Acts 9:23-25; cf. 2 Cor 11:32-33). And when he and Silas were persecuted in Thessalonica, their fellow Christians sent them away by night to a safer city (Acts 17:1-10).

Is avoiding or fleeing from persecution denying Christ? The New

Testament answered this question with an unequivocal no. Jesus thus instructed his disciples: "Whenever they persecute you in this city, flee to the next" (Mt 10:23). This warning is followed by the admonition not to fear those who can kill the body and the obligation to confess Christ before other people.

The New Testament clearly presented an obligation to die for Christ if the only alternative was to deny him. Significantly the list of people to be given over to eternal punishment, that is, to the "second death," is headed by the "cowardly," followed by the unbelieving ("untrustworthy" or "faithless" [Rev. 21:8]). There are, as we have seen, passages in the New Testament that not only discouraged seeking martyrdom but encouraged, both by precept and by example, flight from persecution at least under some circumstances.

The subject of martyrdom in the early church is complex.[16] We cannot deal with the question of why Christians were persecuted but must consider reactions to persecution by those who were persecuted or in danger of death. Christians have reacted to persecution in five different ways: accepting whatever penalties were inflicted, including death; avoiding martyrdom through, for example, bribery or forged documents; fleeing; volunteering for or provoking martyrdom; and apostatizing.

The first of these was always approved and the fifth always condemned during the patristic period. The second, third and fourth were much more problematic and evoked considerable disagreement within the Christian community, especially between rigorists and moderates. The major problem posed by apostasy in the face of persecution was whether the Christian community should receive apostates back into fellowship. That controversy, however, lies outside the purview of this study. When we say that apostasy was consistently condemned by the orthodox community, we are excluding certain heretical groups that were ostensibly Christian (e.g., the Gnostics).

Much more troublesome to the early Christian community were the second, third and fourth responses to persecution: avoiding martyrdom through bribery or forged documents; fleeing; and seeking, provoking or volunteering for martyrdom. The first of these three, though typically condemned, presented the same problem as apostatizing: should the repentant offender be welcomed back into communion after the persecution has subsided? The last two are closely related, since it can be and has been argued that refusing the former is tantamount to doing the latter.

Clement of Alexandria (c. 155-c. 220) writes:

Now we, too, say that those who have rushed on death (for there are some, not belonging to us, but sharing the name merely, who are in haste to give themselves up, the poor wretches dying through hatred to the Creator)—these, we say, banish themselves without being martyrs, even though they are punished publicly. For they do not preserve the characteristic mark of believing martyrdom, inasmuch as they have not known the only true God but give themselves up to a vain death, as the Gymnosophists of the Indians to useless fire.[17]

A few chapters later Clement picks up this subject again:

When, again, He [Christ] says, "When they persecute you in this city, flee ye to the other," He does not advise flight, as if persecution were an evil thing; nor does He enjoin them by flight to avoid death, as if in dread of it, but wishes us neither to be the authors nor abettors of any evil to any one, either to ourselves or the persecutor and murderer. For He, in a way, bids us take care of ourselves. But he who disobeys is rash and foolhardy. If he who kills a man of God sins against God, he also who presents himself before the judgment-seat becomes guilty of his death. And such is also the case with him who does not avoid persecution, but out of daring presents himself for capture. Such a one, as far as in him lies, becomes an accomplice in the crime of the persecutor. And if he also uses provocation, he is wholly guilty, challenging the wild beast. And similarly, if he afford any cause for conflict or punishment, or retribution or enmity, he gives occasion for persecution.[18]

We must not suppose that Clement did not hold martyrdom in high esteem and regard it as an obligation if the alternative was apostasy. He wrote that the true Christian "when called, obeys easily, and gives up his body to him who asks. . . . In love to the Lord he will most gladly depart from this life."[19] But we do see him adamantly opposed to seeking martyrdom. He demonstrated this attitude in practice by fleeing from Alexandria when persecution struck there.

But not all Christians shared his views. Clement's contemporary Tertullian, in his *Scorpiace*, written while he was still a Catholic, spoke of the faithful being hunted down like rabbits.[20] The imagery implies that he regarded flight as legitimate. In his treatise *Patience*, written about the same time, he specified that patience is tested by torture, martyrdom and the inconveniences of flight.[21] But in his *Ad Uxorem*, also written during the same period, he asserted that although flight is permitted as preferable to apostasy, it is not good.[22] This is the first hint of a peculiarity in Tertullian's thought at a time when he was drawing nearer to leaving the Catholic fold for Montanism. After his change of allegiance to this rigorist sect, he wrote *Flight in Time of Persecution*, in which he denounced flight from persecution as a denial of Christ and a sign of cowardice. He explained Jesus' command to his disciples to flee when persecuted as applying only to that time and place, "For, if they had been killed right at the beginning, the diffusion of the Gospel, too, would have been prevented."[23]

Others within Catholicism regarded flight from persecution as tantamount to apostasy or to bribery, to which a fair number had recourse, hence avoiding martyrdom without having to deny Christ by word or by performing pagan rituals. Tertullian, especially as a Montanist, represents a rigorist, Clement a moderate, position on the question. The debate continued well beyond their time as is well illustrated by the case of Peter, bishop of Alexandria, in the early fourth century. During the Great Persecution (303-312) Peter fled from Alexandria to avoid martyrdom. After the persecution subsided, he returned and composed what may originally have been merely a paschal letter but which was later incorporated into the canon law of the Eastern church. In this letter he disparaged those who had volunteered for martyrdom and approved those who had saved their lives by bribery or by flight.[24] Peter's position was not rigorist and is somewhat more liberal than even Clement's, with whom he shared the opinion that the Christian who did not attempt to escape martyrdom shared moral culpability with the persecutors.

Numerous examples of the contrast between the rigorist and moderate positions could be introduced. But the contrast between the martyrdoms of Ignatius (in 98 or 117) and Polycarp (between 155 and 160) should be sufficient. In the letters that he wrote while awaiting execution, Ignatius displayed, as W. H. C. Frend says, "a state of exaltation bordering on mania."[25] His was unequivocally a case of voluntary martyrdom. Polycarp presents quite a different picture. Yielding to the entreaties of his friends, he withdrew from his city to avoid arrest. Ultimately he was apprehended and, when suffering martyrdom, evinced a moving serenity in the face of death that is quite in contrast with Ignatius's passionate desire for martyrdom.[26]

Both Eusebius[27] (c. 265-339) and the anonymous but contemporary author of the *Martyrdom of Polycarp* record the example of a certain Phrygian named Quintus

> who had forced himself and some others to come forward of their own accord. Him the Pro-Consul persuaded with many entreaties to take the oath and offer sacrifice. For this reason, therefore, brethren, we do not commend those who give themselves up, since the Gospel does not give this teaching.[28]

Clement and Peter of Alexandria would have agreed with this last sentence. Tertullian would not have. In his last extant work, addressed to a Roman official named Scapula, Tertullian wrote concerning persecution and martyrdom that Christians, in this case Montanists,

> do not fear these things, but willingly call them down upon ourselves. When Arrius Antoninus [governor of the province of Asia c. 184-185] was carrying out a vehement persecution in Asia, all the Christians of the city appeared in a body before his tribunal. After ordering a few to be led away to execution, he said to the rest, "Wretched men, if you wish to die, you have precipices and ropes to hang yourselves." If it should come into our mind to do the same thing here, also, what will you do with so many thousands of human beings . . . giving themselves up to you?[29]

Aside from this incident, there is little evidence of Christians presenting themselves en masse before officials.[30] But when it did occasionally happen or when individuals or groups volunteered for martyrdom, it undoubtedly smacked of theatrics.

In his invective sketch of Peregrinus, the profligate-turned-Christian-turned-Cynic, Lucian, a second-century Greek satirist, said about Christians that "the poor devils have convinced themselves they're all going to be immortal and live forever, which makes most of them take death lightly and voluntarily give themselves up to it."[31]

Although one need take satirists with a grain of salt, Lucian's assessment is probably not a significant exaggeration of the sentiments of many pagans who may have regarded Christians as suicidal for their willingness to be martyred. But such pagans, including Lucian and the emperor Marcus Aurelius, who regarded Christians as morbid exhibitionists,[32] would probably have been unaware of how many Christians did unobtrusively flee from persecution to avoid martyrdom. Very likely the majority of Christians who were martyred accepted death "voluntarily" when the only alternative was apostasy. Dying voluntarily does not necessarily mean seeking martyrdom. We have already seen that Clement condemned unequivocally those who voluntarily give themselves up to the officials. But he was consistent when he said that the true Christian "will not forsake his creed through fear of death. . . . In love to the Lord he will most gladly depart from this life. . . . With good courage, then, he goes to the Lord, his friend, for whom he voluntarily gives his body."[33]

Boniface Ramsey asserts that in patristic thought, "since martyrdom was a charism, a grace, it could not be demanded as a right; it was a free gift of God."[34] Clement wrote that true Christians are "distinguished from others that are called martyrs, inasmuch as some furnish occasions for themselves, and rush into the heart of dangers." By contrast true Christians, "in accordance with right reason, protect themselves" but, with "God really calling them, promptly surrender themselves, and confirm the call, from being conscious of no precipitancy."[35] Hence one could be certain that God was calling one to martyrdom only if one had done nothing to precipitate it. During an outbreak of plague in Carthage many Christians were distressed because if they died of the pestilence, they would be deprived of the possibility of martyrdom. Cyprian (c. 200-258), in addressing their concern, maintained that "martyrdom is not in your power but in the giving of God, and you cannot say that you have lost what you do not know whether you deserved to receive."[36]

The significance of martyrdom varied according to one's soteriology. To some Christians martyrdom was the only sure means of salvation. Tertullian in his later years is representative of this position. To other Christians martyrdom was one of several means of sanctification leading to salvation. We see this idea heartily emphasized by Clement. Those who held the former position would probably crave martyrdom more than the latter, even though their desire for martyrdom would not necessarily cause them actively to seek it. But even for Clement, martyrdom was the most perfect display of love and was to be desired above any other form of death. Other forms of death could never offer the spiritual glory that martyrdom provided. Hence for those who ardently wished to depart from this life, any form of death, including suicide, would be an obstacle to that one cherished form of death, martyrdom. Accordingly those who most wished to die would seek martyrdom if their theology permitted it. Likely the majority of those who wished to quit life held the position most commonly encountered in the literature, namely, that seeking martyrdom was wrong. The basis for a condemnation of actively seeking that one laudable form of death would *eo ipso* preclude intentionally ending one's own life through some lesser means.

It is likely that the vast majority of Christians before the legalization of Christianity in 313 not only did not seek martyrdom but held that Christ's admonition to flee when persecuted had an abiding validity. Those who believed that one should seek by flight to avoid the most glorious and spiritually fulfilling form of death would be hard pressed to formulate a theological justification for actively seeking to end their lives by their own hand. Hence it is not surprising that in the literature extant from the period before the legalization of Christianity, there is absolutely no mention of Christians who could not succeed in provoking pagans to put them to death committing suicide.

Nevertheless we do no service to the truth if we deny that there have been some aberrations and excesses in the history of Christianity. Some early Christians intentionally provoked pagans to martyr them. It may be perverse obstinacy to insist that such were not suicides.

Sin and Forgiveness

Sin and holiness, diametrical opposites, are frequently contrasted in the New Testament. Christians were regularly reminded what their way of life was like when they were still "dead in their trespasses and sins." They were urged not to revert to their old ways. Peter wrote, "As obedient children, do not be conformed to the former lusts which were yours in your ignorance, but like the Holy One who called you, be holy yourselves also in all your behavior; because it is written, 'You shall be holy, for I am holy'" (1 Pet 1:14-16; cf. Mt 5:48). Spiritual life necessitates death to sin and to self (2 Cor 4:11; 5:15), that is, conformity to the will of God, which Paul describes as "your sanctification" (1 Thess 4:3): "For God has not called us for the purpose of impurity, but in sanctification. Consequently, he who rejects this is not rejecting man but the God who gives his Holy Spirit to you" (1 Thess 4:7-8).

Hence, as the epistle to the Hebrews exhorted, "Pursue . . . the sanctification without which no one will see the Lord" (Heb 12:14). The authors of the New Testament never denied that such striving required considerable effort. "For," as Paul wrote, "the flesh sets its desire against the Spirit, and the Spirit against the flesh; for these are in opposition to one another, so that you may not do the things that you please" (Gal 5:17). The New Testament does not deny either the potential for sin in the Christian's life or the reality of the struggle, but it assures Christians of forgiveness and ultimate victory.[37] Hence despair over sin has no place in the New Testament that could justify, much less encourage, suicide. The New Testament consistently offers salvation to non-Christians who despair over sin; and it consistently promises assurance of restoration and progress in the spiritual life to Christians who fall into sin[38] or are discouraged by the conflict that rages both within and without. To Christian and non-Christian alike, such a message is antithetical to encouraging suicide.

Overall there is considerably more emphasis upon joy in believing and upon ultimate victory over sin in the New Testament and in patristic literature than upon the necessity of the struggle against sin. This is not to say that the latter is not emphasized. The struggle against sin is one aspect of the sanctifying process. It is the active part, that in which the Christian is expected to take the initiative. There is also a rather passive aspect, in which the Christian is expected merely to respond. The first of these is pertinent in a discussion of two of the types of or motivations for suicide that some modern authors attribute to early Christians. The second, as we shall see, is also relevant to a discussion of suicide. We can label the first of these self-discipline, the second God's discipline.

Mortification of the Flesh

The self-discipline to which Christians are called is "mortification," that is, a "putting to death," which is the literal meaning of the Greek word *nekroō*, used in Romans 8:13: "If you are living according to the flesh, you must die; but if by the Spirit you are putting to death the deeds of the body, you will live." Similarly Paul wrote to the Galatians, "The one who sows to his own flesh shall from the flesh reap corruption, but the one who sows to the Spirit shall from the Spirit reap eternal life" (Gal 6:8). Earlier he had urged them, "Walk by the Spirit, and you will not carry out the desire of the flesh" (Gal 5:16). Paul said virtually the same thing to the church in Rome, when he told them to "make no provision for the flesh in regard to its lusts." This is in conjunction with the command to "put on the Lord Jesus Christ" (Rom 13:14). Peter likewise beseeched those to whom he was writing "as aliens and strangers to abstain from fleshly lusts, which wage war against the soul" (1 Pet 2:11). These verses, along with Galatians 5:17 and Romans 7:15-24, reveal a strong dichotomy between the "flesh" and the "spirit" or "Spirit," and have, along with other statements made in the New Testament, sometimes provided the justification for an extreme denigration of the body, a severe asceticism that is based upon a radical dualism.

Writing to the church in Corinth, in which some problems of sexual immorality had arisen, Paul asked, "Do you not know that your bodies are members of Christ?" (1 Cor 6:15). After urging the Corinthians to shun immorality, he exclaimed, "Or do you not know that your body is a temple of the Holy Spirit who is in you, whom you have from God, and that you are not your own? For you have been bought with a price: therefore glorify God in your body" (1 Cor 6:19-20).

"Glorify God in your body." This command, taken out of the broader moral context of New Testament teaching, can justify any use of the body that is construed by an individual as glorifying God. Paul, as we have seen, desired that "Christ shall even now, as always, be exalted [literally, glorified] in my body, whether by life or by death" (Phil 1:20). One who died for Christ certainly glorified God by his or her death. But glorifying God in one's body, other than by martyrdom, is an ambiguous concept. Obviously one did not glorify God in one's body by breaking any of God's commandments, by sinning in any way; hence the command must be understood within the much broader framework of Christian ethics.

Let us now consider that form of self-discipline that sometimes led to death, that is, severe asceticism. Christian asceticism was motivated by a desire to subdue one's propensities to sin. Certain sects have now and then interpreted the doctrine of soteriology as requiring redemptive suffering, that is, earning favor with God through one's own propitiatory suffering. Such thought was sometimes bolstered by a perceived dualism between the spirit and the flesh, the latter being regarded as inherently evil.

A basic principle of the New Testament, however, is that the incarnation demonstrates that the material world was not rendered essentially evil by the Fall. The contrast between spirit and flesh presented in the New Testament is a vital dichotomy, not a dualism. The radical dualism that typified various groups in the early centuries of Christianity (e.g., Gnostics, Marcionites and Manichaeans) that were declared heretical was founded upon a denigration of the entire material realm as essentially evil, leading to two opposite expressions: a sometimes lascivious antinomianism or a severe asceticism. But throughout the early centuries of Christianity there was a tension within orthodoxy between denying that the material realm was evil and desiring to subdue the flesh with its propensities to sin. Sometimes a functional but not theologically radical dualism strained the bounds of orthodoxy by exaggerating the flesh-spirit or body-soul dichotomy of the New Testament into a severe asceticism.

Did the New Testament support abuse of the physical body to any extent approaching a self-discipline that could cause death? Jesus said to his disciples, "If your right eye makes you stumble, tear it out and throw it from you. . . . And if your right hand makes you stumble, cut it off, and throw it from you." He concluded both statements thus: "for it is better for you that one of the parts of your body perish, than for your whole body to go into hell" (Mt 5:29-30).

Paul frequently compared the Christian with the athlete who diligently sought to win the prize through training and said of himself, "I run in such a way, as not without aim; I box in such a way, as not beating the air; but I buffet my body and make it my slave, lest possibly, after I have preached to others, I myself should be disqualified" (1 Cor 9:26-27). Even during Paul's lifetime there were some who were advocating a radical (pre-Gnostic or early Gnostic) dualism. He wrote his epistle to the Colossians in part to counter such teaching: "These are matters which have, to be sure, the appearance of wisdom in self-made religion and self-abasement and severe treatment of the body, but are of no value against fleshly indulgence" (Col 2:23; cf. 1 Tim 4:3). The New Testament clearly asserted that it was the carnal mind—that is, "the mind set on the flesh"—that was "hostile toward God; for it does not subject itself to the law of God, for it is not even able to do so." Hence those who are in that sense "in the flesh . . . cannot please God" (Rom 8:7-8). Abusing one's body, which is described as the "temple of the Holy Spirit," profits nothing. It appears that the New Testament on balance did not encourage any self-discipline or asceticism that could be so severe as to cause one's death.

How did the church fathers feel that Christians should regard forms of suffering other than persecution? Were they to inflict suffering upon themselves in pursuit of sanctification? And what of those afflictions that beset humanity generally? Is God sovereign, and if so, how should Christians' appreciation of God's sovereignty affect their understanding of sanctification and consequently their response to tribulation? We shall begin by considering self-inflicted suffering.

Asceticism, which is the practice of strict self-denial as a spiritual discipline, was a marked feature of early Christianity beginning in the late second or early third century. Clement of Alexandria was the first Christian author to emphasize asceticism as an ideal on the same level as martyrdom. Later, when Christianity became a licit religion and Christians ceased to be martyred for their faith, the ascetic replaced the martyr in the minds of many Christians as the new spiritual hero. The ascetic way of life in its more extreme forms involved a vilification and abuse of the body by those who had withdrawn from society to engage in a determined effort to subdue indwelling sin. Their self-discipline was regarded as a "daily martyrdom."

Mortification of the flesh (i.e., the carnal mind) and denial of self are stressed in the New Testament. But the asceticism that developed in the late second and early third centuries and gained considerable momentum in the fourth went beyond a simple application of New Testament principles. The climate in which Christian asceticism arose was one in which various classical schools of philosophy extolled simplicity and frugality and in which some pagans yielded to the impulse to experience the "flight of the alone to the alone" and withdrew from society. A few of these became severe ascetics who sought suffering for expiatory, propitiatory or purificatory ends by abusing their bodies as the prisons of their souls.[39] They were similar in some of their excesses to members of certain heretical groups, such as the Gnostics, Manichaeans and Marcionites (dualists who conceived of matter, including the body, as inherently evil).

While the New Testament, particularly Paul, speaks of a dichotomy between flesh and spirit, some Christian ascetics strained the bounds of orthodoxy when they exaggerated this dichotomy by abusing the body for the good of the soul. During these centuries there was only a very fine line between a still orthodox but extreme mortification of the flesh and a dualistic, heretical denunciation of the flesh as inherently evil. Although many church fathers did vilify the body, for the most part their appraisal of the body's worth was tempered by their conviction that it was morally neutral, potentially either a temple or a tomb, and must be subservient to the soul in the latter's campaign against evil.[40] Augustine (354-430), who is typically regarded as exemplifying the orthodox spirit in this as in most matters, held that the body was but the slave of the soul. Hence abusing the body accomplished nothing.[41]

Much that the church fathers say about the body strikes our analgesic ethos as severe. Much of it also appears to contradict their stress on the value of life and on health as a good.[42] For the modern audience it is one of the most enigmatic features of Christianity during the third, fourth and fifth centuries. All the church fathers regarded most things and most conditions as potentially good or as potentially evil, depending on the Christian's use of or response to them. Health could be a good thing, or it could be a bad thing, as could sickness or any other form or source of suffering.

How were Christians to respond when they were ill? We shall see in chapter three that they were typically encouraged to seek healing but were admonished not to cling desperately to life. But were they to aggravate the condition, thereby increasing their suffering and thus supposedly derive some spiritual benefit? All the church fathers insisted on a practical self-denial and a subduing of the flesh. The extremes of asceticism of which they approved varied. Clement was mild in that regard compared with Jerome (c. 345-c. 419), who with a hearty fortitude that well matched his often caustic personality bordered on the severe in the self-denial that he both practiced and preached. In one letter Jerome writes that when one's limbs are weak from fasting, Satan may oppress him with illness. What then should he do? Why, respond to the devil just as Paul did, saying "When I am weak, then am I strong" and "Power is made perfect in weakness."[43]

However, in a letter to the lady Paula, whose twenty-year-old daughter, Blaesilla, had recently died, Jerome chides her for fasting. He imagines Christ saying to her that such fasting, which gratifies her grief, is displeasing to him. "Such fasts are my enemies. I receive no soul which forsakes the body against my will." It would be suicide for her to die in this way. Interestingly Blaesilla's death had likely been hastened by her severe self-abasement, which Jerome had then most heartily encouraged. He still approved of it when he wrote to Paula. Toward the end of the letter he rebuked Paula for her public display of grief during the funeral procession. Not only was it a bad witness since Christians were supposed to rejoice in the "homegoing" of loved ones, but also he knew what the Romans viewing the procession were probably saying: The girl was "killed with fasting." "How long must we refrain from driving these detestable monks out of Rome?" "They have misled this unhappy lady."[44] Apparently the fasting in which the already sick Blaesilla had engaged, which probably contributed to her death, was in Jerome's opinion pleasing to Christ. But Paula's fasting was displeasing to Christ because her motivations were wrong. And if she had died because of it, it would have been sinful, and consequently Christ would not have received her soul since it would have forsaken her body against his will.

There are some very fine lines to draw. And we can rest assured that Jerome drew them very close to those extremes of asceticism that earned the status of heresy. Most of the church fathers would not have gone as far as Jerome did in exhorting others to persevere in subduing and denying the flesh. But all shared the view that the soul was of infinitely greater value than the body. They did, however, espouse an obligation to care for the body. Hence the tension between these two obligations as perceived by the Christian community at that time and for a long time after as well.

Once again, as with martyrdom, we do no service to the truth if we deny that there have been some aberrations and excesses in the history of Christianity. Asceticism as a Christian virtue became a form of daily martyrdom, especially after Christians ceased to be a persecuted minority. Although the church quite consistently condemned asceticism if it was based on dualistic heresy or if it was practiced to excess, some Christians undoubtedly brought on an early demise through immoderate mortification of the flesh. Were they suicides? The philosophical principle of double effect (i.e., distinguishing between results that are intended and consequences that are foreseen and even inevitable but not desired) may be marshaled in support of the contention that they were not. Intent is then the criterion. Severe asceticism was practiced not in order to expedite one's death but to purify one's soul.

God's Discipline: Patience and Perseverance in Suffering

Let us turn from self-discipline to God's discipline, from self-imposed austerities to the sufferings and afflictions that are an inevitable part of the human condition. Life becomes exceedingly difficult sometimes, owing to matters over which the individual has no ultimate control, matters that have traditionally been subsumed under the rubric of providence.

For Christians all circumstances that impinge upon and disturb their settled existence can be regarded from a New Testament point of view as discipline. The epistle to the Hebrews teaches that Christ, although God's own Son, "learned obedience from the things which He suffered" (Heb 5:8). Since Christ's divinity and absolute moral perfection are stressed in this epistle, we must assume that this learning of obedience through suffering is not intended as a demonstration of Christ's deficient obedience of which his sufferings were corrective. The passage seems to indicate that in his incarnate state he was in some way edified by his sufferings, for the next verse begins with the statement that by this he was made perfect, that is, complete. Earlier in the same epistle it is explicitly stated that "it was fitting for Him [God], for whom are all things, and through whom are all things, in bringing many sons to glory, to perfect the author of their salvation through sufferings" (Heb 2:10). If in some mysterious way Christ himself, although he was never deficient in obedience, could be taught obedience through suffering; if he, although incarnate God, could be edified and perfected through suffering, so also then could suffering be a most beneficent and edificatory factor in the lives of his followers.

Just as being persecuted for righteousness was a consequence of living a godly life in Christ Jesus, so also was suffering in other forms part of God's edification of his children, according to the epistle to the Hebrews. The passage in question includes a quotation from Proverbs: "My son, do not regard lightly the discipline of the Lord, nor faint when you are reproved by Him; for those whom the Lord loves He disciplines, and He scourges every son whom He receives." The author of the epistle to the Hebrews comments thus:

> It is for discipline that you endure; God deals with you as sons; for what son is there whom his father does not discipline? But if you are without discipline . . . then you are illegitimate children and not sons. . . . [God] disciplines us for our good, that we may share His holiness. All discipline for the moment seems not to be joyful, but sorrowful; yet to those who have been trained by it, afterwards it yields the peaceful fruit of righteousness. (Heb 12:5-11)

This passage says little about the nature of the discipline that God would visit upon his children. It is described as a reproving and a scourging and as something unpleasant, indeed painful. But discipline's effect on the Christian's character, if the discipline was properly received, was salutary and more than sufficient compensation for the pain, since it bore a peaceful fruit of righteousness to those who have been trained by it.

Numerous passages can be adduced from the New Testament where the edificatory aspects of suffering are stressed. It seems that in New

Testament terms suffering was to be viewed as something in which Christians could rejoice, for two reasons: the very fact that Christians experienced and responded as they did to certain kinds of suffering was proof of sonship; and God was using the suffering as a means of causing his children to grow spiritually, if the response to the affliction was right. Perseverance, endurance, standing firm, overcoming—to such were Christians exhorted. Christ had told his disciples that "it is the one who has endured to the end who will be saved" (Mt 10:22 = Mk 13:13; cf. Mt 24:13). The same theme is emphasized in various epistles and especially in the book of Revelation.[45]

Did the New Testament permit or encourage despair in the face of affliction that would justify suicide? We already noted that the author of the epistle to the Hebrews (Heb 12:5-6) urged his readers to avoid two extremes when under God's hand of discipline:[46] making light of God's discipline, or being crushed by or losing heart or courage because of his reproof. Christians were to engage actively in a direct ministry to their fellow sufferers. For example, in the book of Acts, Paul and Barnabas are described as "strengthening the souls of the disciples, encouraging them to continue in the faith" in the face of afflictions (Acts 14:22). The word translated "encourage" also means "exhort," "comfort" or "console," the same word that recurs in the following passage from 2 Corinthians:

> Blessed be the God and Father of our Lord Jesus Christ, the Father of mercies and God of all comfort; who comforts us in all our affliction so that we may be able to comfort those who are in any affliction with the comfort with which we ourselves are comforted by God. For just as the sufferings of Christ are ours in abundance, so also our comfort is abundant through Christ. But if we are afflicted, it is for your comfort and salvation; or if we are comforted, it is for your comfort, which is effective in the patient enduring of the same sufferings which we also suffer; and our hope for you is firmly grounded, knowing that as you are sharers of our sufferings, so also you are sharers of our comfort. (2 Cor 1:3-7)

Several points must be stressed. In this passage the comfort was said to abound through Christ. He was the mediator through whom comfort came. But it was to flow through the sufferer to other sufferers. Suffering was thus seen as a training ground that enabled Christians through participating in Christ's sufferings to participate in and minister to the sufferings of their fellow Christians. The relief that was provided was not the removal of the suffering but a consolation, a comfort in the suffering that transformed it into a positive force in Christians' lives when their response was positive.

In the Gospel of John Christ said, "These things I have spoken to you, that in Me you may have peace. In the world you have tribulation, but take courage; I have overcome the world" (Jn 16:33). "In the world you have tribulation." For Christians it was to be expected and accepted. But no suffering was to be meaningless for them. The ultimate purpose and meaning behind the sufferings of Christians was their spiritual growth. And the ultimate goal in spiritual growth was a close dependence on God, a dependence that was based on a childlike trust. Numerous passages can be adduced from the New Testament that encourage Christians to trust in their heavenly Father. For example, "Be anxious for nothing, but in everything by prayer and supplication with thanksgiving let your requests be made known to God. And the peace of God, which surpasses all comprehension, shall guard your hearts and your minds in Christ Jesus" (Phil 4:6-7; cf. 2 Tim 1:11-12; 1 Pet 4:19; 5:6-7).

The New Testament depicted Christians as children of their heavenly Father who loved them and in spite of any appearance to the contrary was causing all things to work together for their good. Hence they could say with Paul,

> And we know that God causes all things to work together for good to those who love God, to those who are called according to His purpose. . . . For I am convinced that neither death, nor life, nor angels, nor principalities, nor things present, nor things to come, nor powers, nor height, nor depth, nor any other created thing, shall be able to separate us from the love of God, which is in Christ Jesus our Lord. (Rom 8:28, 38-39)

To Christians God was a person to whom they could relate in a spiritual depth commensurate with the degree of their commitment to the person of Christ. The intimacy of this relationship, a relationship based on love and trust, gave meaning to suffering for New Testament Christians and enabled Paul to say of himself and of those of kindred spirit, "We exult in our tribulations" (Rom 5:3). Hence Peter, when writing to some Christians who were deeply afflicted, encouraged them to persevere. Instead of suggesting that they take their own lives, he said, "Let those also who suffer according to the will of God entrust their souls to a faithful Creator in doing what is right" (1 Pet 4:19). Likewise James wrote, "As an example, brethren, of suffering and patience, take the prophets who spoke in the name of the Lord" (Jas 5:10).

Early Christians would have been familiar with the sufferings of the prophets of the Old Testament. As we have already noted in chapter one, Moses in despair had prayed that God would slay him (Num 11:15). So also had Elijah (1 Kings 19:4) and Jonah (Jon 4:3, 8). Jeremiah cursed the day of his birth (Jer 15:10; 20:14-18), as did Job (Job 3:1). Job is the specific example of endurance that James gave: "Behold, we count those blessed who endured. You have heard of the endurance of Job and have seen the outcome of the Lord's dealings, that the Lord is full of compassion and is merciful" (Jas 5:11). It is noteworthy that none of these Old Testament figures, however much they may have wished to depart from life, resorted to suicide. Nor was there any suggestion that they even considered it.[47] The early Christian would undoubtedly have recalled that Job's wife had urged him to curse God and die and that he rebuked her for such advice (Job 2:9-10). Furthermore, Job identified himself with those "who long for death, but there is none" (Job 3:21) and said of himself, "My soul would choose suffocation, death rather than my pains" (Job 7:15-16). Job apparently did not regard suicide as an option even in the midst of his unbearable afflictions. Such was the example of patience in suffering held up to early Christians.

In short, the New Testament encouraged patience, stressed hope, commanded perseverance and so strongly emphasized the sovereignty of God in the life of Christians and the trust that they should exercise, knowing that God will ultimately cause all things to work out for their good, that it is unlikely that suicide to escape from those trials God had chosen to inflict or permit could have been regarded as anything less than a breach of trust.[48]

Even a cursory and random reading of the church fathers reveals that they regarded suffering as an essential aspect of God's sanctifying of his people. This belief, combined with a firm assurance that God is sovereign and an equally firm trust that he does all things for their ultimate good, engendered in them an imperative to preach and practice endurance in the face of all afflictions.

In chapter four we shall see that this fundamental principle provided one of the bases for some church fathers' condemnation of suicide. Although they may have differed from each other significantly in their backgrounds, personalities and emphases, and hence reflect in their writings the diversity of theology that then prevailed within the realm of orthodoxy, yet in the most foundational and essential areas of Christian values they display a profound unity: Christians are subject to the whole range of afflictions that beset fallen humanity in a fallen world. Christians must face even greater sufferings than pagans do, because both God and Satan will buffet them. Satan does so in order to discourage them and hence to tempt them to sin; God does so as paternal chastening (including both training and discipline) that leads to sanctification. Accordingly the Christian must practice patient endurance in defiance of Satan and in resignation to the salutary and salubrious providence of God. It should be noted that both the Greek and the Latin words typically translated as "patience" have the underlying meaning of "patient endurance."

Cyprian (c. 200-258) is an outstanding example. His writings display a passionate and compassionate concern for the spiritual health of his flock. He clearly represents the mainstream of orthodoxy. Furthermore, he does not appear to have directly addressed the subject of suicide or even to have mentioned it in passing. Two of his most pastoral writings are *Mortality*, written during a time of plague, and *The Good of Patience*. In the latter he asserted that "a crown for sorrow and suffering cannot be obtained unless patience in sorrow and suffering precede."[49] For with patience

> we may endure all afflictions. . . . It is a salutary precept of our Lord and Master: "He who has endured even to the end will be saved. . . . " We must endure and persevere . . . so that, having been admitted to the hope of truth and liberty, we can finally attain that same truth and liberty, because the very fact that we are Christians is a source of faith and hope. However, in order that hope and faith may reach their fruition, there is need of patience.

Then, after quoting Romans 8:24-25, Cyprian continued: "Patient waiting is necessary that we may fulfill what we have begun to be, and through God's help, that we may obtain what we hope for and believe." He then quoted Galatians 6:9-10 and commented that Paul here "warns lest anyone, through lack of patience grow tired in his good work; lest anyone either diverted or overcome by temptations, should stop in the middle of his course of praise and glory and his past works be lost." After quoting Ezekiel 33:12 and Revelation 3:11, he said that "these words urge patient and resolute perseverance, so that he who strives for a crown, now with praise already near, may be crowned because his patience endures." He immediately asserted that patience "not only preserves what is good, but also repels what is evil" for "it struggles . . . against the acts of the flesh and the body whereby the soul is stormed and captured." He then enumerated various sins against which patience is the only efficacious defense and states that if patience was strong "the hand that has held the Eucharist will not be sullied by the blood-stained sword."[50] Later he maintained that patience was

> necessary in respect to various hardships of the flesh and frequent and cruel torments of the body by which the human race is daily wearied and oppressed. . . . It is necessary to keep struggling and contending in this state of bodily weakness and infirmity; and this struggle and strife can not be endured without the strength of patience. But different

kinds of sufferings are imposed on us to test and prove us, and many forms of temptations are inflicted upon us by loss of wealth, burning fevers, torments of wounds, by the death of dear ones. . . . The just man is proved by patience, as it is written, "In thy sorrow endure and in thy humiliation keep patience, for gold and silver are tried in the fire (Eccl 2:4-5)."[51]

Cyprian then gave the example of Job: "Thus Job was examined and proved and raised to the pinnacle of praise because of the virtue of patience." He described Job's various afflictions and said that

lest anything at all might remain which Job had not experienced in his trials, the devil even armed his wife against him. . . . Nevertheless, Job was not broken by these heavy and continuous assaults, and in spite of these trials and afflictions he extolled the praise of God by his victorious patience.[52]

A little later he exclaimed:

Let us . . . maintain the patience through which we abide in Christ and with Christ are able to come to God. . . . It is patience that both commends us to God and saves us for God. . . . It vanquishes temptations, sustains persecutions, endures sufferings and martyrdoms to the end. It is this patience which strongly fortifies the foundations of our faith. It is this patience which sublimely promotes the growth of hope.[53]

As the climax of his argument he exhorted, "Let us . . . persevere and let us labor . . . watchful with all our heart and steadfast even to total resignation."[54]

In his treatise entitled *Mortality* Cyprian commented that some Christians were troubled because the plague that was ravaging North Africa

carries off our people equally with the pagans, as if a Christian believes to this end, that, free from contact with evils, he may happily enjoy the world and this life, and, without having endured all adversities here, may be preserved for future happiness. . . . But what in this world do we not have in common with others as long as this flesh . . . still remains common to us?

He gave as examples famine, the ravages of war, drought, shipwreck, "and eye trouble and attacks of fever and every ailment of the members we have in common with others as long as this common flesh is borne in the world."[55]

After giving Job and Tobias as examples of endurance, Cyprian reminded his readers that this

endurance the just have always had; this discipline the apostles maintained from the law of the Lord, not to murmur in adversity, but to accept bravely and patiently whatever happens in the world. . . . We must not murmur in adversity, beloved brethren, but must patiently

and bravely bear with whatever happens, since it is written: "A contrite and humble heart God does not despise."[56]
Hence "the fear of God and faith ought to make you ready for all things" such as loss of property, diseases, loss of wife and children and other dear ones. So

> let not such things be stumbling blocks for you but battles; nor let them weaken or crush the faith of the Christian, but rather let them reveal his valor in the contest, since every injury arising from present evils should be made light of through confidence in the blessings to come. . . . Conflict in adversity is the trial of truth.[57]

Note further Cyprian's emphasis on the activity of God and the passivity of the Christian in death. Cyprian wrote that Christians who died of the current pestilence "have been freed from the world by the summons of the Lord."[58] Later he asserted that "those who please God are taken from here earlier and more quickly set free, lest, while they are tarrying too long in this world, they be defiled by contacts with the world." He then suggested that "when the day of our own summons comes, without hesitation but with gladness we may come to the Lord at His call." For "rescued by an earlier departure, you are being freed from ruin and shipwrecks and threatening disasters!" Therefore "let us embrace the day which assigns each of us to his dwelling, which on our being rescued from here and released from the snares of the world, restores us to paradise and the kingdom." They should consider the loved ones already in heaven and the joys that await them there. "To these, beloved brethren, let us hasten with eager longing! Let us pray that it may befall us speedily to be with them, speedily to come to Christ."[59]

We see that in Cyprian's thought it was God who called; it was he who issued the summons. God took Christians from the world; God freed them; God rescued them; God released them; God restored them to heaven. Christians were passive: they were being freed; they were being rescued; they were being released; they were being restored. This was God's activity. Christians' activity was to yearn for heaven. Hence they should pray for an early departure from life. Yearning for death and praying to die are categorically different from taking one's own life. There is no room here for suicide. Patient endurance of all afflictions, perseverance to the end, final resignation to the will of God in the midst of those situations that God is using to test and to refine the Christian: such thought is antithetical to the taking of one's own life even when one is afflicted by prolonged suffering attendant upon chronic or terminal illness. It is hence not surprising that there is not one example of suicide by the ill in the entirety of patristic literature.

3

Euthanasia in
Early Christianity

A close examination of the vocabulary of health in the New Testament
demonstrates no idea of bodily health that is independent of the larger
concept of reconciliation. The health of the body is not presented as an
absolute good but as one aspect of a much broader concept of well-being
that results from the reconciliation of fallen creatures with their Creator,
which has moral, spiritual and physical implications. Nor does the New
Testament present bodily health as an end in itself, in spite of the
prominence that it enjoys in the Gospel accounts of Jesus' healing
miracles. The presence of sickness and disease are indications of a world
that has been dislocated by sin. When the cosmos is re-created, all that is
imperfect will be made perfect. In the meantime it groans in travail
awaiting the final consummation. And while reconciliation has its present
aspects, its ultimate realization awaits eschatological fulfillment. Jesus'
miracles of healing revealed a glimpse of that fulfillment in which the body
as well as the soul will be redeemed.

Wellness or well-being in the New Testament and throughout the
patristic period was being in a right relationship with God through a
saving, sustaining and vitalizing faith in Christ. The absence of suffering
did not equal wellness or well-being. Hence a person who was suffering
might be regarded as well. God was viewed as the sovereign dispenser of
human suffering. Guilt and suffering were thus linked and placed under

the umbrella of divine justice as were Satan and his demons, who were seen as the unwitting instruments of God's purposes. Ostensibly meaningless suffering highlighted the misery of the human condition, the beauty of the resurrection and the eternal bliss to come. Within the framework of New Testament values, physical health was a good but not an absolute good, much less the supreme good. Physical health could be an obstacle to the supreme good, which was the wellness or well-being that consisted of being in a right relationship with God.[1] The church fathers emphasized that since physical health was by no means essential to well-being, those in poor health could be regarded as being well, either because their poor health was irrelevant to the question of wellness or because their poor health could be an instrument contributing to their well-being. In this sense the highest good of the body was not health or the absence of pain but the soul itself. Health was seen as a blessing from God, a good to be sought for its own sake, like wisdom and friendship.[2] Although health was regarded as a desirable thing, it was only a relative good and hence, depending on its role in the life of the physically healthy person, it could be a lure away from dependence on God.

The Meaning of Sickness
The semantics of disease[3] and physical dysfunction are as broad and imprecise in the New Testament and patristic literature as they are in the common parlance of modern English. Even the most specific of the various terms that are used in the New Testament to describe various sicknesses are precise only symptomatically rather than pathologically and hence are employed more phenomenologically than scientifically. When someone is described as suffering from fever or dysentery, being crippled, paralyzed or blind, having a flow of blood or a withered hand, or as "leprous" or "moonstruck," we can only conjecture what condition is being described, that is, how the condition can be categorized in a manner consistent with continually mutating nosologies and medical paradigms. Even more imprecise is the terminology that is translated by words such as *sick, ill, not feeling well* or *feeling faint* and *sickness, illness* or *disease.* The best attempts at labeling the more specifically designated conditions run aground either immediately on the Scylla of uncertainty or ultimately on the Charybdis of changing nosologies and medical advance. If these conditions had been described in a manner consistent with the predominantly humoral pathology of the time, the same problems would be present, although in a slightly ameliorated form.

Since in the New Testament sickness and dysfunction are not described medically but phenomenologically, we may draw several conclusions from the nature of these descriptions. (1) We shall probably never know with any precision the exact pathological nomenclature of most of the medically related conditions described in the New Testament. (2) In the absence of semantic precision and medically descriptive clarity (from the perspective of either ancient or current nosologies), disease and dysfunction in the New Testament are as open to theological interpretation in the twentieth century as in the first because of their phenomenological description. (3) Hence medical science should not be forced to provide either the context or the tools for understanding the "meaning" of disease in the New Testament.

In this regard H. Roux observes,

Sickness and healing are never approached in the Bible from the medical or scientific point of view, but always from the religious point of view, that is to say, from the viewpoint of the particular relationship which they create or make apparent between the sick person and God. It is not the nature of the sickness, its development or its treatment, which receives attention, but the fact itself envisaged as an event significant of man's destiny or condition within the general perspective of the history of salvation.[4]

Roux's assessment is essentially correct. The New Testament depicts disease as one of many aspects of material (as distinct from moral) evil that resulted from the Fall. Since the Fall was caused not only by human disobedience but also by the serpent's intrigue and deception, both moral and material evil, including disease and death, are the works of Satan. Under the Mosaic covenant Israel was promised blessings that included the removal of sickness. While illness was generally believed to be inflicted on individuals as punishment for sin,[5] in spite of what appeared to be a clear cause-and-effect relationship between disobedience and material evil, including sickness, the godly nevertheless experienced a variety of forms of suffering that included sickness.[6] The most outstanding example is Job.

The eschatological orientation of the later books of the Old Testament project the enjoyment of promised blessings, including the absence or the healing of sickness, into the anticipated messianic kingdom. Hence Jesus is recorded in the Gospels, especially in the Synoptics, as engaging in an extensive healing ministry that included exorcism. Matthew asserts that Jesus' casting out of demons and his healing the sick constituted the fulfillment of Isaiah's prophecy "He Himself took our infirmities, and carried away our diseases" (Mt 8:16-17). Similarly Luke records Jesus' response to the disciples of John the Baptist, who had been sent by John to ask whether he was indeed the Messiah:

At that very time He cured many people of diseases and afflictions and evil spirits; and He granted sight to many who were blind. And He answered and said to them, "Go and report to John what you have seen and heard: the blind receive sight, the lame walk, the lepers are cleansed, and the deaf hear, the dead are raised up, and the poor have the gospel preached to them." (Lk 7:18-23; cf. Mt 11:2-6)

The Evangelists regarded Jesus' miracles in general and his healing miracles in particular as authenticating signs of his messiahship. But there was, they believed, a greater sign:

Then some of the scribes and Pharisees answered Him, saying, "Teacher, we want to see a sign from You." But He answered and said to them, "An evil and adulterous generation craves for a sign; and yet no sign shall be given to it but the sign of Jonah the prophet; for just as Jonah was three days and three nights in the belly of the sea monster, so shall the Son of Man be three days and three nights in the heart of the earth." (Mt 12:38-40; cf. Lk 11:29)

The realization of the sign of Jonah, that is, the death and resurrection of Jesus, became the major emphasis of the post-Easter Christian community. So it is not remarkable that compared with the plethora of healings performed by Jesus in the Gospels, healings in Acts receive comparatively little emphasis, while in the remainder of the New Testament the mention of sickness and healing is so occasional as to be negligible. Furthermore, while in the Gospels there is no instance in which Jesus either refuses or is unable[7] to heal, in the epistles several cases are mentioned of sickness from which the individual simply recovered (Phil 2:25-30; Gal 4:13-15; 2 Cor 1:8-11 may apply to this category), from which no recovery is mentioned (2 Tim 4:20) or from which there was no recovery (i.e., the sickness had to be endured as a chronic condition: 1 Tim 5:23; 2 Cor 12:1-10).

The best-known example of a condition that was not healed is found in 2 Corinthians 12:1-10. Paul writes,

And because of the surpassing greatness of the revelations, for this reason, to keep me from exalting myself, there was given me a thorn in the flesh, a messenger of Satan to buffet me—to keep me from exalting myself! Concerning this I entreated the Lord three times that it might depart from me. And He has said to me, "My grace is sufficient for you, for power is perfected in weakness [*astheneia*]." Most gladly, therefore, I will rather boast about my weaknesses [*astheneiai*], that the power of Christ may dwell in me. Therefore I am well content with weaknesses [*astheneiai*], with insults, with distresses, with persecutions, with difficulties, for Christ's sake; for when I am weak [*astheno*], then I am strong. (2 Cor 12:7-10)

Most scholars believe that Paul's thorn in his flesh was a chronic illness.[8] But while many have been dogmatic, none have been convincing in their efforts to identify the precise nature of this affliction. Nevertheless the following conclusions may be drawn from Paul's description of what appears to have been a chronic illness. These conclusions are consistent with the New Testament understanding of illness as it relates to Christian experience. (1) It is not always God's will for Christians to be free from illness. This is manifested by the negative response to repeated prayers for healing that one finds in the epistles. (2) Weakness, even when it results from sickness or physical dysfunction, may produce spiritual strength, provided that the sufferer submits to the will of God for Christ's sake. (3) Although this "thorn in the flesh" was a messenger of Satan, the fact that it "was given" indicates that ultimately it came from God and hence must be viewed as purposed by divine sovereignty.

Jesus referred to a woman with a severely bent spine as one "whom Satan has bound for eighteen long years."[9] Peter reminds Cornelius that Jesus "went around doing good, and healing all who were oppressed by the devil" (Acts 10:38). It is important to note that in none of the instances of demon possession and exorcism in the New Testament is there a hint that the victims of demonic assault brought it on themselves by sinning. Nor is it ever suggested that while they were in a possessed state, such individuals were especially sinful. Furthermore, forgiveness of sins is never made a condition for or a specified consequence of exorcism. Paul, as we have seen, describes the thorn in his flesh as "a messenger of Satan." He says that it was "given [to] me" *(edothē moi)*. The fact that he specifies no agent suggests that in his mind the agent was God himself. The thorn in Paul's flesh was given in order to keep him from sin, not as a punishment for sin.

The notion that individual suffering is the direct consequence of personal sin had already been rejected by Jesus. When Jesus was told "about the Galileans, whose blood Pilate had mingled with their sacrifices," he replied,

> Do you suppose that these Galileans were greater sinners than all other Galileans, because they suffered this fate? I tell you, no, but, unless you repent, you will all likewise perish. Or do you suppose that those eighteen on whom the tower in Siloam fell and killed them, were worse culprits than all the men who live in Jerusalem? I tell you, no, but unless you repent, you will all likewise perish. (Lk 13:1-5)

The connection between sickness and sin, however, is at least a latent feature of all considerations of sickness in both the Hebrew Scriptures and the New Testament. Although in the New Testament there are occasional instances in which sickness is regarded specifically as punishment, in the teaching of Jesus the direct causal link between individual sickness and personal sin is called into question. Jesus on one occasion forgave sin before healing a paralytic, although no connection between the forgiveness and healing appears to be implied (Mt 9:1-8; Mk 2:1-12; Lk 5:17-26). And he urged another paralytic, in this case after healing him, "Do not sin any more, so that nothing worse may befall you" (Jn 5:14).

Nevertheless Jesus described Lazarus's sickness as having occurred "for the glory of God, that the Son of God may be glorified by it" (Jn 11:4). And when Jesus and his disciples encountered a man who had been born blind, in response to their question "Who sinned, this man or his parents, that he should be born blind?" he replied, "It was neither that this man sinned, nor his parents; but it was in order that the works of God might be displayed in him" (Jn 9:1-3). While Jesus' response does not preclude a direct causal relationship between personal sin and individual sickness, it suggests that he regarded blanket, judgmental assessments as tenuous. The matter is nicely summarized by Raymond E. Brown, who observes that "Jesus was asked about the cause of the man's blindness, but he answers in terms of its purpose."[10] It may be said that throughout the New Testament (not only in the Gospels) disease is viewed primarily in the light of its purpose and meaning and not generally with regard to its etiology or causality.

In describing disease and physical disability, the writers of the New Testament used ordinary language, which renders a precise identification of the conditions they depict problematical in terms of modern medical understanding. But the fact that they described the conditions phenomenologically suggests that they viewed the etiology of disease in naturalistic terms that were derived from the influence of Greek rational medicine. This is true even when the authors attribute a physical disability to divine retribution. The only exceptions are instances of demonic possession or of demonic causality of specific ailments, which are extremely rare. The narratives of the New Testament assume that two levels of causality are operating simultaneously. Even when disease is described solely in terms of proximate causality, supernatural causality is taken for granted; and when disease is spoken of in terms of divine causality, a naturalistic etiology is nevertheless assumed to be operative. In the extremely rare instances in which naturalistic immediate causality gives way to demons causing illness or dysfunction, divine sovereignty remains the nonvariable component. The intention of the narratives always remains the same: to provide an understanding of God's purposes in the realm of disease and physical disability. Hence in approaching the biblical texts we must expect to find a theological rather than a medical understanding of illness.

As in the New Testament, so also in patristic literature, sin always lurked in the background of all conditions of suffering. Without sin there would be no suffering, because the Fall was the ultimate explanation for the miseries of the present. Sin in this sense was impersonal. It is obviously a different matter when one's own sin, especially specific sins, provided the explanation for one's suffering. Some church fathers emphasized the sin of overindulgence as the proximate cause of much illness.[11] Sin, when it was not the proximate cause of an illness as the direct, natural cause, was often allowed as the explanation for God's sending or allowing sickness for the purpose of chastising the sufferer for a specific sin with a view to the sinner's repentance. When in this sense sin was thought to provide the immediate explanation for the suffering of a specific individual rather than of humanity in general, such identification was typically made with a view to salutary self-examination that should not have fostered a despairing sense of guilt since, as we shall see, sickness for correction of specific personal sin or general personal sinfulness was only one of a wide variety of purposes that the church fathers regarded as motivating God to send or permit sickness.

For much of the patristic era three sources of disease or illness were identified, namely, God, demons and natural causality. These were not mutually exclusive. The whole subject of perceived causality of disease (and other forms of suffering, for that matter) is rife with confusion and interpretive problems, especially when considering the role of demons.[12] Demonology occupies a considerable place in the writings of the church fathers, all of whom believed that demons (in the guise of the old pagan gods) were intent on the spiritual destruction of humanity. Pagans believed not only in their own gods but in a plethora of lesser spiritual beings as well. It was, in the words of Michael Green, "an age which was hag-ridden with the fear of demonic forces dominating every aspect of life and death."[13] This was true beginning in the latter half of the second century. In the writings of the apostolic fathers (c. 95-156) there is little mention of demons. But then suddenly a significant increase in references to demonic activity appears in Christian, Jewish and pagan sources.[14] A change was occurring throughout the Mediterranean world, a change for which scholars cannot satisfactorily account. This new environment, the new mental and spiritual outlook, fostered attributing illness to demonic activity to a degree unprecedented in earlier Christian, Jewish, Greek and Roman cultures. Concurrent with the increased interest in demonic activity was the growing appeal of supernatural healing.

Throughout the second half of the second century, reports of super-natural healing in Christianity were confined primarily to sects on the periphery of the orthodox community (e.g., Montanism). References to supernatural healing within the orthodox community were vague and infrequent. But in the third century they became more numerous and specific, and accounts of exorcisms are much more frequently encoun-tered. Beginning in the third century, we find church fathers speaking of healing and exorcism in the same breath.

Accounts from the third century were generally lacking in sensation-alism. But a significant change occurred in the fourth century with a pronounced increase in the number of miracles and in their sensational-istic quality. Now we begin to encounter literature replete with marvels and miracles, many of which must be labeled bizarre even by the most sympathetic reader. Accounting for this change is significantly more difficult than is describing its salient characteristics.[15]

Spiritual Benefits of Sickness

Paul sorrowed over the serious illness of Epaphroditus, whose gradual recovery filled him with joy (Phil 2:25-27), and he was constrained to leave his companion Trophimus sick in Miletus even though he deeply missed him (2 Tim 4:20). In the New Testament sickness does not appear to have been considered a unique form of suffering but rather was included in the assurance that "God causes all things to work together for good to those who love God, to those who are called according to His purpose," for "who shall separate us from the love of Christ? Shall tribulation, or distress, or persecution, or famine, or nakedness, or peril, or sword?" (Rom 8:28, 35). The spiritual benefits that Paul derived from his thorn in the flesh he poignantly describes in 2 Corinthians 12.

The spiritual benefits derived from the suffering peculiar to sickness were a prominent part of the pastoral consciousness of the church fathers. Jerome (c. 345-c. 419), for example, writes to a remarkably healthy centenarian that the health of the righteous is God's gift in which they should rejoice, but the health of the unrighteous is Satan's gift to lead them to sin.[16] Hence he tells another correspondent to rejoice not only in health but also in sickness, saying, "Am I in good health? I thank my Creator. Am I sick? In this case also I praise God's will. For 'When I am weak, then am I strong,' and the strength of the spirit is made perfect in the weakness of the flesh."[17] This is a subject to which Jerome's heart warms: sickness can cause people to adjust their priorities. He describes a young woman who was taught by a burning fever, with which she had suffered for nearly thirty days, to direct her attention to more serious pursuits than the pampering of her person, to which apparently she had been giving more time than Jerome thought appropriate.[18] Ambrose likewise suggests to a correspondent who had been sick that God had sent the sickness to him for the sake of his spiritual health.[19] And in his treatise *Concerning Repentance* Ambrose writes that while sickness restrains one from sin, luxury is a catalyst to sins of the flesh.[20]

Basil of Caesarea (c. 329-379) felt that the primary reason God had bestowed knowledge of medicine on humanity was to provide a model for the cure of the soul. Hence one of the reasons why Christians are permitted to fall ill is so that, through the suffering involved in the disease and in the cure, they may draw valuable instruction to apply to the cure of the soul in need of spiritual medicine, cautery or surgery. While God will not allow Christians to be tried more than they can bear, some are left to struggle with their illnesses and thus become more worthy of reward. Illness can be a punishment for sin, imposed to bring one to repentance. Sometimes God sends or allows sickness to keep the Christian from pride. So Basil admonishes Christians when sick first to ask God to give them understanding of the purpose God has for the sickness and second to pray for healing or, if that is withheld, the strength of character to endure it patiently.[21] When Gregory Nazianzen's father became seriously ill and was surprised that God allowed him to suffer so, his son replied that it was not at all remarkable, since even the great saints of the past were afflicted.[22]

Explicating Paul's advice to Timothy to "use a little wine for the sake of your stomach and your frequent ailments" (1 Tim 5:23), John Chrysostom (349-407) gives twelve explanations for such suffering: so that Christians may not be too easily presumptuous regarding their good works and miracles; so that others may not esteem them more highly than appropriate; so that God's power can be made more spectacular by the service of those who in themselves are infirm; so that their endurance will more strikingly show that they are not striving for temporal rewards; to demonstrate their belief in the resurrection and life eternal; so that others will find encouragement in their example; so that, when exhorted to follow their example, others will be aware that they were also merely frail human beings; so that others may learn whom they ought to consider as blessed, for "whom the Lord loves He disciplines"; because affliction produces patience; so that their faults will be corrected; because their rewards are increased through patient endurance; and because, when Christians give thanks to God in the midst of their afflictions, they deliver a blow to Satan.[23] Such examples could be greatly multiplied.

Care of the Body

If sickness could be of spiritual benefit, should Christians care for their bodies in order to seek to remain healthy? If the eternal Logos became flesh and dwelt among us, the flesh could not be evil in and of itself. One must contrast Paul's statement that "the flesh sets its desire against the Spirit, and the Spirit against the flesh; for these are in opposition to one another" with his assertion that no one ever hated his or her own body (Gal 5:17; Eph 5:29). Then it is evident that the carnal mind is enmity against God (Rom 8:7), and abusing one's body profits nothing (1 Cor 13:3; Col 2:23). Hence the soul should have mastery over, not contempt for, the body, since the body is merely the slave of the will. And the soul is of infinitely greater value than the body. Nevertheless the body has great significance. The coming resurrection attests to that. In the meantime it is the "temple of the Holy Spirit." Although the care of one's body in the New Testament is stressed with a view to guarding it from sin (e.g., 1 Cor 3:16; 6:19-20; 2 Cor 6:16; Rom 14:8), the strong implication is that the body itself deserves care (cf. Eph 5:29).

All church fathers shared the basic presupposition that God's creation was essentially good. One may reasonably assert that any ostensibly Christian writer who classified all created matter as inherently and intrinsically evil was eo ipso not Christian. To insist that such radical dualism as that of the Gnostics, Manichaeans and some Docetists belongs within the broad range of early Christian beliefs that in the aggregate can be regarded as normative is to make of early Christianity something so amorphous as to be infinitely malleable.[24]

The same literature that consistently expressed a yearning for death also consistently expressed a respect for life. The *Shepherd of Hermas,* an anonymous work composed in stages (between c. 90 and c. 150), asserts that one who is harassed by distress *(incommoda)* should be assisted, for "many bring death on themselves by reason of such calamities when they cannot bear them. Whoever therefore knows the distress of such a man, and does not rescue him, incurs great sin and becomes guilty of his blood."[25] This passage suggests that the author regarded the suicide of one who took his own life owing to distress as so serious that anyone who could have helped him but failed to do so not only had committed a serious sin but also was guilty of his blood. Early Christians regarded physical life as a gift of God that was so precious that they viewed the care of the sick as a categorical imperative. We shall return to this subject shortly.

All church fathers held that although humanity and all of nature are fallen, God has provided for people's sustenance through their proper use of nature. Within the history of Christianity there have been dramatic changes in what has been regarded as the proper use of nature for humanity's benefit. And at all times there has been considerable variation within the broad boundaries of Christianity. Since self-denial, much less asceticism, is exceedingly rare today among Christians and within Western society generally, the spiritually motivated desire (expressed in the vast majority of early Christian sources) that Christians should not pamper the body at the expense of the soul or be consumed with the material and temporal to the detriment of the spiritual and eternal may seem severe and is often misunderstood.[26]

In spite of the sometimes extreme ascetic tendencies of the early church, a central tenet of Christian orthodoxy consistently confirms the inherent worth of life and the moral neutrality of the body. Clement of Alexandria (c. 155-c. 220), for example, maintains that those who "vilify the body are wrong. . . . The soul of man is confessedly the better part of man, and the body the inferior. But neither is the soul good by nature, nor, on the other hand, is the body bad by nature."[27] He regarded health as a gift and insisted that the body, as the temple of the Holy Spirit, deserved reasonable care. Clement approvingly quotes Plato's injunction that care must be taken of the body.[28] Tertullian (c. 160-c. 220), who can hardly be regarded as effete, says "I do bathe at the hour I should, one which is conducive to health and which protects both my temperature and my life's blood."[29] To quote more examples would be superfluous.

One's perceptions of the causality of illness greatly affected one's choice of means to employ for healing. The means appropriately employed in attempting to restore health were miraculous (e.g., prayer, the sacraments, exorcism and, beginning in late antiquity, the cult of saints and relics) or natural (employment of physicians or the use of folk medicine, that is, common, especially herbal, substances). Often these two treatments, miraculous and natural, might be combined. A means consistently forbidden by the church, however, was any form of magic (demonic or occult practices, which obviously would include recourse to pagan healing cults).

The choice of which means to employ in the quest for healing can be described in terms of structures of dependence. A Christian was to be dependent on God. Sometimes the line of dependence was direct; at other times it included one or several intermediaries constituting a chain of dependence. The church itself (i.e., its clergy and sacraments) and the saints became variable parts of this chain of dependence linking the Christian with God. Spiritual healing models obviously provided the closest compatibility, a natural model potentially less, and an illicit, magical or pagan model offered a patently incompatible, conflicting and competitive structure of dependence.

The sentiment commonly held by Christians today, that all healing comes from God, whether directly, through prayer or through the use of medicine and the skill of physicians, cannot be accurately attributed to any extant source from the patristic period. All the church fathers were unequivocal in their conviction that healing sometimes came from evil sources. All church fathers took this as a given. Satan and his minions, that is, demons (and early Christians regarded the multitude of pagan deities as demons), were able to heal. No church father dismissed the pagan healing cults as frauds or denied that demons effected cures. Asclepius was a demon to be taken seriously. Furthermore, the church fathers never denied the efficacy of magic. Granted, they regarded some practitioners of magic as charlatans and tricksters. But they never denied the demonically based power of magic since they knew that many pagans employed magic efficaciously for a variety of purposes, including the healing of disease.

We can state categorically that all patristic sources that say anything about medicine share the assumption that the use of physicians and the art of medicine are not essentially and intrinsically inappropriate for Christians. No Christian document from the patristic period entirely condemned on theological grounds the Christian's use of physicians and medicine.[30] But all agreed on one fundamental principle: a Christian's dependence must ultimately be on God and not exclusively on any aspect of his creation, regardless of how appropriate its use is for his creatures. It is within such a structure of dependence that euthanasia in early Christianity must be viewed.

Euthanasia

Jaroslav Pelikan observes that "the core of the Christian faith is pessimism about life and optimism about God, and therefore hope for life in God."[31] The Christian's hope was to be grounded in God's love for humanity, which was itself the source of the love that was to be manifested first to fellow Christians and then to all humanity (1 Jn 4:7-21; Jn 13:35; 15:12; 1 Pet 1:22; 1 Thess 3:12). Love was to predominate in Christians' lives (1 Cor 13:13; Gal 5:6, 22; Eph 3:17-19; 5:2; Col 3:14) to the point that not only should they weep with those who weep (Rom 12:15) but also they should even be willing to lay down their lives for their brothers and sisters (1 Jn 3:16). Another's suffering should elicit Christians' sympathy and concern, and they should attempt to alleviate that suffering. There was a much stronger imperative to alleviate the ills of others than to seek to alleviate one's own sufferings. Christ was the supreme example of this disposition. He had also commanded his followers to love their neighbors as themselves. While concern for another's spiritual needs was regarded as vitally important, it was not to be given in lieu of obvious physical or material necessities (Jas 1:27). The illustrations of charity that Jesus had given to his disciples were practical:

> For I was hungry, and you gave Me something to eat; I was thirsty, and you gave Me drink; I was a stranger, and you invited Me in; naked, and you clothed Me; I was sick, and you visited Me; I was in prison, and you came to Me. . . . To the extent that you did it to one of these brothers of Mine, even the least of them, you did it to Me. (Mt 25:35-36, 40)

"I was sick, and you visited Me." The verb here translated "visited" also means "to be concerned about," "to care for" and "to succor" and was sometimes used to refer to a physician's medical visitation of a patient. One need go no further than the New Testament itself to see the foundation laid for an emphasis on compassion and caring for the sick and the suffering generally that becomes so evident in the early centuries of Christianity.

The gospel as proclaimed in the early centuries of Christianity did not limit itself to the salvation of souls for eternity but also was directed to salvation within the world. It was a gospel not only of God's love to people but also of God's love through them. Christ's commandment to love your neighbor as yourself was not taken as a piece of advice but as a categorical imperative. The care of the destitute generally and of the sick particularly became a duty incumbent on all believers. Adolf von Harnack writes regarding the obligation to visit and care for the sick that "to quote passages would be superfluous, for the duty is repeatedly inculcated."[32] Several sources from the second century stress this duty, one specifying that no one should plead such excuses as squeamishness or being unaccustomed to such activity.[33] Early Christian literature is replete with such admonitions.[34] Although in the early church the care of the sick was urged on all believers, gradually it became more and more the specific duty of deacons and deaconesses who were to report cases of sickness or poverty to the local bishop. After the Christianization of the empire, bishops acquired a civic status similar to that of high government officials and assumed the responsibility of managing large-scale charitable efforts.[35]

On several occasions Christians demonstrated heroism in their care of the sick during outbreaks of the plague. For example, in the mid-third century during a plague that ravaged the Mediterranean area, especially North Africa, Christians engaged in a spectacular degree of activity on behalf of fellow Christians and pagans alike who were suffering from the pestilence. Their zeal was nearly suicidal.[36] Somewhat later we hear of such groups as the *parabolani, philoponoi* and *spoudaioi,* who cared for the sick, especially during epidemics.[37] So well known were the Christians for their acts of charity that the pagan emperor Julian the Apostate (361-363) complained that "the impious Galileans support not only their own poor but ours as well."[38]

In the fourth century Christians began to found hospitals *(xenodochia, nosokomeia, xenones),* together with orphanages and houses for the poor and the aged. Usually such houses were combined into one institution as was the famous charitable complex established by Basil of Caesarea in Cappadocia around 372. Charitable institutions patterned after Basil's spread especially throughout the eastern Mediterranean.[39] Sometimes they were supported by private individuals but more often by monastic communities (of which such institutions were sometimes a part) or by bishops. Usually they were administered by bishops from church funds. These institutions were recognized as distinctly the product of Christian charity, as is illustrated again by the reaction of the emperor Julian, who urged the chief priest of Galatia to establish similar pagan philanthropic institutions in every city.[40] The intention clearly was to emulate Christian medical and other charitable institutions, for, as E. R. Dodds suggests, it was the Christians' success in creating a community that cared both for its own and for others that was "a major cause, perhaps the strongest single cause, of the spread of Christianity."[41]

Although there were some limited philanthropic efforts by classical pagans[42] (for the most part these efforts came after the advent of Christianity), such activity was not grounded in any foundational premise of inherent human value.[43] The concept of inherent human value ultimately provided the basis for Christianity's ethics of respect for human life. And this respect for life manifested itself in a positive way in caring and curing and in a negative way in the resounding condemnation of abortion, infanticide (including child exposure)[44] and sexual immorality. This first espousal of an idea of inherent human value in Western society, not limited exclusively to one race, as was generally the case with the Jews, depended on the principle of the imago Dei, that is, that every human being is formed in the image of God.[45]

All church fathers who commented on medicine and physicians also placed significant limitations on Christians' recourse to them. One must not rely exclusively on them. One must rely on God as the source of the skill of the physician and of the efficacy of medicine, for God may choose to heal through them, to heal without them or to withhold healing. Although they thought it proper to desire and to seek the restoration of

health when one was ill, the church fathers regarded excessive concern
for the body and a desperate clinging to life as a sad contradiction of
Christian values. Cyprian (c. 200-258), writing in Carthage to his fellow
Christians while the city was being besieged by plague, was disturbed
both by their fear of death and by their efforts to preserve their lives.

> What madness it is to love the afflictions, and punishments, and tears
> of the world and not rather to hurry to the joy which can never be taken
> from us. . . . How absurd it is and how perverse that, while we ask that
> the will of God be done, when God calls us and summons us from this
> world, we do not at once obey the command of His will. We struggle
> in opposition and resist, and in the manner of obstinate slaves we are
> brought with sadness and grief to the sight of God, departing from
> there under the bond of necessity, not in obedience to our will. . . . Why,
> then, do we pray and entreat that the kingdom of heaven may come, if
> earthly captivity delights us? . . . Let us be ready for every manifesta-
> tion of God's will; freed from the terror of death, let us think of the
> immortality which follows.[46]

Basil of Caesarea, instructing his monks about the proper use of the
medical art, was governed by principles similar to those that motivated
Cyprian. Basil wrote,

> Whatever requires an undue amount of thought or trouble or involves
> a large expenditure of effort and causes our whole life to revolve, as it
> were, around solicitude for the flesh must be avoided by Christians.
> Consequently, we must take great care to employ this medical art, if it
> should be necessary, not as making it wholly accountable for our state
> of health or illness, but as redounding to the glory of God.[47]

John Chrysostom described a woman who had been urged by her
Christian friends to employ supposedly efficacious but magical means
for the cure of her critically ill child. Chrysostom praised her refusal
to resort to such illicit means even though she thought they would
restore her child to health. He then lamented the low level of spiritual
life and the skewed priorities of so many professing Christians who
were little concerned with heaven, although they were willing to
undergo anything for the sake of this life. He urged his audience to be
ready for death and asked them why they clung to the present life.[48]
Similarly Augustine (354-430) preached that just as the martyrs, even
though they loved life, did not cling to it but willingly gave it up when
God chose to remove them,[49] so also should those afflicted with seemingly hopeless illness. He pointed to the irony that so many, when faced
with troubles, cry out, " 'O God, send me death; hasten my days.' And
when sickness comes they hasten to the physician, promising him

money and rewards."[50] Augustine was grieved at

> what things men do that they may live a few days. . . . If, on account
> of bodily disease, they should come into the hands of the physician and
> their health should be despaired of by all who examine them; if some
> physician capable of curing them should free them from this desperate
> state, how much do they promise? How much is given for an altogether
> uncertain result? To live a little while now, they will give up the
> sustenance of life.[51]

Paradoxically physical life was worth little to early Christians, but it was
also of inestimable value. Christians were frequently urged to give their
lives willingly as martyrs if the only alternative was denying Christ.
However, although they should seek healing, whether miraculous or
medical or both, when they were sick, they should not cling to life but
should regard their sickness as potentially the God-given vehicle for their
homegoing. And under all circumstances the care of the soul was to take
precedence over the care of the body.

In classical antiquity, as we saw in chapter one, taking on a case that
could not be successfully treated was regarded as the physician's ethical
duty by virtually no one. The advent of Christianity created no change in
this aspect of medical deontology. But Christianity did introduce moral
obligations that were alien to the Greek and Roman ethos. One of these
was an obligation to care—not an obligation to cure, but an obligation to
care—a categorical imperative to extend compassion in both word and
deed to the poor, the widow, the orphan and the sick. This was a truly
revolutionary change in attitude to the sick, and we continue to feel its
effects.

But to go to extreme lengths to forestall death in cases where little or
nothing could be done was clearly denounced in early Christian literature
as a tragic contradiction of Christian values. Nevertheless the fact that
Christians were encouraged to trust in the sovereign will of God and to
place their destiny in his hands in such circumstances must not be
construed as evidence that they placed a low value on human life and
employed suicide or euthanasia when they were afflicted with extreme
suffering.

The church fathers were convinced that the art of medicine could be
used for egregious and sinful ends, especially in abortion and some forms
of medical experimentation. Although early Christians lived in a secular
milieu in which suicide by the ill was frequently practiced and its probity
seldom questioned, we are confident that, in the entirety of patristic
literature, there is not a single example of Christians committing suicide,
asking others' assistance in doing so or requesting others to kill them

directly in order to escape from the grinding tedium of chronic, or the severe suffering of terminal, illness. The only ethical issues raised by illness in patristic literature are the tendency of some Christians to seek medical care without first pondering the spiritual dimensions of their suffering; their having recourse to pagan or magical healing alternatives; and their occasionally frantic struggles to find and cling to even a meager hope of recovery. Not only is suicide by the ill never raised as an ethical issue in the literature of early Christianity, but also there is not a scintilla of evidence that the preferential position that Christianity gave to the sick included an expedited final exit. The goodness of God and his sovereignty are foundational in patristic theology, and patient endurance of affliction is regularly and consistently stressed as an essential Christian virtue. Hence it is not surprising that patristic texts are void of any reference to suicide by the ill in the Christian community. As we shall see in the next chapter, however, general condemnations of suicide to escape suffering and of assisting others in taking their own lives are sufficiently inclusive to embrace euthanasia.

4

Suicide in
Early Christianity

The only suicide recorded in the New Testament is that of Judas, and the event is reported without comment (Mt 27:5; Acts 1:18), although it is reasonable to assume that he would hardly have been regarded as a model of Christian probity. Suicide comes up incidentally on a few other occasions. Some scholars see Satan's suggestion that Jesus throw himself from the pinnacle of the temple as an effort to have him take his own life (Mt 4:5-6; Lk 4:8-9). When Jesus said, "Where I am going, you cannot come," the Jews erroneously suggested that he might be contemplating suicide (Jn 8:21-22). Neither condemnation nor approbation of the act may be read into this event. There is, however, one suicide prevented in the New Testament. When Paul and Silas were miraculously freed from prison in Philippi, the jailer was at the point of killing himself. As an alternative to suicide, Paul offered him salvation, which he joyfully accepted (Acts 16:25-34). Finally, self-destructive tendencies appear in some cases of demon possession, as in Mark's account of the Gerasene demoniac (Mk 5:1-20) and of the mute boy (Mk 9:14-29). In the latter instance the boy's father told Jesus that from childhood the demon had "often thrown him both into the fire and into the water to destroy him" (Mk 9:21-22). This is the closest that the New Testament comes to the nebulous realm of suicidal psychoses. The New Testament contains no other references to suicide.

Christian Condemnations of Suicide Before Augustine

Although suicide is a topic that excited little comment in Christian literature before Augustine, twelve church fathers condemned the act at least in passing.

An anonymous author of the *Shepherd of Hermas,* a work that was composed in stages between 90 and 150, contended that one who was harassed by distress *(incommoda)* should be assisted, for "many bring death on themselves by reason of such calamities when they cannot bear them. Whoever therefore knows the distress of such a man, and does not rescue him, incurs great sin and becomes guilty of his blood."[1] This suggests that the author held the suicide of one who resorted to such a deed because of distress as so serious a matter that whoever could have helped but failed to do so was guilty not only of a serious sin but also of the suicide's blood.

Justin Martyr (c. 100-165) envisaged a pagan suggesting, "All of you, go kill yourselves and thus go immediately to God, and save us the trouble." Justin responded, "If . . . we should kill ourselves we would be the cause, as far as it is up to us, why no one would be born and be instructed in the divine doctrines, or even why the human race might cease to exist; if we do act thus, we ourselves will be opposing the will of God."[2] L. W. Barnard, in his insightful study of Justin, says on the basis of this passage that Justin "shows us men and women . . . who thought it a duty to preserve life so long as God delayed to take it."[3]

There is a difference between a duty to preserve one's life and a duty not to take it, a distinction made by Justin in the context surrounding the passage quoted. In this context he juxtaposed Christians' refusal to kill themselves and their willingness to die for their faith. This passage, although it is an unequivocal condemnation of suicide for Christians, was only an explanation provided to pagans of why Christians did not kill themselves. Justin appears not to have felt it incumbent upon himself to provide any moral explanation or scriptural defense of his position. Although his argument is sufficiently Platonic to be familiar to educated pagans, it contains ingredients that even Platonists would find unpalatable: Christians must not kill themselves because God wanted them in the world and humanity needed them. If there were no Christians not only would there be no one to instruct pagans in the truth, but since God sustained the world for his people's sake, the human race would cease to exist if all Christians were removed from the face of the earth.

A similar message is contained in the late-second-century, anonymous *Epistle to Diognetus:*

The soul is locked up in the body, yet is the very thing that holds the body together; so, too, Christians are shut up in the world as in a prison, yet are the very ones that hold the world together. Immortal, the soul is lodged in a mortal tenement; so, too, Christians, though residing as strangers among corruptible things, look forward to the incorruptibility that awaits them in heaven. The soul, when stinting itself in food and drink, is the better for it; so, too, Christians, when penalized, increase daily more and more. Such is the important post to which God has assigned them, and it is not lawful for them to desert it.[4]

The similarity of the reasoning of Justin and of the author of the *Epistle to Diognetus* is striking. It represents a Christianized form of the Platonic argument that God has assigned people to a post that they must not abandon.

The *Clementine Homilies*, falsely attributed to Clement of Rome (late first century to early second century) but written in their present form probably in the mid-fourth century, were based on an original composed in the late second or early third century. Although the *Homilies* display a marked Ebionite or Elkesaite orientation, in many ways their theology was not inconsistent with contemporary orthodoxy. In *Homily* 12 the apostle Peter encountered a pagan woman who, because of a variety of afflictions, was considering committing suicide. He admonished her, "Do you suppose, O woman, that those who destroy themselves are freed from punishment? Are not the souls of those who thus die punished with a worse punishment in Hades for their suicide?"[5] This was a novel position, that suicide would compound one's future punishment; hence it is unfortunate that we cannot know whether this incident was in the original or added by a fourth-century redactor.

Of all the church fathers none was more significantly influenced by Greek philosophy than Clement of Alexandria (c. 155-c. 220). To him Greek philosophy was a *praeparatio evangelica* that contained more truth than falsehood. He eagerly drank from the springs of the pagan past, rejoicing in the plethora of wisdom that he felt God had revealed to the Greeks, partially through a supposed early acquaintance with Hebrew Scripture. Nevertheless he did not accept all that these philosophers offered. How could he? Not only did they frequently contradict each other, but also they were often at variance with Scripture. Clement's style, however, was not to draw attention to points of disagreement but, as a means of apologetics, to emphasize primarily matters of consonance. Sometimes he was rather obscure; at other times he could easily be misunderstood, especially when he drew the reader's attention to certain philosophical tenets, not to endorse them but rather to illustrate a particular Christian truth. Here is a pertinent example:

> The philosophers also allow the good man an exit from life in accordance with reason, in the case of one depriving him of active exertion, so that the hope of action is no longer left him. And the judge who compels us to deny Him whom we love, I regard as showing who is and who is not the friend of God. In that case there is not left ground for even examining what one prefers — the menaces of man or the love of God.[6]

An "exit from life in accordance with reason" was the suicide permitted by certain philosophical schools. The Christian also had an "exit from life in accordance with reason," said Clement, and that was martyrdom. But, as we saw in chapter two, Clement unequivocally condemned seeking martyrdom and strongly encouraged flight in the face of persecution. Hence this cannot be taken as an endorsement of suicide, as is made even more clear from Clement's discussions of suffering and sanctification that are scattered throughout his *Stromateis.*

Even when he is addressing the topics of suffering and sanctification, Clement's terminology is so philosophical, his vocabulary so peppered especially with Stoic jargon, that he can be easily misunderstood especially if sentences, even paragraphs, are taken out of context. The concept of *apatheia* (insensibility to suffering) is central to Stoic thought. It was also of vital importance to Clement. But in Clement it was significantly informed by those essential scriptural principles that were basic to other church fathers' values. So also for Clement suffering was an essential aspect of Christian growth, and he frequently stressed God's paternal, sovereign care of his people. He said, for example, that the true Christian

> will never . . . have the chief end placed in life, but in being always happy and blessed, and a kingly friend of God. Although visited with ignominy and exile, and confiscation, and above all, death, he will never be wrenched from his freedom, and signal love to God. The charity which "bears all things, endures all things" is assured that Divine Providence orders all things well.[7]

Clement enlarged on these themes later:

> Though disease, and accident, and what is most terrible of all, death, come upon [the true Christian], he remains inflexible in soul, —knowing that all such things are a necessity of creation, and that, also by the power of God, they become the medicine of salvation, benefiting by discipline those who are difficult to reform; allotted according to dessert, by Providence, which is truly good. . . . He undergoes toils, and trials, and afflictions, not as those among the philosophers who are endowed with manliness, in the hope of present troubles ceasing, and

of sharing again in what is pleasant, but knowledge has inspired him with the firmest persuasion of receiving the hopes of the future. [He] withstands all fear of everything terrible, not only of death, but also poverty and disease, and ignominy, and things akin to these. . . .[8]

Penury and disease, and such trials, are often sent for admonition, for the correction of the past, and for care for the future. Such a one prays for relief from them, in virtue of possessing the prerogative of knowledge, not out of vainglory . . . having become the instrument of the goodness of God. . . . He is not disturbed by anything which happens; nor does he suspect those things, which, through divine arrangement, take place for good. Nor is he ashamed to die, having a good conscience, and being fit to be seen by the Powers. Cleansed, so to speak, from all the stains of the soul, he knows right well that it will be better with him after his departure.[9]

The *apatheia* that Clement lauded as a Christian ideal could never logically lead to suicide:

By going away to the Lord . . . *he does not withdraw himself from life. For that is not permitted to him.* But he has withdrawn his soul from the passions. For that is granted to him. And on the other hand he lives, having put to death his lusts, and no longer makes use of the body, *but allows it the use of necessaries, that he may not give cause for dissolution* [emphases added].[10]

This is a magnificent blending of certain Stoic principles that are compatible with Clement's Christianity. But it is a Stoicism that had been Christianized to such a degree that suicide was permitted neither in the active sense of withdrawing from life nor in the passive sense of causing the dissolution of the body by failing to provide it with "necessaries."

For Clement Job was the outstanding example of endurance. The Christian "will bless when under trial, like the noble Job. . . . He will give his testimony by night; he will testify by day; by word; by life, by conduct, he will testify."[11] Later he mentioned Job once more: "And indeed Job, through exceeding continence, and excellence of faith, when from rich to become poor, from being held in honour dishonoured, from being comely unsightly, and sick from being healthy, is depicted as a good example for us, putting the Tempter to shame, blessing his Creator."[12]

Clement's contemporary Tertullian (c. 160-c. 220) also stressed the necessity of patient endurance:

Let us strive, then, to bear the injuries that are inflicted by the Evil One, that the struggle to maintain our self-control may put to shame the enemy's efforts. If, however, through imprudence or even of our own free will we draw down upon ourselves some misfortune, we should submit with equal patience to that. . . . But if we believe some blow of misfortune is struck by God, to whom would it be better that we manifest patience than to our Lord? In fact, more than this, it befits us to rejoice at being deemed worthy of divine chastisement. . . . Blessed is that servant upon whose amendment the Lord insists, at whom He deigns to be angry, whom He does not deceive by omitting His admonition. From every angle, then, we are obliged to practice patience, because we meet up with our own mistakes or the wiles of the Evil One or the warnings of the Lord alike.[13]

Later Tertullian gave Job as the most significant example of patient endurance:

Far from being turned away by so many misfortunes from the reverence which he owed to God, he set for us an example and proof of how we must practice patience in the spirit as well as in the flesh, in soul as well as in the body, that we may not succumb under the loss of worldly goods, the death of our dear ones, or any bodily afflictions. What a trophy over the Devil God erected in the case of that man! What a banner of His glory He raised above His enemy . . . when [Job] severely rebuked his wife who, weary by now of misfortunes, was urging him to improper remedies. . . . Thus did that hero who brought about a victory for his God beat back all the darts of temptation and with the breastplate and shield of patience soon after recover from God complete health of body and the possession of twice as much as he had lost.[14]

Here also there was no room for suicide. The most basic principles of patient endurance for the Christian militated against the very thought of suicide. Tertullian, after mentioning that Christ "tells us to give to the one who asks," remarked that "if you take His command generally, you would be giving not only wine to a man with a fever, but also poison or a sword to one who wanted to die."[15] Giving wine to the febrile was thought to be very harmful. Tertullian included assisting in suicide in the same category. The thought was that one would not supply the means if asked. Elsewhere he classified anyone who "cuts his own throat" as demented or insane, and the context suggests that such a one was demon possessed.[16]

Tertullian remarked that some pagans, "led by the impulses of their own mind, put an end to their lives." Under this rubric he included the Roman matron Lucretia; the legendary Carthaginian queen Dido; the wife of Hasdrubal, the Carthaginian general who surrendered to Scipio; Cleopatra; and the philosophers Heraclitus, Empedocles and Peregrinus—the latter, after a brief stint as a Christian, became a Cynic and ended his life by self-immolation during the Olympic Games in 165.[17]

Tertullian's assessment of these suicides and of those who sacrificed their lives or bravely endured horrible sufferings was that "if earthly glory accruing from strength of body and soul is valued so highly" that pagans would undergo such things "for the reward of human praise," then the sufferings that Christian martyrs endure "are but trifling in comparison with the heavenly glory and divine reward."[18]

In his *Apology* Tertullian compared Lycurgus, who had "hoped to starve himself to death because the Spartans had amended his laws," with the Christian, who, "even when condemned, gives thanks."[19] Later he mentioned Empedocles' and Dido's self-immolation. Here he became sarcastic: "Oh, what strength of mind!" he exclaimed about the former, and about the latter, "Oh, what a glorious mark of chastity!" He said that he would "pass over those who by their own sword or by some other gentler manner of death made sure of their fame after death." Regarding these suicides, he commented that "such recklessness and depravity, for the sake of glory and renown, raise aloft among you the banner of courage." But in the opinion of pagans, the Christian who "suffers for God, is a madman."[20]

Tertullian did not condemn these pagan suicides, at least not directly. His sole purpose, as Timothy Barnes expresses it in his study of Tertullian, is contrast: "If glass is so precious, how valuable must be a genuine pearl! Why should Christians hesitate to die for the truth, when others die for false ideals such as their own glory?"[21]

Lactantius (c. 240-320) was a Latin rhetorician whose accomplishments attracted the attention of the emperor Diocletian, who appointed him professor of oratory in Nicomedia. He was converted to Christianity, and when the Great Persecution began (303), he felt compelled to resign his position. He turned to writing Christian apologetics directed on the one hand to educated pagans and on the other to Christians who were troubled by philosophical attacks against their faith. The major argument of his *Divine Institutes* is that "pagan religion and philosophy are absurdly inadequate. Truth lies in God's revelation, and the ethical change which the teaching of Christ brings points conclusively to its accuracy."[22]

The first two books of the *Divine Institutes*, "Concerning False Religion" and "Concerning the Origin of Error," attempted to refute polytheism. The third book, "Concerning False Wisdom," tried "to prove the falsity of pagan philosophy, its contradictions, and its uselessness in practice."[23] The remainder of the work was devoted to demonstrating the truth of Christianity. Lactantius's major statement on suicide appears in book 3. Discussing the Pythagoreans and Stoics, both of whom believed in the immortality of the soul (although the latter regarded it as right to take one's own life under some circumstances), Lactantius said that many of them, "because they suspected that the soul is immortal, laid violent hands upon themselves, as though they were about to depart to heaven." He then gave as examples the suicides of Cleanthes, Chrysippus, Zeno, Empedocles, Cato and Democritus. He asserted that

> nothing can be more wicked than this. For if a homicide is guilty because he is a destroyer of man, he who puts himself to death is under the same guilt, because he puts to death a man. Yea, that crime may be considered to be greater, the punishment of which belongs to God alone. For as we did not come into this life of our own accord; so, on the other hand, we can only withdraw from this habitation of the body which has been appointed for us to keep, by the command of Him who placed us in this body that we may inhabit it, until He orders us to depart from it. . . . All these philosophers, therefore, were homicides.[24]

Some years after completing his *Divine Institutes*, Lactantius was asked to produce an epitome of it. It is interesting to note that the space he devoted to suicide in this much shorter abridgment is more than in the original. In the *Epitome* he asked whether we should approve those

> who, that they might be said to have despised death, died by their own hands? Zeno, Empedocles, Chrysippus, Cleanthes, Democritus, and Cato, imitating these, did not know that he who put himself to death is guilty of murder, according to the divine right and law. For it was God who placed us in this abode of flesh: it was He who gave us the temporary habitation of the body, that we should inhabit it as long as He pleased. Therefore it is to be considered impious, to wish to depart from it without the command of God. Therefore violence must not be applied to nature. He knows how to destroy His own work. And if any one shall apply impious hands to that work, and shall tear asunder the bonds of the divine workmanship, he endeavours to flee from God, whose sentence no one will be able to escape, whether alive or dead. Therefore they are accursed and impious, whom I have mentioned above, who even taught what are the befitting reasons for voluntary death; so that it was not enough of guilt that they were self-murderers, unless they instructed others also to this wickedness.[25]

In his *Divine Institutes* Lactantius had condemned suicides as worse than homicides on the Christianized Platonic grounds that suicides desert the place to which God had appointed them. In his *Epitome* he added the offenses of attempting to flee from God by committing violence against nature and encouraging others to do likewise. In his second work his tone was even more vitriolic and outraged than in the first: suicides were not only homicides but were impious as well.

Lactantius's contemporary, Eusebius (c. 265-339), wrote,

> It is worthy of note that, as the records show, in the reign of Gaius . . . Pilate himself, the governor of our Saviour's day, was involved in such calamities that he was forced to become his own executioner and to punish himself with his own hand: divine justice, it seems, was not slow to overtake him. The facts are recorded by those Greeks who have chronicled the Olympiads together with the events occurring in each.[26]

Eusebius clearly regarded Pilate's suicide from despair as God's just penalty, a condemnation for his sin of sentencing Jesus to death by crucifixion.

Eusebius quoted from the anti-Montanist work of Bishop Apollinarius of Hierapolis, written during the reign of Marcus Aurelius, the following account of the deaths of Montanus (the founder, in the late second century, of the charismatic and prophetic sect that bears his name) and one of his prophetesses, Maximilla:

> It is thought that both of these were driven out of their minds by a spirit, and hanged themselves, at different times; and on the occasion of the death of each, it was said on all sides that this was how they died, putting an end to themselves just like the traitor Judas. . . . But we must not imagine that without seeing them we know the truth about such things, my friend: it may have been in this way, it may have been in some other way, that death came to Montanus . . . and [his] female associate.[27]

Neither Eusebius nor his source would vouch for the accuracy of this account. Including it, however, they suggested that death by suicide was appropriate for two whom they regarded as notorious heretics.

Basil of Caesarea (c. 329-379), in one of his canonical letters (so called because their contents — they deal with aspects of church discipline — became part of the canon law of the Eastern church), wrote that a woman who had an abortion was guilty not only of the murder of the fetus but also of "an attempt against her own life, because usually the women die in such attempts."[28] There may have been no precedent for Basil's regarding an abortion as tantamount to making an attempt on one's own life because of the high probability of the mother's death owing to the dangers involved in procedures then available. Nevertheless it is obvious that Basil was speaking for and to a community that regarded even an attempt on one's own life as sinful.

John Chrysostom (349-407) was a fervent and eloquent preacher whose concerns were primarily pastoral. In his *Commentary on Galatians,* when he was dealing with Galatians 1:4 (Jesus "gave Himself for our sins, that He might deliver us out of this present evil age [or evil world], according to the will of our God and Father"), he criticized those heretics who regarded the material world as evil. He took the words "evil age [or world]" to mean

> evil actions, and a depraved moral principle. . . . Christ came not to put us to death and deliver us from the present life in that sense, but to leave us in the world, and prepare us for a worthy participation of our heavenly abode. Wherefore He saith to the Father, "And these are in the world, and I come to Thee; I pray not that Thou shouldest take them from the world, but that Thou shouldest keep them from the evil," i.e., from sin. Further, those who will not allow this, but insist that the present life is evil, should not blame those who destroy themselves; for as he who withdraws himself from evil is not blamed, but deemed worthy of a crown, so he who by a violent death, by hanging or otherwise, puts an end to his life, ought not to be condemned. *Whereas God punishes such men more than murderers, and we all regard them with horror, and justly; for if it is base to destroy others, much more is it to destroy one's self* [emphasis added].[29]

Chrysostom maintained that encouragement to suicide was a reasonable consequence of dualistic heresy. But as far as he was concerned, true Christians—"we all" would be the orthodox—regarded suicides with horror, and justly so. This would be a preposterous statement if there had been even a strong minority sentiment in the orthodox Christian community that would justify suicide to escape "this present evil world."

Ambrose (c. 339-397), Augustine's mentor, was much influenced by both Neo-Platonism and Stoicism.[30] His position on suicide, however, seems to have been no more affected by Stoicism than was that of Clement of Alexandria. In *Death as a Good* he commented on Paul's statement "for to me to live is Christ and to die is gain":

> For Christ is our king; therefore we cannot abandon and disregard His royal command. How many men the emperor of this earth orders to live abroad in the splendor of office or perform some function! Do they abandon their posts without the emperor's consent? Yet what a greater thing it is to please the divine than the human! Thus for the saint "to live is Christ and to die is gain." He does not flee the servitude of life like a slave, and yet like a wise man he does embrace the gain of death.[31]

Once again we see the Christianized form of the Platonic argument against suicide.

Elsewhere Ambrose wrote to his sister Marcellina,

> You make a good suggestion that I should touch upon what we ought to think of the merits of those who have cast themselves down from a height, or have drowned themselves in a river, lest they should fall in

the hands of persecutors, seeing that holy Scripture forbids a Christian to lay hands on himself.[32]

Then, after giving an example of suicide by a virgin to preserve her chastity, he described an instance of a woman's endurance under torture leading to death, implying that suicide undertaken to avoid persecution was wrong but suicide done to preserve virginity was laudable. It is noteworthy that Ambrose asserted that Scripture forbade suicide and seems to have assumed that his addressee would share this opinion. This appears to be the earliest extant blanket appeal to Scripture by a church father for a condemnation of suicide.

Very similar were the views of Jerome (c. 345-c. 419). In a letter written to the lady Paula, who was distraught over the death of her daughter, Blaesilla, he said,

> Have you no fear, then lest the Savior may say to you: "Are you angry, Paula, that your daughter has become my daughter? Are you vexed at my decree, and do you, with rebellious tears, grudge me the possession of Blaesilla? You ought to know what my purpose is both for you and for yours. You deny yourself food, not to fast but to gratify your grief, and such abstinence is displeasing to me. Such fasts are my enemies. I receive no soul which forsakes the body against my will. A foolish philosophy may boast of martyrs of this kind; it may boast of a Zeno, a Cleombrotus, or a Cato. My spirit rests only upon him 'that is poor and of a contrite spirit and that trembleth at my word; Is. 66:2'."[33]

Elsewhere Jerome qualified this otherwise unlimited condemnation of suicide: "It is not ours to lay hold of death, but we freely accept it when it is inflicted by others. Hence, even in persecutions it is not right for us to die by our own hands, except when chastity is threatened, but to submit our necks to the one who threatens."[34]

There is no suggestion in the writings of these church fathers that for contemporary Christians suicide either was an attraction or posed a theoretical, much less a practical, problem. All the evidence points in the opposite direction.

"Approved" Suicides Prior to Augustine

Eusebius is the earliest church father to record any examples of Christians committing suicide. These suicides are of three categories, all having this in common: they took their lives under extreme duress.

1. Those who killed themselves to avoid being arrested and subjected to extreme suffering. We have found only one instance. It is recorded by Eusebius and occurred during the Great Persecution (303-312):

> Need I rekindle the memory of the martyrs at Antioch, who were

roasted over lighted braziers, not roasted to death but subjected to prolonged torture? Or of others who plunged their hands right into the fire sooner than touch the abominable sacrifice? Some of them were unable to face such a trial, and before they were caught and came into the hands of their would-be destroyers, threw themselves down from the roofs of tall houses, regarding death as a prize snatched from the scheming hands of God's enemies.[35]

Eusebius recorded this incident with neither approval nor disapproval. As we saw, Ambrose implicitly and Jerome explicitly condemned suicide to avoid the tortures that typically attended martyrdom.[36] Both, however, were born decades after the legalization of Christianity, but Eusebius lived through the Great Persecution. This fact may suggest why the latter did not condemn the act. Augustine (354-430) was extremely thorough in his various analyses of suicide. Yet, as we shall see, he made no reference to this category of self-killing by Christians, although he appears to have scoured both pagan and Christian literature for references to suicide. Hence it is reasonable to conclude that such types of suicide by Christians had occurred very rarely while Christians were still a persecuted minority.

2. Those who had already been arrested but dramatically ended their lives before being executed. We know of only two examples, both recorded by Eusebius. The first occurred in Alexandria in 249 under Decius:

Next they seized the wonderful old lady Apollonia, battered her till they knocked out all her teeth, built a pyre in front of the city, and threatened to burn her alive unless she repeated after them their heathen incantations. She asked for a breathing-space, and when they released her, jumped without hesitation into the fire and was burnt to ashes.[37]

The second was during the Great Persecution:

There was a conflagration in the palace at Nicomedia, and through a groundless suspicion word went round that our people were responsible. By imperial command God's worshippers there perished wholesale and in heaps, some butchered with the sword, others fulfilled [*teleioō* = perfected, made perfect or complete] by fire; it is on record that with an inspired and mystical fervour men and women alike leapt on to the pyre.[38]

Such suicides were not without precedent. As we have seen in chapter one, such dramatic suicides by Jews about to be martyred were lauded in 2 Maccabees and 4 Maccabees and in the Talmud. But such were apparently very rare among Christians, and Augustine evidently was unaware of their occurrence.

3. Virgins and married women who committed suicide to avoid sexual defilement. As we have seen, both Ambrose and Jerome assumed the probity of suicide to preserve chastity. Here we enter into an anomaly in early Christian thought: the approbation of suicide to preserve chastity, especially to preserve virginity. Only a minority of the sources surveyed mentioned it; the few that did, approved it.[39] The earliest of these was Eusebius. He told of a virtuous woman and her two virgin daughters at Antioch who threw themselves into a river to escape the salacious designs of the Roman soldiers.[40] Later, after describing the endurance of martyrs under the most severe tortures, he wrote,

> As for the women, schooled by the divine word, they showed themselves as manly as the men. Some underwent the same ordeals as the men, and shared with them the prize of valour; others, when dragged away to dishonour, gave up their souls to death rather than their bodies to that dishonour [*phthora* = "moral corruption"].[41]

Then he gave an example of a "most noble and chaste" married lady in Rome who, when faced with imminent threat of sexual violation,

> stabbed herself to the heart, dying instantly. Her dead body she left to the emperor's pimps; but by deeds that spoke more loudly than any words she proclaimed to all men then living or yet to come that the only unconquerable and indestructible possession was a Christian's virtue.[42]

Eusebius's approval of these cases is obvious.

We have already noted that Ambrose appears to approve such suicide. The remarks of the leading twentieth-century authority on Ambrose, F. Homes Dudden, are worthy of inclusion:

> On one occasion Ambrose was requested by his sister Marcellina to state his opinion concerning virgins who committed suicide to avoid violation. He did not, however, express himself very clearly. On the one hand, he told the story of the suicide of St. Pelagia of Antioch and of her mother and sisters in a manner which suggests that, if he did not actually commend, he certainly did not condemn their act. On the other hand, he spoke with unqualified admiration of another Antiochene virgin, who, being sentenced to violation in a brothel, on account of her refusal to sacrifice, prepared to undergo the penalty, without anticipating it by suicide. In relating the incident, he said, "A virgin of Christ may be dishonoured, but she cannot be polluted. Everywhere she is the virgin of God and the temple of God. Places of infamy do not stain chastity; on the contrary chastity abolishes the infamy of the place."[43]

Ambrose's reasoning, as expressed in the last three sentences quoted here from his treatise *Concerning Virgins*, corresponds closely to Augustine's, who on these grounds condemned suicide even to preserve chastity.

Jerome was unequivocal in his approbation of these acts of suicide. For him they were the only exception to his firm conviction that suicide was illicit for Christians. In order to appreciate why such an exception was made by these church fathers, one must be aware of the extent to which the early Christian community recoiled from what it regarded as the gross immorality of pagan culture. Early Christian sources condemned nearly all aspects of pagan immorality as related features of a society that they regarded as rotten to its core because of sin. With sweeping strokes of moral indignation, early Christian apologists condemned gladiatorial shows and cruel executions, along with abortion, infanticide, homicide generally and a broad variety of sexual practices ranging from homosexuality to adultery, from fornication to perversions within the marriage bond. The range of imagination employed in sexual activities by the pagans and the open display of it appears to have caused the early Christian community to react more strongly against sexual sins than against any other realm of contemporary immorality. And the numerous injunctions in the New Testament to refrain from sexual sins supported Christians' moral indignation.

But these factors alone were not sufficient to produce a climate conducive to regarding the preserving of one's chastity as a higher moral obligation than refraining from suicide. Sexual abstinence is occasionally praised or recommended in the New Testament, and as early as the late first or early second century Ignatius calls Christian women who voluntarily remain virgins Christ's brides and jewels. But it was not until the mid- to late second century that some sources began to suggest that celibacy was a higher good than marriage and an essential quality for the true ascetic. That virginal celibacy was continuing to grow in esteem, gradually becoming nearly the highest virtue, is illustrated by the fact that instances of Christian women committing suicide to preserve their chastity are not found before the fourth century.

We do no service to the truth if we deny that there have been some aberrations and excesses in the history of Christianity. Christian women who killed themselves to avoid sexual defilement, especially during times of persecution, were venerated by their fellow Christians. Were they suicides? Although the philosophical principle of double effect (i.e., distinguishing between results that are intended and consequences that are foreseen and even inevitable but not desired) may be marshaled in support of the contention that they were not, only those who are willing will be convinced by such an approach.

This one category of suicide first caught Augustine's attention and caused him to address the subject of suicide.

Augustine

All the implicit and explicit condemnations of suicide in Christian literature prior to or contemporary with Augustine were encapsulated and
elaborated by Augustine.[44] No figure in the early centuries of Christianity
had a more significant influence on later Western Christian thought than
he. So similar was he to his Eastern contemporaries, Basil of Caesarea,
Gregory Nazianzen and Gregory of Nyssa (the Cappadocian fathers),
and to John Chrysostom that to see him as a spokesman for Western as
opposed to Eastern Christianity would be simplistic. Yet there is in
Augustine's works a melody that is hauntingly medieval in many of its
nuances. The end of his long life marked a watershed in Western history.
When he died in 430, Rome had been sacked twenty years earlier by the
Goths, and Roman North Africa was falling to the Vandals. The unity of
the Mediterranean world was beginning to disintegrate as its western half
was increasingly affected by forces from the north, some already Christianized, and was slowly being drawn into an emerging European, rather
than a strictly Mediterranean, ethos.

Hence we need to approach Augustine as something of a Janus figure.
His influence on medieval Christianity was enormous. Much more important for the present study is a consideration of the extent to which his
values resembled those of his Christian antecedents and contemporaries
as they pertain to suicide. As early as Rousseau, some scholars have
claimed that Augustine took his arguments against suicide from Plato's
Phaedo and not from the Bible. It is common to find modern scholars
making such amazing claims as "there is little reason to think that
Augustine's position is authentically Christian."[45] Our survey of patristic
literature demonstrates that it is inaccurate to maintain that Augustine
formulated what became the Christian position on suicide. Rather, by
removing certain ambiguities, he clarified and provided a theologically
cogent explanation of and justification for the position typically held by
earlier and contemporary Christian sources.

Augustine's best-known discussion of suicide is found in book 1 of the
City of God. This is a digression that he could not have intended to be a
systematic and comprehensive treatment of the moral issues involved in
a consideration of suicide, regardless of the extent to which portions of
the latter were used as authoritative by later generations. His discussion
of suicide must be appreciated within the context of his immediate
purposes in formulating a position to which a consideration of suicide is
only incidental.

In his introductory letter to the first installment of this work, published
in 414, Augustine said that he had undertaken the writing of the work in

order to defend the City of God, that is, the community of those "predestined to reign with God from all eternity" (as he eventually defines it),[46] against the pagans. Just four years earlier (410) Rome had been captured and ravaged by Alaric and his Goths. This had sent a shock wave throughout the empire. Even though pagan temples had been closed by imperial decree about two decades earlier and public worship of the traditional deities forbidden, the city of Rome had remained largely pagan, especially its upper classes, who had clung tenaciously and defiantly to their ancient religious practices refined by the increasingly popular Neo-Platonism that had become nearly a religion itself. The sack of Rome was, in the pagans' opinion, the final proof of the gods' displeasure with the official neglect of their worship. In response to such sentiments Augustine began, essentially as an encouragement to his fellow Christians in the face of troubling accusations by pagans, what was, over the next thirteen years, to evolve into the *City of God*.

Shortly after finishing this massive work, Augustine wrote his *Retractations* in which he described the schema of the *City of God*. Here he said that the first five books were designed to refute those who tied the prosperity of the empire to the favor of the gods and adversity to their disfavor.[47] Book 1 begins with the assertion that Christianity had mitigated rather than aggravated the violence of the recent sack of Rome in particular and of war in general. Christians had shown a clemency antithetical to the typical savagery of the pagans (*City of God* 1.1-7). Augustine argued that prosperity and adversity affected both the good and the bad alike (1.8-9). Christians lost nothing when deprived of temporal goods, even of life itself, since all must die sooner or later (1.10-11). Furthermore it was not a matter of great concern whether the dead bodies of Christians were abused and left unburied, as happened in several instances during the recent sack of Rome. Nevertheless, if possible, Christians paid respect to the bodies of their dead (1.12-13). Augustine then described the consolations that Christians experienced when in captivity and reminded the pagans of their own Regulus, who, centuries before, had endured captivity in an exemplary manner for the sake of his religion, albeit a false religion (1.14-15). Some pagans had taken great delight in pointing out that even Christian women had been sexually violated by the barbarian Goths during their ravaging of Rome. Augustine replied that the virtue of one thus violated was not polluted (1.16). Here Augustine detoured into a discussion of suicide by women to preserve their chastity.

Augustine then crafted intricately reasoned condemnations of different motivations for suicide: a desire to escape from or avoid temporal troubles; a desire to escape from or avoid another's sinful actions (suicide to protect one's chastity would be included here); guilt over past sins; a desire for the better (i.e., eternal) life; and a wish to avoid sinning. He emphatically maintained that if there were any just cause for suicide, it would be the last. He made only passing mention of martyrdom in this digression on suicide, and that was in his refutation of the pagans' approval of suicide to avoid captivity. He said that the patriarchs, prophets and apostles certainly did not do so, and in reference to the apostles he quoted Jesus' admonition that when his disciples were persecuted in one city, they should flee to another (*City of God* 1.22). He would shortly be devoting much attention to the subject, but it would not be to the martyrdom of fellow Catholics; rather, it would be to the courting of martyrdom by and the "heroic" suicides of members of a schismatic or heretical group, the Donatists.[48]

The Donatist movement was named after its leader, Donatus, who was bishop in Carthage from 313 to about 355. The movement had been formed two years earlier by rigorists who condemned what they regarded as the laxness of the church in accepting back into fellowship those who had apostatized during the Great Persecution under Diocletian. It was essentially a protest movement by those who regarded themselves as the one true and holy church. The Catholics, they maintained, because of their toleration of low standards of holiness, were apostates. The Donatists saw themselves as upholders of purity of discipline in the face of Catholic compromise with the world and its system, including the ostensibly Christian emperors. From its inception the sect was both on the offensive and on the defensive; its members were the church of the righteous who alone were pure.

The schismatic basis for the Donatist movement evoked a negative response both from the Catholic church and from the emperor Constantine, who, beginning in 317, attempted to coerce them back into the fold. Persecution encouraged rather than discouraged these rigorists and merely confirmed them in their convictions. They appear to have been only spasmodically persecuted until early in the fifth century, when a series of repressive measures were promulgated by imperial edict. In 415 the death penalty was specified for those Donatists who continued to assemble.

Augustine greeted these draconian measures with enthusiasm, except for the death penalty, which he consistently opposed in principle: it, like suicide, removed any possibility of repentance.[49] Furthermore it provided the Donatists with the martyrdom that so many of them seem to have wanted. Augustine's position on coercion had changed over the years along with his evolving ecclesiology. Earlier he had maintained that only spiritual measures should be used against heretics. Now he advocated force to bring them into the Catholic Church, for outside the Catholic Church there could be no salvation. He applied the *cogite intrare* of Luke 14:23 to the treatment of heretics by civil authorities, hoping that by these measures they would be saved when reason and instruction had failed.

Undoubtedly a catalyst to Augustine's change of heart on the question of religious coercion were those aspects of the Donatist movement that he found exceptionally objectionable: their provoking persecution through acts of violence and obnoxious defiance and their "heroic" suicides. The most noteworthy practitioners of these tactics that Augustine so loathed were the Circumcellions, a fringe group of Donatists who were generally an embarrassment to the more moderate members of the sect. The Circumcellions often roamed the countryside, inciting peasants and slaves to rebellion, engaging in indiscriminate as well as systematic acts of violence, destroying Catholic churches, harassing, sometimes maiming and occasionally even killing Catholic clergy. They once attempted to kill Augustine by an ambush that he escaped only by having accidentally taken the wrong road on a journey.[50] It is impossible to determine with accuracy when it is fair to saddle the entire Donatist movement with complicity in the actions of the Circumcellions or to know when the fanatical actions of the latter were an extension of the ideology of the former, especially in their provoking of martyrdom and in their "heroic" suicides.

Augustine, perhaps unfairly, attributed both of these acts indiscriminately to the Donatists generally. In one of his earliest anti-Donatist works, the *Contra Litteras Petiliani*, written between 401 and 405, he asked, "If you are suffering persecution, why do you not retire from the cities in which you are, that you may fulfill the instructions" of Christ to flee when persecuted? Why are you always "eager to annoy the Catholic Churches by the most violent disturbances, whenever it is in your power, as is proved by innumerable instances?"[51] But what disturbed him far more was their practice of "heroic" and very dramatic suicides. Just before committing suicide, they would shout *Deo laudes*: "You are so furious, that you cause more terror than a war trumpet with your cry of 'Praise to God'; so full of calumny, that even when you throw yourselves over precipices without any provocation, you impute it to our persecutions."[52] This was written before the death penalty had been imposed against Donatists who persisted in assembling, and apparently Augustine's point was that their propensity to suicide was so ingrained that their acts of self-destruction could not be mitigated by the claim that it was done to avoid being put to death by their persecutors.[53]

Three major themes in Augustine's anti-Donatist writings did not appear in his digression on suicide in book 1 of the *City of God*.

1. Provoking martyrdom was a form of suicide and hence a sin. Persecution by pagans had become a moot point by that time. Consequently Augustine's treatment of voluntary martyrdom, since it involved those outside the orthodox community who were responding to efforts by the Catholic Church to compel them to enter the orthodox fold, differed somewhat in force and emphases from earlier condemnations of voluntary martyrdom by members of the orthodox community.

2. "Heroic" suicides by these same folk, when they were unable to provoke others to martyr them, had no known parallel in earlier Christian experience. While the circumstances were novel, Augustine's condemnation of such suicides was consistent with the position that he had already articulated in book 1 of the *City of God*.

3. In an anti-Donatist letter written in 420, Augustine maintained that "it is not lawful to kill another, even if he wishes and asks for it and has no longer the strength to live, as is clearly proved [when] King David ordered the slayer of King Saul to be put to death, although he said that he had been importuned by the wounded and half-dead king to kill him with one blow and to free his soul struggling with the fetters of the body and longing to be released from those torments."[54] That Augustine regarded it as a sin to aid in the suicide of one who strongly desired to die but did not have the strength to kill himself is clearly stated here but only adumbrated in another anti-Donatist letter written four years earlier in which he comments that "bodily safety behooves to be so guarded that it is the duty of those who love their neighbour to preserve him even against his own will from harm."[55]

4. In one of his last anti-Donatist treatises (Augustine *Letter* 204, written in 420), Augustine argued that the Donatists' suicides violate the foundational Christian principle of patient endurance. In his treatise on patience, written five years earlier, he had condemned suicide precisely on these grounds. In 426 or 427 Augustine published book 19 of the *City of God* along with the remainder of the work. In this, the last section of his magnum opus, is his final discussion of suicide. Here patient endurance is the foundational principle for his ultimate condemnation of suicide as encouraged by various pagan philosophical schools.

Augustine's most frequently cited discussion of suicide, which is also his earliest thorough treatment of it, is his digression on suicide in book 1 of the *City of God*, which he could not have intended to be a systematic theological, much less philosophical, analysis of the subject. Augustine entered the discussion convinced that suicide was a reprehensible sin and a crime. He was speaking to his fellow Christians, who would not have been particularly surprised by anything that he was saying because they held the same basic values as Augustine and his older contemporaries who had already penned condemnations of suicide. The fact that in his discussion of suicide his general condemnations of the act are almost incidental to his main line of argument is in itself compelling evidence for the stability of a tradition of condemnation of suicide. If it were not for the exception that a few church fathers had made of some virgins "martyred" by their own hand to preserve their chastity in the face of persecution, the subject of suicide would almost certainly never have come up in book 1 of the *City of God*, and the only discussion of it in that work would then be that in book 19.

Augustine based his condemnation of suicide most fundamentally on the same presuppositions and values that caused the earlier church fathers to condemn the act. His position is more developed than theirs. Earlier sources assumed that suicide was a sin. The only difference between Augustine and his predecessors who dealt with suicide is that in book 1 of the *City of God* he attempted to answer possible objections to the traditional Christian condemnation of suicide. His defense of the traditional position was fourfold.

1. Scripture neither commanded it nor expressly permitted it, either as a means of attaining immortality or as a way to avoid or escape any evil.

2. It must be understood to be forbidden by the sixth commandment: "You shall not murder."

3. If no one on his own authority had a right to kill even a guilty man, then one who killed himself was a homicide.

4. The act of suicide allowed no opportunity for repentance.

Did Augustine formulate the Christian position on suicide? The answer must be an unequivocal no. He based his condemnation of suicide most fundamentally on the same presuppositions and values that had caused the earlier church fathers to condemn the act. Recall the terms with which they had condemned it: it is opposed to the will of God (Justin); it is not lawful *(Epistle to Diognetus)*; suicides are punished more severely than others *(Clementine Homilies)*; it is not permitted (Clement); God punishes suicides more than homicides, and we all justly regard them with horror (John Chrysostom); nothing can be more wicked than suicide (Lactantius); the sin of abortion is compounded by the dangers of the procedures that render it virtually an act of attempted suicide (Basil); Christ will not receive the soul of a suicide (Jerome); Scripture forbids Christians to lay hands on themselves (Ambrose). Augustine was the first Christian on record to discuss the issue thoroughly, although a century earlier Lactantius had already devoted several pages of his *Divine Institutes* to suicide and then amplified his treatment of the subject in his *Epitome.*

Did Augustine contribute anything new to the Christian position? Here the answer must be a qualified yes, for three reasons.

1. Although it is unlikely that any of the earlier sources that we have cited would have disagreed with any of his arguments except regarding suicide to preserve chastity, nevertheless this was a significant disagreement. It is both ironic and intriguing that in this one area of dispute, as we shall see in chapter five, Augustine did not carry the day.

2. In his unequivocal and absolute condemnation of suicide, Augustine had painted himself into a corner. If committing suicide to preserve chastity was a sin, what was one to think of those women who had killed themselves during times of persecution and were then venerated as martyrs? Augustine's only explanations were either that divine authority instructed the church that they should be thus honored, or that these "martyrs" had followed a divine command that was personally revealed to them. The latter was the only explanation that he could imagine for the one "justifiable" suicide in Scripture, that of Samson. Hence one could commit suicide only when one was the recipient of an unmistakable and entirely unambiguous command from God to do so. Augustine was noticeably uncomfortable with this apparently unavoidable conclusion.[56]

3. The thoroughness with which he discussed suicide — in books 1 and 19 of the *City of God* and in his various anti-Donatist writings — resulted in his marshaling a much larger array of arguments against suicide than had any of his predecessors. His appeal to the sixth commandment is interesting as the earliest example in the history of moral considerations of suicide. But it would be significant only if earlier church fathers had attempted to justify their condemnations of suicide by recourse to specific injunctions in Scripture, which they did not.

There is no evidence that before Augustine's time suicide was a debated issue in the Christian community. Martyrdom, however, was. The probity of provoking or volunteering for martyrdom was hotly disputed before the legalization of Christianity. Furthermore, those few "approved" suicides that we encounter in early Christian literature occurred under the extreme duress of persecution or imminent sexual violation. It was the questionable probity of the latter that had stimulated Augustine to deal with suicide per se, bolstered by the antics of Donatist Circumcellions. Why was suicide not a debated issue within the Christian community?

Surely not because the church fathers were reluctant to condemn sin and to confront their fellow Christians for their moral failings. Many of them warmed to that task with an enthusiasm of moral vigor, and they dealt not only with matters specifically prohibited by Scripture but also with *adiaphora* (gray areas) as well. Nevertheless there does not appear to be even one exhortation to refrain from suicide even in the writings of those authors who condemn the act unequivocally. The absence of a debate over suicide should not suggest that Christians were indifferent to suicide as an ethical issue. It appears not to have been a sufficiently attractive and viable option for them to have regarded it as a threat to the moral integrity of the Christian community.[57]

The condemnations of suicide that we encounter prior to Augustine's time are comparatively rare because they are not part of the broad moral indignation voiced by church fathers against pagan depravity. Their outrage, especially against abortion and infanticide, was greatly stimulated by the perceived helplessness of the victim, whether a fetus or an infant. So also with gladiatorial combat and viciously cruel forms of torture and execution. Even acts of sexual immorality were more severely condemned when there were victims such as slaves who were forced to be the objects of their owners' lusts or of their greed when they were compelled to act as prostitutes for their owners' profit. The moral indignation of Christian authors was especially animated by the helplessness of the victims of others' sins. Suicide, as practiced by pagans, did not evoke passionate denunciation, for it is not an act in which an innocent party is victimized but an act in which one harms only oneself.

Most important, the whole of the New Testament's and the church fathers' theology, morality and values militated against suicide, especially when it was done to avoid suffering.

5

Euthanasia & Suicide
in the Middle Ages

Augustine is typically credited with having formulated the subsequent Christian position on suicide and by doing so effecting a considerable change in the attitude of the Christian community. He ostensibly turned Christianity from gently condoning or even strongly supporting suicide to vitriolically condemning the act. The evidence that we have given in earlier chapters shows that this claim is not true. What is especially intriguing, indeed ironic, is that in the only matter relevant to suicide in which Augustine disagreed with any earlier or contemporary church fathers (women committing suicide to preserve their chastity), he did not carry the day. Numerous examples could be given of theological justifications of such suicides by Roman Catholic casuists and moral theologians from the Middle Ages to the present. One influential work must suffice as an illustration, and that is Hermann Buzembaum's *Medulla Theologiae Moralis*. First printed in 1648, it has enjoyed numerous reprintings. According to Buzembaum, it is "not deemed suicide . . . if a virgin, to preserve her chastity, were 'to embrace even certain danger of death,' so great a good was her 'integrity.' "[1] Suicide by virgins to preserve their chastity has remained a gray and disputed area, and through the casuistic philosophical principle of double effect (i.e., justifying good results that are intended at the expense of evil consequences that are foreseen and even inevitable but not desired) it is not classified as suicide. And it has continued to be morally defended in spite of such great thinkers in Catholic tradition as Augustine and Aquinas.

Thomas Aquinas (1225-1274) stands even higher than Augustine as an authoritative figure in Roman Catholicism. In his *Summa Theologiae,* while discussing martyrdom,[2] Aquinas condemns suicide by virgins to preserve their chastity. His main discussion of the act, however, occurs earlier, in his section on homicide,[3] which contains his classic treatment of suicide. Here he follows Augustine closely, allowing no exceptions to the condemnation of suicide (except the hypothetical case of a direct, personal command of God). Aquinas's argument is significantly shorter and much more concise than Augustine's various treatments of the subject. Aquinas's position is based on three "reasons" why it is "altogether unlawful to kill oneself." (1) It is unnatural, that is, contrary to the inclination of nature, for everything seeks to keep itself in being, and it is contrary to charity because every person should love himself or herself. (2) It is an offense against and an injury to one's community because one belongs to one's own community. (3) It is a usurpation of God's power to give and take away life.

Aquinas's argument against suicide begins with a quotation of Augustine's application of the sixth commandment to suicide,[4] after which Aquinas gives the three reasons for regarding suicide as "completely illegal" *(omnino illicitum).* The remainder of his discussion is an elaboration of these three reasons. Suicide is contrary to justice and to "that charity which a man owes to himself" and is therefore a sin. It is "a sin against justice when considered in relation to the community and to God." He then distinguishes between lawful killing of a malefactor and suicide, asserting that "nobody is a judge in his own cause."

Aquinas's next section begins with the assertion that free will makes one a master of oneself. One's free will is limited, however, to the management of one's life. Hence, since the passage from this life to "a more blessed one" is not the province of man's free will, one may not kill oneself. The same applies to suicide when it is committed to escape from the miseries of this life; to punish oneself for having committed some sin; to avoid (in the case of a woman) being sexually violated; and to avoid a sin that one is in fear of committing. While considering the second and third instances, Aquinas stresses that suicide deprives one of an opportunity for repentance.

Aquinas then deals briefly with the problem presented by the suicides of Samson and those virgins "celebrated in memory by the Church" who committed suicide to preserve their chastity. He quotes Augustine's assertion that they must have acted under the command of the Holy Spirit.

He concludes his discussion of suicide by citing Razis[5] as an example of the "sort of courage" that is cowardice rather than true courage, which is the ability to bear afflictions. He cites both Aristotle and Augustine as authorities for this conclusion.

What, if anything, new did Aquinas add to the traditional Christian arguments against suicide? Margaret Pabst Battin maintains that two arguments originated with Aquinas: "1) that suicide is forbidden because it attempts to usurp God's judgment over 'the passage from this life to a more blessed one'; and 2) the warning that suicide is 'very perilous' because it leaves no time for repentance."[6] She is wrong in regard to the latter, for Augustine emphasizes that point. In regard to the former, she appears at first glance to be technically correct. Aquinas may have been the first to employ this argument, articulated in this precise way, in condemning suicide. However, a fervent belief in the sovereignty of God undergirds Augustine's entire *City of God* and conditions his and other church fathers' discussions of suicide throughout. Furthermore, Aquinas's point here is nothing more than the Christianized form of the Platonic argument against suicide that several church fathers, beginning as early as Justin Martyr, had employed in condemning suicide.

Aquinas originated neither of the other two reasons that he gives for the absolute illicitness of suicide, although his use of them as two of only three foundational principles for the condemnation of suicide was new. In reference to the first of these, we should note that in book 19 of the *City of God*, Augustine agrees with those philosophers who maintain that the first and greatest command of nature is to shun death and make continued existence one's aim. His conclusion is that the compulsion to end one's life thoroughly defeats nature. Also, in his *De Libero Arbitrio*, written shortly after his conversion, he uses the assertion, as an oblique argument against suicide, that existence is eo ipso a good and that even a miserable and unhappy existence is better than nonexistence. He further maintains that no one should be ungrateful to the goodness of his Creator for his existence.[7]

Aquinas's second reason, for which he cites Aristotle as his authority, is an argument that would not have seemed particularly compelling during Augustine's time, when civilization appeared to have been teetering on the brink of destruction. But it was a central verity of the late medieval ethos. The highly corporate structure of life in Aquinas's time fostered a deontology predicated upon community. It is not remarkable that Aquinas included the principle of community in his treatment of suicide. It was thoroughly Aristotelian. So was Aquinas. And it was in the most vivid of ways foundational for contemporary concepts of obligations, as we shall see later in this chapter when dealing with physicians' obligations. It would truly have been remarkable if Aquinas had not had recourse to this principle as an essential element in his argument against suicide; it would have been equally remarkable if Augustine had.

There are two matters that neither Augustine nor Aquinas considered in their discussions of suicide, both of which were matters of interest to some members of late classical but Christianized society and the medieval community. One of these involves mitigating or extenuating circumstances affecting the suicide. The one mitigating or extenuating factor was insanity or demon possession. In late antiquity John Chrysostom[8] and John Cassian[9] dealt with a phenomenon known in Greek as *athumia* and in Latin as *acedia,* a condition subsumable under the catchall rubric of melancholy, to which monks were especially susceptible. Numerous examples of suicide or of contemplated or attempted suicide owing to this condition are preserved by medieval sources. Early medieval penitentials wrestled with suicides by the insane or demon possessed. A good example is the Penitential of Theodore (c. 668-690):

> *Of Those Who Are Vexed by the Devil:* If a man is vexed by the devil and can do nothing but run about everywhere, and [if he] slays himself, there may be some reason to pray for him if he was formerly religious. If it was on account of despair, or of some fear, or for unknown reasons, we ought to leave to God the decision of this matter, and we dare not pray for him. In the case of one who of his own will slays himself, masses may not be said for him; but we may only pray and dispense alms. If any Christian goes insane through a sudden seizure, or as a result of insanity slays himself—there are some who celebrate masses for such a one.[10]

Here we enter into a quagmire of confusion that demands a thorough analysis well beyond the scope of this chapter. Since many modern scholars assume that in the early Middle Ages demonic causality was accepted for most disease and certainly for mental illness, natural causes such as despair, fear, sudden seizure and "unknown reasons" may take us by surprise. But such explanations occur with frequency. There is, however, much vagueness in the literature. This vagueness arises from two different sources. First, there was much inexactness in identifying the causes of mental illness. The second source of vagueness is the failure of modern readers to penetrate adequately into the early medieval structure of reality in which final and immediate causality are often melded and an intermediate (typically demonic) causality mingled in with the former two. Any one of the three may be specified as the cause of a particular condition and then interpreted by the modern reader as the author's perceived sole cause, whereas the author's choice of that cause was predicated upon his desire to emphasize one without intending to make it appear the exclusive cause.

It must be sufficient that the reader be aware that during the period between Augustine and the Renaissance and Reformation insanity or demon possession rendered suicide not as clear an issue as we might assume based on some modern discussions of that period. This held true not only in the ecclesiastical realm but in secular law as well. Henry of Bracton, an English jurist living in the thirteenth century, for example, exempted suicide by the insane from criminal considerations.[11]

The second matter with which neither Augustine nor Aquinas dealt that was a concern to the medieval community is the question of temporal penalties against the suicide. While ecclesiastical law and practice involved questions of the propriety of administering the sacraments for the deceased's soul and proper manner of burial, secular law went much further. When considering the latter, we enter into a chamber of horrors including such customs as exposing the suicide's body at crossroads with a stake driven through the heart and confiscating all his temporal goods — to the obvious detriment of his family.

Augustine may have known of earlier pagan customs (which were localized and quite rare) of dishonoring a suicide's corpse. It is less likely that he was acquainted with contemporary practices in Europe. He advocates nothing similar. Nor does he suggest anything like the denying of sacraments and burial rites to suicides, policies adopted by regional church councils throughout the Middle Ages.[12] Glanville Williams, after citing the action of the Synod of Nimes in 1284 that "refused suicides even the right of quiet interment in holy ground," comments:

> This canonical development was undoubtedly influenced in part by the writings of St. Augustine; but he had not demanded any punishment for the deed. In fact, as has been seen, Augustine was prepared to justify some historic suicides as specially commanded by God, and, consistently with this theory, he felt himself constrained to admit that even in his own day a person might rightly make away with himself by special command of God: "only let him be very sure that the divine command has been signified." Such a theory is obviously inconsistent with the anathematizing of the suicide's corpse by way of punishment, for what ecclesiastic can say, after the event, whether the divine command was signified or not? There is another reason for absolving Augustine from sole responsibility for these laws. The severe penalty of depriving burial rites smacks of the pagan practice of dishonouring the corpse, and Bayet[13] consequently maintains, with much force, that

it represents an irruption into the church of the pre-Christian popular horror of suicide. Like so much else in ecclesiastical practice and belief, it is a pagan intrusion upon the simple philosophy of the Gospels.[14]

Even this absolving of Augustine of responsibility for ecclesiastical and secular practices that were common during the Middle Ages and much later is inadequate because it hinges on the false premise that Augustine introduced something new into the Christian attitude toward suicide. Williams is correct in seeing some medieval and later practices as "a pagan intrusion upon the simple philosophy of the Gospels," but he demonstrates a lack of discernment of the nature of this "simple philosophy of the Gospels" by attributing attitudes to the early Christian community that are inconsistent with the values consistently expressed both in the New Testament and in patristic literature. Furthermore, he sees pagan intrusions into Augustine's thought:

> Augustine's third argument [against suicide] was stoical in conception, though he rejected the Stoics. The truly great mind, said Augustine, will bear the ills of life. The argument reappears from time to time in the proposition that suicide is an act of cowardice. Now, the only line between cowardice and caution (or wise retreat) is that the coward does not do what he ought to do. To brand the suicide as a coward is, therefore, to beg the question whether there is a duty to go on living.[15]

This quotation reveals a misunderstanding, common to many modern scholars, of the most fundamental principles of Christian thought that permeate Scripture and Christian literature generally. As we have already emphasized and will continue to emphasize, these fundamental principles of Christian thought encourage patience, stress hope, command perseverance and rest so firmly on the foundational belief in the sovereignty of God in the life of Christians and the trust that they should have, based on the conviction that God will cause all things to work together for their ultimate good. It is unlikely that suicide for such reasons as Augustine and Aquinas condemn, including suicide (assisted or otherwise) to expedite death in the face of painful illness, would have been regarded by the vast majority of Christians, past and present, as anything less than a breach of trust.[16]

Sin and Sickness

At all levels of medieval society it was commonly believed that one must suffer for one's sins, either in this life or in purgatory, although usually in both. The suffering attendant upon sickness was not excluded from the realm of spiritually meritorious and expiatory suffering. Sin was conceptually linked with sickness in three ways. First, sin was regarded by medieval authors as the cause of sickness in the sense that without sin there would have been no material evil. Second, the fact that all people, even the most righteous, were regarded as sinners at least by nature and often by choice or oversight made one's own general sinfulness a readily available explanation for one's own sicknesses. Third, sometimes sickness was attributed to specific sin.

The last is seldom encountered except in denunciations of and warnings to entire communities, and then the emphasis was often on general moral laxity, which makes it nearly indistinguishable from the second category. Sin was commonly regarded as the immediate cause of plague or at least the catalyst behind God's sending the plague. This was collective sin. Individual sin was seldom seen as the cause of sickness. One notable exception was leprosy, which was associated with a variety of sins, but especially with lust and pride.[17] By a strange irony to which medieval Roman Catholic theology was conducive, lepers were regarded as chosen by God for the privilege of suffering in this life in lieu of purgatory.[18] The majority of people who were afflicted with sickness in the Middle Ages obviously did not suffer from leprosy. During the long course of time, only a small minority died of plague. Some people when ill may have been burdened with a sense of guilt. If medieval Roman Catholic theology in some ways fostered such an attitude, it did not, however, actively encourage it as a morbidly obsessive response to illness.

In medieval spiritual literature there is a marked appreciation of God's hand in Christians' suffering and of the salutary role of sickness in their lives. Gregory I, who was pope from 590 to 604, wrote in his pastoral handbook that "the sick are to be admonished to realise that they are sons of God by the very fact that the scourge of discipline chastises them." Their priests were to encourage them to "preserve the virtue of patience."[19]

Bede (c. 673-735) thus described his contemporary the Abbess Aethelburh:

> Now in order that her strength, like the apostle's, might be made perfect in weakness, she was suddenly afflicted with a most serious bodily disease and for nine years was sorely tried, under the good providence of our Redeemer, so that any traces of sin remaining among her virtues through ignorance or carelessness might be burnt away by the fires of prolonged suffering.[20]

Aethelburh eventually succumbed to her disease. Bede also wrote that the saintly Germanus's merits were augmented by the sufferings that an accident had inflicted on him. According to Bede, Germanus was healed miraculously after a relatively short bout of suffering.[21] Typical of the views expressed in the literature of that time is Bede's account of the afflictions of Bishop Benedict and of his colleague Sigfrid:

> And not long after, Benedict also began to be wearied by the assault of illness. That the virtue of patience might be added, to give conclusive proof of such great zeal for religion, Divine Mercy laid them both up in bed by temporal illness that, after sickness had been conquered by death, God might restore them with the endless rest of heavenly peace and light. Sigfrid, punished . . . by long internal suffering, drew toward his last day, and Benedict, during three years, gradually became so paralyzed that all his lower limbs were quite dead . . . to exercise him in the virtue of patience. Both men sought in their suffering ways to give thanks to their Creator, and always to be occupied with the praises of God and with teaching the brethren.[22]

This level of spirituality could not have been typical of all people during the early Middle Ages. Many people undoubtedly admired the spiritual fortitude of the sanctified suffering of a special, holy minority. Whether they emulated them is another matter. While the well-being of this minority might be increased by suffering, the well-being of the semi-Christianized pagans of the early Middle Ages was disrupted, perhaps destroyed, by serious sickness. Their frantic quest for physical healing, as is manifested in our sources, suggests that their well-being was primarily material and temporal.

Between 541 and 767 sixteen waves of plague swept Europe.[23] These plagues proved to be most useful in pastoral efforts to wean the flock from the material to the spiritual, from the temporal to the eternal. Plague

> mainly had the effect of making them more amenable to certain Christian beliefs and practices. Seen as one element in a whole set of calamities and signs, the plague settled in people's minds a concrete expectation of the Last Judgement. . . . [It] explained calamities as retribution for collective sin, instilled notions of a wrathful God . . . and gave rise to an apocalyptic and millenarian mentality.[24]

Pope Gregory I, who had assumed the papacy during an outbreak of the plague, was virtually obsessed with it.

> [He] preached a sermon declaring the plague to be a punishment from God and calling upon the people to do penance and repent of their sins. He ordered them to pray and sing psalms for three days, and at the end of that time arranged for a massive city-wide litany. . . . No less than eighty people dropped dead of the plague during the procession.[25]

A century and a half later, Bede expressed amazement that a recent episode of plague had not turned the Anglo-Saxons from their sinful ways,[26] and on another occasion he called the plague "a blow sent by God the Creator."[27] An individual's personal holiness did not protect against the plague. Nor was being afflicted with it regarded as an indication of personal sin. Plague and all other sicknesses were generally seen as sent for the purpose of adjusting people's priorities to focus more on spiritual and eternal realities than on material and temporal matters. Regardless of the level of one's personal sanctity, repentance was always appropriate in the face of illness.

The church's reaction to the Black Death of 1348-1349, the most horrible pestilence ever to afflict Europe, is well illustrated by the actions of Pope Clement VI when the plague hit Avignon, then the seat of the papacy. He hired physicians to care for the stricken, ordered various measures taken to hinder contagion and conducted a special mass to implore an end to the plague.[28] Clement also gave special indulgences to encourage the clergy to minister to those afflicted with plague. These indulgences were regarded as absolving the sins of those to whom they were granted so that their sins would not require expiation in purgatory. It appears that dying of plague came to be considered by some as potentially expiatory in itself. John of Saxony, who wrote a treatise on plague during the first half of the fifteenth century, complained that some people disregarded physicians' prophylactic advice during times of plague. Of the several reasons that he gave for this attitude, one was a prevailing fatalism, for some people believed that "the time of one's death has been established for every individual." Another reason was

> the desire and hope for death. For I recall that in a certain great pestilence in Montpellier, when many men wished to die, on that account the pope gave to the dying absolution from punishment and guilt and thus they hoped to be carried to heaven immediately, and therefore they did not want physicians to prolong their lives.[29]

Assisted Suicide and Euthanasia

Medieval Roman Catholic theology fostered dependence on the church for spiritual well-being, for salvation, for eternal life. It provided a climate that was entirely inimical to suicide. As Robert Barry remarks,

> The continuation of the ancient Christian prohibition of suicide into Medieval Christianity was extraordinarily effective. What is striking about the history of suicide in the Middle Ages is that there were few notable suicides between 400 and 1400 A.D. among orthodox[30] Christians. Catholic doctrines and attitudes had so permeated society during this era that individuals did not find suicide to be an efficient means of resolving personal, financial or political issues. Medieval Catholicism had given such emphasis to repentance, confession, and penance that suicide to escape shame virtually disappeared. In antiquity, suicide on

account of poverty was not uncommon, but medieval society removed the stigma of poverty far more than other societies, and, as a result, there were an insignificant number of suicides. Catholicism's emphasis on the value of the life of poverty and simplicity destroyed the grounds of suicide to escape the shame of poverty.[31]

The same may be said about suicide to escape painful illness. In medieval Roman Catholic theology, death was in a sense the most significant moment of one's life. And the church jealously guarded its prerogatives, responsibility and authority in that sphere. This is well illustrated by a canon of the Fourth Lateran Council of 1215:

> As sickness of the body may sometimes be the result of sin—as the Lord said to the sick man whom he had cured: "Go and sin no more, lest something worse befall you"—so we by this present decree order and strictly command physicians of the body, when they are called to the sick, to warn and persuade them first of all to call in physicians of the soul so that after their spiritual health has been seen to they may respond better to medicine for their bodies; for when the cause ceases so does the effect. This among other things has occasioned this decree, namely that some people on their sickbed, when they are advised by physicians to arrange for the health of their souls, fall into despair and so the more readily incur the danger of death. If any physician transgresses this our constitution, after it has been published by the local prelates, he shall be barred from entering a church until he has made suitable satisfaction for a transgression of this kind. Moreover, since the soul is much more precious than the body, we forbid any physician, under pain of anathema, to prescribe anything for the bodily health of a sick person that may endanger his soul.[32]

Three matters in this canon are germane to our study: bodily illness sometimes has a spiritual cause, in which case the sacrament of confession will restore the patient to health; for the possible benefit of the body and for the definite benefit of the soul, the physician of the body must have the patient summon the physician of the soul (i.e., the priest) for the sacrament of confession before continuing treatment; and since the soul is of inestimably greater value than the body, the physician of the body must not do anything for the benefit of the patient's body that is to the detriment of the latter's soul.

Writing about a century before Lateran IV, the author of an anonymous treatise on medical etiquette suggests to his fellow physicians:

> When you reach [a patient's] house and before you see him, ask if he has seen his confessor. If he has not done so, have him either do it or promise to do it. For if he hears mention of this after you have examined

him and have considered the signs of the disease, he will begin to despair of recovery, because he will think that you despair of it too.[33] Such advice does not necessarily indicate a high level of personal piety on the part of this anonymous physician. He was a member of a society that held firmly the conviction that confession before death was necessary for the health of one's soul. Hence it is not surprising that after Lateran IV similar advice appears in the extant writings of several physicians. A treatise probably wrongly attributed to the physician Arnald of Villanova, written in the late thirteenth or early fourteenth century, thus advises physicians:

> When you come to a house, inquire before you go to the sick whether he has confessed, and if he has not, he should immediately or promise you that he will confess immediately, and this must not be neglected because many illnesses originate on account of sin and are cured by the Supreme Physician after having been purified from squalor by the tears of contrition, according to what is said in the Gospel: "Go, and sin no more, lest something worse happens to you."[34]

So striking is the similarity of this to the canon of Lateran IV that there seems to be a direct influence of a rubric of canon law on a secular piece of medical literature. The same applied to the following passage in an anonymous plague treatise written in 1411:

> If it is certain from the symptoms that it is actually pestilence that has afflicted the patient, the physician first must advise the patient to set himself right with God by making a will and by making a confession of his sins, as is set forth according to the Decretals: since a corporal illness comes not only from a fault of the body but also from a spiritual failing as the Lord declares in the gospel and the priests also tell us.[35]

Consider the incongruity of a physician who believes in the efficacy of confession for the healing of some physical ills and ensures that his patients summon a priest and make confession, in those cases in which the illness persists and medical treatment proves ineffective, either suggesting suicide to his patients or yielding to their requests to help them commit suicide.

Insofar as the iconography of the *Ars moriendi* literature[36] in the Middle Ages illustrates socioreligious realities, suicide (assisted or otherwise) would have been starkly contradictory of the drama being played out in the death chamber. The dominant personas are spiritual beings, demons and angels, who are struggling for the dying person's soul. The clergy are there administering the sacraments and giving solace and encouragement. Obligated to be there but hovering in the background are the physicians—impotent in the face of immanent death. What this literature depicts is a *psychomachia*, a battle for the soul of the dying person. These treatises typically contain, among other matters, a variety of quotations on death from Christian sources and advice for the dying person on practicing the virtues of faith, hope, love, humility and detachment while fleeing the vices of faithlessness, despair, impatience, pride and worldliness. The demons are suggesting, among other sins, the destruction of the sufferer's soul by suicide.

Did physicians assist their patients in committing suicide during the Middle Ages? It would be rash to answer this question with a categorical negative. It would be even more rash to suggest that such occurrences were other than so extremely rare as to be virtually anomalous. The subject comes up in the literature of medical ethics from the early and high Middle Ages only in rather potted paraphrases of the Hippocratic Oath.[37] In a sense it would have been surprising if it had been particularly stressed, especially given the well-established emphases in Christian teaching on the sinfulness of both murder and suicide, on the *imago Dei* as the basis for intrinsic worth of human life, and on the imperative to care for the ill, succor the suffering and comfort the dying. It would be patently absurd to suggest a positive attitude toward euthanasia based on the absence of direct prohibitions of it in this literature.

The only reference to euthanasia that we have located in the writings of physicians of the late Middle Ages is in a plague treatise written by the physician Sigmund Albichs in 1406: "The . . . physician should refrain from administering anything to the patient that will cause him to die quickly, for then he would be a murderer."[38]

Recall the final stipulation of the canon of Lateran IV: because the soul is inestimably more precious than the body, physicians must do nothing for the good of their patients' bodies that would be detrimental to the latters' souls. Commentators on this canon were concerned with sinful means that a physician might employ or recommend for the restoration of health. They do not, however, refer to euthanasia.

The canon of Lateran IV that immediately precedes the canon that we have been considering is regarded by many historians as the most significant piece of ecclesiastical legislation from the Middle Ages. This canon required that all Christians confess annually under pain of severe sanctions. This requirement stimulated an outpouring of treatises in which all manner of sins of omission and of commission were subjected to detailed scrutiny, including those peculiar to various vocations. Short, handy versions of these treatises, known as confessional manuals, were made available to priests to aid in their interrogation of penitents. All contain a section on the sins of physicians and surgeons. We emphasize again the imaginative thoroughness of these treatises and manuals.

Nowhere in these works' sections on the sins of physicians and surgeons does the subject of their assisting a suffering or dying patient commit suicide or engaging in "mercy killing" arise until quite obliquely in this passing comment in the confessional manual written by the post-Tridentine moral theologian Martin Aspilcuetta (better known as Navarrus) in 1568: A physician sins by giving anyone a medicine that he knows is harmful, "even if he administers it out of pity or in order to please the patient."[39] Such an act, although it is broader than euthanasia, includes it. Note that it is sinful even if the physician is motivated by pity or by the patient's wish. Navarrus cites as his authority the commentary of the canon lawyer Panormitanus, written sometime after 1421, on a rubric of canon law that has nothing to do with suicide or euthanasia. Panormitanus had remarked that those who had the responsibility of caring for the ill sin if, motivated by "a sort of pity," they yield to the "corrupted desire" of the ill.

In some of the sections of this literature that are devoted to the sins of physicians and surgeons appear brief discussions of the sins of the sick. It is as if the authors were at a loss for a better place in which to locate such considerations. In two of the treatises that we have studied there are some stipulations that are germane to our subject. The more thorough of the two reads as follows:

> If a sick man intentionally consumes harmful food or drink, he sins; likewise if he does this from feigned or improbable ignorance, because according to God one is expected to love one's own body. Next it can be said that if he does not believe that it would be deadly, although he believes that his sickness would be aggravated by it, he does not sin mortally, or at least not so gravely, i.e., mortally or venially and more or less commensurate with the quantity of the noxious substance taken. In this the extent of one's offence against charity is manifest. That which is done against charity is a mortal sin according to all theologians. The ones who attend him also sin if they supply such things intentionally or through improbable ignorance. Finally, whenever, in the opinion of physicians,[40] one is not expected to live because of his ill health, and he takes anything from which death or further sickness results, he sins gravely and commensurate with the quantity of the noxious substance taken.[41]

Such passages, addressed to the sick, demonstrate an unequivocal condemnation of suicide to escape illness. But why is there so little attention paid to the subject of euthanasia in the sections of this literature that were crafted for the confessional interrogation of physicians and surgeons? It appears that it was as far from the minds of moral theologians and canonists that a priest should ask a physician or surgeon, during his annual confession, whether he had killed any patient at the patient's request or supplied him with the means to do so as it was to ask him whether he had raped his patient's wife, stolen his property or burned down his house. The lack of concern with assisted suicide in these sections of treatises on moral theology and of confessional manuals of the late Middle Ages is compelling evidence that physicians' and surgeons' practicing euthanasia must have been so rare as to be negligible.

Withdrawing Medical Treatment

By the late Middle Ages physicians were expected to be involved with the dying patient. They had not always been. As we have seen in chapter two, in classical antiquity taking on a case that could not be successfully treated was regarded as the physician's duty by virtually no one. Many would have regarded a physician who took on a hopeless case as acting unethically, being propelled by mercenary motives or by a desire to experiment at the expense of the patient. Likewise, if a patient's condition became hopeless, no one would have regarded the physician as obligated to stay with him until the end; if he did stay, many would castigate him for the same reasons. The physician's role was to attempt to cure the ill or to provide prophylactic advice to the healthy. What business did he have with the dying? most people would have asked.

Such was the case throughout the early Middle Ages. The advent of Christianity, as we saw in chapter three, created no change in this aspect of medical deontology. But Christianity did introduce moral obligations that were, at least as categorical imperatives, alien to the Greek and Roman ethos. One of these was an obligation to care—not an obligation to cure but an obligation to care—a categorical imperative to extend compassion in both word and deed to the poor, the widow, the orphan and the sick. This was truly revolutionary, and we continue to feel its effects. While this change effected immediate results (e.g., the creation of the first hospitals), it did not impose on physicians any sense of obligation to take on hopeless cases or to stay with those patients whose condition had become hopeless. Granted, the Christian qua physician should be compassionate. But the physician qua physician had no obligation to minister in any way to the dying.

As an aside, however, we bring to readers' notice a sixth-century physician, Alexander of Tralles. He vigorously and repeatedly maintained that it was sinful not to apply any and every remedy that might possibly save a patient's life, even amulets and magical incantations and spells.[42] Not only were his priorities in conflict with those of the church, but also we see in his concerns perhaps the earliest hint of a physician's expressing a moral, indeed a religious, obligation to preserve life, based in this case on the reasoning that the supposedly greater sin of not doing all in one's power to save a patient was justifiably avoided by the ostensibly lesser sin of using magical remedies. This position will not be taken by the theologians of the high and late Middle Ages.

In the high Middle Ages, because of the convergence of two factors, an obligation for physicians to attempt to treat the dangerously ill or hopeless began to emerge. The first of these was a fundamental redefinition of the practice of medicine from a right to a privilege. Heretofore anyone who wished to practice medicine could call himself a physician and engage in practice: one's training and reputation were one's only credentials. The ethics of the medical "profession" consisted of traditional etiquette and popular morality alone. But in the high Middle Ages, beginning in the twelfth century in the kingdom of Sicily, a few governments imposed medical licensure requirements. Even more important, because they were more prevalent, were the burgeoning medical and surgical guilds that negotiated with either municipal, royal or ecclesiastical authorities for a monopoly for their services (just as other guilds, such as of artisans, did for theirs). This was also a form of licensure. In the case of medical and surgical guilds, their negotiations included guarantees, for instance, to treat all in need of medical care, irrespective of their condition, and not to desert the hopeless. Medical licensure requirements imposed from above generally included these stipulations as well.[43]

This change of the practice of medicine from a right to a privilege was not isolated and unique. Medieval society, which was becoming increasingly urbanized, was also becoming increasingly structured. For nearly every legitimate occupation there was a legitimating organization. Everyone was to have a defined and legally sanctioned role in society. And to every role certain obligations seemed virtually inherent. Hence Thomas Aquinas could say of the duties of the king,

> Nor has he the right to question whether or not he will so promote the peace of the community, any more than a physician has the right to question whether he will cure the sick committed to him. For no one ought to deliberate about the ends for which he must act, but only about the means to those ends.[44]

Such an articulation of the most essential obligation of a physician as a sine qua non of being a physician reflects a much more compelling social reality in the high and late Middle Ages than it could have at any time earlier in Western civilization.

The second factor that helped to foster in physicians a sense of duty to stay with terminal patients came from the moral theologians whom we considered earlier. The focal point of their discussion was whether the physician should receive his fee if his patient dies. Antoninus of Florence, writing in the late fifteenth century, asserted that "desperate cases which, according to the judgments of men, are held to be fatal, sometimes the diligent physician is able to cure, but rarely. . . . Therefore, clear to the end the physician ought to do what he can to cure the patient."[45] The question, however, still remained as to whether physicians should receive a fee for treating incurable cases. Antoninus's opinion was that

> because the physician was created as an instrument of nature, the instrument of medicine should not be entirely withdrawn from the patient as long as nature does not succumb. Therefore, the physician does not sin by accepting a stipend for the treatment of an illness which, following the principles of the art of medicine, he believes is incurable.[46]

The physician must not hide that knowledge from those who have the immediate care of the patient or cause unnecessary expenses or promise entirely to cure him. He thus can justly receive his stipend,

> as he displays in the care of his patient faithful attendance and true counsel . . . because the physician does not know what God has arranged concerning the patient, whether he will recover or die, although, according to the art of medicine, he ought to die. Therefore it is licit for the physician to pursue a cure and to accept a stipend clear up to the end or nearly.[47]

There is a statement attributed to Pope Symmachus, quoted in the *Decretum* of Gratian (c. 1140), to the effect that "there is not a great difference whether you inflict something fatal or allow it. He is proved to inflict death on the weak who does not prevent this when he is able to."[48] Although this says nothing directly concerning physicians, Joannes Teutonicus, in what became known as the *Glossa Ordinaria* (c. 1216) to the *Decretum,* commented on this passage that the physician is obligated to treat both the poor and the rich gratis rather than to allow them to die. This gloss is the locus classicus for moral theologians' discussion of the question of whether a physician is obligated to cure gratis rather than to allow a sick person to die.

Thomas Aquinas considered the problem of the extent to which the physician is morally obligated to treat the poor gratuitously. Beginning with the remark "Nobody can possibly help out all those in need," he then writes that kindness ought first to be shown to those with whom one is united in any way *(propinqui).* In respect to others, if a man "is in such dire straits that it is not immediately obvious how else he is to be helped [then] one is bound to come to his assistance." Thus a lawyer is not always obligated to defend the destitute. "Otherwise he would have to give up all other work and devote himself exclusively to the cases of the poor. And the same considerations apply to the doctor in connexion with the care of the poor."[49] Astesanus de Asti, writing in the early fourteenth century, follows Aquinas closely when discussing lawyers' obligations to defend the poor gratis, adding that "the same must be said concerning a physician as to the care of paupers."[50] The other moral theologians and authors of confessional manuals rely also on Joannes Teutonicus's gloss on the passage from the *Decretum,* considering the obligation especially to exist if the alternative to free care is the death of the patient.

Generally the position in this literature is as follows, with slight variations: A physician is obligated to give care and counsel gratis to a sick pauper, "for he is proved to inflict death on the weak who does not prevent it when he is able to." He ought to give care and medicines gratis rather than to allow a patient to die. This applies not only to the pauper but also to the rich. The physician should not only give care gratis but should even provide the medicines at his own expense for a sick rich man who is not willing to pay him anything, rather than to allow him to die. Antoninus of Florence here stipulates that the physician is thus obligated only if the patient or his relatives have called him. If the patient recovers, the physician can then demand his fee from him; if the patient dies, from his heirs. In the former the grounds are that he has rightly managed the patient's affair; in the latter that he had rightly begun to conduct the affair, although the outcome did not follow. Nor may it be objected that the physician did it for charity *(causa pietatis),* unless he is united in some way *(propinquus)* to the patient. He is both able and obligated to treat such a man and can afterward demand a fee, even if the patient refuses to allow himself to be treated, just as we can drag a person from a building that is about to collapse and confer a benefit on one against one's will. It must be assumed that the patient, by refusing treatment, is insane.

Not only was the medieval ethos uncongenial to euthanasia, but also it fostered in physicians a sense of obligation neither to refuse to take on nor to desert hopeless cases. This latter development was in some instances imposed by secular governments and by physicians and surgeons themselves through their negotiated guild regulations, but it was encouraged by the church as well. It is here that we find an incipient though only tacit disapproval of withholding medical treatment to hasten death. This, however, must be balanced by the insistence of the moral theologians and authors of confessional literature that the patient does not sin if he disobeys his physician, because the physician does not hold a position of authority over him.

Structures of Dependence

In the early Middle Ages, as various groups of pagans were incorporated into the church, they brought with them a folk paganism, essentially pantheism, that was so much a part of the rhythm of their lives that it remained for most of them a vitally real if officially suppressed and experientially submerged current of their subconscious being and identity. All had in common the same alternative to their folk paganism. That was Roman Catholicism, which consistently declared their folk paganism to be both real and evil, and could tolerate no alternative to itself. Accordingly the church sought to channel their individual and communal impulses and wants into sources of actualization and fulfillment that were within the ordered structure of dependence: Roman Catholic liturgy, sacraments and the cult of saints and relics. The church also permitted certain strictly pagan practices to continue as long as they were conducted in the vicinity of churches and not in traditional sites such as sacred groves.

Attempts to deal with relapses into paganism or participation in pagan practices varied. Roman law had consistently forbidden malicious magic but even after the Christianization of the empire had tolerated benevolent magic. The church vigorously condemned both. In the early Middle Ages, moreover, not only did the church continue its fight against both types of magic, but also secular law declared both illicit and severely punished those who practiced either. Numerous church synods and councils had addressed the problem of continuing pagan practices. Walter Ullmann observes that the conciliar "decrees against superstition are so numerous that one is justified in the assumption that [the practices that they repeatedly prohibited] were general and widespread." Commenting on the motivation behind these conciliar actions, he suggests that the promulgators of such decrees "cared for what may be termed the public health of society, public health understood not in terms of physical well-being, but in terms of protecting and if necessary immunizing and inoculating the mind of the people against infectious diseases of a pandemic kind."[51] A major focal point of secular and ecclesiastical legislation against magic was that used for physical healing.

Inculcating into the people a nearly palpable dependence on the church for well-being in life, in death and in the hereafter was the church's most urgent goal. And so it remained during the high and late Middle Ages. The church continued condemning magical healing practices, but beginning in the twelfth century we find magic denounced not as paganism any longer but as heresy. The only mechanisms for healing that were not condemned were those that the church either dispensed or attempted to regulate. Of the former there was a rich variety, most spectacularly a multitude of healing shrines. The latter, however, was a mixed blessing.

Johann Geiler von Kaiserberg, a German priest and professor of theology, preached a series of sermons in 1498 and 1499. In one sermon, entitled "Sick Fools," Geiler discussed seven follies of the ill.[52] The first four involved their relations with physicians. Ill fools scorn medicine, deceive or disobey their physician, follow the physician's advice belatedly or distort it so that it does not help. These were simply foolish. The remaining three were sinful, although the first was transitional and only potentially sinful. The ill sought medicine and advice from "old women and from others who have never learned medicine." Or they searched "for medicine and health from witches and exorcisoresses of the devil." The last and most serious folly was "to neglect one's duty to God—to make use of medicine and not desire the help of God."

The penultimate folly of the ill in Geiler's list is the perpetual concern of the medieval church that people would seek healing through spiritually dangerous means. Magic was outside the licit structure of dependence. Medicine, however, was within it. But we must note Geiler's last point.

By the late Middle Ages the existence of a recognized medical profession whose monopoly was guaranteed by both state and church, whose responsibilities were defined and as much as possible enforced by the church, and whose medical theory was not discordant with orthodox theology and whose techniques were not religiously illicit was useful in providing a traditionally acceptable, nonspiritual source of healing clearly distinct from the sometimes magical alternatives feared by ecclesiastical authorities. Yet this alliance of the church with orthodox medicine as practiced by a recognized and licensed profession still remained uneasy. For the propensity of the sick was to neglect their duty to God, that is, to make use of medicine and not desire the help of God. This was a frequently repeated concern throughout the first fifteen hundred years of Christianity (and well beyond, although little in contemporary evangelicalism), where the attitude criticized was one of independence, an attitude of sufficiency to maintain or restore one's health without reference to one's Creator. The church could exhort, threaten and plead against that attitude but could not effectively regulate or control the attitudes of the sick or of physicians toward the medical art, which was itself regarded not only as being a gift of the Creator but also as having a dangerous potential to lure people away from submission to him. Hence in the *Ars moriendi* literature there is much less emphasis against suicide than against clinging to life, against seeking from the physicians support for a probably vain hope of restoring one's bodily health when one's attention should be focused on the health of one's soul.

6

Euthanasia & Suicide Since the Middle Ages

The teachings of Augustine formalized and consolidated traditional Judeo-Christian opposition to suicide and euthanasia as an unacceptable form of murder. This view has remained a central tenet of Christian doctrine ever since despite vast changes in the structure and culture of both the church and society. The Middle Ages of Roman Catholic dominance built directly on Augustinian teachings. But even as the Reformation and Counter Reformation shook the traditional church, suicide and euthanasia remained an anathema among nearly all Christian denominations and sects. As this chapter describes, only with the increased secularization of the West did public attitudes toward suicide begin to change, a process that has not occurred in Islamic regions of the world, where the Qur'an's express prohibition of suicide governs social norms.

The Renaissance
The Italian Renaissance was concurrent with the late Middle Ages, the Northern Renaissance with the Reformation. Renaissance means "rebirth," in this case a rebirth of interest in Greek and Roman cultures, the *studia humanitatis*, hence "humanities," "humanism" and "humanist." The Italian Renaissance has traditionally been seen as representing a radical shift from the theocentrism of the Middle Ages to an anthropocentrism, that is, from a God-centered to a human-centered focus. This perspective

is that the Renaissance was inherently pagan and hence anti-Christian. With the rebirth of interest in the classics, light had at last broken in on the darkness with which the oppressive force of Christianity, especially medieval scholasticism and ecclesiastical tyranny, had enveloped Western civilization. Finally the fresh air of an atmosphere conducive to the flowering of human dignity and potential, so long suppressed by the church, wafted from Italy northward across Europe. This view of the Renaissance is still perpetuated in some textbooks and classrooms.

The spirit of the Renaissance experience, however, although it was affected significantly by its appreciation and adoption of various classical ideas that are reflected in its literature and art, was Christian in its marrow. Sometimes scholars enthuse that a classical Greek or Roman would have felt much more at home in Renaissance Italy than in any medieval milieu. But it is safe to say that this hypothetical Greek or Roman would have felt so alien to both that he or she would have felt only slightly less foreign in the atmosphere of Renaissance Italy than in medieval environs. And that person's alienation would have been precipitated by the predominantly Christian presuppositions undergirding nearly all intellectual and artistic expressions. The much-glorified anthropocentrism of the Renaissance ambience was significantly tempered by a vital, though not always compatible, christocentrism. The human dignity that is typically touted as such a hallmark of the Renaissance was far from any inferred pagan antecedent. The Renaissance articulation of the theme of human dignity was unambiguously founded on the reality of God's creation of humans in his own image and belief in redemption in Christ. Human multipotentiality and self-determination in Renaissance thought must be seen within that framework, as must euthanasia and suicide.

Some scholars assert that the glorification of humanity and the stress of individualism, coupled with the essential secularism of the Renaissance, precipitated a marked change in attitudes toward suicide. One writes, "As the humanists freed men to live, they brought them the right to die."[1] It would, however, be another two centuries before this dramatic shift took place. Although Greek philosophy was immensely popular and influential during the Italian Renaissance, the strongly favorable attitude of Stoicism toward suicide seems to have been overpowered by the equally strong condemnation of the act by the Greek philosophical school that was then most esteemed, Platonism. And even Neo-Stoic humanists (e.g., Justus Lipsius [1547-1606]), urging Christian patience and Stoic imperturbability in the face of suffering, labeled suicide as ethically unacceptable. The strongest bulwark against the acceptance of classical advocacy of suicide, however, was the persistence of the church's unequivocal condemnation of the taking of one's own life.

No text in the history of euthanasia is more controversial and more controverted than a short passage written by Sir Thomas More (1478-1535), lord chancellor of Henry VIII, who was beheaded for refusing to swear allegiance to the latter as supreme head of the English church. More left to posterity as his most intriguing work his *Utopia* (from the Greek *eu topos*, "a good place," and *ou topos*, "no place"). In this entertaining and sometimes puzzling trifle, More describes the Utopians' care for the incurable as consisting of conversation and relief of pain. Priests and magistrates urged terminally ill persons whose pain could not be relieved to kill themselves or allow others to do so, because they had become burdens both to themselves and to others.

> This, they say, he would do wisely, for by death he would lose nothing but suffering. Since he would be acting on the advice of the priests, who are the interpreters of God's will, he would act rightly and virtuously. Those who are moved by these arguments either starve themselves to death of their own accord or through the aid of an opiate die painlessly. If a man is not persuaded to this course, they do not force him to it against his will, nor do they lessen their care of him. To choose death under these circumstances is honorable.[2]

Needless to say, this passage has aroused considerable excitement on the part of those who are eager to defend euthanasia. As loyal a Catholic as Sir Thomas More, who gave his life for his church, is a highly prized compatriot in the advocacy of euthanasia. But is More to be taken seriously here? We quote one scholar's circumspect appraisal:

> The work is clearly satirical and contains much social criticism of Tudor society, but it is unlikely that More intended it to be a philosophical treatise whose imaginary descriptions were to be taken as serious suggestions for the reform of society. C. S. Lewis argues, convincingly, I think, that its purpose was entertainment: it is "a holiday work, a spontaneous overflow of intellectual high spirits, a revel of debate, paradox, comedy and (above all) of invention, which starts many hares and kills none."[3] There is so much that is amusing, even outrageous, in the customs of the Utopians that it is difficult to sort out that which is to be taken seriously from that which is not. If More did not intend to suggest that we make chamber pots out of gold and silver or that prospective spouses examine their future mates naked to find hidden blemishes, it is not likely that he had in mind to recommend an organized system of euthanasia. It is much easier for More's readers who live in the late twentieth century, when discussion of euthanasia is commonplace, to lift this passage out of its imaginative context and

give it more seriousness than its author intended. More was an orthodox Catholic who, as lord chancellor, was severe in his prosecution of heretics and hardly the kind of person to recommend so strongly condemned a practice as suicide. Long after *Utopia* was published, More suggested that it . . . might better be burned. Perhaps he felt that passages that were meant to entertain were being taken too seriously.[4] The only significant thinker of the Renaissance who challenged the traditional Christian condemnation of suicide was Michel de Montaigne (1533-1592). His *Essais* reveal a skeptical, secular, even pagan worldview. Much influenced by Pyrrhonian skepticism, Epicureanism and Stoicism, Montaigne enjoyed examining all aspects of any question, coming to no forceful conclusion, suspending judgment, as it were. In book 2.3, where he deals with suicide, it is not so much that he advocates personal moral or natural freedom to take one's own life if one rationally chooses to do so, as he calls into question religious and philosophical constraints against it.

The Renaissance reintroduced to the Western world the writings of the classical philosophical schools that favored suicide as a morally acceptable alternative to shame, suffering and dependence on others. The influence of pagan philosophical justifications of suicide was only gradual. Their full impact was not realized until the Enlightenment.

Reformation Europe

During the sixteenth century the Reformation ended the unity of the Christian church in the West. Despite their growing differences over church hierarchy, the sacraments and even the authority of canon law, religious leaders remaining loyal to the Roman pope and those breaking away to form new Protestant churches continued to condemn suicide as contrary to God's will. The breakdown in religious and political authority associated with the Reformation did not appreciably impact practices properly categorized as either physician-assisted suicide or euthanasia.

Early Protestants knew suffering firsthand. Many were persecuted for their faith. Even more suffered in the political turmoil and widespread warfare spawned by the Reformation. Others succumbed to the plague and other infectious diseases that ravaged Europe during this same period. Protestantism was nurtured in a crucible of physical suffering. Confronting this situation, early Protestant leaders generally accepted human affliction as inevitable and appreciated it as a potential spiritual blessing for believer and nonbeliever alike. Accordingly physical afflictions were to be endured for as long as they lasted, even unto natural death. This is exemplified in the teachings of the two guiding figures of the Reformation, German Reformer Martin Luther (1483-1546) and French Reformer John Calvin (1509-1564).

"Because nothing else is so effective in taming the flesh as are our cross and the suffering we must bear," Luther wrote in his preface to the eighth chapter of Romans, "He comforts us in our suffering by assuring us of the support of the spirit, of love, and all created things."[5] In this and other advice about enduring physical illness to its end, Luther wrote from intense personal experience. Throughout his remarkably active life, and in spite of his apparently enjoying the stamina and energy of one who possessed an iron constitution, Luther was plagued with bouts of serious illness, including heart problems, kidney and bladder stones, a ulcerated leg, severe constipation and hemorrhoids, migraine headaches, melancholy and recurrent respiratory difficulties. He did not view such illnesses as divine punishment but as the natural consequences of humanity's fallen state to be countered with both prayer and medication. He felt God's presence and power especially in his sickness. Luther penned the great hymn of faith, "A Mighty Fortress Is Our God," upon recovering from an illness so grave that at one point his basic life signs were undetectable to his physician. "Though life be wrenched away," he concluded in that hymn about the believer's victory through God over all spiritual foes, "They cannot win the day, / The Kingdom's ours forever!"

Inspired by his own intense experience, Luther developed a rich theology of health and illness. Perhaps his most oft-quoted adage in this realm is "Affliction is the best book in my library."[6] Church historian Carter Lindberg noted, "Luther did not think suffering good in itself nor something to be sought for self-improvement, but when encountered it could be the locus of wellness." Another Lutheran scholar added, "Luther found healing precisely in his sickness, not in escaping from it." Afflictions could serve to increase individuals' recognition of their utter dependence on God and therefore should be accepted when they came. While Luther did not believe that Christians should unduly cling to this life, he never condoned suicide as a means to hasten death for the dying. To the contrary, he expressly condemned it as the work of the devil. In an age before pain medication, Luther bore his grave illnesses until his natural death, and they enriched his theology. "It is not by understanding, reading, or speculating that one becomes a theologian," he once observed, "but through living, dying, and being damned."[7]

The founder of the Presbyterian tradition, John Calvin, from his youth on, was a driven man in spite of having a congenitally weak constitution. He frequently suffered from a deep feeling of guilt and inadequacy because of his lack of energy and habitual fatigue. He appears to have been very conscious of his own aging and inevitable death. One scholar remarks:

> His last letters, as he continued to drive himself, are full of clinical detail. . . . It was rather as though he were trying to impose some kind of order on the horror of his physical disintegration by the precision and detachment of his observations. Even dying had, for Calvin, to be put to use, as in the description of his singularly complex pathology that he prepared for the medical faculty of Montpellier. His ailments included, by his own account, arthritis, kidney stones, unspecified intestinal disorders, hemorrhoids, bleeding from the stomach, fever, muscle cramps, nephritis, and gout.[8]

Yet Calvin clearly rejected suicide and euthanasia. Despite affliction or hardship, Christians should "not generate either hatred of the present life, or ingratitude toward God," he warned in his great theological work, *The Institutes of the Christian Religion.* Instead Christians should recognize life as a gift from God, and they should "be prepared to remain in it during the Divine pleasure," thus repeating intentionally or inadvertently the Christianized Platonic argument that Christians had employed since at least the second century. Calvin called it "a station in which the Lord hath placed us to be retained by us till he call us away." The French Reformer put this theology into practice when ministering at the deathbed of his followers. In several letters he described the protracted final illnesses of friends and family — diseases that were allowed to run their course until, as Calvin described it in one such letter, the sufferer "gave up his pious soul to Christ."[9]

Calvin's repudiation of suicide as a means to escape affliction reflected his theology of suffering. Sickness came into the world with sin, Calvin believed, but God used it for spiritual healing. "For He afflicts us not to ruin or destroy us but, rather, to free us from the condemnation of the world," he asserted in the *Institutes.* "When we recognize the Father's rod, is it not our duty to show ourselves obedient teachable children rather than, in arrogance, to imitate desperate men who have become hardened by their evil deeds?" Acknowledging that "the heavenly physician treats some more gently but cleanses others by harsher remedies," Calvin concluded that while God "wills to provide for the health of all, He yet leaves no one free and untouched, because He knows that all, to a man are diseased." Christians should accept physical affliction with faith, he added, knowing that "a man [is] truly submitted to God's yoke only when he yielded his hand and back to His rod." Fittingly, in his prayer for the sick, Calvin asked God "to show them Thy fatherly kindness, chastening them for their profit; to the end that in their hearts they may turn unto

Thee, and being converted, may receive perfect consolation, and deliverance from all their woes." Escape from suffering through suicide or euthanasia was never condoned. Rather Calvin admonished believers to "leave the limits of our life and death to His decision."[10]

English Protestant Reformers generally retained the traditional Christian repudiation of suicide as well. For example, the first Reformed Archbishop of Canterbury, Thomas Cranmer (1489-1556), a distinguished theologian who led the Church of England into the Protestant camp and drew up the Anglican *Book of Common Prayer*, denounced a suicide as "cursed of God, and damned forever." Also in the sixteenth century Anglican theologians George Abbot (a future Archbishop of Canterbury) and John King (later Bishop of London) taught that the sixth commandment, "Thou shall not kill," forbade suicide. They expressly adopted the positions of Augustine and Thomas Aquinas on this issue.[11]

As Calvinism spread into Britain during the seventeenth century, with its followers striving to purify Anglicism of any surviving Roman Catholic taint, suicide remained anathema to religious leaders. It is important to be aware that although the early Protestants, including the English Reformers, adopted the traditional Christian position on suicide, that articulated by Augustine and Aquinas, they differed subtly from their Roman Catholic contemporaries. While the latter were then inflexibly rigid, Protestants were less convinced that under all circumstances suicide was absolutely and categorically a damnable sin.[12] This is neatly illustrated by a conversation in 1600 in which a Jesuit, John Gerard, and George Abbot discussed whether suicide was an unforgivable sin:

"But," said the doctor [Abbot], "we don't know whether this was such a sin."

"Pardon me," I [Gerard] said, "it is not a case here of our judgement. It is a question of God's judgement; He forbids us under pain of hell to kill anyone, and particularly ourselves, for charity begins at home."

The good doctor was caught. He said nothing more on the point.[13] The suicides of melancholics especially troubled Protestants, particularly the suicides of those who had earlier demonstrated a deep personal piety.

In 1637 a prominent Anglican cleric with Puritan leanings named John Sym wrote an influential tract condemning suicides as "certainly and infallibly damned souls and body for evermore without redemption." Nevertheless "he argues that in the case of disordered minds those who take their own lives cannot be held to be beyond the possibility of redemption."[14] Theologian John Owen (1616-1683), known as the Calvin of England, taught believers to accept affliction and not despair unto death, because affliction may have a divine purpose. "God may deliver you, first of all, by sending you an affliction to mortify your heart," he counseled.

Similarly English Puritan leader Richard Baxter (1615-1691) advised Christians to seek the best medical care for their illnesses, yet he warned them to bear with incurable diseases and death. Baxter, who endured persistent ill health and described his own preaching as that of "a dying man to dying men," instructed the sick to teach the well how to live. This instruction appears in *A Christian Directory*, published in 1673. *A Christian Directory*'s subtitle begins *A Sum of Practical Theology and Cases of Conscience*. The word *sum* is short for *summa* (i.e., a single, comprehensive statement covering everything within its purview). The treatises of moral theology of the high and late Middle Ages, which we considered in chapter five, were *summae confessorum*, to be used by the priest in the confessional, and dealt with "cases of conscience," hence casuistry.

Baxter's *A Christian Directory* is one of the most influential Protestant successors to this genre, although obviously it was not designed for use in the confessional. It contains a section entitled "Advice Against Self-Murder"[15] in which, among the various motivations for committing suicide, physical pain and terminal illness receive no mention. Melancholy can drive one to suicide, he says here. Earlier in the volume is a section entitled "Directions to the Melancholy About Their Thoughts"[16] in which he also discusses suicide. In his extensive sections entitled "Directions for the Sick" and "Directions to the Friends of the Sick, That Are About Them,"[17] he makes no mention of any temptation on the part of the sick, even those painfully ill or terminal, to expedite their own deaths. Nor does he caution the friends of the sick in this regard. And in his pages on "The Duty of Physicians"[18] there is no hint that physicians could realistically expect either to be asked by their patients to put a permanent end to their suffering or to be moved to consider doing so at their own initiative.

Another genre that was born in the Middle Ages, the *Ars moriendi*, was sustained by Protestant divines. A multitude of treatises on spiritual euthanasia, that is, on "dying well," were written.[19] Perseverance in the face of death, resting and trusting in the certainty of God's promises and the sufficiency of Christ's redemptive sacrifice—such was the theme of this literature, a hallmark of historic, creedal Christianity throughout the centuries. Hence it is not surprising that in the authoritative Westminster Larger Catechism of 1647, English Calvinists denounced suicide and euthanasia by directing Christians "to preserve the lives of ourselves and others, by . . . patient bearing of the hand of God."[20]

During the mid-1600s a flood of English Puritan antisuicide tracts appeared in response to both an increase in self-murder during the social chaos associated with the English civil war and two religious works questioning traditional teachings on the subject. The first of these two works, *The Anatomy of Melancholy*, was by the Anglican cleric Robert Burton (1577-1640), who published it under a pseudonym in 1621. The second, *Biathanatos*, was written by the poet John Donne (1572-1631) before he became an Anglican priest and while he still struggled with his personal salvation. It was not published until fifteen years after his death, however. Both works challenged the traditional position that all who commit suicide were eternally damned. Donne's work also suggested grounds on which one could rightly take one's own life. A host of Anglican theologians, both traditional and Puritan, took issue with these works and effectively countered them. "By 1705," as one academic analysis of this period concluded, English "clergymen had ceased to mention *Biathanatos* in sermons on suicide. Suicide still continued to increase but the arguments in defense of it were becoming atheistic rather than deistic."[21]

In England during the years following the civil war of the mid-1600s, the most widely read Christian repudiation of suicide appeared in John Bunyan's great religious allegory, *Pilgrim's Progress*. At the time, Bunyan (1628-1688) was a popular (though much persecuted) Calvinistic Baptist preacher. As any ordinary English reader of that or later generations knows, the book's hero, Christian, was sorely tempted to commit suicide to avoid torture and death at the hands of Giant Despair, who imprisoned Christian and his traveling companion, Hopeful, in the "nasty and stinking" dungeon of Doubting Castle after they had trespassed across the giant's domain on their pilgrimage to the promised land. After he "beats them fearfully," Giant Despair urges the two pilgrims to kill themselves: "'For why,' he says, 'should you choose life, seeing it is attended with so much bitterness.'" Christian initially agrees, telling Hopeful, "My soul chooseth strangling rather than life; and the grave is more easy for me than this dungeon."

Hopeful stands firm on faith, however, and delivers Bunyan's earnest plea for all Christians to resist the lure of suicide even in the face of an imminent and painful death. "Indeed our present condition is dreadful, and death would be far more welcome to me than thus for ever to abide: but yet let us consider, the Lord of the country to which we are going hath said, Thou shalt do no murder, no not to another man's person; much more then are we forbidden to take his counsel to kill ourselves," Hopeful declares. "And moreover, my brother, thou talkest of ease in the grave; but hast thou forgotten the Hell whither, for certain, the murderers go? For no murderer hath eternal life." Taking heart from Hopeful's words, Christian places his faith in obedience to God and finds unexpected release toward the promised land.[22]

This allegorical account could stand for Bunyan's own life. A peasant turned soldier and then preacher during the social turmoil of the English civil war, Bunyan suffered periods of deep spiritual and psychological despair, grave physical illnesses and prolonged imprisonment. Yet he resisted the temptation to kill himself at a time when suicide seemed epidemic in the land and penned the most widely read repudiation of the practice ever written in English. Bunyan's religious beliefs, which stand in the mainline of the evangelical and fundamentalist traditions, reject suicide even in the face of death. Euthanasia and physician-assisted suicide are clearly incompatible with his viewpoint.

As Bunyan and other religious leaders in the then generally Protestant regions of northern and western Europe reaffirmed the historic Christian repudiation of suicide, leaders of the Counter Reformation reasserted those doctrines in the still largely Roman Catholic areas of southern and eastern Europe. Jansenist and Jesuit theologians lead the way, but as in England with Bunyan, it was probably a popular religious writer who had the most influence. The writer, a French mystic known as Brother Lawrence (c. 1605-1691), who lived at the same time as Bunyan, reached an enormous audience throughout Roman Catholic Europe with the collection of his thoughts published under the title *The Practice of the Presence of God*. His attitude toward enduring suffering unto death was reflected in a letter to a gravely ill friend included in that book. "I do not pray that you may be delivered from your pains, but I pray God earnestly that He would give you strength and patience to bear them as long as He pleases," Lawrence wrote. "Seek from Him the strength to endure as much, and as long, as He shall judge to be necessary for you. The men of the world do not comprehend these truths." As such, he noted, "they consider sickness as a pain to nature, and not as a favor from God; and seeing it only in that light, they find nothing in it but grief and distress." In contrast Lawrence admonished his friend to find comfort in the knowledge that God "often sends diseases of the body to cure those of the soul."[23] For the mystic Lawrence and more militant leaders of the Counter Reformation, practicing the presence of God meant patiently accepting one's condition until one's natural death.

During this period hardened theological opposition to suicide as an escape from illness influenced developments within medical ethics and practice. As we described in chapter five, by the late Middle Ages the Judeo-Christian principle of the sanctity of life was wedded to the socioreligiously defined expectations attached to those who were en-trusted with the privileged monopoly of medical practice. By the late sixteenth century the simple desertion of the incurable by physicians must have become relatively rare. The Reformation-era English scholar Francis Bacon (1561-1626) wrote that "in our times, the physicians make a kind of scruple and religion to stay with the patient after he is given up."[24] He leveled no criticism against their continued attendance on the terminally ill but castigated them for failing to give more diligence to finding or developing cures for conditions thought incurable.

This basic change in attitudes toward the responsibility of a physician to his patient is neatly illustrated by contrasting positions of two popes, one from the late twelfth and the other from the mid-eighteenth century. Both have to do with the situation of a physician entering holy orders. In the late twelfth century Pope Clement III responded to a physician who requested admission to holy orders but was troubled that he may have unknowingly incurred, as a result of his medical practice, an irregularity that would, if known, be an obstacle to his admission to orders. Clement replied that the applicant should search his memory to ensure that he had never, even unintentionally, harmed patients by any treatment administered to them.[25]

When Pope Benedict XIV addressed the same situation in the mid-eighteenth century, he stated that a physician who wished to enter orders should first obtain a precautionary dispensation because the physician cannot be certain that he never failed to employ some available means to save the life of a deceased patient.[26] There is a vital change: in the twelfth century the concern was with possible harm inflicted on a patient actively; in the eighteenth it was with harm that resulted passively. In the first the question was, Did you ever harm patients by the treatment you gave them? In the second it was, Did you ever harm patients by failing to give them the treatment you should have given? These two documents by themselves prove nothing, but they illustrate a fundamental change both in physicians' sense of responsibility to their patients and in popular expectations, a change rooted at least in part in a redefinition of medical practice from a right to a privilege.

So it is well before the advent of modern medicine that physicians were expected to do all that they can to cure a patient and that they not desert the patient in extremis. Beginning with the late Middle Ages and increasingly during the Renaissance and Reformation, they were depicted lingering in the background in the death chamber, not able to do anything but obligated to be there. The major change in modern times is in the capacity of the medical profession to cure disease and prolong life and the often unrealistic expectations of society that physicians should be able to perform miracles. This has in part resulted from a changed view of nature.

Granted, ever since the time of Hippocrates and Plato dispute has intermittently arisen over the question of whether the physician works with or against nature in the treatment of illness. Bacon's plea that physicians seek to prolong life through finding cures for supposedly incurable conditions has blossomed into an attitude that in such a quest it is humans against nature, the "conquest" of disease involving human ingenuity thwarting nature's purposes. Nevertheless the principle of the sanctity of life had long before been allied with the physician's obligation to do all he could for the patient and to stay with the patient to the end.

The Reformation did little to alter Christian thinking on suicide, euthanasia and suffering. Luther, Calvin and the English Reformers clung to traditional beliefs on these subjects even as they rejected other doctrines associated with Roman Catholicism. Leaders of the Counter Reformation maintained their church's historic stance in this area as well. For nearly all Christians of the era, the sixth commandment provided sufficient warrant to condemn all forms of suicide and euthanasia. If any change occurred, it appeared in the increased professional commitment of physicians to stay with patients until their natural deaths. Yet other ideas were spreading across the lands of Western Europe with the dawn of the secular Enlightenment.

The Enlightenment in Western Europe and America

During the eighteenth century Christian dominance over Western thought and ethics weakened as the successes of the scientific revolution in offering rational, empirical explanations for natural phenomena became apparent to many educated Europeans. Reason and experience increasingly replaced revelation as sources for knowledge and understanding. Renewed interest in ancient Greco-Roman philosophies and in the ideas brought back to Europe from the voyages of discovery to India, China and other non-Christian lands fed the intellectual ferment. The era became known as the Enlightenment, and even the most entrenched codes of conduct were subjected to reexamination in the light of reason and experience.

For many Enlightenment philosophers individual freedom and autonomy became the rightful objectives of society. The new ideas were strong enough to bring down age-old monarchies throughout Europe and embolden English colonists in North America to throw off imperial rule. These new ideas naturally led many people to question traditional religious strictures against self-murder. "During the eighteenth century, the controversy between opponents and defenders of suicide became more pronounced," one analysis of the subject noted. "Individualism and subjectivism inclined philosophers toward the forces of nature and the resources of the thinking-self to explain existence; skepticism and religious indifference began to spread throughout society."[27]

This process did not lead to widespread acceptance of an individual's right to commit suicide, however. Most earlier leaders of the scientific revolution, such as René Descartes, Nicolaus Copernicus, Isaac Newton, Gottfried Leibniz, Blaise Pascal and Robert Boyle, had either publicly defended or not challenged traditional Christian doctrines regarding suicide. All of these scientists remained Christians, though some developed highly idiosyncratic beliefs. Many of their intellectual descendants during the Enlightenment, while broadly questioning Christianity, nevertheless devised sophisticated rational objections to suicide. Perhaps the most influential of these Enlightenment opponents of suicide was the great German philosopher Immanuel Kant (1724-1804).

On the basis of reason and experience Kant sought to develop a necessary and universal system of moral behavior. In his *Fundamental Principles of the Metaphysics of Morals* he concluded that morality consisted in always acting in ways that could serve as universal laws, that treat humans as ends rather than means and that the actor accepts as making universal law by its maxims. Applying these categorical imperatives to suicide, Kant wrote of the self-murderer:

> His maxim is: From self-love I adopt it as a principle to shorten my life when its longer duration is likely to bring more evil than satisfaction. It is asked then simply whither this principle founded on self-love can become a universal law of nature. Now we see at once that a system of nature of which it should be a law to destroy life by means of the very feeling whose special nature it is to impel to the improvement of life would contradict itself, and therefore could not exist as a system of nature; hence that maxim cannot possibly exist as a universal law of nature.

Reinforcing this conclusion, Kant observed:

> He who contemplates suicide should ask himself whether his actions can be consistent with the idea of humanity as an end in itself. If he destroys himself in order to escape from painful circumstances, he uses a person merely as a means to maintain a tolerable condition up to the end of life. But a man is not a thing, that is to say, something which can be used merely as means.

Thus Kant concluded regarding situations directly equivalent to physician-assisted suicide and euthanasia, "To observe morality is far more important [than life]. It is better to sacrifice one's life [by continuing to live] than one's morality [by suicide]. To live is not a necessity; but to live honorably while life lasts is a necessity."[28]

Many if not most Enlightenment thinkers also condemned suicide, among them Dutch rationalist Benedict de Spinoza (1632-1677), Jewish philosopher Moses Mendelssohn (1729-1786) and French political theorist Jean-Jacques Rousseau (1712-1778), but rational empiricism led some to support it as a natural human right. The influential French writers Montesquieu (1689-1755) and Voltaire (1694-1778) boldly defended the practice, for example, with the latter wittily replying to Kantian-type arguments about civic duty, "The republic will do very well without me after my death, as it did before my birth."[29]

The leading Enlightenment apologist for suicide, however, was British empiricist David Hume (1711-1776). Believing that no theory of reality is possible in either revelation or reason, Hume concluded that there can be no knowledge of anything beyond experience. His experience led him to a utilitarian view of morality: An individual owed a duty to society only so long as society benefited the individual in return. "All our obligations to do good to society seem to imply something reciprocal," he reasoned, "but when I withdraw altogether from society [such as by suicide], can I be bound any longer?" More particularly this line of reasoning led Hume to maintain that individuals who did not benefit from living bore no obligation to live. "If upon account of age and infirmities I may lawfully resign my office," he asked, "why may I not cut short these miseries at once by an action which is no more prejudicial to society?" Looking at the issue from the perspective of society, Hume concluded that if one becomes a net burden rather than a benefit to society, then "resignation of life must not only be innocent but laudable." Adding his own revealing retort to arguments about one's general duty to live, Hume observed that "the life of a man is of no greater importance to the universe than that of an oyster."[30]

Tempering his empiricism with reason, however, the other great English political philosopher of the Enlightenment, John Locke (1632-1704), reached a different conclusion. Looking at the condition of people in nature, Locke found them in "a state of liberty, yet it is not a state of license, though man in that state has an uncontrollable liberty to dispose of his person or his possessions, yet he has not liberty to destroy himself." This restriction stemmed from Locke's deist beliefs that people were the "workmanship" of a creator, which "makes all servants of one sovereign master, sent into the world by his order and about his business—they are his property, whose workmanship they are, made to last during his, not one another's pleasure."[31] Locke's political philosophy in general and his views on suicide in particular profoundly influenced a generation of American deists during the Revolutionary era, including Thomas Jefferson, John Adams and Thomas Paine, and contributed to England's maintaining its law against suicide until 1961, long after similar laws were repealed in most Western nations.

The campaign to repeal laws against suicide began during the Enlightenment, gaining force in North America following the American Revolution and on the European continent after the French Revolution. This process did not necessarily reflect a change in the societal view of suicide, however. On the one hand many opponents of suicide, such as Adams and Jefferson, supported the repeal of statutes outlawing the practice on the grounds that the state should not punish innocent heirs by confiscating a suicide's property. On the other hand some defenders of suicide nonetheless maintained that the state could sanction the act. The decriminalization of suicide did not lead to the immediate legalization of attempted suicide, however, and most states maintained or added laws against assisted suicide. States used these laws to discourage suicide to the extent possible without heaping further penalties on the families of those who killed themselves.

The Enlightenment may have legitimated the debate over the morality of suicide and euthanasia among rationalists, but it did little to soften opposition to those practices among Christians. The Roman Church remained steadfast in its damnation of suicide as contrary to Scripture and natural law. During the late 1700s Hume's support of suicide unleashed an avalanche of opposition sermons, tracts and books from English religious leaders both inside and outside the established church, including the Bishop of Norwich's 1784 *Letters on Infidelity*. Methodist evangelist John Wesley (1703-1791) denounced suicide as a "horrid crime" and proposed discouraging the practice by publicly hanging the body.[32] The English separatist minister and hymn writer Isaac Watts (1674-1748) had already penned a popular tract against suicide. In it he attributed growing interest in the act to Enlightenment atheism. The emotional evangelism of Wesley, Watts and other gifted preachers of the period prevented Enlightenment rationalism from overwhelming Christianity in England. A series of religious revivals in America beginning with the Great Awakening of the mid-1700s had the same impact on the United States. Soon the Enlightenment itself waned even among secular intellectuals as Romanticism displaced rationalism. Both England and the United States entered the nineteenth century with a broad public consensus against suicide and euthanasia.

The Modern United States Before Life-Support Technology

The cultural and legal status of physician-assisted suicide and euthanasia changed little in the United States during the nearly two hundred years from the formation of the republic until the advent of modern medical life-support technology in the second half of the twentieth century. The issue remained a topic of intellectual debate, as it had been during the Enlightenment, with philosophers disagreeing among themselves over the morality of the practice. Some physicians and family members participated in hastening the death of suffering patients, as some surely had throughout the Christian era and before. Pneumonia was commonly called the old man's friend, and mortally wounded soldiers were put out of their misery on the body-strewn battlefields of the Civil War. Rumors circulated about terminally ill monarchs and millionaires receiving aid in dying from their physicians. Yet while society seemed to accept these acts as a private matter, it never condoned them, and most religious leaders remained firmly opposed to all forms of suicide and euthanasia.

This period in the legal history of suicide in the United States is bracketed by two episodes. The first followed the American Revolution, as the newly independent states rapidly moved to decriminalize the act of suicide. The second occurred during the 1950s and 1960s, as the drafters of the Model Penal Code debated and ultimately retained criminal sanctions against assisted suicide and euthanasia. These episodes reveal much about social attitudes toward the practice of hastening death for the terminally ill.

The American colonies inherited the English common law against suicide. In his authoritative eighteenth-century compilation of English common law, which was widely used in America at the time of the Revolution, William Blackstone wrote, "The suicide is guilty of a double offense, one spiritual, in evading the prerogative of the Almighty, and rushing to his immediate presence uncalled for, and the other temporal, against the sovereign [or state], who has an interest in the preservation of all his subjects, the law therefore ranked this among the highest crimes."[33] The established punishment for suicide aimed at discouraging the act through forfeiture of the suicide's estate to the crown and an ignominious burial. There is little evidence that the law was vigorously enforced in America, however. Quaker leader William Penn abolished the penalty of forfeiture for suicide in his colonies of Pennsylvania and Delaware in 1701, and other colonies moved to mitigate the punishments in certain cases. These efforts did not necessarily reflect an acceptance of suicide but rather a desire not to punish innocent heirs.

Once the colonies gained independence, most of the new states quickly ended criminal penalties for suicide. A classic 1796 legal treatise by the future chief justice of Connecticut, Zephaniah Swift, explained the motive. In it he denounced the act of suicide as "abhorrent to the feelings of mankind" but noted, "there can be no greater cruelty, than the inflicting of a punishment, as the forfeiture of goods, which must fall solely on the innocent offspring of the offender." Rejecting the traditional justification that the penalty deterred the practice, Swift further betrayed his revulsion of suicide by explaining, "It is evident that where a person is so destitute of affection for his family, and regardless of the pleasures of life, as to wish to put an end to his existence, that he will not be deterred by a consideration of their future existence."[34] Even states that did not promptly decriminalize suicide ceased to impose penalties against it. By 1824 the great Massachusetts jurist Nathanial Dane commented regarding laws against suicide nationally, "But this kind of law since the American revolution has very rarely been executed; not one instance is recollected among the scores of self-murders remembered. It seems to have become a general practice to consider those who kill or destroy themselves as being insane."[35]

During this era any waning Enlightenment-era arguments in favor of suicide met stiff resistance. One of the leading religious figures of the day was Jonathan Edwards's grandson, Yale University president Timothy Dwight. Just as Edwards helped launch the First Great Awakening, Dwight played a leading role in the Second Great Awakening or Great Revival of the Early National Period, which revitalized Christianity in the wake of Enlightenment deism and disbelief. One commentator concluded that Dwight "did more than any one man in the newborn United States of America to stem the tide of atheism and advance the cause of the Christian faith." In his preaching and academic writing, Dwight denounced suicide as a testimony of "enormous corruption."[36]

Other eighteenth-century evangelical Christian leaders shared Dwight's condemnation of suicide and added a rich theology of suffering. The premier Anglo-American evangelist of the century, C. H. Spurgeon (1834-1892), who enjoyed a wide following on both sides of the Atlantic, offered perhaps the best example. He was afflicted throughout his later life with grave and often incapacitating illnesses, leading him once to comment, "I have suffered many times from severe sickness and frightful mental depression, sinking almost to despair." Yet he carried on his active public ministry despite an earnest desire to end the pain even through death. "Flesh and blood cannot bear the strain, at least such flesh and blood as mine," he confessed at the age of forty-five. "I would, if it were God's will, escape from such frequent illness: [But] that must be according to His will and not mine." Spurgeon's appreciation of the spiritual value of his suffering deepened throughout his life. Shortly before his death, he reflected: "I venture to say that the greatest earthly blessing that God can give to any of us is health, with the exception of sickness. Sickness has frequently been of more use to the saints of God than health has." Spurgeon saw similar blessings from the suffering caused by the illness of a loved one, which he said "might teach us lessons nowhere else to be learned so well. Trials lead us to the realities of religion."[37]

In the United States the great Princeton theologian A. A. Hodge (1823-1886), one of the founders of the modern school of biblical inerrancy, agreed that Christians should recognize and endure sickness as God's "fatherly chastisement—a proof of love for our good, not a mark of anger or displeasure for sin." He observed, "Some of the holiest saints have been the greatest sufferers and for the longest time." Accordingly he firmly rejected suicide and euthanasia.[38] At least on these matters, he spoke for a united evangelical church. Unlike Wesley in England a century earlier, however, American church leaders did not oppose the removal of criminal sanctions against suicide.

The decriminalization of suicide created uncertainty in some quarters regarding the legality of assisted suicide, which had been a related crime under the common law. State courts and legislatures quickly resolved the issue. "I apprehend that if a man murders himself, and one stands by, aiding in and abetting the death, he is as guilty as if he had conducted himself in the same manner," the Massachusetts high court ruled in 1816. "And if one becomes the procuring cause of death, though absent, he is accessory."[39] This ruling clearly covered physician-assisted suicide, and it served as precedent within the state long after Massachusetts repealed its sanctions against suicide. The reason for decriminalizing suicide (not wanting to penalize innocent heirs after the actor was outside the reach of the law) did not apply to the case of assisted suicide, in which the actor remained within the reach of the law. And by outlawing the latter act, the state could make it harder both for people to commit suicide and for others to encourage it. Persons considering suicide are already in a vulnerable state. This is particularly true of the elderly and infirm, who are the prime subjects of physician-assisted suicide and euthanasia. Assistance from third parties increases the risk of abuse, mistake and duress and can raise questions about who instigated the act. With these concerns in mind, states typically maintained their laws against assisted suicide despite decriminalizing suicide, with many of them passing new statutes expressly covering the matter.

Thus evidence of societal attitudes toward suicide as reflected in the law suggests that while Americans sympathized with the suicide's family, they did not condone the act. Confronted with a case of assisted suicide after the decriminalization of suicide, for example, the Kentucky Supreme Court decreed, "In this case, it would be impossible to punish the principal; but it is not believed that under any sound reasoning the accessory would thereby go scot free."[40] In 1872 the Ohio Supreme Court faced the case of a defendant named Blackburn who was charged with murder for supplying poison for a suicide. "It is immaterial whether the party taking the poison took it willingly, intending thereby to commit suicide, or was overcome by force," the court concluded. "The lives of all are under the protection of the law, and under that protection to their last moment. The life of those to whom life has become a burden—of those who are hopelessly diseased or fatally wounded—nay, even the lives of criminals condemned to death, are under the protection of the law equally as the lives of those who are in the full tide of life's enjoyment."[41] This ruling unquestionably covered the situation of physician-assisted suicide for the terminally ill, and a host of court decisions from various states adopted similar reasoning in cases of euthanasia. In the latter instances, all courts maintained that consent is no defense to a charge of murder.[42]

Despite the firm legal restrictions against assisted suicide and euthanasia that remained largely unchanged during the nineteenth and twentieth centuries, the judicial system tended to exhibit increasing leniency if the victim was terminally ill or severely incapacitated. Even in the Blackburn case, the Ohio court noted that "the atrocity of the crime, in a moral sense, would be greatly diminished by the fact that suicide was intended" by the victim.[43] By the 1920s the exceptions threatened to swallow up the rule.

During the 1920s and the 1930s, in any number of highly publicized criminal prosecutions brought against family members or physicians who hastened the death of a suffering person, juries refused to indict or convict the actor or judges suspended the sentence of those convicted. The *New York Times* reported an epidemic of four separate "mercy killings" in February of 1925, only one of which went to trial. That case involved Colorado physician Harold E. Blazer, who chloroformed his mentally retarded thirty-two-year-old daughter. In its opening statement the defense argued that the daughter "was better off dead than alive" and that she "had no place in the scheme of life." It contrasted this image with its description of the defendant as a devoted father who lovingly ended his daughter's suffering because he could no longer care for her.[44] The trial, which attracted nationwide attention, ended in a hung jury. In a pair of New York cases a decade later, a Nassau County grand jury refused to indict a husband for asphyxiating his cancer-stricken wife, and an Italian immigrant named Repouille received a suspended sentence from a New York City judge after being convicted of gassing his brain-damaged teenage son.

These cases reflected an ambivalence toward punishing people for participating in compelling cases of assisted suicide and euthanasia, yet they do not necessarily demonstrate a general acceptance of such acts.

Most such cases date from the early twentieth century, when leading biological and social scientists accepted a particularly grim view of genetic determinism that saw no hope for those born with severe mental disabilities or for their descendants. Many of these experts advocated such so-called eugenic remedies as sexual sterilization and euthanasia for the mentally ill and retarded. Parallel with the movement to promote eugenics, related organizations promoted the legalization of voluntary euthanasia for the terminally ill.[45]

As a result of these efforts, laws mandating sterilization for the mentally ill and retarded were enacted in thirty-five American states and most European countries, but only Nazi Germany succumbed to the lure of legalized euthanasia. Roman Catholics and conservative Protestants united to oppose both eugenics and euthanasia, with the biting satire of British essayist G. K. Chesterton, a convert to Roman Catholicism, doing as much as anything to debunk them in the popular mind. Yet many modernist ministers embraced these seemingly scientific ideas, such as the Unitarian minister who cofounded the Euthanasia Society of America in 1938, and successive deans of St. Paul's Cathedral in London who helped lead the English eugenics and euthanasia movements. After the full horror of Nazi practices were exposed following World War II, however, programs of forced sterilization and efforts to legalize euthanasia lost support. Yet before that time, and in light of all the clamor for eugenics and euthanasia, it was hardly surprising that juries and judges often gave the benefit of the doubt to defendants in particularly compelling cases involving those practices.

Selective refusals to enforce laws against assisted suicide and euthanasia reflected a pragmatic approach to the law, not a repudiation of it. The high incidence of failures to indict or convict in such cases during the mid-1900s supports the view that, as one legal commentator wrote at the time, "If the circumstances are so compelling that the defendant ought to violate the law, then they are compelling enough for the jury to violate their oaths. The law does well to declare [euthanasia] unlawful. It does equally well to put no more than the sanction of an oath in the way of an acquittal."[46] A 1925 *New York Times* editorial on the Blazer case drew a similar distinction between outlawing euthanasia in general and exempting certain compelling cases from the law. "Dr. Blazer had no more legal right to kill his unfortunate daughter than has the Superintendent of any asylum for imbeciles to put all of his charges out of the way," the *Times* noted in an obvious reference to pending eugenic proposals. "But the circumstances in this Colorado case were peculiar, and again most people will feel, though they could not prove, that Dr. Blazer did something so different from murder that he should be sentenced neither to death nor to imprisonment."[47]

During this period when juries frequently acquitted persons charged with euthanasia in compelling cases, they would nevertheless hand down convictions if the facts appeared to justify it. For example, about the same time that Repouille received a suspended sentence for gassing his thirteen-year-old retarded son, another defendant, John F. Noxon, was sentenced to die for electrocuting his mentally retarded infant child. Although the two cases bore surface similarities, Repouille evoked sympathy because of his prior efforts to care for his child and the painless method of death.[48] No general law to legalize euthanasia could make such fine distinctions, and few people would want to let defendants like Noxon go free. Despite impassioned campaigns to legalize euthanasia, all such proposals were soundly defeated outside Germany. The tenor of debate was reflected by a proponent's plea made shortly before the British parliament crushingly rejected a 1950 bill to legalize voluntary euthanasia. "I believe that posterity will look back on this refusal you are going to make this afternoon," he bitterly complained, "as people look now on the burning of witches—as a barbarious survival of medieval ideas, an example of that high-minded cruelty from the entanglement of which it has taken mankind so many centuries to emerge. In that day we few, we five or six [supporters] shall, I believe, be remembered."[49]

After this defeat in parliament, a leading proponent of the bill, legal theorist Glanville Williams, brought his campaign for legalizing euthanasia to the United States through his role as a special consultant to a committee of the American Law Institute (ALI) charged with drafting a model criminal-law code. The ALI had already prepared model statutes for other areas of the law, and states had widely adopted them. The so-called Model Penal Code represented its most ambitious project to date. Williams had reason for optimism because the committee was led by the renowned law professor Herbert Wechsler, who had publicly endorsed euthanasia during the 1930s. Further support for Williams's position came from Joseph Fletcher, a provocative Episcopal theologian whose theory of situation ethics had stirred renewed interest in the morality of euthanasia among liberal American Christians. Fletcher published a defense of voluntary euthanasia in 1954 and later advanced arguments for involuntary euthanasia in certain situations. The former reflected his view that the sick and infirm should not be forced to endure "unnecessary" pain without hope for their recovery; the latter added his notion that personhood was so tied to the ability to reason that individuals lacking that capacity could be put to death out of compassion for their lost personhood.[50] Fletcher later became the guiding spirit behind the

Euthanasia Educational Fund, which sought to promote public acceptance of mercy killing.

Fletcher's thoughts on euthanasia encountered immediate opposition
from a host of influential Christian theologians, ranging from the neo-or-
thodox Karl Barth, a Swiss scholar with an enormous following in the
United States, through Princeton theologian Paul Ramsey to the neo-
evangelical Carl F. H. Henry, a founding faculty member at Fuller
Theological Seminary. "We must start with the unequivocal fact that
when self-destruction is the exercise of a supposed and usurped sovereignty of man over himself it is a frivolous, arbitrary and criminal violation
of the [biblical] commandment," Barth maintained. Making an exception
only for situations exemplified in the Bible by the deaths of Samson and
the early Christian martyrs, he argued, "If a man kills himself without
being ordered to do so [by God], then his action is murder."[51] Barth and
Ramsey stressed the view that life is a gift from God that humans should
not throw back in the face of the giver. Both of these mainline theologians
and the evangelical Henry emphasized the sanctity of all human life,
created in the image of God, as a central biblical tenet and linchpin of
Christian ethics. Their writings on the subject during the postwar era,
coupled with the concurrent rise of neo-orthodoxy and neo-evangelicalism within American Protestantism, helped solidify religious opposition
to euthanasia during the 1950s.

The movement for legalizing euthanasia, which had grown within some
liberal secular and religious circles in the United States during the 1920s
and 1930s, appeared to crest and break during the 1950s. Opinion
surveys, one of which showed growing popular support for both eugenics
and euthanasia based largely on the public response to individual compelling cases, reversed direction as Americans began to realize how Nazi
Germany had applied such concepts as a general practice.

When the drafters of the Model Penal Code took up the issue, they
rejected Williams's proposals, which took the form of suggesting that
criminality in this area should turn on the presence of a selfish motive on
the part of the actor, in favor of a blanket prohibition of assisted suicide
and euthanasia. With respect to assisted suicide the drafters noted, "The
wiser course is to rely on mitigation in the sentence when the grounds for
it appear."[52] One observer suggested that the about-face by Wechsler on
the issue may have resulted from his experiences as an advisor at Nazi
war trials during the late 1940s.[53] In the official commentary to the Model
Penal Code, the ALI maintained that "the interests in the sanctity of life
that are represented by the criminal homicide laws are threatened by one
who expresses a willingness to participate in taking the life of another,

even though the act may be accomplished with the consent, or at the request, of the suicide victim."[54] In the years following publication of the Model Penal Code, eight states added new statutes outlawing assisted suicide, and eleven other states revised their existing laws on the subject to conform with the model code. At last count thirty-five states expressly outlaw assisted suicide, and all fifty classify euthanasia as murder.

No one did more to influence the Model Penal Code on this point than a young law professor named Yale Kamisar. Appalled by Williams's proposal and fearful of its reception within the ALI committee, Kamisar penned a landmark law-review article in 1958 that set the tone for subsequent legal debate about physician-assisted suicide and euthanasia by amassing "utilitarian" arguments against them. Williams had pled for the right of rational persons who suffer from incurable, painful afflictions to choose death. "I am perfectly willing to accept civil liberties as the battlefield, but issues of 'liberty' and 'freedom' mean little until we begin to pin down *whose* 'liberty' and 'freedom' and for *what* need and at *what* price," Kamisar countered. "I am more concerned about the life and liberty of those who would needlessly be killed in the process or who would irrationally choose to partake of the processes." He singled out those "who, though they go through the motions of 'volunteering,' are casualties of strain, pain or narcotics to such an extent that they really know not what they do." Kamisar also highlighted the dangers of abuse and duress in dealing with the most likely candidates for euthanasia, the elderly and infirm. "I submit too," Kamisar added, "that the possible radiations from the proposed legislation, *e.g.*, involuntary euthanasia of idiots and imbeciles (the typical 'mercy-killings' reported by the press) and the emergence of the legal precedent that there are lives not 'worth living,' give additional cause to pause."[55]

Due in part to Kamisar's persuasive arguments, the revival of religious neo-orthodoxy and neo-evangelicalism among Christians, and the shadow cast by Nazi practices, the United States entered the final third of the twentieth century with a solid consensus opposed to euthanasia and physician-assisted suicide. For the first time since the Enlightenment, the topics were all but beyond the range of polite conversation in the United States. The practices still occurred and were not harshly punished, but prudent politicians and pundits did not openly discuss the merits of decriminalization. Secular and religious leaders generally agreed on the proper public policy regarding this issue, even if they might disagree in their reasoning. Yet revolutionary developments in medical technology soon shattered the consensus and returned the topic to center stage of public debate.

7

The Right-to-Die
Movement

In 1974, after imbibing a particularly potent mix of hallucinatory drugs and alcohol at a party near her New Jersey home, twenty-one-year-old Karen Ann Quinlan lapsed into a coma. She was rushed to a hospital and placed on a respirator but never recovered consciousness. Seven months later, after extensive counseling from his Roman Catholic priest—who advised that although church doctrine strictly forbade euthanasia, it permitted the termination of extraordinary medical treatment in hopeless cases—Quinlan's father requested that the respirator be turned off. Fearing that the act would violate state law, the hospital refused, and the father went to court.

The ensuing case became front-page news across the country and in a new context returned the old issue of euthanasia to the center of public debate. The old hypothetical examples of dying patients' hastening death gave way to the new realities of patients' being kept alive on medication and machinery without prospect of recovery. The secular philosopher's academic argument for rational suicide became a public cry for the so-called right to die, and a popular movement by that name emerged. Quinlan presented a sobering case in point. Before the development of modern respirators, the experts testified, she would have quickly died from her overdose. Now Quinlan could be kept alive indefinitely on a breathing machine. But she would never communicate or move; she would live on in a persistent vegetative state. Few Americans seemed to want that result, certainly not her father. Public opinion sided with his agonized plea for relief. After lower courts initially refused his request based on traditional laws against euthanasia, in 1976 the New Jersey Supreme Court issued a landmark decision declaring that Quinlan had a constitutional right to die. The ruling gained added force when the United States Supreme Court declined to review it.[1]

The legal precedent from the Quinlan case became muddled at this point because the labored court opinion confused whether the right belonged to the father, who exercised it on his own behalf, or to the patient, with the father acting as a surrogate. Most commentators agreed that under existing law, competent patients could refuse medical treatment for themselves, but Quinlan was unable to do so. The dispute centered on how to refuse treatment where patients could not speak for themselves.

From his post at Princeton University, near the center of controversy in New Jersey, Christian ethicist Paul Ramsey, who had argued vigorously against euthanasia in the 1950s, reentered the fray. "The *Quinlan* case has gone a long way toward obliterating the distinction between voluntary and involuntary euthanasia," Ramsey worried. "The court *imputed* to Karen a will to die; it did not discover it. Then the court permitted others also to impute a will to die to an uncomprehending patient and to act in behalf of that patient's privacy so construed. It does not matter *who* is the designated agent; *others* now have an extraordinary extralegal power to bring death." What troubled him most was that Quinlan never chose to turn off her respirator. Instead, Ramsey noted, the court assumed that she would want to die, in part "because the 'overwhelming majority' of us would want to do so" in a similar situation.[2] Many conservative Christians denounced the ruling as an opening wedge for euthanasia, but liberal Christians tended to hail it as an enlightened advance in individual freedom—and the public widely supported it.

A further issue left unresolved by *Quinlan* involved the type of treatments that could be terminated upon request. Quinlan's father asked only to stop the respirator, a technology that both he and the court considered extraordinary. When asked in court if he also wanted power to discontinue tube feeding, Quinlan's father said no—that was her nutrition! Clearly he perceived a distinction between extraordinary treatment that postponed death and ordinary care necessary to sustain life, a distinction that made a profound difference in this case when Quinlan confounded the medical experts by living on for nine years in a coma without a respirator. At the time many Roman Catholic and some Protestant ethicists stressed the difference between ordinary and extraordinary medical procedures, but legal critics complained that no clear line divided the two categories. Even though eating and drinking are natural acts, they asked, what is ordinary about giving artificial nutrition and hydration to comatose patients? And if Quinlan's wishes controlled, why should it matter what procedures were ended? Such questions highlighted the role that advances in modern medical technology played in the right-to-die debate.

Medical Aspects

The medical factor is brought in focus by a story told by Lutheran bishop Lowell O. Erdahl about the mother of premature twins being kept alive on modern neonatal life-support systems. "One child, though tiny, was normal; the other was blind and severely deformed," he noted. "As the mother looked at the normal child, she thanked God for the medical technology that enabled hope for a full and meaningful life, but as she looked at the deformed child who seemed destined for a world of darkness and suffering, she silently cursed the same technology that sustained its life."[3]

Erdahl's story emphasizes the mixed reactions of many Americans to modern medical technology. Hardly more than a generation ago, health-care providers could do little to postpone the death of a severely and incurably ill patient. Procedures already existed to prevent or cure previously fatal or permanently incapacitating illnesses and injuries from smallpox to skull fractures, and nearly everyone welcomed them. But increasingly after 1960, a variety of life-sustaining procedures became available that could forestall death for a significant period of time. Some of these, like kidney dialysis, offered no hope for cure but some chance for continued active life. Others, such as cancer chemotherapy, might either slow the disease process or cure it. Still others, like respirators, could give time for other treatments to work or the body to heal itself. These modern medical miracles seemed like curses to some people when they did not lead to recovery (as they did for the normal twin in Erdahl's story), but rather to a prolonged and more painful death (as presumably happened with the other twin).

The technological onslaught against disease engendered at least two fundamental concerns that helped spur the right-to-die movement. One involved the objection that in some cases so-called life-sustaining procedures prolong (perhaps painfully) the dying process beyond the control of patients and their families. Another was the high cost of high-tech medicine and the heavy financial burden that it placed on patients, their families and society. The medical aspects of both merit close examination.

The first concern has multiple facets. "Before the day of dialysis machines and ventilators, people died if they went into kidney or respiratory failure. These technologies have saved many lives, but they have also raised legitimate fears in many that their dying process might be unnecessarily prolonged," Adventist physician Robert C. Orr concluded from his experience as director of clinical ethics at Loma Linda University Medical Center. "Many patients fear that the 'technological imperative'—the inclination to use a treatment just because it is available—will be the value used in making decisions for them."[4]

A recent study of nearly five thousand dying patients in five major teaching hospitals found a basis for these fears. While a third of these critically ill patients asked not to have cardiopulmonary resuscitation in the event of heart failure, for example, the doctors in half of those cases never issued a do-not resuscitate order, and even when they did so, it took an average of twenty-two to seventy-three days (depending on the type of medical specialist involved), with nearly half of the orders finally issued within a day or two of the patient's death. Over a third of the patients spent at least ten days in intensive care on respirators. "We don't decide to let patients die in peace until almost the last moment," study codirector Joanne Lynn of George Washington University Medical Center observed. "This is hard on patients, their families and the health professionals who care for them."[5]

The situation is aggravated because patients are less likely now than in the past to know the doctor who is treating them. Advances in medical knowledge and technology have spawned a cadre of specialists. "Instead of having one family doctor, many patients see several specialists," Orr noted. "And because the patients or their doctors are more likely to move away than in the past, or because their employer may change to a more competitive managed-care plan with different physicians (as in HMOs), they do not develop the long-standing, trusting relationship that used to be more common in the past." Christian physician Rob Roy MacGreagor, chief of the infectious diseases section at the University of Pennsylvania School of Medicine, put it in historical perspective. "Until around 1900, there was very little a doctor could do to affect the course of any disease," he commented. "The physician in that day was primarily a counselor and the interpreter of disease, conducting the patient through the course of the illness. Today he is a soldier—an aggressor against disease." The result for patients and their families, he warned, can be "a dehumanizing spiral in which each organ failure is met by still another life-support procedure," which they find increasingly difficult to understand or control.[6]

Further, more people confront these situations now than ever before.

As George Bernard Shaw once remarked, the ultimate statistic is that one out of one dies. Yet, before the advent of modern medical procedures, people died younger and quicker than they do today. For example, heart attacks that once caused sudden death are now routinely treated by drugs and angioplasty, with bypass surgery and heart transplants offering additional options in serious cases. Life-threatening strokes can be monitored with magnetic imaging technology and successfully treated with chemicals that draw blood off the brain. Many potentially fatal infectious diseases are now fully controlled through vaccinations. New treatments reduce the risk of death from injuries, wounds and burns.

As a result of such medical advances, more people grow old—the average life span jumped 50 percent during the twentieth century—and face the prospect of long-term degenerative diseases, such as cancer and Alzheimer's disease. Others, who would have quickly succumbed in an accident or life-threatening medical event, now live on in a coma or other seriously incapacitated state. These situations can raise profound questions about when to end treatment—questions that arose less often in an earlier era. At the beginning of the twentieth century most people in the United States died at home without receiving medical treatment, and only a tiny percentage died in a hospital. Today over 85 percent of all Americans die in a hospital, and in many of these cases somebody must make a decision to stop further medical treatment.[7]

The issue of patient control over end-of-life medical care does not arise only in situations where patients receive more treatment than they want, but also where they receive less. The core finding of Lynn's study was that physicians tended to enter do-not-resuscitate orders when they deemed them appropriate, not when the patient asked for them. A related question occurs when patients or their families request continued life-sustaining treatment after their physician gives up hope. Increasingly during the 1990s health-care providers have formalized a concept of "medical futility" and claimed the authority to terminate treatment that falls within this category. Thus, for example, the professional treatment guideline on medical futility now maintains that life-support treatment "can be limited without the consent of patient or surrogate when the intervention is judged to be futile," which it defines as treatment "that would be highly unlikely to result in a meaningful survival for the patient." Reporting on a recent study of a thousand intensive-care-unit physicians, one researcher noted that "the vast majority of the doctors admitted to unilaterally either discontinuing or withholding life support because they considered the case would be futile," sometimes without informing family members or contrary to family wishes.[8]

A case in point involved Catherine Gilgunn, a seventy-one-year-old woman who suffered from a Jobian litany of illnesses. While she was in the prestigious Massachusetts General Hospital following a mastectomy for breast cancer, she had a series of seizures that resulted in brain damage and left her comatose on a respirator. Even though he knew that Gilgunn would have wanted continued treatment no matter what, her doctor (backed by the hospital's aptly named Optimum Care Committee) entered a do-not-resuscitate order on her chart. Over the vigorous protests of her daughter, Gilgunn was taken off the respirator and later died in the hospital. The daughter filed suit, but the court upheld the hospital's decision.

Commenting on the ruling, medical ethicist and law professor Alexander Morgan Capron worried, "The greatest danger at the moment, is that people . . . will be misled by media coverage into thinking that the law has now placed the decision about which treatment should be used (especially with critically ill patients) solely in physician's hands."[9] For some people this is especially worrisome in the context of recent efforts to contain health-care costs, such as by Medicare and insurance payment methods that reimburse providers based on diagnosis rather than service; HMOs that charge a flat per-member fee; and widespread reliance on unreimbursed hospital care for needy patients. All encourage health-care providers to provide as little treatment as possible for a satisfactory outcome, which some critics charge may excessively curtail end-of-life care.

These worries highlight the second medically related concern driving the right-to-die movement: exploding health-care costs. This concern is doubly linked to the advent of modern medical technology. Not only does that technology enable people to live longer and thereby consume more health care, but also newer treatments tend to be much more costly than older treatments.

The raw figures are staggering. Between 1960 and 1995 health spending in the United States has increased at more than twice the rate of inflation and now consumes nearly 15 percent of the nation's gross national product. In 1960 Americans spent about $130 per person on health care, with most of it paid by individuals or private insurers. In 1995 the figure topped $3,000 per person, with most of it coming directly or indirectly from the government. Health care now far surpasses defense as the largest category in the federal budget, and the growth in this area has become a leading cause of the federal budget deficit. The government spent $175 billion on Medicare in 1996, which was nearly $10 billion more than it took in from the payroll taxes that are supposed to fund the system. And payments are predicted to rise dramatically in the coming years, up at least 50 percent by 2001. If nothing changes in the system, government actuaries predict that the Medicare deficit will increase twelvefold over the next decade and balloon to over $350 billion in 2020, as baby boomers qualify for coverage. The Medicare *deficit* would then exceed total defense spending by nearly a third.[10]

Much of this federal spending and many private dollars go for end-of-life treatment. Between Medicare and Medicaid, the government pays for the care associated with two-thirds of all deaths that occur in the United States. One out of every twelve dollars spent on heath care in the United States pays for intensive-care treatment, and nearly 30 percent of all Medicare payments are attributable to patients in their last year of life.[11] Neither of these categories of spending would disappear if the terminally ill died without treatment. Most intensive-care patients fully recover, and much of the treatment given to patients in the last year of life occurs before death becomes imminent. Yet such figures factor into right-to-die advocacy. At the public-policy level, this was reflected in the much-publicized declaration of Colorado governor Richard A. Lamm, "Elderly people who are terminally ill have a duty to die and get out of the way," and by Oregon's efforts to end Medicaid funding of certain treatments for persons nearing the end of life so that more could be spent on those expected to live.[12] At the private level, such thinking influences the countless elderly and terminally ill persons who justify their decision to refuse life-sustaining treatment or to commit suicide as a way to conserve family resources.[13]

The social history of kidney dialysis in the United States illustrates the intersection of medical technology, health-care costs and the right-to-die movement. Kidneys cleanse the blood of impurities collected from throughout the body, and if they fail a person gradually becomes poisoned by his or her own bodily wastes. Prior to 1960 kidney failure inevitably caused death. In that year, however, in one of the historic triumphs of modern medical technology, Belding Scribner of Seattle invented a shunt that could be implanted in a patient's vein and used repeatedly for dialysis, or machine cleaning of the blood. Before this invention, dialysis required direct access to the patient's veins, which became unusable after multiple incisions.

This technological development posed an ethical dilemma, however. Kidney failure is usually a permanent condition. Therefore, until the later introduction of kidney transplant techniques, each new dialysis patient became a regular user for the rest of his or her life. And the process was expensive and time-consuming, commonly requiring patients to visit hospitals as often as one day per week or more. There were not enough kidney dialysis machines to go around during the 1960s, and the price of treatment was beyond the reach of many people who needed it for survival. Seattle, the birthplace of the technology, led the way in forming an elite screening committee, locally known as the "God Committee," that determined which patients should receive dialysis. Otherwise healthy male breadwinners most often got the nod. In other places throughout the country, hospital selection committees performed the task of selecting which kidney patients would live and which would die. Such rationing processes still occur in many parts of the world, such as in England, where the government health-care system does not offer dialysis treatment to some elderly people with kidney failure.

In the United States, Congress finally resolved the dilemma in 1971, after enough patients and their families complained. Seattle's most powerful federal lawmaker, Senate Appropriations Committee chair Warren Magneson, crafted a budget amendment that extended Medicare coverage for dialysis treatment to *all* Americans who needed it regardless of their age or health condition. Basing his conclusions on usage at that time, Magneson asserted that no more than twenty thousand persons would need dialysis per year, for an estimated annual cost of about $75 million. This was less than the price of a new aircraft carrier, he argued—an effective analogy in an era when money flowed freely to fight the Vietnam and cold wars. Yet his projections proved far off the mark.

With payment coming from the federal government, kidney dialysis suddenly became a certain source for hospital profits. Machines were installed in heath-care facilities throughout the country, within easy access of nearly all kidney patients. And pressure grew to use these machines. As dialysis became widely available, "anyone in kidney failure was promptly placed on dialysis regardless of medical prognosis," according to an analysis by Judith Wilson Ross and William Winslade. "Families began to beg that [terminally ill] patients not be given dialysis, though these requests were seldom honored, whether they came from the family or the patients themselves." By 1980 more than sixty thousand patients were receiving dialysis in the United States at an annual cost sixteen times higher than Magneson projected only eight years earlier. Both figures have continued to far exceed predictions, contributing to the insolvency of the Medicare system.[14]

One example of how the kidney dialysis story affects individual treatment decisions was related in 1987 by Surgeon General C. Everett Koop, a devout Christian and renowned physician who had collaborated with apologist Francis Schaeffer in raising right-to-life issues within the evangelical Protestant community a decade earlier. The high cost of health care was then becoming a major concern in Washington. Koop, himself a senior citizen, told the story of his eighty-seven-year-old mother's death from uterine cancer. "She was in a coma, during which people actually asked me if I wanted to put her on dialysis. That would have been ridiculous for personal, spiritual, and economic reasons," he commented. Speculating about a similar choice that might face him, Koop added, "If my kidney shut down tomorrow, let's say, after a severe infection, I don't know how long I would want to be on dialysis. It would be foolish and a waste of resources for me to have a kidney transplant at my age. I would probably opt to clean up my affairs, say good-bye to my family, and drift out in uremia."[15] That choice has not yet confronted Koop, however, and he lived on to champion the Clinton administration's failed 1994 health-care reforms, which would have inevitably led to some rationing of treatment by imposing a global budget on health-care spending.

Cultural Aspects

As concerns over the public cost and patient control of life-sustaining treatment intensified during the 1970s and 1980s, Americans increasingly claimed a right to refuse such treatment and thereby to allow the dying process to proceed without medical intervention. Quinlan's plight represented a particularly compelling case that captured the nation's attention. The story told by Koop about his mother's death without dialysis was probably more representative of what was occurring in the United States and illustrates that the right-to-die movement (broadly defined to include those claiming personal and familial rights to refuse medical treatment that merely prolongs the dying process) drew support from Christians. While it is a vanity to throw the gift of life back in the face of God, Ramsey observed in this context, it is also a vanity to clutch too strongly to temporal life when the greater gift of eternal life awaits.[16]

Francis Schaeffer's death offered another example. The decision came on Easter Sunday of 1984. Schaeffer, a world-famous champion of the Christian right-to-life movement, had been dying from cancer for several years. As his condition worsened, he had moved with his wife, Edith, from their long-time residence in Switzerland to a new home near the Mayo Clinic in Minnesota. Extensive treatment allowed him to write and lecture to very near the end. But when final treatment decisions had to be made, Schaeffer was no longer able to make them himself. A team of Mayo doctors called his wife aside, and the leading consultant asked her, "He is dying of the advancing cancer. Do you want him to be placed in intensive care on machines? Now is the time to make the choice."

Edith Schaeffer knew precisely what she and her husband wanted. "You men have already done great things during these last years and these last few weeks. You fought for life and gave Fran time to complete an amazing amount of work," she replied, reflecting on the distinction that her husband had drawn between preserving life at all costs and prolonging death. The time had come for her husband to go home, surrounded by the familiar things he loved. Soon he was home, in a bedroom with a large window overlooking colorful flowers put there each day in pots because it was still winter in Minnesota. Treasured memorabilia from Switzerland filled the room, and his favorite music by the masters flooded the air. Ten days after leaving the hospital, amid the sounds of Handel's *Messiah*, Francis Schaeffer died without the treatment that could have prolonged his death. His wife had made their home into a hospice.[17]

Perhaps the most tangible evidence of the right-to-die movement's social impact on America was the rapid spread of hospices, a development that had distinctly Christian roots in the person of Anglican physician Cicely Saunders of London. Saunders had studied under Oxford scholar C. S. Lewis before World War II and traveled in Christian circles that included Dorothy L. Sayers. While serving as a nurse during the war and a social worker immediately after it, Saunders became interested in the plight of the terminally ill, and serving them became her ministry. She attended medical school to learn ways to control the pain of dying cancer patients, and in 1967 she founded the first modern hospice, St. Christopher's, as a place where she could apply that knowledge to the terminally ill.[18] The hospice is now a part of Britain's public health service, and hundreds of people still go to St. Christopher's each year to die with the latest palliative care but without other treatment. Similar institutions exist throughout Great Britain.

The hospice concept first came to the United States in the mid-1970s, just as the right-to-die movement began to grow. The timing was perfect. Hospices provided a way for terminally ill patients to access the latest pain therapy in settings that, unlike hospitals or nursing homes, did not push life-sustaining medical treatments on them. Within a decade after the first American hospice opened in 1974, over 1,000 of them had sprung up across the country, serving a total of about 150,000 patients annually. Approximately one-third of these programs were sponsored by religious organizations, and nearly all offered a spiritual component to patients who wanted it. Clearly many Americans welcomed this way of dying without life-support technology, though even many hospice patients do not reject such treatment until death is imminent. And the number of Americans who use hospices continued to grow, reaching 300,000 patients in 1994.[19]

Despite the rapid public acceptance of hospice care for the terminally ill, many physicians proved reluctant to acquiesce in a patient's request to terminate life-sustaining treatment, at least until they agreed that death was imminent. Retired New York University philosophy professor Sidney Hook, a renowned advocate of secular pragmatism, experienced this reluctance firsthand in 1984, when he was eighty-one years old. Weakened by a serious stroke, paralyzed on one side, tormented for days with violent hiccups that prevented digestion, and suffering from an awful pleurisy that made him feel as if he were drowning, Hook asked his physician to end all life-sustaining medical treatment. The doctor refused, saying it was premature. "A month later, I was discharged from the hospital," Hook recounted. "In six months, I regained the use of my limbs. I have resumed my writing and research." He lived for another decade, yet always maintained that the doctor should have honored his request. Using arguments reminiscent of those of David Hume, Hook argued in a widely distributed newspaper article that elderly people, who have little to gain, should be allowed to avoid the agony he suffered. The brief article generated more mail to Hook than anything that he had ever published, with almost all of the letters supporting his stance and many of them describing similar situations involving relatives.[20]

Hook's argument captured the growing sense among Americans that they should have the right to die when and how they want. Public-opinion surveys consistently found widespread support for the right to refuse life-sustaining treatment. In 1983, for example, one national poll found that 63 percent of its respondents favored a terminally ill patient's right to die, nearly double the support found in 1950. A 1990 poll conducted for *Time* placed this figure around 80 percent. In a sensational Chicago case from the 1980s, the father of a severely handicapped infant unplugged his child's hospital respirator after the physician refused to do so. Prosecutors charged the father with murder, but the grand jury refused to indict him. Despite record numbers of reported instances in recent years, there have been few convictions for euthanasia and none for stopping life-sustaining treatment.[21] Linking themselves with the more popular cause, the nation's two main pro-euthanasia organizations changed their names and missions to focus on advocating the right to refuse life-sustaining treatment, with the Euthanasia Society of America becoming the Society for the Right to Die and the Euthanasia Educational Fund becoming Concern for Dying.

Both organizations, which formally merged in the early 1990s, worked together to normalize the right to refuse life-sustaining treatment within mainstream American culture. The public tended to think of this right in connection with terminally ill or comatose patients, like Quinlan, but these groups also asserted it for persons like Dax Cowart. As a young man during the mid-1970s, Cowart suffered third-degree burns over much of his body in a propane-gas explosion. He begged his rescuers to let him die and endured months of excruciating treatment against his persistent pleas to stop it. He would have died without modern medical technology; with it, he barely survived. Like Hook, he later maintained that his health-care providers violated his right to refuse treatment. They claimed that he lacked the capacity to refuse rationally. "The physicians say that when a patient is in that much pain, he is not competent to make judgements about himself. It's the pain talking," Cowart explained. "And then when narcotics are given to subdue the pain, they say it's the narcotics talking. It's a no-win situation."[22]

Even though Cowart had a realistic chance to recover from his injuries while Quinlan did not, they were similar in that both lacked the legal capacity to refuse life-sustaining treatment. Cowart even tried to commit suicide in the hospital but was prevented by his attendants. More than anything, the fear of such helplessness to die drove the right-to-life movement. As long as people were able, they could always commit suicide; and if they were competent, they could probably manage to stop life-sustaining treatment. But what about when they lapsed into a coma like Quinlan or became hopelessly captive of their physicians like Cowart? How could they ensure their right to refuse treatment? These questions seemed to pose a legal problem and brought forth a legal response.

Legal Aspects

The evolving public sense of a right to die was reflected in the law, and the law in turn influenced public attitudes. This should be expected. In a republic such as the United States, the people ultimately determine the law by controlling who writes and interprets it. Voters directly elect legislators, who enact statutes governing procedures for terminating life support. Judges, who are either elected or chosen by elected officials, then apply these statutes and principles of constitutional and common law to individual cases. As more Americans demanded ways to protect themselves and prevent their close relatives and friends from being kept alive "like Karen Ann Quinlan," as many people expressed it at the time, judges and legislators devised appropriate mechanisms for doing so, including the judicial doctrine of substitute judgment and the legislative techniques of living wills, durable powers of attorney for health care and statutory surrogates.

The problem that the law faced was that under traditional legal principles, only competent persons possess authority to refuse life-sustaining medical treatment for themselves. In the absence of a free and informed choice to decline treatment made by the patient at a time when the relevant facts are known, the law gave the benefit of any doubt to life by presuming that the patient wants treatment. This was an acceptable assumption when medicine could do little to prolong the life of dying persons. As it became possible to prolong the dying process, however, this presumption lost validity. The *Quinlan* court reflected this when it wrote, "We have no doubt, in these unhappy circumstances, that if Karen were herself miraculously lucid for an interval (not altering the existing prognosis of the condition to which she would soon return) and perceptive of her irrecoverable condition, she could effectively decide upon discontinuance of the life support apparatus, even if it meant the prospect of natural death." And the court was so sure that she would opt to end treatment that it authorized her father to exercise this right based on his "best judgment . . . as to whether she would exercise it in these conditions."[23] In short, in the language of later court rulings that labored to clarify the *Quinlan* ruling, he was empowered to act as her surrogate decision-maker by rendering his substitute judgment as to what she would choose.

As courts in various states grappled with this issue in a stream of right-to-die cases that followed in *Quinlan*'s wake, fine differences developed. All accepted the basic but revolutionary notion that the next of kin or other fitting person could make a decision to terminate treatment on behalf of an incompetent patient. But some, like the New York Court of Appeals, maintained that "clear and convincing evidence" of the patient's wish to refuse treatment was needed to overcome the traditional presumption to the contrary. Others, like the New Jersey Supreme Court in *Quinlan*, gave more leeway to the surrogate. Regardless of their opinions on terminal health care, it became important for people to express their wishes in advance and thereby leave clear evidence as to whether they would or would not want treatment in the event that they became incompetent.

The most common vehicle for expressing these opinions became known as a living will. Using such a document, persons can direct in advance that certain treatments be discontinued or continued if they become terminally ill (or, in some states, comatose) and are then incapable of participating in treatment decisions. The first living wills date from the 1960s, shortly after life-support technology began to transform terminal health care, but they did not become commonplace until after the *Quinlan* decision legitimated their use. Almost overnight living wills came into vogue, and the legislatures of a dozen states rushed to confirm and define their authority. Legislation was not needed for courts to accept living wills as clear evidence of patient wishes (and the New Jersey legislature never involved itself in the issue after *Quinlan*), but especially in states without a court decision on point and also in those where the legislature wanted to formalize the process, statutes were passed to authorize living wills.

Shortly after the *Quinlan* decision in 1976 and partly in response to that widely publicized case, California became the first state to pass living-will legislation. The bill excited widespread comment. At the time public-opinion surveys revealed widespread support for such legislation. The twenty-six-million-member American Association for Retired Persons endorsed the concept, as did many mainline Protestant denominations. Americans United for Life (AUL), the National Right to Life Committee, Koop, and others in the prolife community tended to oppose it, with Koop and the AUL leader Edward R. Grant later warning that "passage of the living wills will make further proposals for more direct forms of euthanasia more palatable." Yet the California law expressly excluded voluntary euthanasia, and this led Ramsey to support it. On the critical issue of involuntary euthanasia, he hoped that legislation allowing people to refuse terminal health care in advance for themselves would discourage courts from giving that power to others acting on behalf of incompetent patients, a practice he saw as more akin to involuntary euthanasia. In light of the *Quinlan* decision, Ramsey commented, "Legislation is our last resort if I am correct in believing that the common law's ancient protection of life—against any private decision makers and against any consensus—is eroding."[24]

Over the following fifteen years nearly every state except New Jersey enacted some form of living-will statute. Each was the product of political compromise, and they differed in their details. Some statutes specified that the directives took effect only when death was imminent even with treatment, but others simply required that the patient be terminally ill or in a permanent vegetative state. A few states authorized the termination of extraordinary treatment, while others broadly covered all forms of terminal health care.

Major disagreements developed over the issue of tube feeding. Early living-will statutes typically did not mention tube feeding, and physicians often terminated it along with other forms of treatment. Some patients like Quinlan lived on unless tube feeding stopped. Providing food and water, even if it goes through a tube, has powerful symbolic significance for many people, however, and withholding them can cause added suffering. "For I was hungry and you gave me something to eat; I was thirsty and you gave me something to drink," Jesus said in Matthew 25:35. More critically some Christian ethicists argued that terminating nutrition and hydration *caused* rather than *allowed* death. In 1982 the Baby Doe case focused public attention on this issue for the first time. Baby Doe was born with Down's syndrome and a blocked esophagus. The blockage, which prevented food from reaching the stomach, was easily correctable with surgery. Because they did not want a Down's child, however, the parents refused to permit the operation or intravenous feeding. Hospital doctors petitioned for a court order directing treatment, but the courts refused, and Baby Doe died. No subsequently passed living-will statute in any state ignored the issue. Some expressly excluded the termination of artificially administered nutrition and hydration. Most required that individuals decide the matter for themselves by indicating their preferences on the form document.

By this time lawmakers realized that living wills were more complicated than they first thought. People differ about what types of life-sustaining treatments they want terminated and when they want it done. No statutory form can accurately reflect the wishes of everyone. Further, as Koop and Grant cautioned at the time, "No one can even theoretically contemplate all of the factors that will be operating when he becomes terminally ill."[25] Living wills communicate only a general desire to refuse life-sustaining treatment, not detailed instructions. Many individuals care deeply about these details when it comes to their own life and death. As it is said, the devil is in the details.

Although living wills remained an option in nearly every state, a second form of advance treatment directive gained popularity during the mid-1980s. Technically called a "durable power of attorney for health care," or DPA, it allowed people to designate in advance who could make treatment decisions for them if they became incapacitated. The concept originated for financial dealings, but by 1990 most states had passed statutes extending it to the health-care context. Unlike a living will, with its all-or-nothing approach to treatment, a DPA designates a decision-maker who can tailor treatment to the actual illness. Further, it works during any incapacitating illness, not just a terminal one. Nevertheless the final decisions are left to another. "Thus," prolife attorney James Bopp warned at the time, "durable power of attorney is very dangerous since there is no real limitation on the right of the third party to withdraw treatment or care when the patient is incapacitated."[26] While some limits can be included in the terms of a DPA, the best protection lies in people first choosing a decision-maker who shares their values and then communicating their wishes to that decision-maker as fully as possible. In many instances this is preferable to letting the law designate a surrogate after the patient becomes incapacitated, especially for people with a close friend or relative who would be more likely to know or carry out their wishes than their next of kin, who is the likely legal designate.

Living wills and DPAs never lived up to the expectations of their proponents. Studies indicated that although most Americans supported the concept of advance treatment directives, only 15 to 25 percent of adults completed them. Figures were much lower among minority groups and the poor. Hoping to raise these figures, Congress in 1990 passed a law requiring every hospital and nursing home in America to inform all incoming patients and residents about their rights to execute advance directives. Additional targeted interventions tested strategies to promote the use of living wills and DPAs. Nothing worked. After one particularly massive intervention among an elderly population that seemed receptive to the concept, for example, researchers found that only 35 percent of the targeted whites and 2 percent of the targeted blacks completed a living will. "Even when patients have executed a written directive, they do not discuss that directive with families, the named proxy, or health care providers," another research team found. "Even the most detailed written directive is likely to be of limited value if there has been no communication among patient, provider team, and proxy decisionmaker." Reinforcing this conclusion, other studies found that living wills had little actual impact on treatment. They had more legal form than medical substance.[27]

To clarify who possesses the right to refuse life-sustaining treatment for incompetent patients without advance treatment directives, several states have enacted statutes automatically giving this authority to the next of kin. These statutes never displace DPA decision-makers or court-appointed guardians but fill the gap where there are no such surrogates.

In 1993 the National Conference of Commissioners on Uniform State Laws combined all of these statutory developments into its Uniform Health-Care Decisions Act that is likely to become the model for future state laws in this field. Under it people can designate DPA decision-makers, execute a living will or do both—in which case the living will's instructions for health care guide the decision-maker. Significantly, those instructions include the options of either receiving or rejecting life-sustaining treatment and offer a separate choice regarding artificial nutrition and hydration. For any person without an advance treatment directive, decision-making authority passes to the next of kin, beginning with a spouse and followed by adult children, parents and adult siblings, in that order. If no such relative is available, then it goes to "an adult who has exhibited special care and concern for the patient."[28]

The Uniform Act included one key provision that wipes out the traditional legal presumption in favor of providing life-sustaining treatment. This clause directs a surrogate to make each treatment decision in accordance with the patient's instructions and wishes "to the extent known to the surrogate," but where those wishes are not known it allows that "the surrogate shall make the decision in accordance with the surrogate's determination of the patient's best interest."[29] Thus under the act a surrogate can end life-sustaining treatment, including tube feeding, for a terminally ill or comatose patient even if there is no evidence that the patient would want it ended. The *Quinlan* court had only authorized Quinlan's father to act within his "best judgment" regarding whether Quinlan would have wanted to end life support. Most courts have hesitated to move much beyond such subjective standards involving the patient's own wishes in authorizing the termination of life-sustaining treatment; the patient's right to die is at stake, not the surrogate's right to let the patient die. This was dramatically illustrated when New York's highest court rejected a mother's plea to discontinue life-prolonging therapy for her mentally retarded adult son, who had cancer. Because the patient had been retarded for life, he could never have formulated a reasoned preference regarding medical treatment. As such, the court ruled, no one could speak for him, and the legal presumption favoring treatment must control.[30] This is a prolife position, if only at the margins.

The New Jersey Supreme Court narrowly held to this line in an important ruling that clarified many of the issues left open by its *Quinlan* decision. The later case involved Claire Conroy, an eighty-four-year-old recluse who had lived alone all of her adult life until she was placed in a nursing home by her closest relative, a nephew, in 1979. By 1983 she was confined to her bed in a semifetal position. She suffered from heart disease, hypertension, diabetes, eye infections and bedsores. Her left leg was gangrenous. Conroy could not speak, properly swallow, or control her bowels. She received food and water through a relatively painless tube that extended from her nose down her throat to her stomach. Yet Conroy could move her upper body somewhat and would scratch herself and pull on her bandages. She moaned when moved or fed. Despite her greatly diminished mental capacity, her eyes sometimes followed individuals in the room, and she smiled when her hair was combed or her body rubbed.

Based on a medical diagnosis that Conroy would never improve, her nephew requested the end of tube feeding. Believing the resulting death would be painful, her doctor refused. "She's a human being," the doctor said, "and I guess she has a right to live if possible." The nephew then sought a court order to remove the feeding tube.

Conroy died before the final court ruling in 1985, but the court rendered a decision anyway to clarify the doctrine of substituted judgment as applied to incompetent patients like Conroy. According to that ruling, where "clear evidence" exists that the patient would have refused treatment, then a surrogate can make the same decision on the patient's behalf. Where there is only "some evidence" that the patient would refuse treatment, then a surrogate can end treatment only where "the burdens of the patient's continued life with the treatment outweigh the benefits of that life." If there is no indication of the patient's wishes, then the legal presumption favoring treatment prevails unless that treatment is inhumanely painful. Treatment must never be terminated from a patient who previously expressed a clear wish that it continue.[31] The delicate balance struck by the *Conroy* court between patient autonomy and the law's preference for life is typical of judicial reasoning in this field.

In its only decision involving the constitutional right of patients to refuse life-sustaining treatment, the United States Supreme Court effectively upheld the type of balance struck in *Conroy*. That 1990 decision involved the fate of Nancy Cruzan, a thirty-two-year-old Missouri woman who had remained in a coma for seven years following a car accident. Her parents sought to end tube feeding and thereby her life. Although it recognized that patients possess a right to refuse life-sustaining treatment that surrogates can exercise on their behalf, the Missouri Supreme Court refused to grant the Cruzans' request because, under its state law, "no person can assume that choice for an incompetent in the absence of the formalities required under Missouri's Living Will statutes or the clear and convincing, inherently reliable evidence absent here."[32]

On appeal the U.S. Supreme Court upheld this approach, which applied a prolife presumption favoring treatment to the case of a permanently comatose patient where no clear evidence showed that the patient would have wanted otherwise. After discussing various state-court decisions, including *Quinlan* and *Conroy*, the Supreme Court observed, "We note that many courts which have adopted some sort of substitute judgment procedure in situations like this, whether they limit consideration of evidence to the prior expressed wishes of the incompetent individual, or whether they allow more general proof of what the individual's decision would have been, require a clear and convincing standard of proof for such evidence." Rejecting the argument of Cruzan's parents that close family members should have the right to speak for an incompetent patient "even in the absence of substantive proof that their views reflect the views of the patient," the *Cruzan* court maintained that the constitution does not require "the State to repose judgment on these matters with anyone but the patient herself."[33] States may maintain that the traditional legal presumption favoring treatment can be overcome only by patients themselves, with advance treatment directives serving as one means for them to do so.

The *Cruzan* decision completed the fifteen-year-long legal revolution that began with *Quinlan* and witnessed the enactment by every state of statutes authorizing the use of advance treatment directives. In *Cruzan* the Supreme Court acknowledged the existence of a constitutionally protected liberty interest in refusing life-sustaining treatment that a surrogate could exercise on behalf of an incapacitated patient so long as sufficient evidence existed regarding the patient's wishes, and the court assumed that the right would include the termination of "lifesaving hydration and nutrition." The justices implicitly sanctioned the use of advance treatment directives.[34] By doing so the Supreme Court confirmed everything that the right-to-die movement reasonably had sought with respect to the right to refuse medical treatment. In its lead editorial the next day the *New York Times* hailed the *Cruzan* decision as "a monumental example of law adjusting to life."[35] Yet forces within the right-to-die movement drove some of its leaders beyond seeking a right to refuse treatment to demanding the options of physician-assisted suicide and euthanasia.

8

From the Right to Die
to the Right to Be Killed

Depending on one's perspective, the step from terminating life-sustaining treatment to euthanasia can be either a small shuffle or a large leap. The case of Claire Conroy, discussed in chapter seven, illustrates the point. With the aid of a nasogastric tube, Conroy barely clung to life in a near-comatose condition. Exercising her legal right to refuse tube feeding would lead to certain death by a gradual process of starvation and dehydration, which her doctor thought would be somewhat painful for her. The New Jersey Supreme Court ruled that her nephew could exercise this right on her behalf and have the tube removed. Why not give Conroy a lethal injection and let her die quickly and painlessly? How different can that be?

In part the extent of the difference between terminating treatment for Conroy and euthanizing her depends on whether one looks solely at the ends or also at the means. So far as the law is concerned, by removing her feeding tube Conroy (through her surrogate) exercised her general right to keep others from interfering with her body, with death as a foreseeable byproduct. As a means under the law, this differs dramatically from intentionally administering a fatal dose of poison, which is a classic form of murder. Using a Kantian analysis, the former act of defending personal bodily integrity could be a norm for human behavior, while the latter act of willful killing could never be one. Similarly for the doctor, stepping back to permit a terminally ill patient to die is a traditional role for physicians; administering a lethal drug has been historically taboo for them, at least since the end of antiquity. The end result from either course of action is the same, however. In both a legal and a medical sense Conroy is dead.

In thinking about whether legalized euthanasia follows logically from the right to refuse life-sustaining treatment, should one look at the similarity in the end result or the dissimilarity in the means of getting to it? There are weighty public-policy reasons for drawing a sharp line here. These are examined in chapter nine. In the abstract, however, it is somewhat like looking at an Escher drawing and trying to decide if the stairs are going up or down. If one focuses on legal rationale and medical procedure, then the stairs are going up from terminating treatment and away from euthanasia. But if one focuses on the end result, death, then the stairs are going down from terminating treatment toward euthanasia.

Slippery-Slope Arguments

The decisive first step toward normalizing voluntary euthanasia for all competent persons and involuntary euthanasia for certain incompetent ones is legalizing physician-assisted suicide, even in a limited form. This is suggested by the results of a series of three initiative elections conducted in West Coast states during the early 1990s, all of which were instigated by the pro-euthanasia Hemlock Society. The first two of these initiatives, in California and Washington State, sought to legalize physician-assisted suicide and voluntary euthanasia for competent, terminally ill adults. In both states preelection polls showed the initiatives passing by twenty or more percentage points until opponents launched media campaigns explaining the arguments against these practices, with a particular focus on the possible consequences of legalized euthanasia. Voters in both states ultimately rejected the measures by nearly identical eight-point margins. The third initiative, filed in Oregon, sought to legalize only a limited form of physician-assisted suicide. It passed by a razor-thin 51-to-49 percent margin. Many factors contributed to this outcome. Given the closeness of the vote, however, the Oregon initiative would have lost had it authorized euthanasia, yet that option must inevitably follow under the most basic notions of equal treatment for similarly situated people.

The legal strategy of first securing a limited right for physician-assisted suicide was also reflected in simultaneous court suits. After the Washington State initiative failed, its proponents filed an action in federal court to gain by judicial decree what they had lost by popular vote. But now they asked only, as the trial judge carefully described it, for "adults who are mentally competent, terminally ill, and acting under no undue influence the right to voluntarily hasten their death by taking a lethal dose of physician-prescribed drugs."[1] At the same time East Coast proponents of legalized euthanasia filed a similarly narrow suit in a New York federal court, again seeking only a right for physician-assisted suicide. In both cases the plaintiffs included terminally ill AIDS and cancer patients who claimed to suffer from unmanageable pain. A detailed analysis of these cases follows in chapter nine. Suffice it to note here that the strategy led to the first ever federal-court decisions finding a constitutional right to hasten death through lethal medication.[2]

The wedge-entering victories for physician-assisted suicide beg the question, as legal scholar Yale Kamisar put it, "How does active voluntary euthanasia differ from assisted suicide?" The former occurs when the final act, the one that actually causes death, is performed by someone other than the person who dies, he explained. The latter takes place when that final act is performed by the person who dies but someone else provides assistance, such as supplying the means of death. Although Kamisar argues that this distinction can diminish toward insignificance in actual cases, its seems to make a difference to courts and voters. For example, the Michigan Supreme Court wrote in a 1995 case involving suicide doctor Jack Kevorkian, "Recent decisions draw a distinction between active participation in suicide and involvement in the events leading up to the suicide, such as providing the means." In particular the court cited two recent cases near the borderline in which defendants were convicted of murder, which is how the law treats euthanasia. One defendant had held a terminally ill man in position during self-strangulation; another defendant had aimed the rifle for his dying wife to shoot herself. Kamisar suggests that these acts, while wrongful, differ little from assisted suicide.[3]

To drive home his point Kamisar offered a hypothetical situation that is likely to arise in the context of physician-assisted suicide. "Consider the following cases," he asks. "A competent patient who has clearly made known her wish to die accomplishes her purpose by swallowing a lethal dose of medication which her physician has (a) placed under her pillow or on the night table next to her bed; (b) placed in her hand; (c) put in her mouth. How should we characterize these cases?" Kamisar classified the first two cases as assisted suicide because "the lethal process has not yet become irreversible" by the physician's act: "The patient still has a choice." He saw the third case as "a very close call" so long as the patient could spit out the medication: "If so," Kamisar wrote, "the patient still retains the final choice."[4] In contrast, when presented with the same hypothetical cases, the chief editor of the *Journal of Law, Medicine and Ethics* characterized the second and third cases as euthanasia because the physician was an "active participant in an overt act directly causing death."[5] If these two legal experts cannot agree on the line separating physician-assisted suicide from euthanasia, then it would seem beyond the ability of jurors called upon to apply the distinction, especially since criminal defendants enjoy the benefit of any reasonable doubt.

Despite these similarities in the actual practice of the two acts, the public appears less concerned about physician-assisted suicide than about voluntary euthanasia. Kamisar attributed this in part to the historical experience that "assisted suicide is less widely condemned by the criminal law." New York Medical College psychiatry professor Herbert Hendin, an expert in the psychology of suicide, added that, as opposed to euthanasia, "assisted suicide has been seen as protecting against potential medical abuse since the final act is in the patient's hands." Whatever the reason, as Kamisar concluded from his own experience arguing the law in this field, "Assisted suicide causes less alarm than active euthanasia and generally commands more support."[6] As such physician-assisted suicide has become the opening-wedge demand for proponents of euthanasia.

In both their courtroom advocacy and their initiative campaigns, proponents arguing for the legalization of physician-assisted suicide have relied on compelling cases of competent, terminally ill patients who suffer from unmanageable pain and cry out for relief through death. From his first law-review article on the subject in 1958, Kamisar has conceded such cases but maintained that a few compelling instances do not necessarily make for good public policy. Rather he saw this as a proper place for discretion by prosecutors, juries and judges charged with enforcing a general law.[7] The drafters of the Model Penal Code recommended this approach to the law against assisted suicide (see chapter seven). Nevertheless, on close examination even these compelling cases offer thin support for physician-assisted suicide because they so rarely arise and provide no effective limiting criteria.

From an objective standpoint, for example, unmanageable pain should rarely be a factor. As a result of work by Cicely Saunders and other experts in the field of pain management, nearly all terminally ill patients can obtain sufficient relief from their physical pain. That is the purpose of hospice — and it works. Based on her years of experience treating dying patients with proper pain management at her hospice in London, Saunders reports that none of them have asked for physician-assisted suicide or euthanasia. "We never directly or indirectly suggest they should take this step, and it is worth noting that as the hospice approaches 20,000 patients who have received our care, only three inpatients and two home care patients have taken their own lives," she noted in 1995.[8] Similarly Memorial Sloan-Kettering Cancer Center pain expert Kathleen Foley found in her work that suicide requests "dissolve with adequate control of pain and other symptoms."[9] There may come a point in the dying process when adequate pain medication depresses respiration to the point where the patient dies, but this is proper medical practice, not physician-assisted suicide or euthanasia.[10] Once such patients are allowed to die with pain medication, there may be no one left who qualifies for physician-assisted suicide under the narrow criteria proposed by some of its proponents.

The real issue is not objective pain but subjective suffering and a false sense of control. Many people fear death and its approach. "When euthanasia is requested, the doctor is being asked to act upon someone else's subjective suffering—variable from person to person, eternally unverifiable, and always, in principle reversible," asserts Daniel Callahan, founding director of America's preeminent secular institution for bioethical study, the Hastings Center. "No evidence could establish that a person is not suffering the severe and unrelenting suffering he claims."

Subtly replacing "unmanageable pain" with "pain or suffering" as the qualification for physician-assisted suicide vastly increases the number of eligible candidates, especially since for some people the notion of suicide addresses the suffering that they associate with impending death. "Our culture supports the feeling that we should not tolerate situations we cannot control," Hendin notes. "Assisted suicide and euthanasia [provide] an illusion of mastery over the disease and the accompanying feelings of helplessness. Determining when death will occur becomes a way of dealing with frustration." Yet it is a false sense of control that comes from capitulation: rather than cheating death, the suicide gives up early. "Fear of uncontrolled pain is no longer a major feature of the justifying arguments" for physician-assisted suicide, Albert Jonsen of the University of Washington Medical School concludes. "Autonomy, not pain or its merciful alleviation, is the principal and even sole justifying argument."[11]

Terminal illness represents an even less effective limiting criteria for physician-assisted suicide than that offered by suffering. In this respect Kamisar asks:

Why should the non-terminal nature of a person's suffering disqualify her as a candidate for assisted suicide? If personal autonomy and the termination of suffering are the key factors fueling the right to assisted suicide, how can we exclude those with non-terminal illnesses or disabilities who might have endured greater suffering over a much longer period of time? Why should a quadriplegic or a person afflicted with severe arthritis have to continue to live what she considers an intolerable existence for a number of years? Why doesn't such a person have an equal claim—or even a greater one—to assisted suicide?[12]

The force of this reasoning was illustrated by an analogous case involving the right of Elizabeth Bouvia to refuse life-sustaining treatment. Bouvia was a mentally competent, twenty-eight-year-old paraplegic who was physically dependent on tube feeding. In 1985 she sought to end her life by refusing further tube feeding. The Los Angeles county hospital where she resided refused this request on the grounds that the state law allowing patients to refuse life-sustaining medical treatment applied only to the terminally ill, and Bouvia had a long life expectancy. The court disagreed, holding that Bouvia could not be denied an equal right to refuse life-sustaining treatment because she was not terminally ill.[13]

Current competence is hardly a more durable criterion. The series of right-to-die cases from *Quinlan* to *Cruzan* that serve as the foundation for claiming a right to physician-assisted suicide involved incompetent patients. The whole point of living wills is to allow people to exercise their right to refuse treatment after they become incompetent. Once competent patients gain a right to receive physician-assisted suicide, others will assert it on behalf of incompetent patients who had expressed a wish for it or formally requested it in their living will.

One peculiar byproduct of allowing only competent patients to commit physician-assisted suicide is its tendency to force rapidly deteriorating patients to rush into suicide before they become incompetent. How much better to enjoy life while one is competent and leave suicide until later. In 1996 the *Journal of the American Medical Association* published the living will of a physician from North Carolina. "If I ever suffer irreversible central nervous system damage to the point that I do not recognize my family, I believe it would be best for me to die," he wrote. "If physician-assisted death is legal, that is what I choose."[14] Clearly he did not expect that this choice, if then legal, would be limited to competent patients. Yet it stretches the accepted definition of physician-assisted suicide to think of this doctor committing it after he can no longer even recognize his family. He would probably need enough aid in dying to constitute euthanasia.

As narrow limits on the right to receive physician-assisted suicide must logically slip away in practice, so too will the arbitrary line between it and voluntary euthanasia. Most leading proponents of physician-assisted suicide are on record favoring euthanasia. They often equate the two acts or refer to them under a common euphemism, such as "physician-assisted death." One of them, Timothy Quill, a University of Rochester medical-school professor who instigated the lawsuit challenging New York's law against assisted suicide, signed onto a 1994 statement published in the *New England Journal of Medicine* that concludes, "To confine legalized physician-assisted death to assisted suicide unfairly discriminates against patients with unbelievable suffering who resolve to end their lives but are physically unable to do so. The method chosen is less important than the careful assessment that precedes assisted death."[15]

The same type of reasoning that logically expands the criteria of those eligible for physician-assisted suicide applies with equal force for euthanasia. Once these practices are permitted for some, they must be allowed for all who determinedly demand them, or at least who did so while competent. "Proponents of an expansive 'right to die' have had considerable success in overcoming resistance step by step, blotting out one distinction after another," Kamisar warned in 1995. "The one formidable distinction that remains is the one that is presently under attack — 'the historic divide' between the termination of medical treatment and the active intervention of another to promote or to bring about death. If . . . this bridge falls, the flimsy bridge between assisted suicide and active voluntary euthanasia seems sure to follow."[16]

Selling Death

The slippery slope from the right to refuse life-sustaining medical treatment to the legalization of euthanasia is greased by indiscriminate use of the seductive slogan "the right to die." For many Americans during the 1970s and 1980s, it solely meant the right of permanently incapacitated and terminally ill patients like Karen Ann Quinlan to refuse further life support. Perhaps it should have been called "the right to limit treatment" or "the right to let die." A recent statement by a national council for state courts explains, "There is a significant moral and legal distinction between letting die (including the use of medications to relieve suffering during the dying process) and killing (assisted suicide/euthanasia). In letting die, the cause of death is seen as the underlying disease process or trauma. In assisted suicide/euthanasia, the cause of death is seen as the inherently lethal action itself."[17] Over time, however, some Americans broadened the notion of a right to die to include suicide, physician-assisted suicide and euthanasia. More precisely it grew to mean the right to be dead or the right to be killed on demand.

This transformation did not occur overnight. In 1976 interviews and surveys of those supporting the Quinlan family's efforts to turn off their daughter's respirator found many people staunchly opposed to euthanizing her, even though they undoubtedly thought that the two acts would lead to the same end result. Even Quinlan's father could not countenance the termination of tube feeding for her, and she lived on for nine years. Yet the profound impact of the *Quinlan* case on public opinion regarding the right to refuse treatment was not lost on those who wanted more. "Supporters of assisted suicide and euthanasia have found the ultimate marketing technique to promote the normalization of assisted suicide and euthanasia: the presentation of a case history designed to show how necessary assisted suicide or euthanasia was in that particular instance," Hendin notes. "Those who participate in the death (the relatives, the euthanasia advocates, the physician) are celebrated as enhancing the dignity of the patient, who is usually presented as a heroic, fully independent figure."[18]

A growing number of books and movies feed the public interest in mercy killing, with many of them glorifying the act. In 1985, for example, NBC television correspondent Betty Rollin wrote a popular book that told how she assisted the suicide of her mother, who was slowly and painfully dying from ovarian cancer. "Mother, you don't have to. No one can force you to have chemotherapy," Rollin reported telling her mother after the cancer returned. When her mother later expressed a wish to die, Rollin supplied the method and means of suicide—a laborious process involving a doctor in the Netherlands. On the appointed day of death, family members gathered to reminisce and then watch their mother swallow the lethal drugs as directed by the Dutch physician. Rollin reported her own words of encouragement, "You're doing it, Mother. You're doing it. You're doing great"; and her mother's triumphant reply, "Remember, I am the most happy woman. And this is my wish."[19] After reading the book, *Christianity Today* editor Beth Spring asked, "Why did Rollin not spend her energies lobbying for better pain control for her mother?"[20] But it undoubtedly stirred others to embrace the legalization of physician-assisted suicide at home without the need for covert dealings abroad.

About the same time a popular made-for-television movie dramatized the sensational 1985 trial of Roswell Gilbert, a retired engineer who shot his wife to end her suffering from Alzheimer's disease. Prior to the shooting, the wife apparently asked Gilbert, "Please, let me die," but the jury found him guilty of murder. Far from condemning the act, the television version ended with a fictional scene in which Gilbert, portrayed by actor Robert Young—best known as the television father who knows best and the caring doctor Marcus Welby—urged the legalization of euthanasia. Other books and movies from the period, including *This Far and No More* and *Baby Girl Scout*, related similar stories. "Modern psychology tells us that when a person in deep distress talks about suicide, it is really a cry for help and for care," medical ethicist Joseph J. Piccione observed at the time. "When this cry comes to the ears of a society which affirms the goodness of life at all stages, the response is to control the pain and to be present and to love the person. When a society changes to a utilitarian view of life, to an ultimate kind of consumerism in which life is possessed until it is no longer enjoyable, then the cry for death will be taken at face value."[21] Rollin, Gilbert and the other self-styled heroes of this literary genre promoted the latter course, yet their stories could just as easily be presented as arguments against mercy killing.

A 1993 *New York Times Magazine* cover article about a dying Seattle woman's assisted suicide offered a case in point. The article was arranged by Ralph Mero, a Unitarian minister who heads Compassion in Dying, a Seattle-based organization that has fought to legalize mercy killing through educational campaigns, lobbying efforts and lawsuits. Members of the group also work directly with dying patients and their doctors, and Mero wanted to publicize this compassionate process in action. A woman named Louise, who was dying of a degenerative neurological disorder, had been referred to Mero by her doctor after she had expressed a desire to die. Louise then agreed to let the reporter write an article about her death. Proponents of physician-assisted suicide would consider it a puff piece, but based on his expert analysis as a leading psychiatrist and suicidologist, Hendin concluded that "the account serves equally to illustrate how assisted suicide made both life and death miserable for Louise."[22]

According to the article, "Louise had mentioned suicide periodically during her six years of illness, but the subject came into sudden focus in May during a somber visit to her doctor's office." Her symptoms had not changed, but she tells her doctor, "I'm starting to die." The doctor agrees and then does a test confirming brain deterioration. She would rapidly become mentally incapacitated, the physician warns, and die within months or weeks. "I can't do that," Louise replies, "I don't want that." The article then reports, "Her doctor, Louise thought, looked both sad and relieved. 'I know, I know,' the doctor said. 'But it has to come [from] you.' " They are both referring to suicide now, and Louise confirms, "That's what I'd like to do, go for as long as I can and then end it." The doctor tells Louise of another patient whom she has helped to die, assures Louise that she will prescribe the appropriate medication and contacts Mero about the case. "What has happened between Louise and her doctor? The doctor's quick affirmation that Louise is starting to die, even before the MRI scan confirms the decline, is disturbing," Hendin comments on the article. "The doctor's relief when Louise indicates that she is choosing

194 ─────────────────────────────────── A Different Death

suicide gives us some feeling about her attitudes toward patients in Louise's condition."

The pace of the story quickens. Mero meets with Louise and offers to be with her when she dies. She confirms that suicide is her choice and tells him that all she wants "these next few weeks is to live as peacefully as possible." Hendin interprets this as a desire to spend "what is left of her life in an environment of loving leave-taking," which sounds like the hospice ideal. "Yet," Hendin notes with respect to the rest of this account, "the closeness before dying that Louise seemed to want is lost in the flurry of activity and planning for her death as each of those involved with her dying pursues his or her own requirements." Mero and Louise's mother are busy planning the act. The reporter needs to be in Seattle at the right time. The doctor apparently wants to be out of town and also worries that Louise might wait too long. "If she loses her mind and doesn't do this, she's going into a hospital," the doctor tells the others. "But the last thing I want to do is pressure her to do this." The reporter hurries to Seattle and, after Louise speaks of wanting a week to relax with her mother, blurts out, "Your doctor feels that if you don't act by this weekend you may not be able to." When her mother confirms this prognosis and says it is all right to be afraid, Louise shoots back, "I'm not afraid. I just feel as if everyone is ganging up on me, pressuring me. I just want some time."

But Louise did not have much time. The end came quickly, though not quite so soon as the doctor predicted, and the pace of activity never slowed. Louise picks a day during the next week. Mero, the reporter, Louise's mother and a friend are there when Louise swallows the lethal dose of barbiturates; the doctor, as planned, is not. The death is slower than expected—seven hours—and Mero implies the he would have used a plastic bag if it had lasted much longer. "Everyone—Mero, the friend, the mother, the doctor, and the reporter—all become part of a network pressuring Louise to stick to her decision and to do so in a timely matter," Hendin comments. "Although the mother, friend, and physician may have acted out of good intentions in assisting suicide, none appears to have honored Louise's need for a 'peaceful' parting. None seems to have been able to accept the difficult emotions involved in loving someone who is dying and knowing there is little one can do but convey love and respect for the life that has been [and is being] lived. The effort to deal with the discomfort of Louise's situation seems to drive the others to 'do something' to eliminate the situation." If this is death with dignity and compassion in dying, as its proponents claim, then the practice falls short of the promise. "The patient, who may have said she wants to die in the hope of receiving emotional reassurance that all around her want her to live, may find that like Louise she has set in motion a process whose momentum she cannot control," Hendin concludes.

If Louise's story leaves doubts about Compassion in Dying, then Derek Humphry's life should raise concerns about the Hemlock Society. No one has done more to promote voluntary euthanasia in the United States than has Humphry, a former journalist from England whose Oregon-based Hemlock Society leads the fight for legalized mercy killing across the country. His books, which glorify mercy killing for the terminally ill and instruct readers how to commit rational suicide, have sold more than a million copies. For many people, Humphry maintained, "just knowing how to kill themselves is in itself a great comfort." In an observation that runs like a common thread though pro-euthanasia literature, he attributed this comfort to a sense of personal "control and choice" over death, or empowerment, that comes from having the right to assisted suicide or voluntary euthanasia. After reviewing that literature Hendin concluded, "The more one knows about individual cases, the more apparent it becomes that needs other than those of the patient often prevail. 'Empowerment' flows toward the relatives, the doctor who offers a speedy way out if he cannot offer a cure, or the activists who have found in death a cause that gives meaning to their lives."[23]

Humphry's preoccupation with suicide began in England on the day before Easter 1975, when he helped his first wife, Jean, to kill herself. She was painfully dying from bone cancer; he had stored up barbiturates by their mutual agreement. She insisted that he pick the time and tell her when it came. "Is this the day?" she asked one morning. "This is the day," he answered, and handed her a cup of coffee laced with the lethal drugs. Humphry married an American named Ann Wickett a year later and at her urging retold the suicide story in a sensational book, *Jean's Way,* that became an immediate bestseller in England and was later made into a movie and play. "Reading between the lines of this book," commentator Thomas W. Case noted, "I think the title might well have been 'Derek's Way.'" It certainly became Humphry's cause for life, especially after his new celebrity status led the police in England, where assisting suicide remained a serious crime, to begin investigating the case. Although the case was dropped, Humphry and Wickett moved to Los Angeles, where they founded the Hemlock Society to promote voluntary euthanasia or, as they sometimes termed it, "rational and planned self-deliverance." They devoted themselves full time to the cause, organizing chapters, lecturing widely and publishing a series of popular books on the subject, including his 1989 runaway American bestseller, *Final Exit.*

Death intervened again in 1986, when Wickett's elderly parents committed a double suicide. Both parents suffered serious health problems. According to Wickett's popular book about the episode, *Double Exit,* her father first raised the issue with her solely about himself. Humphry then got the drugs and Wickett sent them to her father. Three days before the final act, with Humphry and Wickett then staying with her parents, her mother declared, "We want to go together. We're a burden. We have no future." To this Case asks, "When did our society start considering old folks a burden rather than a source of love and wisdom?" and "Did she really want to die, or was she just afraid to live without her husband?" Humphry and Wickett agreed to help, but Humphry wanted to leave when Wickett's sister, the parents' primary caregiver, began asking questions about their role in the planned suicides. "Then go, and let's get a divorce," Wickett responded. They compromised by getting a motel room and later told police that they were in it when the deaths occurred. Actually they mixed the drugs with 7-Up and took the mixture to her parents. Wickett spoon-fed her mother in one bedroom while Humphry watched her father feed himself in another. These spouses, who did not want to live apart, died in separate rooms.

The marriage between Humphry and Wickett ended three years later, when he left after she was diagnosed with breast cancer. He retained control of the thirty-thousand-member Hemlock Society. She survived the cancer but soon resigned her position with the society and committed suicide. "Derek: There. You got what you wanted," Wickett wrote in her suicide note. "Ever since I was diagnosed as having cancer, you have done everything conceivable to precipitate my death."

Humphry denied Wickett's accusations and attributed them to her "emotional illness." They have not seemed to tarnish the reputation of the society, which has continued to flourish. Two years after Wickett's death, it finally won its first statutory victory after a string of defeats when Oregon voters narrowly approved a ballot measure to legalize physician-assisted suicide for the terminally ill. Humphry's direct role in the campaign capped his years of writing and speaking that had laid the foundation for victory. Not long after this victory, the society broadened its mission statement to support assisted suicide and voluntary euthanasia for "all mentally competent adults," not just the terminally ill and permanently incapacitated.

In Oregon as elsewhere, proponents of physician-assisted suicide and euthanasia have used compelling cases of suffering individuals to gain popular acceptance for these practices. Firsthand accounts of persons like Humphry and Rollin, who risked prosecution to help a close relative or friend die, lead some who reject these options for themselves to support their legalization for others. In 1986 a Roper poll commissioned by the Hemlock Society was one of the first national public-opinion surveys to indicate majority support for mercy killing. Nearly two-thirds of those surveyed answered yes when asked "whether or not doctors should be allowed by law to end the life of a suffering terminally ill patient if the patient requests it." The society's question incorporated compelling circumstances into its wording. Similarly phrased questions generated equally positive responses in a series of later surveys.

But a neutrally worded poll conducted for the National Hospice Organization by Gallup pollsters in 1996 confirmed the trend. Exactly half of those responding said that doctor-assisted suicide should be legal. Only one in three indicated that they would choose it for themselves if they became terminally ill, however, with this figure roughly the same for all age groups. Over one in two said that they would *never* choose that way to die.[24] This nearly even split in public opinion was apparent in the hotly contested initiative campaigns to legalize physician aid in dying during the early 1990s.

Ballot Measures and Beyond

Public opinion on an issue usually affects lawmaking indirectly through its influence on legislative and judicial decisions. Early efforts by the Hemlock Society to obtain statutory sanction for "physician aid in dying," a term that covered both physician-assisted suicide and voluntary euthanasia performed by doctors, failed in various state legislatures around the country. Growing public acceptance of such practices had little apparent impact on legislators. Everywhere medical and religious groups joined in successfully opposing the concept as unwise and unethical. At the time courts seemed to offer no better prospect for a breakthrough, so the Hemlock Society turned to the ballot box. In some states, particularly in the West, voters can directly enact statutes through the initiative and referendum process. Increasingly since about 1975, the process has become a common way to deal with controversial issues (such as immigration control and tax relief) in the Pacific coast states of California, Washington and Oregon. These three states, together with New York, were the centers of support for the Hemlock Society. The society was founded in California and later moved its headquarters to Oregon. Ballot measures offered a logical way for it to publicize, legitimize and attempt to legalize physician aid in dying.

After several false starts in which pro-euthanasia activists failed to secure enough signatures to get their measures on the ballot in California and Washington State, Humphry's Hemlock Society and Mero's Compassion in Dying managed to place the issue before Washington voters in November 1991. The result was an unusually bitter and nationally followed campaign. As late as mid-October, polls showed the initiative favored by a two-to-one margin among state residents, but this may have been due to widespread support for a provision in the measure clarifying an ambiguity in state law so that living wills could be used to direct the termination of tube feeding. At first few people seemed to notice that the measure also allowed living wills to authorize euthanasia for terminally ill or permanently comatose patients. Competent patients with six months or less to live would have a right to receive either physician-assisted suicide or euthanasia. Two doctors had to confirm patient eligibility, but neither needed to have the knowledge of psychiatry necessary to examine the patient's mental state. Further, the initiative did not require either that the doctors have a prior medical relationship with the patient or that the patient be a state resident, which raised the prospect of euthanasia clinics or spas springing up along the Pacific coast.

Opponents of the initiative launched a massive educational effort during the final weeks before the election, stressing the lack of safeguards in the measure and the risk of abuse under it. The state and national medical associations actively denounced the initiative. Washington's small Roman Catholic population, which was deeply divided on most political issues, united to oppose it, as did the evangelical community. A coordinating Anti-euthanasia Task Force organized a media campaign that featured C. Everett Koop and other respected medical leaders. Proponents countered with compelling cases of dying patents, but they were clearly on the defensive.

On the day of the vote in Washington State, opposing opinion pieces in the *New York Times* captured the essence of the state and national debate over the initiative. "For those terrified of ending their lives in pain and degradation that they lack the ability to end," former Harvard Law School dean James Vorenberg wrote, "the carefully limited and protective procedures of the Washington initiative offer promise." Yale Kamisar countered with questions:

If Washington State voters today approve what is euphemistically called the "death with dignity" or "aid in dying" referendum, . . . how many patients will choose euthanasia because they feel obligated or pressured to do so in order to relieve their relatives of financial pressures or emotional strain? How many severely ill patients will feel that to reject euthanasia, once it is acceptable and others are "doing it," would be selfish or cowardly? . . . Are these the kind of pressures we want to inflict on a very sick person?[25]

In the end Washington voters were more concerned about Kamisar's questions than Vorenberg's promise and defeated the measure, 54 percent to 46 percent.

Both sides realized that the issue would soon return. "We are grateful that the citizens of Washington state have turned back a measure that would have extended the permission to kill, but we know that this is not the end of the matter," read a statement issued by thirteen prominent national Jewish and Christian leaders. "The well-organized campaign for legalized euthanasia cruelly exploits the fear of suffering. . . . But to deal with suffering by eliminating those who suffer is an evasion of moral duty and a great wrong. We may think we care when we kill, but killing is the rejection of God's command to care and of his help in caring." For his part, Humphry vowed to continue the battle with another initiative campaign. "The great debate of the 1990s about the right to choose to die will be settled in California next year with a much more carefully framed law."[26]

The Hemlock Society did try again in 1992 with a similarly broad initiative to legalize both physician-assisted suicide and euthanasia. The battleground shifted to California, which raised the stakes and the costs, but the pattern held. Proponents again began with a huge lead in the polls. That lead gradually dwindled, however, as opponents shifted the focus from the concern for individual cases to the consequences of a general rule. The final margin of defeat was the same as in Washington State.

Opponents of the California and Washington initiatives often saw special significance in holding the line against euthanasia in such secular states. "If radical, liberal Washington State" is reluctant to embrace aid in dying, a leader of the Christian Action Council asserted, "that tells us that the center on this issue is far more reluctant than is generally perceived." Yet a poll conducted by the Harvard School of Public Health suggested that ideology and religion had little impact on a person's position on this issue. When first presented with the Washington initiative, for example, respondents favored it by about the same margin as respondents in the early Washington State polls. Roman Catholics, Protestants and Jews all supported it by roughly similar percentages; even a plurality of self-proclaimed born-again Christians said that they would vote for the initiative.[27] The same sort of education that California and Washington voters received through their initiative campaigns is needed nationwide, regardless of whether the audience is compassionate liberals, pragmatic moderates or libertarian conservatives.

Stung by these two defeats, the Hemlock Society set its sights on its home state of Oregon and in 1994 tried again with a ballot measure that appeared safer than the earlier ones. "The major concerns expressed by opponents of physician-aided dying and those who are still undecided center on the issue of safeguards. The Hemlock Society has spent more than a decade developing a system of safeguards for such legal change," the society's executive director claimed. "These safeguards are included in the Oregon Death with Dignity Act, which will appear on the ballot in November. In our view, this act is the finest, safest piece of legislation ever proposed for physician-aided death." In particular the measure only authorized physicians to prescribe lethal medication for competent Oregon residents diagnosed as having six months or less to live and expressly proscribed "lethal injection, mercy killing or active euthanasia"—all acts that the society endorses. Further, the act mandated a formalized request and informed consent process, required the "attending physician" to get a second opinion and directed patient counseling if either physician thought that the "patient may be suffering from a psychiatric or psychological disorder, or depression causing impaired judgment." According to the Hemlock Society leader, "All these measures would help to assure that physician-aided dying would be a treatment option chosen only by those who are absolutely sure of their own desires and who are acting in a truly voluntary and informed way."[28]

Opponents doubted the sincerity and efficacy of these safeguards. For example, health-law professor Alexander Morgan Capron, who helped shape national policies for the termination of life-sustaining treatment, dismissed the safeguards as meaningless. Providing a residency requirement for patients and calling the doctor an "attending physician" would not limit the practice to local citizens with an established doctor-patient relationship, he explained, because anyone can claim residency and "the 'attending' is simply the patient's current physician." Further, he noted, "The protection against mental illness or depression inducing a suicide is likewise a weak reed, not only because counsellors need not be independent of the referring physician but also because the average physician is a poor detector of mental illness and depression."

Most critically, however, Capron maintained that once physician-aided dying becomes available to some terminally ill patients, it must extend to those with longer life expectancies and who cannot self-administer drugs. "Having slid out onto the slopes," he concluded, "the citizens of Oregon may soon discover just how slippery they can be, as their law expands to encompass a range of death-dealing actions that go beyond even those that would have been authorized by the initiative measures previously rejected in California and Washington State." Admittedly Capron's general opposition to physician-assisted suicide may have colored his views on the initiative, but even the pro-euthanasia physician Sherwin Nuland, author of the award-winning *How We Die,* agreed that the Oregon initiative lacked adequate safeguards. Expanding on these concerns, the Roman Catholic archbishop of Portland added that its approval "would surely affect all the elderly by making them face the question: 'Am I, too, perhaps a burden to my family and society?' Would the 'right to die' become a duty to die?"[29]

Such questions clearly troubled Oregon voters. Polls indicated a steady decline in support for the measure as opponents explained its inherent problems. Both gubernatorial candidates, one of whom was a physician, opposed the measure, and the American Medical Association (AMA) actively campaigned against it. "We felt it was a national issue," an AMA board member explained. "We felt it was fundamentally inappropriate for physicians to be asked to participate in such acts." If the campaign had gone on a few more days, the measure probably would have lost. But on election day it passed by a 32,000 vote margin, 51 to 49 percent. On November 8, 1994, Oregon became the first jurisdiction in the Western world to pass a statute authorizing physician-aided death.[30] Even in the Netherlands the practice is tolerated under a court-made exception to the general law against killing rather than under a permissive statute.

Although medical groups and physicians took the lead in opposing the Oregon initiative, by 1994 an increasingly vocal minority within the medical community had begun to question the profession's traditional stance on the issue. This phenomenon affected the Oregon election when the state medical association decided not to take a position on the initiative and left it to the AMA to campaign against it. Interested commentators ranging from the National Right to Life Committee to Jack Kevorkian viewed this decision by the Oregon State Medical Society as a decisive factor in the election. An Oregon physician on the AMA board of trustees noticed a "schism" by age within his state medical group, with young doctors tending to support the initiative, which he blamed on "a yuppie society coming up that wants instant gratification. They're not used to stress, and do not want to face the difficulties of life. People look for an easy way out." One such young doctor, a teacher at Oregon's medical school, countered that "the practice of 'sedating to death' terminally ill patients, often without their knowledge or consent, with increasing doses of morphine is already an everyday occurrence that needs to be brought out of the closet." In that sense, he argued, the practices authorized by the initiative were nothing new and would be more honest than current procedures.[31]

The young doctor raised a significant issue. Survey data and individual accounts testify that a significant number of the physicians and nurses who care for the terminally ill occasionally help their patients to die. For example, one respected oncologist stunned a conference on death and dying by confiding that he kept count of his patients who had asked to die. "There were 127 men and women," he said, "and I saw to it that 25 of them got their wish." A 1996 survey of intensive-care nurses found that 17 percent of them reported having received requests from patients or patients' relatives for euthanasia or assisted suicide, and 16 percent reported engaging in such practices. Other surveys indicated that a rising percentage of doctors endorse the concept of physician-assisted suicide, though most respondents typically maintained that they would not per-form it themselves.[32] New York physician Timothy Quill did as much as anyone to legitimize discussion of this issue within the medical community when in 1991 he published an article in the *New England Journal of Medicine* describing his role in a particularly compelling case of physician-assisted suicide. This admission led to the filing of criminal charges, but a grand jury refused to indict him. Subsequently he became an activist for the cause, culminating in his role as the lead plaintiff in a major lawsuit challenging the constitutionality of his state's law against assisted suicide.

Quill's lawsuit, which ultimately wound its way to the United States Supreme Court, exemplified a shift in the legal battle over euthanasia rights. Prior to the mid-1990s partisans on both sides of the issue treated it as a statutory matter. Accordingly, after its victory in Oregon, the Hemlock Society unveiled plans to seek similar statutes in a half-dozen other states. But the losing side in Oregon went to court, claiming that the new Oregon statute allowing physician-assisted suicide violated the constitutional rights of terminally ill patients to due process and equal protection of the law. Meanwhile Compassion in Dying, the losing side in neighboring Washington State, went to court claiming that the old Washington statute barring physician-assisted suicide violated those same constitutional guarantees. Both challengers, who had lost at the ballot box, won in the courtroom, throwing the two statutes into legal limbo until appellate courts could resolve the conflicting trial-court rul-ings. The cases finally ended up in the U.S. Supreme Court, along with Quill's lawsuit. In the peculiarly American way of transforming moral and ethical issues into constitutional ones, the battle over euthanasia rights entered a new chapter.

9

Current Legal Issues in Physician-Assisted Suicide

"The call came in the middle of the night," said a 1988 letter to the prestigious *Journal of the American Medical Society (JAMA)* from an anonymous gynecology medical resident at a large private hospital. "A nurse informed me that a patient was having difficulty getting rest, could I please see her." The letter went on, "I grabbed the chart from the nurses station on my way to the patient's room, and the nurse gave me some hurried details: A 20-year old girl named Debbie was dying of ovarian cancer. She was having unrelenting vomiting, apparently as the result of an alcohol drip administered for sedation. Hummm, I thought, very sad.

"I entered and saw an emaciated, dark-haired woman who appeared much older than 20," the letter recounted. "She had not responded to chemotherapy and was being given supportive care only. It was a gallows scene, and cruel mockery of her youth and unfulfilled potential. Her only words to me were, 'Let's get this over with.'" The medical resident described his decision to administer a lethal dose of pain-killing morphine sulfate. "Debbie looked at the syringe, then laid her head on the pillow with her eyes open, watching what was left of the world," he recalled. "I injected the morphine intravenously and watched to see if my calculations on its effects would be correct." They were. First the patient's labored respiration calmed to normal. "Within four minutes the breathing rate slowed even more, then became irregular, then ceased," the young doctor concluded. "It's over, Debbie."[1]

But the episode was not over so far as the law was concerned, and it was just the beginning for society as a whole. Both the AMA and *JAMA* are headquartered in Chicago. After the letter was published, local prosecutors served a grand-jury subpoena on *JAMA*, demanding all its documents relating to the letter. Among other things, the prosecutors wanted to know the letter writer's identity and whether he had acted within their jurisdiction. If so, a criminal indictment for murder or assisted suicide might result. Even though the AMA opposes physician-assisted suicide and euthanasia, its journal resisted the subpoena on the basis of a state law protecting journalists from being forced to reveal their sources. Without further evidence the criminal investigation floundered. Yet the prosecutors' response foreshadowed the litigation over euthanasia and physician-assisted suicide that would arise with increasing frequency across the United States in the years to come.

Debbie's case raises many questions for prosecutors and society. Was it against the law for the doctor to relieve Debbie's suffering? And if so, should the law be enforced? As we have seen, traditional Anglo-American laws against suicide have long since been repealed throughout the United States. No American state outlaws either suicide or attempted suicide. Yet most states maintain laws against assisting others to commit suicide, and every state outlaws murder. In Debbie's case these latter laws could be invoked, but do they really apply when the victim is dying anyway and the doctor is acting to alleviate pain? And if they do apply, are they constitutional? In a variety of different contexts, courts and legislatures across America have been grappling with these questions ever since the furor over the *JAMA* letter refocused public attention on them. At the time University of Chicago physician and ethicist Mark Siegler commented about *JAMA*'s decision to publish the letter: "This could change medicine profoundly and irreversibly. It undermines the profession if the public believes that doctors have the power to kill people and occasionally do."[2] But in Debbie's case, maybe that is what the public wants.

Most of the legal, legislative and public battles over this issue center on laws against assisted suicide. Debbie's case may have gone beyond that, crossing into the realm of euthanasia and murder, but proponents of euthanasia typically frame the issue more narrowly by focusing on the right or liberty of competent, terminally ill patients to obtain medical assistance in committing suicide. "On the question you ask depends the answer you get," Justice Felix Frankfurter once observed about judicial proceedings, and on this issue proponents are most likely to get what they want by presenting compelling cases of dying patients asking their physicians for means to avoid the seemingly meaningless pain and indignity of terminal illnesses.[3] These scenarios directly implicate statutes against assisted suicide. These laws and the arguments for and against their constitutionality have become the focal point of the euthanasia debate in modern America. They merit close examination.

The Law Against Assisting Suicide

Criminal penalties have been imposed for assisting suicide from the dawn of the Anglo-American legal system. As we have seen, it was a felony to commit suicide under traditional English common law, and it always has been unlawful to aid and abet the commission of a felony. These common-law crimes were carried over to the thirteen original American colonies and remained good law after the colonies became states in 1776. Acting under the influence of Enlightenment thinking, however, most states decriminalized suicide following the American Revolution either by legislative enactment or by judicial decree. This left the prohibition against assisting suicide in doubt. Courts in some states continued to punish assisting suicide as a common-law crime, while courts in other states did not. New York became the first state to address this issue legislatively when in 1828 it enacted a criminal statute providing, "Every person deliberately assisting in the commission of self-murder shall be deemed guilty of manslaughter in the first degree."[4] As new states and territories were carved out of the American West during the mid-1800s, most of their legislatures used New York criminal law as a model in enacting statutes against assisted suicide. The legislature of the new Washington Territory did so in 1854 as part of its second legislative act. In 1997 the legacy of these two early enactments became the subject of constitutional challenges to laws against assisted suicide before the United States Supreme Court. As such they took on special significance.

The New York statute against assisted suicide has changed little over the years. In 1881 it was included in the state's new penal code even though that code expressly decriminalized suicide. New York's 1881 code was the work of David Dudley Field, a giant in American legal history. Inspired by what Napoleon had done for French law in the early 1800s, the New York legislature appointed a commission led by Field to reorganize the entire body of state civil and criminal law into a systemic code. Field and his commission labored for eighteen years, from 1847 to 1865. All or part of the resulting Field Codes were adopted in dozens of American states and by English-speaking countries and colonies throughout the world.

Regarding suicide, Field's penal code provided, "Although suicide is deemed a grave public wrong, yet from the impossibility of reaching the successful perpetrator, no forfeiture [or penalty] is imposed." With regard to assisted suicide, however, his code maintained, "Every person, who willfully, in any manner, advises, encourages, abets or assists another person in taking his own life, is guilty of aiding suicide." Further, in a section seemingly speaking to the situation of physician-assisted suicide, the code added, "Every person who willfully furnishes another person with any deadly weapon or poisonous drug, knowing that such person intended to use such weapon or drug in taking his own life, is guilty of aiding suicide, if such person thereafter employs such instrument or drug in taking his life."[5] When New York finally adopted its version of Field's penal code in 1881, it classified assisted suicide as "manslaughter in the first degree."[6] Ten other American states or territories enacted laws against assisted suicide modeled on the Field penal code, including Washington State in 1909.

By 1900 most American states had statutes or clear judicial precedent establishing assisted suicide as a crime. During that era no court apparently even considered a claim that such a statute might violate the federal constitution, much less hold that it did so. The constitutional provision now claimed by some to protect a person's right to assisted suicide, the Fourteenth Amendment (which guarantees to all U.S. citizens a certain measure of liberty and equal protection under state law), was originally ratified just as Field's commission was completing work on its penal code. There is no indication that anyone then perceived any conflict between the two. On the contrary, a state-by-state analysis conducted by a team of scholars led by Thomas J. Marzen concluded that when the Fourteenth Amendment was ratified following the Civil War, "twenty-one of the thirty-seven states, and eighteen of the thirty ratifying states prohibited assisting suicide."[7] All of these twenty-one states maintained their laws against assisting suicide in the years to come, and other states joined them by adopting the Field penal code. At the least this suggests that the legislators who ratified the Fourteenth Amendment did not see it as creating constitutional protection for assisting suicide.

New York did not again change its laws relating to suicide until 1965. At that time it deleted its statutory declaration that suicide was a "grave public wrong" but retained its law against assisted suicide. The classification of the crime was reduced, however, to second-degree manslaughter.[8] The issue was reexamined two decades later at the instigation of Governor Mario Cuomo, who appointed a blue-ribbon task force of doctors, ethicists and religious leaders to examine public policy regarding the right to die. After a ten-year investigation, in 1994 the task force concluded that patients should be allowed to refuse life-sustaining medical treatment (including artificially administered nutrition and hydration) but that physician-assisted suicide and euthanasia should not be allowed. No changes were recommended in the law against assisted suicide.[9] It remained unchanged until it was challenged in *Quill* v. *Vacco,* one of the two cases ultimately reviewed by the U.S. Supreme Court in 1997.

The appeal also involved the Washington State law against assisted suicide that was challenged in the companion case of *Compassion in Dying* v. *Washington* (which went to the High Court under the name *Washington* v. *Glucksberg*). Like most states, Washington does not outlaw suicide or attempted suicide. Rather the law at issue proscribes aiding or causing the suicide of another. It provides, "A person is guilty of promoting a suicide attempt when he knowingly causes or aids another person to attempt suicide."[10] This is a broad prohibition. Nothing in the statute focuses on physicians as actors or on the elderly, terminally ill or those in pain as recipients. It was intended to protect life and discourage suicide without regard to the victim's condition.

As noted, restrictions against assisted suicide were in place in Washington even before the region became a state. The second bill passed by the first territorial legislature for Washington in 1854 provided, "Every person deliberately assisting another in the commission of self-murder, shall be deemed guilty of manslaughter."[11] That law or one similar to it has remained on the books in Washington ever since. This long history for the Washington State bar against assisted suicide does not in and of itself make it a good rule. As the progressive jurist Oliver Wendell Holmes once observed, "It is revolting to have no better reason for a rule of law than that it was laid down in the time of Henry IV."[12] Yet Washington State's age-old stance against assisted suicide does not run afoul of this dictum. In its present form the Washington law reflects the relatively recent influence of the Model Penal Code, which was crafted by the leading criminal law scholars of the mid-twentieth century. The drafters of the Model Penal Code considered the arguments in favor of legalizing assisted suicide but ultimately decided to retain that traditional feature of Anglo-American criminal law (see chapter seven). In the past thirty years, following the publication of the Model Penal Code, eight states passed new statutes specifically outlawing assisted suicide, and eleven other states, including Washington in 1975, revised their existing statutes.

The people of Washington reconsidered their law against assisted suicide in the current medical context during the 1991 initiative campaign. At that time, after extensive public discussion of the issues on both sides of the question, state voters rejected the initiative measure that would have legalized physician-assisted suicide. A year later the Washington State legislature added a provision expressly excluding physician-assisted suicide from the practices permitted under that state's living-will statute.[13] Thus, like the New York statute, the Washington State law has been reexamined in light of recent developments in terminal health-care practices. And like such statutes throughout the country, its constitutionality was never seriously questioned until the litigation leading up to the 1997 Supreme Court ruling. That litigation and the legal arguments made by both sides in it lie at the heart of the public-policy debate over euthanasia in the United States. We shall examine it in great detail throughout this chapter.

Liberty Interests After *Casey*

Even though states have outlawed suicide practices since the beginning of the republic without engendering constitutional challenges, the recent litigation did not arise totally without legal precedent. Those precedents are important. In particular proponents of a constitutional right to physician-assisted suicide rely primarily on two earlier Supreme Court decisions. One is misapplied; the other is flawed.

The most obvious Supreme Court precedent for these constitutional challenges is the 1990 decision in *Cruzan* v. *Director*, in which the Supreme Court expressly "inferred" that a competent person has a "constitutionally protected liberty interest in refusing unwanted medical treatment." The court in *Cruzan* was grappling with the vexing issue of how to apply the due process clause of the Fourteenth Amendment to current controversies. That clause declares that states may not infringe individual liberty without due process, but it has long been interpreted to have substantive content so as to protect certain individual rights (such as the freedoms of speech and religion) from state restriction.

Yet, as the *Cruzan* decision stressed, individual liberty interests are something less than constitutional rights and must be balanced against countervailing societal interests to determine which controls. In that case societal interests in protecting life overcame the Cruzan family's liberty interest in refusing life-sustaining medical treatment on behalf of Nancy Cruzan at least to the extent that the state could demand clear and convincing evidence that Nancy would have wanted the end of treatment. Further, the majority opinion in that case clearly distinguished the situation from suicide with the observation "Moreover, the majority of States in this country have laws imposing criminal penalties on one who assists another to commit suicide. We do not think a State is required to remain neutral in the face of an informed and voluntary decision by a physically-able adult to starve to death."[14]

In the lower court challenges to the Washington State law against assisted suicide, both the trial court and the Ninth Circuit Court of Appeals twisted the *Cruzan* opinion to protect assisted suicide. For example, the trial judge wrote in her decision:

In *Cruzan,* the Supreme Court considered whether a competent person has a constitutionally protected liberty interest in refusing unwanted, life sustaining medical treatment including artificially delivered food and water essential to life. In his majority opinion, Justice Rehnquist acknowledged that this principle "may be inferred from our prior decisions," and that "the logic of the cases . . . would embrace such a liberty interest." He then assumed for the purposes of the case before the Court that the United States Constitution would grant a competent person a constitutionally protected right to refuse lifesaving hydration and nutrition.

The trial judge went on to inquire "whether a constitutional distinction can be drawn" between the situation in *Cruzan* involving the withdrawal of life-sustaining medical treatment and the case of competent, terminally ill patients who wish to hasten death with a doctor's aid. "In other words," she asked, "is there a difference for purposes of finding a Fourteenth Amendment liberty interest between refusal of unwanted treatment which will result in death and committing physician-assisted suicide in the final stage of life?" She neglected to note that the *Cruzan* decision all but answered this question in the negative in its comment approving state laws against assisted suicide.[15]

In its decision upholding the trial-court decision in *Compassion in Dying,* the Ninth Circuit also relied on the ruling in *Cruzan* without noting the Supreme Court's favorable reference to laws against assisted suicide. In particular the Ninth Circuit concluded "that *Cruzan,* by recognizing a liberty interest that includes the refusal of artificial provision of life-sustaining food and water, necessarily recognizes a liberty interest in hastening one's own death."[16] Yet the *Cruzan* decision never suggested that this applied to physician-assisted suicide or euthanasia and all but stated that it did not.

Despite ultimately ruling in favor of physician-assisted suicide on other constitutional grounds, the Second Circuit appellate panel in *Quill* v. *Vacco* disagreed with the Ninth Circuit regarding due process. In *Quill* the Second Circuit set forth the recognized tests for determining whether a claimed right (in this case, to physician-assisted suicide) constitutes a fundamental liberty under the substantive component of the due process clause of the Fourteenth Amendment. No right to any form of suicide has direct textual support in the language of the Constitution. The Constitution expressly declares a variety of individual rights, such as the right to the freedom of speech or religion, but never mentions suicide. With respect to such nontextual rights the Second Circuit quoted from established Supreme Court precedent as follows:

> Rights that have no textual support in the language of the Constitution but qualified for heightened judicial protection include fundamental liberties so "implicit in the concept of ordered liberty" that "neither liberty nor justice would exist if they were sacrificed." . . . Fundamental liberties also have been described as those that are "deeply rooted in this Nation's history and tradition."

The Second Circuit concluded that neither of these tests was satisfied regarding a right to assisted suicide. "Indeed, the very opposite is true," the *Quill* court wrote, adding:

> The Common Law of England, as received by the American colonies, prohibited suicide and attempted suicide. . . . Although neither suicide nor attempted suicide is any longer a crime in the United States, 32 states, including New York, continue to make assisted suicide an offense. . . . Clearly, no "right" to assisted suicide ever has been recognized in any state in the United States.

Based on this historical record, the Second Circuit declined the invitation to create a substantive due process right to assisted suicide. In doing so it quoted the Supreme Court's apt warning from a 1986 decision, "The Court is most vulnerable and comes nearest to illegitimacy when it deals with judge-made constitutional law having little or no cognizable roots in the language or design of the Constitution."[17] That should have settled the matter. Nothing that the Supreme Court wrote in *Cruzan* ordained a different result.

The Ninth Circuit was influenced by the later and much more troubling U.S. Supreme Court decision in *Planned Parenthood* v. *Casey*. The plurality opinion in *Casey* resulted from the labored effort by several moderate justices, most whom had been appointed by Presidents Ronald Reagan or George Bush, to find a new rationale to uphold abortion rights. Initially partisans on both sides of the abortion issue hailed *Casey* as a victory. For those opposed to abortion, it gave states greater authority to discourage abortion. For those supporting abortion rights, it nevertheless reaffirmed the core holding of *Roe* v. *Wade* that women have the ultimate right to choose an abortion at least during early stages of pregnancy.

Yet this apparent middle-of-the-road compromise incorporated a radical shift carrying profound implications. *Roe* v. *Wade* relied on an individual's so-called right to privacy, which is never expressly set forth in the Constitution but rather had been conjured up by liberal Supreme Court justices during the 1960s out of what even they described as "penumbras, formed by emanations" from the text of the Bill of Rights.[18] A series of

Republican presidents from Richard Nixon to Bush vowed to appoint federal judges who would foreswear such judicial conjuring and instead strictly construe the Constitution from its text.

In an effort to follow this approach without overturning the result in *Roe* v. *Wade*, moderate Republican appointees on the Supreme Court allied themselves with their liberal colleagues in *Casey* to shift the basis for abortion right from the implicit right of privacy to the explicit liberty interests protected by the Fourteenth Amendment. That amendment does not say anything about abortion. It was adopted following the Civil War to help ensure liberty for freed slaves. Yet to stretch its general language ("no State shall deprive any person of life, liberty, or property without due process of law") to include abortion rights, the lead opinion in *Casey*, over the howls of Justices William Rehnquist, Antonin Scalia and other dissenters, declared:

> It is . . . tempting . . . to suppose that the Due Process Clause protects only those practices, defined at the most specific level, that were protected against government interference by other rules of law when the Fourteenth Amendment was ratified. . . . But such a view would be inconsistent with our law. It is a promise of the Constitution that [that] is a realm of personal liberty which the government may not enter.[19]

With this the moderates had kicked the textual props out from under constitutional interpretation just as effectively as had their liberal predecessors.

The *Casey* decision exceeded the *Roe* decision in inviting judicial activism in the realm of individual rights. In *Casey* the plurality broadly defined the liberty protected by the Fourteenth Amendment to include those matters "involving the most intimate and personal choices a person may make in a lifetime, choices central to personal dignity and autonomy." The justices obviously wrote this with abortion in mind, but by trying to state a general principle, they created a limitless category. They only made matters worse by adding, "At the heart of liberty is the right to define one's own concept of existence, of meaning, of the universe, and of the mystery of human life."[20] This would make fine Fourth-of-July oratory, but it provides no basis for defining the limits of governmental power, which is the function of the Constitution. Undoubtedly for Charles Manson, murder was an intimate and personal choice central to his autonomy, just as taking LSD defined Timothy Leary's concept of meaning and the universe, but surely this does not suggest that the government could not outlaw such activities.

Legal commentators from across the spectrum of opinion have recognized the problems with this approach. In his dissent Justice Scalia warned that under the plurality's reasoning in *Casey*, constitutionally protected liberty interests could include "homosexual sodomy, polygamy, adult incest, and suicide." Conservative Christian legal commentator Charles Colson responded that the dissenting justice's "list is too short: The truth is that *liberty* could now encompass virtually any decision by which an individual expresses his sense of 'selfhood.'" He added, "The Court endorsed a philosophy of the autonomous individual defining his or her own reality in complete isolation—even to the point of taking the life of another person. But if autonomous, personal choices may not be circumscribed in any way by the state, the rule of law is impossible."

University of Texas law professor John Robertson was equally harsh. He compared the task of constitutional interpretation under *Casey* to playing "tennis without a net" and saw it as a continuation of the earlier right-to-privacy rulings. "The whole project of constitutionalizing the resolution of a serious public policy dispute presupposes that the text of the Constitution and the history of its interpretation play a significant, indeed a definite, role in how that dispute is resolved," Robertson wrote regarding the physician-assisted suicide cases. "But the decisional privacy cases of the past thirty years have not been decided in that way at all. What has happened instead is that the whole process of constitutionalizing has been debased in ways that cry out for correction."[21]

Predictions of Scalia, Colson, Robertson and others that the *Casey* rationale would lead judges to embrace a right to physician-assisted suicide and more came true in *Compassion in Dying* v. *Washington*. The trial-court judge started this ball rolling by basing her analysis of the Washington State law against assisted suicide squarely on the *Casey* court's claim that "the right to define one's own conception of existence, or meaning" lies at the heart of the liberty interests protected by the Fourteenth Amendment. As this was not enough to guarantee her result, the judge proceeded to exaggerate the weight of the liberty interest at stake. This is apparent from examining how she defined the relevant liberty interest. She stated:

> There is no more profoundly personal decision, nor one which is closer to the heart of personal liberty, than the choice which a terminally ill person makes to end his or her suffering and hasten an inevitable death.[22]

Even assuming that this is true—and it appears to be a subjective observation (for example, some might view the decision to kill others as more profoundly personal and yet courts have upheld the constitutionality of compulsory military service)—it does not necessarily answer the question of whether a terminally ill person has a profound personal liberty interest in committing physician-assisted suicide.

To make the connection between a personal right to commit suicide, which is the subject of the judge's premise, and a right to commit physician-assisted suicide, which is the subject of her conclusion, evidence must show that persons need physician assistance to exercise their liberty interest in hastening death. If that evidence shows that a terminally ill person can easily hasten death without a physician's assistance, such as by using traditional suicide methods or drug doses readily available in the popular literature, then a law against physician-assisted suicide should not significantly burden the person's liberty interest. At most the law would discourage persons from choosing death, which the state is clearly free to do. Alternately, if the evidence shows that many of the persons who need a physician's assistance to commit suicide are physically unable to self-administer drugs and therefore require a lethal injection or some other form of euthanasia, then the trial court's limited holding that allowed "terminally ill adult patients to hasten death by prescribing suitable medication for self-administration by the patient"[23] would not significantly advance this liberty interest. In either event the decision would lack justification. Yet the evidence necessary to connect a terminally ill person's liberty interest in hastening death with physician-assisted suicide is absent, probably because it does not exist. Her decision jumps from one to the other.

In the initial appeal of this ruling to a three-judge Ninth Circuit panel, Judge John Noonan (writing for the majority) attempted to correct the trial court's flawed reasoning. Asserting that any effort to base a limited right to physician-assisted suicide for the terminally ill on the general language in *Casey* regarding individual autonomy proved too much and hence proved nothing all, Noonan astutely observed:

> If at the heart of the liberty protected by the Fourteenth Amendment is this uncurtailable ability to believe and to act on one's deepest beliefs about life, the right to suicide and the right to assistance in suicide are the prerogative of at least every sane adult. The attempt to restrict such rights to the terminally ill is illusory. If such liberty exists in this context, as Casey asserted in the context of reproductive rights, every man and woman in the United States must enjoy it. . . . The conclusion is a reductio ad absurdum.[24]

Judge Noonan's logic presumed that courts would not stretch *Casey* to its logical conclusion of establishing a universal right to assisted suicide. Yet that was precisely where the Ninth Circuit seemed headed.

Following Judge Noonan's decision upholding the Washington State law against assisted suicide, the entire Ninth Circuit took the unusual step of reconsidering the case *en banc*. In a split decision a majority of the twelve-judge reviewing court followed the trial court in relying on *Casey*. "The district judge in this case found the [Supreme] Court's reasoning in *Casey* 'highly instructive' and 'almost prescriptive' for determining 'what liberty interest may inhere in a terminally ill person's choice to commit suicide,'" the majority declared. "We agree. Like the decision of whether or not to have an abortion, the decision how and when to die is one of 'the most intimate and personal choices a person may make in a lifetime,' a choice 'central to personal dignity and autonomy.' " Thus, they concluded, "a statute that prohibits doctors from aiding terminally ill persons to hasten their deaths by providing them with prescription medications unconstitutionally *burdens* the liberty interests of the terminally ill."[25]

All the arguments that Judge Noonan and others leveled against the trial court decision also apply to the final Ninth Circuit decision. Yet in large part it represents a logical result of following the flawed definition of constitutionally protected liberty asserted in *Casey*. The Second Circuit in *Quill* v. *Vacco* managed to avoid this pitfall (only to fall in another) by qualifying the broad principle of *Casey* with earlier Supreme Court pronouncements suggesting that there must at least be historical support for judge-made constitutional rights. To expand on Robertson's analogy, if giving constitutional status to individual rights not mentioned in the text of the Constitution is like playing tennis without a net, then doing so without either a textual or a historical basis is like doing so without a net and lines. Judges become free to constitutionalize whatever strikes their fancy as being intimate and personal. This is more appropriate for gods and philosopher kings than for life-tenure, appointed judges in a democracy.

Although the Ninth Circuit relied primarily on *Casey* in finding a substantive right for assisted suicide within the due process clause, it vainly tried to concoct some historical authority to give added legitimacy to its holding. Its opinion reversed Judge Noonan's panel decision that, like the Second Circuit, found "that 'a constitutional right to aid in killing oneself' was 'unknown to the past.'" Responding expressly to this finding and implicitly to the Second Circuit, both of which look to American history to determine if a right to assisted suicide might be such a part as our cultural tradition as to be implicit within our Constitution, the Ninth Circuit opinion stated that "our inquiry is not so narrow. Nor is our conclusion so facile. The relevant historical record is far more checkered than the [panel] majority would have us believe."[26] The court could find both Greco-Roman and Enlightenment acceptance of suicide but went far afield in trying to find Judeo-Christian roots for the practice. The result is a sad commentary of judicial misuse of history.

We discussed the judicial mishandling of this history in our introduction and tried to set the record straight in chapters one through four. Now, to put the matter in context of the Ninth Circuit's ruling, we reiterate that there was no moral acceptance of suicide within the historical Judeo-Christian tradition, and this is especially true for the early Christian church. No recognized historian has documented instances of early Christian church leaders condoning suicide, as that term is commonly understood as the voluntary taking of one's own life. To the contrary, they uniformly condemned self-murder.

Even the Ninth Circuit opinion recognized that the influential bishop and Christian scholar Augustine (354-430) denounced suicide as a "detestable and damnable wickedness" and that thereafter "the Christian view that suicide was in all cases a sin and crime held sway for 1,000 years," but it suggested that Augustine's opposition to a previously tolerated practice turned the Christian church against it.[27] Yet the historical record shows continued church opposition to suicide from the earliest days. Regarding the pre-Augustinian period, one Jesuit scholar recently observed:

> The early orthodox Christian church issued few official moral condemnations of suicide, or of any action for that matter, even though the great proportion of early Christian writers condemned deliberate self-killing vigorously. The lack of "official" condemnations of suicide, however, does not mean that the early Church endorsed or permitted it. The early Church produced many theological and moral writings against suicide, and these views later came to be expressed in councillor and juridical documents after Constantine granted legal status to the Church.[28]

In deeds as well as words, early Christians rejected suicide and euthanasia (see chapters two through four).

In contrast to the consistent historical record of early church opposition to suicide, the Ninth Circuit writes, "The early Christians saw death as an escape from the tribulations of a fallen existence and as the doorway to heaven."[29] In particular the court cites the early Christian martyrs, who died rather than renounce their faith, as examples of the acceptance of suicide among early Christians and quotes from a two-hundred-year-old history of the Roman Empire to describe the nature and extent of the practice. Yet submitting to forced martyrdom is not equivalent to modern practices of voluntary suicide, and modern scholarship suggests that earlier historians grossly exaggerated both the number of early Christian martyrs and the eagerness with which they met their fate. One of the most famous early Christian martyrs, Justin, preached and taught against suicide.

The Ninth Circuit also turned to the Bible to support its position. Here too, however, its reliance is misplaced. The court wrote:

The stories of four suicides are noted in the Old Testament—Samson, Saul, Abimlech [sic], and Achitophel [sic]—and none is treated as an act worthy of censure. In the New Testament, the suicide of Judas Iscariot is not treated as a further sin, rather as an act of repentance.[30] There are other examples of suicide recorded in the Bible but many more examples of faithful Jews and Christians resisting the temptation to commit suicide. Of the five biblical suicides identified by the Ninth Circuit, all but Samson were by persons alienated from God, and Samson died as a captured warrior in an act intended to kill Israel's enemies. These persons are not models for Jewish or Christian behavior, and their suicides underscored their depravity. There is no biblical acceptance of suicide. In asserting otherwise the Ninth Circuit relied on the writings about suicide of Alfred Alvarez and Émile Durkheim, neither of whom was either a theologian or a historian. Their writings do not provide historical support for early Christian acceptance of the type of suicide at issue in this case.

Further, the test that the Ninth Circuit apparently is trying to satisfy with its analysis of historical attitudes toward suicide describes fundamental liberties as those that are "deeply rooted in this Nation's history and tradition."[31] By its terms this test looks only to American history and tradition, which is what the Second Circuit did in finding no right to assisted suicide under the due process clause. The same result should follow for the Washington State law against assisting suicide at issue in the Ninth Circuit case. If the history and tradition of this statute are any guide, they strongly support upholding it as constitutional. Stripped of any historical support for its holding, the Ninth Circuit decision is left resting on the rotten foundation of *Casey* and its standardless claim to constitutionalize intimate and personal decisions. Yet even this reliance is misplaced, for even *Casey* does not support a right to physician-assisted suicide for the terminally ill.

Countervailing State Interests

Under *Casey* and *Cruzan,* as the Ninth Circuit concedes, finding a liberty interest in assisted suicide does not end the constitutional inquiry. Individual liberty interests are something less than constitutional rights, the Supreme Court has stressed, and must be balanced against societal interests to determine which controls. The state, in its defense of the statute against assisted suicide, raised a variety of countervailing societal interests in support of the law, two of which have proved particularly significant in persuading policy makers of the need for such statutes: discouraging suicide generally and protecting the elderly and infirm.

"During the course of this litigation, the state has relied on its interest in the prevention of suicide as its primary justification for its statute," the Ninth Circuit commented in its decision. "As the state notes, in 1991, suicide was the second leading cause of death after accidents for the age groups 15-19, 20-24, and 25-34 and one of the top five causes of death for age groups 35-44 and 45-54. These figures are indeed distressing."[32] Yet even this recitation does not capture the awful force of the state's suicide statistics.

Suicide is a major social concern in both the state of Washington and the country as a whole. It now ranks as one of the top causes of death in the United States, with over 25,000 cases reported annually. In Washington State suicide takes twice as many lives annually as all infectious diseases and over two-thirds as many deaths as automobile accidents. The state vigorously seeks to combat both of these other causes of death and logically attempts to discourage suicide as well. In the United States suicide by young people has increased dramatically in recent years, with persons aged 15 to 24 years now committing about 20 percent of all suicides. The number of suicides by persons in that adolescent and young adult age group is nearly as high as that by all Americans over 65 years of age, who are the typical target population for physician-assisted suicide. Further, there are twice as many suicides by persons aged 25 to 44 as by senior citizens. These figures are even more dramatic among some ethnic groups, such as Native Americans, where the suicide rate is over twice as high for youth as for adults and four times higher for youth than for senior citizens. In Washington State the relative youth of suicide victims is suggested by the state statistic that the average number of years lost by each suicide is over twice that lost by each cancer death.

Advocates of physician-assisted suicide tend to focus on cases involving the elderly, particularly by those who are terminally ill. The issue is far from simple even in those most compelling cases, however. A leading suicide researcher, David Clark, observes that "the major studies all agree in showing that the fraction of suicide victims struggling with terminal illness at the time of death is in the range of 2% to 4%." Even among senior citizens, Clark adds, most dying by suicide "were in relatively good health."[33] Further, University of Rochester geriatric psychiatrists Yeates Conwell and Eric Caine note that "90 to 100 percent of [suicide] victims die while they have a diagnosable psychiatric illness, an observation that is equally true in suicides among the elderly." Such illness typically involves treatable depression. In this respect Conwell and Caine warn that

many doctors on the front lines, who would be responsible for implementing any policy that allowed assisted suicide, are ill equipped to assess the presence and effect of depressive illness in older patients. In the absence of that sophisticated understanding, the determination of a suicidal patient's "rationality" can be no more than speculation, subject to the influence of personal biases about aging, old age, and the psychological effects of chronic disease.[34]

This observation implicates the ruling in *Compassion in Dying*, which on its face would extend the authority to prescribe lethal drugs to all physicians, not just to those trained in geriatric psychiatry.

In addressing the state's first interest of preventing suicide, the trial-court judge noted, "The State's interest in preventing suicide by prohibiting any manner of assisted suicide in actuality arises out of its apprehension of the 'slippery slope' problem. The State is concerned that allowing any exception to a total ban will encourage the gradual development of a more permissive attitude toward suicide." After conceding "the general validity" of this concern, the court dismissed it by stating, "The court has no doubt that the legislature can devise regulations which will define the appropriate boundaries of physician-assisted suicide for terminally ill individuals, and at the same time give due recognition to the important public policy concerns regarding the prevention of suicide."[35] This bald affirmation, which presumes Solomonic wisdom for the part-time state legislators of Washington, provides a peculiar basis for voiding an earlier enactment by those same solons.

More critically, the trial court incorrectly characterizes the real slippery slope here. It is not that a narrow exception to the law against assisted suicide will encourage greater acceptance of suicide but how constitutionally to limit that exception and thereby keep from broadly authorizing the practice of assisted suicide and euthanasia. It is not as easy as the trial court suggested. Admittedly, the line between physician-assisted suicide and the termination of life-sustaining treatment is not always a neat one. No line is, and that creates the slippery slope. Yet the line that the trial judge drew between the terminally ill, whom she would give a right to assisted suicide, and other seriously ill persons, whose rights she did not address, is a particularly difficult one to maintain. The Ninth Circuit as much as conceded this point when, in its decision affirming the trial court ruling, it noted, "Our conclusion is strongly influenced by, but not limited to, the plight of mentally competent, terminally ill adults. We are influenced as well by the plight of others, such as those whose existence is reduced to a vegetative state."[36] The slippery slope beckons.

The plaintiffs in *Compassion in Dying* v. *Washington* only claimed a right to physician-assisted suicide, in which the victim performs the final act. The Ninth Circuit decision, however, also left open the door for euthanasia, in which the physician performs the final act. "While we place euthanasia," the court noted, "on the opposite side of the constitutional line we draw for purposes of this case, we do not intimate any view as to the constitutional or legal implications of the practice."[37] This comment reflected a realistic view of the decision's inevitable consequences. Washington and every other state condemn euthanasia as murder. Yet some otherwise competent, terminally ill persons physically are unable to perform a final, death-causing act. If physician-assisted suicide is a constitutional right for such people, then how can they be denied a right to demand death when and how they choose because they cannot perform the final act by themselves?

Similarly, even though the plaintiffs limited their claims to the rights of adults, why should minors be excluded? A Florida court recently ruled that a mentally competent minor had the same right to refuse life-sustaining medical treatment as an adult.[38] A similar extension will inevitable follow for a liberty interest in physician-assisted suicide. The Ninth Circuit decision in *Compassion in Dying* v. *Washington* slid far beyond this point when it noted, "Finally, we should make it clear that a decision of a duly appointed surrogate decision maker is for all legal purposes the decision of the patient himself."[39] Under this principle the parent or other surrogate of a person who is incompetent to make decisions due to age or infirmity could authorize the physician-assisted death of that person. There is no certain end to this downward slide. Granting constitutional protection to a terminally ill patient's liberty interest in physician-assisted suicide will initiate an avalanche of predictable equal-protection challenges destined to broaden the impact of the initial ruling.

This process is illustrated in the famous pair of U.S. Supreme Court decisions protecting an individual's constitutional right to obtain contraceptive devices. In 1965 the first decision found that married persons have a constitutionally protected privacy right to obtain contraceptives despite a state law outlawing such devices. When the state then reenacted the restriction for unmarried persons, the Supreme Court struck it down on equal-protection grounds.[40] Once a constitutional right to assisted suicide is recognized, even in a limited form, equal-protection analysis will surely extend it beyond all bounds. Suicide will inevitably become more common if the practice of physician-assisted suicide is legalized. This is evident from the Dutch experience, which we describe in chapter ten.

Proponents of legalization counter that even though the number of suicides may increase, not all suicides are bad. In particular, they contend, suicide may constitute a dignified, rational, pragmatic way to deal with terminal or degenerative illness. This view was reflected in the Ninth

Circuit opinion. "While the state has a legitimate interest in preventing suicide in general, that interest, like the state's interest in preserving life, is substantially diminished in the case of terminally ill, competent adults who wish to die," the majority wrote. "In the case of a terminally ill adult who ends his life in the final stages of an incurable and painful degenerative disease, in order to avoid debilitating pain and a humiliating death, the decision to commit suicide is not senseless."[41] However, few if any patients fit this description. Modern pain management techniques, such as are readily available through hospices and hospitals, can prevent debilitating pain and enhance life quality for dying patients in nearly all cases, though there may come a point where the appropriate medication may contribute to death. This is common medical practice everywhere in the United States, and no legal change is required for it to continue. Unrealistic hypothetical cases or isolated tragic examples should not control overall public policy, especially given the weighty societal interest in discouraging suicide generally. Individual physicians can and do deal with the exceptional cases as they arise.[42]

Beyond the general societal interest in discouraging suicide through laws against assisting the act, there lies a particularly compelling reason for specifically barring physician-assisted suicide. "In upholding Washington's statute, the majority of the three-judge panel relied heavily on the state's interest in preventing the exercise of undue, arbitrary or unfair influences over the individual's decision to end his life," the Second Circuit majority acknowledged. "There is a far more serious concern regarding third parties that we must consider—one not even mentioned by the majority in the panel opinion. That concern is the fear that infirm, elderly persons will come under undue pressure to end their lives from callous, financially burdened, or self-interested relatives, or others who have influence over them. The risk of undue influence is real—and it exists today."[43]

There is good reason for concern about the risk of unintended undue influence, especially when one is dealing with the elderly. "Ageism," Yale Kamisar writes, "may manifest itself in a failure to recognize treatable depression, the view that an elderly person's desire to commit suicide is more 'rational' than a younger person's would be, or, more generally, the attitude that the elder has every reason to be depressed." That could lend to easy acceptance of physician-assisted suicide for physically ill senior citizens without sufficient study of their motives. In a leading book on suicide, George Colt observes, "Although we shrink from the idea of elderly suicide and euthanasia, we encourage it by our neglect and indifference." Sociologist Menno Boldt states, "Suicidal persons are succumbing to what they experience as an overpowering and unrelenting coercion in their environment to cease living." That sense of coercion could only be increased by condoning physician-assisted suicide. In her analysis of the subject, ethicist Sissela Bok concluded that "the possibility of abuses and errors" in the practice of euthanasia, especially in cases involving the "senile" and the "powerless," outweigh the potential benefit of the practice for some compelling cases.[44]

On the testimony of such experts, state legislators reasonably could find that this coercion might intensify in a state that sanctions physician-assisted suicide. They could conclude that if physician-assisted suicide is legal, freely discussed and openly practiced, then more people, especially the infirm and the elderly, will see it as the socially accepted way to save society, their family and themselves from the burdens of old age and serious illness. Even if legislators could not prove that legalizing physician-assisted suicide for the terminally ill would unduly encourage these and other people to take their own lives and increase the likelihood of duress and mistake in this area, they have a reasonable basis for outlawing the procedure. Given the gravity of this concern, it should sustain the statute.

Further, where undue influence from third parties is not present, those diagnosed with terminal illness might choose physician-assisted suicide not because they want to die but because they fear either the pain or the loss of control that may come at a later stage of illness. Should physician-assisted suicide be condoned, then a patient might accept that route without fully exploring the alternatives of pain management, which can be effective in nearly every case, and advance treatment directives, which can protect a person's control over future life-sustaining treatment. A Hastings Center report on this subject dismissed the argument for assisted suicide as a means to avoid a painful death by observing, "If medicine's capacity for relieving pain and suffering were fully tapped, there would probably be no significant foundation for this argument." It has endorsed advance treatment directives as preferable means to preserve self-determination over terminal health-care decisions.[45]

By adopting the name "Compassion in Dying" the organization promoting physician-assisted suicide in Washington State professed a sincere concern for the rights and interests of the infirm. But legislators reasonably could believe that on balance a law against assisted suicide helps the terminally ill much more than it hurts them. It protects them from the duress and mistakes that could lead vulnerable human beings to premature death. At the least this is a determination—a balancing of societal benefits and burdens—that is best left to the legislative process rather than to judicial fiat.

Equal Protection for Unequal Acts

The Fourteenth Amendment not only protects liberty interests but also guarantees equal protection under law for similarly situated people. This provides a second basis for challenging the constitutionality of laws against assisted suicide under the curious rationale that terminally ill persons who do not require life-sustaining treatment should have the same right to die as those persons who do require such treatment. Persons in the latter group can hasten their death by directing their physician to withhold or withdraw treatment, it is argued, but those in the former group need a physician's aid in dying to achieve the same result. It is somewhat like saying that rich people can buy a yacht but poor persons need aid in buying — and the state should equalize the two groups. Having found that laws against assisted suicide unconstitutionally restricted the liberty interests of terminally ill persons, the Ninth Circuit never reached the equal protection issue. Having found no such constitutional violation, however, the Second Circuit turned to the equal protection challenge.

The level of judicial scrutiny afforded an equal-protection claim depends on the nature of the challenged distinction. For example, any governmental action treating persons differently because of their race or religion is subject to strict scrutiny and requires a compelling state interest that cannot be addressed by any less restrictive means. In contrast, governmental distinctions based on social categories need only have some rational relationship to a legitimate state purpose. For instance, the government may choose to build highways instead of subways (even though the decision favors car owners over those who rely on mass transit) so long as it rationally advances some legitimate state interest, such as improving transportation.

In *Quill* v. *Vacco* the Second Circuit correctly identified the lower level, "rational basis scrutiny," as the appropriate standard of judicial review under the equal protection clause of the Fourteenth Amendment for statutes outlawing assisting suicide, but then proceeded to find equality where there is none. After setting forth the various standards of equal protection scrutiny, the panel explained:

> Indeed, applying the foregoing principles to the New York statutes criminalizing assisted suicide, it seems clear that: 1) the statutes in question fall within the category of social welfare legislation and therefore are subject to rational basis scrutiny upon judicial review; 2) New York law does not treat equally all competent persons who are in the final stages of fatal illness and wish to hasten their deaths; 3) the distinctions made by New York law with regard to such person do not further any legitimate state purpose; and 4) accordingly, to the extent

that the statutes in question prohibit persons in final stages of terminal illness from having assistance in ending their lives by the use of self-administered, prescribed drugs, the statutes lack any rational basis and are violative of the Equal Protection Clause.[46]

In particular, on the crucial issue of equating types of terminally ill persons, the court wrote that "those in the final stages of terminal illness who are on life-support systems are allowed to hasten their deaths by directing the removal of such systems; but those who are similarly situated, except for the previous attachment of life-sustaining equipment, are not allowed to hasten death by self-administering prescription drugs."[47] Yet the court's opinion offered no medical, ethical or historical authority—no authority of any type other than its own reasoning from prior decisions—for equating the two groups.

The absence of authority on this point is striking because it deals with one of the central issues in Western medical ethics. Although some medical ethicists and physicians agree with the court's position, the great weight of both secular and religious authority maintains that there is a fundamental difference between allowing patients to die by withholding or withdrawing medical treatment and hastening death though a medical intervention. This distinction dates at least as far back in Western medical tradition as the Hippocratic Oath, which is attributed to the ancient Greek physician Hippocrates and is still widely recognized. That oath imposes no ethical obligation to treat the terminally ill but enjoins physicians from ever assisting in a person's suicide or euthanasia.

The major Anglo-American medical associations vigorously maintain this distinction. Thus, for example, the American Medical Association's current Code of Medical Ethics condemns physician-assisted suicide as "fundamentally inconsistent with the physician's professional role" and states that it "must be distinguished from withholding or withdrawing life-sustaining treatment, in which the patient's death occurs because the patient or the patient's proxy, in consultation with the treating physician, decides that the disadvantages of treatment outweigh its advantages and therefore treatment is refused."[48] The British Medical Association took a similar position in its 1988 *Euthanasia Report,* which concluded, "There is a distinction between an active intervention by a doctor to terminate life and a decision not to prolong life (a nontreatment decision)."[49]

Leading medical ethicists also accept this distinction. For example, a committee of medical ethicists working under the auspices of the Hastings Center concluded in a 1987 report that helped shape the right to refuse life-sustaining treatment:

Some persons who accept this right of patients to decide to forgo treatment are concerned nevertheless that the values supporting it, and in particular self-determination, necessarily imply that voluntary euthanasia and assisted suicide are also justified. We disagree. Medical tradition and customary practice distinguish in a broadly acceptable fashion between the refusal of medical interventions and intentionally causing death or assisting suicide.

Elaborating on this distinction, the report explained:

Our society forbids assisting suicide or active euthanasia, even if the motive is compassionate. This prohibition serves to sustain the societal value of respect for life and to provide some safeguards against abuse of the authority to take actions that shorten life. It also encourages us to provide decent and humane care to those who suffer, and to those who are dependent, ill, or impaired. Since these people are already vulnerable to being mistreated, undertreated, or avoided, eroding the legal prohibition of active euthanasia might well further endanger them. Respecting the individual's liberty to direct his or her own life requires, however, that patients generally be allowed to refuse medical interventions.[50]

These observations provide strong public-policy reasons for outlawing both assisted suicide and euthanasia.

An exhaustive study of the issue by the twenty-four-member New York State Task Force on Life and the Law reached a similar conclusion in 1994, after a decade of careful deliberation. In its two-hundred-page report, this broad-based, expert panel, which included physicians, unanimously recommended maintaining the law that the Second Circuit struck down as unconstitutional only a year later. "Few states have ever provided a more cogent explanation for any public policy, and none has ever furnished a more coherent defense of the ban against assisted suicide," one legal commentator noted. "If the Task Force Report couldn't pass muster with the Second Circuit, it is virtually impossible to think of a rationale that would." Similarly Kamisar sighed, "To be sure, any American legislature remains free to reject the Task Force report as a matter of public policy. But how can it be said that a legislature that is impressed by the same *non*religious arguments against assisted suicide that influenced the Task Force and arrives at the same conclusions the Task Force did has acted *unconstitutionally?*"[51]

In a joint statement on the issue published in *JAMA*, four of America's premier physician-ethicists, Willard Gaylin, Leon R. Kass, Edmund D. Pellegrino and Mark Siegler, declared, "Generations of physicians and commentators on medical ethics have underscored and held fast to the distinction between ceasing useless treatments (or allowing to die) and active, willful, taking of life." In a statement that denounces the Second

Curcuit's ruling, these four distinguished scholars added, "Neither legal tolerance nor the best bedside manner can ever make medical killings medically ethical."[52]

The only evidence that the court offered to support its equal-protection holding was the citation of New York State statutory and common law regarding the right of terminally ill persons to refuse life-sustaining treatment. It then quoted Justice Scalia's concurring opinion in *Cruzan* as authority for dismissing "the action-inaction distinction" as irrelevant, leading to the Second Circuit's conclusion that there is no legally meaningful distinction between "ordering the discontinuance of . . . artificial life-sustaining processes" and "writing a prescription to hasten death." In both cases, the court wrote, "The ending of life by these means is nothing more nor less than assisted suicide."[53] Justice Scalia never intended for his comment to endorse a constitutional claim for assisted suicide but rather used what he perceived as the obvious constitutionality of laws against assisted suicide to argue that a state could also limit a patient's authority to refuse treatment.

Mainstream medical and ethical opinion simply does not equate the two actions. As the 1987 Hastings Center report concluded, "A reasonable, if not unambiguous, line can be drawn between foregoing life-sustaining treatment on the one hand, and active euthanasia or assisted suicide on the other."[54] The Second Circuit ignored this line and ordered the state to do likewise. Either the distinction separating terminating life-sustaining treatment from prescribing lethal medication is sufficient to satisfy rational basis scrutiny, or many of America's most respected medical ethics and physicians are irrational regarding an issue of central concern to their profession.

Jews and Christians have consistently opposed suicide and euthanasia on biblical grounds. They should continue to stand firm. Yet they cannot expect society to defer to biblical principles without showing that those principles advance public policy. On this issue that showing is easy. Mainstream medical ethics agrees with religious teachings. Society will need to hear the compelling public-policy arguments against physician-assisted suicide, not just the biblical commands, or it will be seduced by the siren song of physician-assisted suicide, a song that sings of painless passings and dignified death without warning about the dark shoals of abuse, mistake, duress and undue influence that lie just beneath the surface calm of physician-assisted suicide.

10

Euthanasia Practices Today

What would happen in the United States if physician aid in dying became a general legal right and common medical practice? Proponents project a self-limiting number of compelling cases in which competent, pain-wracked, terminally ill patients exercise a reasoned right to receive "compassion in dying" and "death with dignity" through physician-assisted suicide. In contrast opponents predict a widespread practice of euthanasia fed by duress, abuse, mistakes, subtle coercion and changing societal norms. Because of the historic legal and medical rejection of both assisted suicide and euthanasia throughout the world, neither side can draw on much current experience to support its projections and predictions. The little experience that exists, however, points toward the opponents' grim predictions.

Proponents' own words and acts belie the projection of limiting the practice to physician-assisted suicide. In 1992, for example, Timothy Quill advocated legalizing only physician-assisted suicide and opposed practicing euthanasia "because of the risk of abuse it presents." In particular he expressed concern about "the risk of subtle abuse from doctors" and commented that the "balance of power between doctor and patient is more nearly equal in physician-assisted suicide than in euthanasia." Perhaps he based this observation on his own experiences as a doctor, but Hastings Center president Daniel Callahan shot back that Quill's arguments "do not cite any empirical studies to show there is less coercion and a greater balance of power. There are no such studies. The claim is pure assertion, and not a very plausible one at that. To insinuate the idea of suicide into the mind of someone already grievously suffering can surely be no more difficult than insinuating the idea of euthanasia." In any event, confronted with an actual case a year later, Quill wrote approvingly about a physician who crossed over the line to euthanasia in treating an AIDS patient: "The patient wanted to take the barbiturates he had saved for an overdose, but was too weak to feed them himself. Faced with this moment of truth, the doctor helped his patient swallow the pills." In 1994 Quill endorsed the statement "To confine legalized physician-assisted death to assisted suicide unfairly discriminates against patients with unbelievable suffering who resolve to end their lives but are physically unable to do so."[1]

Many other leading proponents do not even attempt to draw a line between the two practices. In his popular writings on the subject, Derek Humphry uses the terms "assisted suicide" and "euthanasia" almost interchangeably and often confuses the two practices. He termed his own actions in assisting his wife's suicide as a "euthanasia experience." Similarly, in a 1992 piece about the practice of "euthanasia" among the elites, Humphry claimed, "Well off or well connected people often have medical friends who, in secret, will pass out lethal drugs or actually make the injection." He apparently drew no distinction between these two alleged medical practices, even though the former assists suicide and the latter involves euthanasia.[2] In his philosophical writings on the subject Ronald Dworkin also lumped together the two acts. "The argument over euthanasia has suddenly exploded into front-page news," he observed in the introduction to a 1993 book. "Doctors are now beginning openly to admit what the profession once kept secret: that doctors sometimes kill patients who ask to die, or help such patients to kill themselves."[3] Neither proponents nor practitioners seem to treat physician-assisted suicide differently from euthanasia. The one flows logically from the other in theory and practice.

Dworkin's book suggests just how far the logic of euthanasia extends. The author, an eminent legal philosopher, considered three types of patients and found them all appropriate subjects for physician aid in dying. Two were standard targets: gravely ill but competent patients and the permanently comatose. A third type, conscious but incompetent patients, best illustrated his thinking. Dworkin used the example of Margo, an Alzheimer's disease patient described in an earlier medical journal article. According to the article, Margo lived at home with an attendant. The article's writer, a medical student, visited her daily and described her condition. He would often find her joyfully reading a mystery novel, but "her place in the book jumped randomly from day to day." She loved to listen to music and repeatedly enjoyed the same song as if for the first time. And she happily painted, but she always created the same "drawing of four circles, in soft rosy colors." The medical student concluded, "Despite her illness, or maybe somehow because of it, Margo is undeniably one of the happiest people I have known. There is something graceful about the degeneration her mind is undergoing, leaving her carefree, always cheerful." Margo is typical of many Alzheimer's disease patients.[4]

Conceding that it might be difficult emotionally to euthanize a person like Margo, Dworkin maintained that we should do so if, "when fully competent," she had executed an advance directive requesting it for dementia. "We all do things because we like the experience of doing them," he reasoned, but it is our "critical interests" that give meaning to our lives and should be honored above all else, especially in our death. In this case, he concluded, "we must judge Margo's critical interests as she did when competent to do so." By Dworkin's logic it is compassion "toward the whole person" not to let Margo live with dementia even though she enjoyed her altered state of life and did not want death. Her advance directive should control. Even without an advance directive, Dworkin asserted, family members should be able to request euthanasia for Margo based on "the shape and character" of her life and their knowledge of her "critical interests." Yet honoring Margo's so-called precedent autonomy or her family's view of it dishonors her current autonomy. More critically, who can judge the value of Margo's continued life? Traditional practice let nature or God determine the timing of Margo's death. Dworkin would assign the decision to Margo's former self. It could pass on to the doctor or society. Should euthanasia become a common practice, people like Margo will be as vulnerable as the comatose and terminally ill.[5]

These writings by Quill, Humphry and Dworkin provide some clue into the practical consequences of crossing the line between allowing patients to die and hastening their death. None of these three proponents would hold the line at either physician-assisted suicide or competent, terminally ill patients. In their writings they all hail actual cases that go far beyond these limits. An analysis of current euthanasia practices points to similar consequences. That analysis is limited, however. In the mid-1990s Oregon and Australia's Northern Territory became the first two jurisdictions to enact statutes authorizing physician-assisted suicide, but legal challenges have prevented implementation of either law. The only systematic, public practice of physician-assisted suicide in the United States has involved the renegade acts of Jack Kevorkian. Internationally the Netherlands has become the leading center for euthanasia under a series of permissive court rulings. These examples offer further evidence of the likely results of legalizing such practices in the United States and have received close examination from proponents and opponents alike.

Jack Kevorkian

Jack Kevorkian's first suicide patient bore striking similarities to Margo in Dworkin's hypothetical case. This patient's name was Janet Adkins. She suffered from early-stage Alzheimer's disease and had a life expectancy of at least ten years with the illness. Certainly she was not terminally ill by any conventional understanding of that term, though Kevorkian asserts that "every disease that shortens life no matter how much is terminal."[6] Only under such an expansive definition would Adkins qualify as terminally ill. Unlike Margo, however, Adkins could still express her wishes, and she wished to die. In fact she wanted to die before the disease robbed her of her competence. She did not want to become like Margo. This realistic scenario undermines the smug assurance commonly offered by euthanasia proponents that, as one of them put it, "obviously, the terminally ill person will not seek to hasten inevitable death until the end stages of the terminal illness has been reached."[7] Like Adkins, many patients diagnosed with an incurable illness may want to die before the disease progresses. If they have a right to euthanasia or assisted suicide, then they may exercise it long before their death is imminent. Kevorkian publicly professes, "The patient decides when it's best to go," and he maintains, "I'm for absolute autonomy of the individual."[8]

Adkins got her wish in 1990 with the assistance of Kevorkian, who was then an obscure retired pathologist in Michigan. As a former pathologist, he had not been Adkins's attending physician and was not a specialist in treating her illness. He further lacked the special training in psychiatry necessary to evaluate a patient's mental state. But having worked with the dead all of his professional life, Kevorkian had an abiding interest in helping people die painlessly; given the macabre nature of his paintings and writings, some people would say he had an interest in death generally. Recently retired from his medical post, he now felt free to act on his interests. Kevorkian also had a tinkerer's knack with machinery, which he used to build various suicide delivery systems. For Adkins he employed one that allowed her to self-administer poison intravenously. The machine worked as planned, and Kevorkian made no attempt to conceal his role in the death. The media picked up on the sensational story of a physician who volunteered to help patients die and made him famous overnight. Prosecutors reviewed the case but did not press charges because Michigan lacked a law against assisted suicide. Some opponents of physician-assisted suicide denounced the episode as the grim consequences of the euthanasia movement. Proponents within the medical community typically dismissed it as an extreme case that showed the need for regularizing the practice within health-care facilities. Among rank-and-file supporters of euthanasia, however, Kevorkian became something of an antiestablishment hero, a role he clearly relished.

People from across the country began asking Kevorkian for assistance in dying. He would evaluate their cases to determine, in his own words, "if the wish of the patient is medically justified." Yet Kevorkian never clearly identified his medical criteria for assisted suicide—certainly his criterion was not terminal illness. He did interview patients extensively and recorded their suicide requests on videotape. Typically they came to Michigan for the procedure, and Kevorkian never charged them a fee. Each new assisted suicide brought added publicity, with Kevorkian's name soon becoming a household word and his practice the subject of countless jokes. To most people he became Dr. Death, a nickname that he first gained thirty-five years earlier during his medical training because of his interest in photographing patients at the moment of death.[9]

"I think that the American public is puzzled about you," journalist Andy Rooney mused on *Sixty Minutes*. "They don't know whether you're a medical philosopher or a nut. Which are you?"

Conceding that he was "probably both," Kevorkian replied, "You might say I'm a philosophic nut, or a nutty philosopher. It doesn't matter. Words don't mean anything."[10]

Perhaps Kevorkian's most famous assisted suicides occurred late in 1991 at a Michigan state park. Kevorkian had begun moving his practice around to avoid surveillance, and he had even equipped a suicide van. These deaths occurred in a cabin, however. Two people died side by side, Sherry Miller, a forty-three-year-old with multiple sclerosis, and Marjorie Wantz, a fifty-eight-year-old with pelvic pain from botched surgery. Neither was terminally ill, and even Kevorkian acknowledged that Wantz would not die from her condition. Wantz had been treated in mental-health hospitals for a depression and was taking excessive amounts of a sleep aid known to cause suicidal impulses in some people. Kevorkian hooked the older patient up to his suicide machine but could not find a suitable vein in Miller's emaciated arms. For the younger patient he improvised with a canister of carbon monoxide attached to a face mask.

The Michigan legislature responded by passing a law against physician-assisted suicide. The state medical establishment suspended Kevorkian's license to practice medicine, which curtailed his access to drugs. "And then, when I use gas," Kevorkian sneered, "they scorn it."[11] The police began closely monitoring his activities and searched his home for materials that could cause death. Yet when Kevorkian was prosecuted under the new statute for later acts, once in Detroit during 1994 and once in Pontiac a year later, the jurors acquitted him.

The Detroit case involved the suicide of Thomas Hyde, a thirty-year-old man with Lou Gehrig's disease, a degenerative condition that inevitably causes death. Kevorkian again supplied the mask, a carbon monoxide canister and a deathbed in the back of his van. The patient opened the valve, and Kevorkian delivered the body to the hospital in the van. When the jury acquitted Kevorkian on these facts, some proponents of physician-assisted suicide hailed it as jury nullification. "The jury thought Kevorkian was justified in what he did precisely because it thought that Hyde was under no duty to live, and could end his life if he so chose," one legal commentator wrote. Kevorkian's lawyer boasted, "No jury will ever convict Jack Kevorkian." But Yale Kamisar attributed it to the wording of the assisted-suicide statute, which included an exception for medical acts intended to "relieve pain or discomfort." The judge instructed jurors that the prosecution must prove "beyond a reasonable doubt" that Kevorkian "intended solely to cause death." After hours of deliberation and a tentative 7-to-5 vote for conviction, the jury opted to acquit. "I don't think it is our obligation to choose for someone else how much pain and suffering they should endure," one juror told the press. Moving testimony of Hyde's wretched condition certainly contributed to the verdict, as did the certainty that death was Hyde's wish.[12]

By this time Kevorkian was speaking widely on the need for euthanasia and denouncing the medical and legal professions for opposing it. In 1994 he launched an unsuccessful campaign for Michigan voters to establish a state constitutional right for physician-assisted suicide. In his public statements Kevorkian cited the medically and legally approved practice of terminating artificial nutrition and hydration as being much more "brutal" than his method of hastening death. "When you say a person should be allowed to die," Kevorkian told Rooney on *Sixty Minutes*, "inject them quickly and painlessly, not let them wither away and starve to death." This simply made "common sense" to him: Any other practice resulted from "religious fanaticism and dogma," he claimed. "You're basing your laws and your whole outlook on natural life on [Judeo-Christian] mythology," Kevorkian charged. "That is why you have all these problems in the world."[13]

In May 1996, after Michigan's ineffective statute against assisted suicide expired, prosecutors indicted Kevorkian under the common law for assisting in the suicides of Miller and Wantz. Kevorkian again maintained that he intended "to relieve their pain and suffering. Their death was an unfortunate but necessary consequence of the only way that could be done." Clearly unrepentant for his actions, Kevorkian assisted in his twenty-eighth suicide during a break in the court proceedings. Yet the jury again acquitted him. Once again his clear showing that his patients wanted to die and that he did not encourage them in any way was crucial to his successful defense strategy.[14]

Following this final acquittal, his fifth, Kevorkian picked up the pace of his activities. He assisted in ten more suicides over the next few months. His thirty-eighth assisted suicide, in August 1996, raised particular concerns. It involved a depressed, overweight woman afflicted with chronic fatigue syndrome, a treatable condition that is never fatal. She was forty-two years old, the mother of two children, and a recent victim of spousal abuse. Some proponents of euthanasia thought Kevorkian had gone too far. "He's been a little too enthusiastic to help people," a leading suicidologist noted, "and I think that is another case of that." An expert in chronic fatigue syndrome called Kevorkian's act "a mistake." *Newsweek* reprinted an editorial cartoon showing a smiling Kevorkian defining dandruff, a hangnail and athlete's foot as terminal diseases.

Yet those were the logical results of Kevorkian's avowed acceptance of the "absolute autonomy of the individual" in choosing death. When he was asked in an interview if he believed that he was the right person to represent the cause of physician-assisted suicide, however, Kevorkian merely conceded, "They criticize me, 'You're not the poster child for this.' Fine, the reason I'm doing this in a fashion that is not entirely acceptable to everyone is because of the prosecutor and the intimidation." But when the interviewer went on to ask the retired pathologist what he liked to do for fun, Kevorkian gave a telling answer: "Irritate people."[15]

It remains uncertain if Kevorkian's practices helped or harmed his cause. "In thinking about this issue, do not be misled by the ghoulish aspects of this case. Only someone with the near-fanatical convictions of a Dr. Kevorkian would be prepared to stand up to the organized might of the medical and legal establishments," one proponent commented on Hyde's suicide. "Once assisted suicide is legal, then the process can be done above board by ordinary physicians and patients freed of the complications of a protracted legal struggle." This commentator and many others point to the Netherlands as a better example of how physician aid in dying should operate.[16] That depends on one's perspective, however. Between his commitment to individual autonomy and his concern over prosecution, Kevorkian has carefully documented his patients' death wishes. Even critics concede that these people wanted to die, at least at the time that Kevorkian helped them to do so. This is less clear in the Netherlands, where physician-assisted suicide and euthanasia are practiced by respected physicians in public hospitals. And its example should offer a better illustration than Kevorkian's renegade acts of what would happen in any American state that legalized such practices.

Dutch Death

Despite its small size, the Netherlands has maintained a distinctive national culture and identity. Famous for its art, flowers and battle against the sea, the country once nurtured one of the most theologically conservative and culturally influential national churches in Protestant Europe. Churches within this Dutch Reformed tradition remain strongly evangelical in North America and the Netherlands' former overseas colonies, but they have all but died out in their homeland. Only a few hundred thousand of the country's more than thirteen million people regularly attend any church, making the Netherlands one of the least churched places in the world. Since the 1960s it has become a European center for legalized drugs and prostitution. Casino gambling is also endemic. More recently it has become the one place in the world where euthanasia is openly practiced. Social commentators typically attribute the radical Dutch acceptance of once forbidden activities as a reaction to the culture's former strict religiosity. Stern, self-imposed social conformity still exists, they posit, but now it manifests itself in a secularized Calvinism that exalts individual autonomy in seeking pleasure and avoiding pain. Tolerance has become the highest virtue and intolerance the only remaining sin.[17]

Although the Netherlands Penal Code outlaws both euthanasia and assisted suicide, a series of decisions by various Dutch courts have made those laws all but unenforceable against physicians. The first such ruling came in 1973 and set the stage for all that followed. In it a lower court in Leeuwarden suspended the sentence of a physician who had euthanized her invalid mother. Courts often show mercy in such situations on a case-by-case basis, but the Leeuwarden court went further. Based on expert testimony from a district medical inspector regarding the acceptance of euthanasia within the Dutch medical community, the court fashioned a general exception to the penal code. A summary by a leading Dutch legal commentator indicates that the court ruled that physicians should not be punished for euthanasia "if the patient is incurably ill; the patient suffers unbearably; the patient has requested the termination of his life; and the termination of the patient's life is performed by the doctor who treats the patient or in concert with him."[18] These became the initial guidelines for permissible euthanasia in Holland. The defendant did not meet them because she had not been her mother's treating physician. Further, court records did not establish that the patient was incurably ill. But the physician received a suspended sentence, and an important legal precedent was set for other doctors.

The practice of euthanasia apparently began to increase from this point, with only scattered prosecutions. In 1984 one such prosecution (known as the Alkamaar case from the district where it arose) finally reached the Dutch Supreme Court after a doctor was convicted for giving two lethal injections to a ninety-five-year-old woman in deteriorating health who had repeatedly requested death. The Supreme Court reversed the conviction and directed a lower court to reconsider the case in light of the question "Whether the euthanasia practiced by the accused would, from an objective medical perspective, be regarded as an action justified in a situation of necessity (beyond one's control)?"[19] This odd wording reflected the court's attempt to bring the practice under the statutory defense of necessity, which was traditionally used to excuse criminal acts done to save life but here was extended to cover a procedure ostensibly done to alleviate suffering. With this excuse tied to an "objective medical perspective," the lower court solicited the opinion of the Royal Dutch Society for the Promotion of Medicine (KNMG). The result was a set of guidelines, much like those issued by the Leeuwarden court a decade earlier, establishing when physicians could perform euthanasia and assisted suicide without fear of prosecution. These guidelines remained somewhat vague but were generally understood to require that the patient voluntarily request the procedure and experience intolerable and irreversible suffering.

From this modest beginning the practice of euthanasia rapidly spread across the Netherlands. The number of cases officially reported to the government rose annually, starting at 17 in 1984, surpassing 100 by 1987, then 500 in 1991, exceeding 1,000 a year later and reaching nearly 1,500 by 1994. Yet, because of lax reporting requirements, these figures probably represented only a fraction of the total. To ascertain more accurate figures, the Dutch government commissioned a survey of deaths for the year 1990. This official survey found that out of 129,000 deaths during the year, 2,300 were requested euthanasia, 400 were physician-assisted suicide, and 1,000 were euthanasia without explicit requests. Another 1,350 death were from pain medication administered with the explicit purpose of ending the patient's life, 450 of which occurred without explicit requests. Combining these figures produces a total of about 5,000 cases, or nearly 4 percent of all deaths in the Netherlands that year. An official task force replicated this study for 1995, finding that the total had jumped by 27 percent in five years, to nearly 6,400 cases, which represented nearly 5 percent of all deaths.[20] Even these figures may understate the total, with some estimates running as high as 20,000 per year, or nearly one out of seven deaths. A leading Dutch advocate of euthanasia commented in the late 1980s, "I don't have good data, but from talking to other doctors—from doctors who call for advice or talk to me at meetings—maybe 15% of cancer patients get euthanasia."[21]

The most striking finding in the official surveys involved the extent of involuntary euthanasia despite clear guidelines requiring patient requests in all instances. In nearly half of the involuntary cases physicians did not consult with family members but took it upon themselves to perform the procedure. A governmental commission led by Dutch Attorney General Jan Remmelick reviewing the 1990 survey expressed little concern with these involuntary cases, finding that most involved incompetent patients in "death agony." In these instances, the Remmelick commission concluded, "the intervention by the doctor can easily be regarded as an action that is justified by necessity." Only a "few dozen" cases were said to involve competent patients who should have participated in the decision. Yet the survey indicated that one quarter of all patients euthanized involuntarily were at least partially competent at the time, and 28 percent had a life expectancy of a week or more. The most common reason for euthanasia given by doctors in these cases was the absence of any prospect for improvement rather than pain or suffering.[22]

Rather than dismiss these cases of involuntary euthanasia as exceptions, the authors of the 1990 survey commented that "once one accepts euthanasia and assisted suicide, the principle of universalizability forces one to accept termination of life without explicit requests, at least in some circumstances." Fitting this comment, an earlier Dutch study of euthanasia practices found that more requests for hastening patients' deaths came from family members than from patients and that family members and health-care providers often pressured patients to request death. For example, a Dutch medical journal tells of one instance in which one spouse gave her invalid husband a choice between euthanasia or going to a nursing home. He chose euthanasia, and his doctor, who knew about the ultimatum, performed the act. In a case at the other end of the age spectrum, a lower court recently acquitted a Dutch physician for euthanizing a handicapped newborn. The infant could not request euthanasia, but her parents did so after refusing treatment for their child. Both official surveys found over half of all Dutch doctors willing to suggest the option of euthanasia to patients who did not raise the option themselves.[23]

The official survey also found that in practice euthanasia was not limited to patients experiencing intolerable and irreversible suffering, even though this was required under the original guidelines. When they were asked about the reasons patients gave for requesting euthanasia, physicians reported that patients cited a "loss of dignity" more often than they cited "pain."[24] In one recent case, occurring after the official survey, the Dutch Supreme Court confirmed that the requisite suffering could be psychological rather than physical. The case involved a deeply depressed fifty-year-old woman who repeatedly requested to die. Her psychiatrist eventually helped her to commit suicide even though she had no physical illness. "The ruling recognizes the right of patients experiencing severe psychic pain to choose to die with dignity," the psychiatrist's attorney declared. New York Medical College psychiatrist and suicidologist Herbert Hendin commented that it illustrated the " 'slippery slope' that moves society inexorably from assisted suicide to euthanasia, from euthanasia for terminally ill to patients who are chronically ill, from physical suffering to mental suffering, from voluntary requests for euthanasia to killing at the discretion of the physician." Boston University health-law professor George Annas added, "If you're worried about the slippery slope, this case is as far down as you can get."[25]

In less than a decade, the survey found, euthanasia had become integrated into the practice of medicine. Over half of the physicians questioned for the 1990 study reported that they had euthanized patients or assisted in their suicides, and only 1 in 8 said that they would never do so. A subsequent survey found that nearly every hospital in the Netherlands, and most nursing homes, permitted euthanasia, with many leaving the matter entirely to physicians. Of the few nursing homes that refused to permit euthanasia or physician-assisted suicide, nearly half had religious affiliations. While patients opposed to euthanasia can opt for one of these nursing homes, they have virtually no choice regarding hospitalization. One newspaper investigation found that many of the elderly in the Netherlands actively resist going to hospitals for fear of euthanasia, and some carry cards stating, "Please don't euthanize me if I can't speak for myself."[26]

These survey data belied claims that euthanasia was carefully limited by narrow safeguards in the Netherlands. After reviewing the 1990 survey, Callahan concluded, "The Dutch situation is a regulatory Potemkin village, a great facade hiding non-enforcement." British legal commentator John Keown added:

The hard evidence of the *Survey* indicates that, within a remarkably short time, the Dutch have proceeded from voluntary to non-voluntary euthanasia. This is partly because of the inability of the vague and loose *Guidelines* to ensure that euthanasia is only performed in accordance with the criteria laid down by the courts and the K.N.M.G. It is also because the underlying justification for euthanasia in the Netherlands appears not to be patient self-determination, but rather acceptance of the principle that certain lives are not "worth" living and that it is right to terminate them.

In a particularly egregious case reported to an American congressional committee reviewing the Dutch experience, one doctor allegedly "terminated the life of a nun a few days before she otherwise would have died because she was in excruciating pain, but her religious convictions did not permit her to ask for death." Far from enhancing patient autonomy, evidence from the Netherlands amply supports the conclusion, set forth in the *Hastings Center Reports*, that the practice of euthanasia in that country has given physicians "even more power over the life and death of their patients."[27]

This result was reflected in a popular 1994 Dutch television documentary entitled *Death on Request*, which was intended to project the opposite image. The program opened with a physician, Wilfred van Oijen, getting dressed for work, and then followed him through a routine day that included a visit with Cees van Wendel, an elderly man dying of amyotrophic lateral scelorosis (ALS) who had agreed to have his death filmed. Although the documentary was supposed to present the fulfillment of the patient's euthanasia request, the physician played the leading role in this performance. "In the two house calls van Oijen makes to Cees, of most interest is the tension between the film's professed message—that all want release from illness, the patient most of all—and the message conveyed by what is actually filmed," Hendin commented on the documentary. "The relationship depicted is between van Oijen and Antoinette, the patient's wife, who has called the doctor and clearly wants her husband to die."[28]

During the physician's first visit, the wife sat stiffly in the room with her husband. She never touched him and insisted on answering all the questions posed to him even though he could still communicate in a slurred whisper and by typing messages on a computer. She alone answers the key question about wanting to die. "When Cees begins to cry, the doctor moves sympathetically toward him to touch his arm, but his wife tells the doctor to move away and says it is better to let him cry alone," Hendin observed. "Virtually the entire film is set up to avoid confronting any of the patient's feelings or how the relationship with his wife affects his agreeing to die." A subsequent visit by a consulting physician was similarly formal, with the wife answering for her husband.

Van Oijen's second house call occurred in the early evening of the patient's birthday, the time chosen for death. Van Wendel marked the occasion by drinking a glass of port, followed by a remark that sleep is usually a little death but this time will be a lot of death. Van Oijen laughed, but the wife merely complained about how slowly the day had gone. She then helped her husband into bed, where the doctor administered an initial shot to put the patient into a deep sleep. No one said goodby. After a few minutes the doctor gave the lethal injection. "Antoinette asks if this was good, presumably wanting to know if it was 'good' to kill Cees," Hendin commented on this scene. "Van Oijen reassures her. They leave Cees alone very quickly. On the way into the next room, Antoinette takes a note Cees wrote to her about their relationship and what it meant to him and reads it to the doctor. She seems to want to convey to him that they in fact once had a relationship."

Death on Request probably presented the practice of euthanasia in the Netherlands as favorably as possible. The filming was arranged by the Dutch Voluntary Euthanasia Society, a group that promotes the right of individuals to choose physician aid in dying. Yet even in this instance, which clearly would be categorized as voluntary rather than involuntary euthanasia, questions of control haunt the episode. "One leaves the film feeling that death with dignity requires more than effective management; it requires being accorded personhood," Hendin concluded. "Throughout the film, Cees's wife denies him such personhood, as does the doctor, who never questions her control over all the patient's communication and even the doctor's communication with Cees. The doctor and wife took away Cees's personhood before ALS had claimed it." This is death, Dutch style.

Case Studies from the Netherlands

Case studies offer the best way to show the practice of euthanasia in the Netherlands. University of Virginia medical school professor Carlos F. Gomez compiled twenty-six such case studies based on interviews with various Dutch health-care providers during the late 1980s and included them in *Regulating Death: Euthanasia and the Case of the Netherlands.*[29] With his permission, five of these studies follow. They illustrate euthanasia in a variety of different contexts.

Widow. The patient was an eighty-nine-year-old widow who lived by herself. She had suffered a stroke six years previously, from which she had partially recuperated. She came in to this doctor's care shortly after her return from the hospital when she moved to a smaller house in another neighborhood. Since her return she had become increasingly unable to care for herself. For "about three years" she had asked the doctor about euthanasia and once had threatened to kill herself if the doctor did not accede to her request. The doctor had suggested psychotherapy, which she declined, and at one point the doctor tried to put her on antidepressant medication ("which I am never sure she would take"). The family doctor had contacted the visiting nurse in the area, asking her to visit this patient on a regular basis. The doctor had also arranged for the local welfare department to send a part-time aide to help the patient with cooking and heavier tasks. The patient's mood would lift periodically, but she mentioned euthanasia "almost every time she would visit me."

The woman's requests became so persistent that the doctor agreed to accede if she told a son who lived a good distance away. The woman refused and said her son had nothing to do with this matter. The patient then called a neighbor, who came with the patient to visit the physician. The neighbor helped the woman plead her case and suggested that if this doctor would not perform euthanasia, the neighbor would help the patient to find another doctor who would. The doctor finally agreed, and a week later he euthanized the patient in her home (no one else was present) by giving her a solution of orphenaldrine and pentobarbital to drink. She died within the half-hour after drinking the solution. The doctor then notified the son that evening that his mother had passed away suddenly but did not tell him of the circumstances. The cause of death was listed as "cardiac arrest"; the public prosecutor was not notified.

Man with AIDS. A thirty-two-year-old man with AIDS had been admitted twice previously to this hospital: once for a persistent cough, during which time the diagnosis of AIDS was established; the second time for a bout of *pneumocystis carinii* pneumonia, from which he had recovered temporarily.

"This case I remember well because from the beginning the man said 'I want to die.' Right away, before we had started anything." The patient, who was estranged from his family, was accompanied on his hospital visits by his lover, and the hospital had accommodated their needs by giving them a private room: "In cases like this, we always try to make a difficult situation much easier; we always let the boyfriend stay in the hospital; it makes the patient better, less lonely."

During his previous admission for pneumonia, the patient had requested euthanasia over the protests of his lover. The attending physician suggested a psychiatric consultation and at least a trial period of therapy. The psychiatrist concurred: "He said it was much too soon; maybe the desire to die came from the shock of the scary disease." The patient responded reasonably well to the treatment, but prior to discharge, he asked to speak alone to the doctor: "He said to me: 'This time, I am saved, but next time, no. I have seen this disease and prefer death.' What do you say to such a thing? Was he angry at me for saving his life?" The physician, as a precautionary measure, asked the psychiatrist and a member of the terminal-care team to speak to the patient before he was discharged: "These patients do not get better, only worse; he would be back, and then, it was necessary for someone else to know the problem here."

In fact the patient returned "very soon, he was very ill and was brought by the boyfriend." Again the patient brought up the desire to die and was emphatic about not starting treatment: "He said only drugs to make me feel better, not to cure." The physician contacted the terminal-care team, which sent a representative: "Not a doctor, but someone to put the request on paper." Shortly afterward ("the next morning") the request was approved: "But the problem was the boyfriend, who really needed some help too. Finally I said, 'If your friend wants this, if he is so sick, why do you act this way and make him suffer more?'"

Over the lover's protests, the patient was euthanized that day by giving him an oral euthanasic: "It is like an ice-cream mixture [milkshake]. I put in Norflex [orphenadrine] and pentobarbital, and then he drank it. Within the hour he was dead."

The prosecutor was notified "and took so much time with this case. I don't know if the boyfriend made accusations, but for several days, the prosecutor [kept] coming back. He asked if there was another doctor involved, and I said, 'The whole hospital is involved,' but he wanted a name, so I said, 'Talk to the hospital administrator, he can give the names of all the doctors here, just pick one.'" After a few weeks of deliberation the prosecutor dropped the case.

Elderly woman. The patient, a seventy-five-year-old woman, had been diagnosed with an inoperable brain tumor. Several rounds of radiation therapy had left her weakened. "She did not want anything else, and the doctor she had seen here had made a promise that if the radiotherapy did not work, she could have euthanasia." This promise took the form of an interview with the terminal-care team: "Before therapy, she wanted to be sure nothing would go too far; she already had lost her husband with cancer, and I think she was very afraid of what she had seen with his disease."

On the advice of her doctor, the terminal-care team agreed to the contract: "This is a case I do not understand very well; she was not my patient at the beginning, but only at the end. When I saw her, she was already very weak, and she asked, 'Are you the doctor that is going to end this?'" The physician consulted several times with the original doctor on the case, and he also spoke with the terminal-care team. Before proceeding with the patient's request, the physician suggested that she speak with a psychiatrist; the patient declined. The physician then suggested that the family be called in, "but she said her family had died when her husband had died; the rest did not matter." The physician looked at the records of the terminal-care team, "and there were many written requests for euthanasia, and everyone on the committee said it was appropriate."

The patient was given an oral euthanasic and expired. The prosecutor who was called to the case did not even speak with the physician who performed the euthanasia but with the hospital administrator: "I was only asked by the administrator to sign some papers; this was very strange, but I believe now that the hospital has some agreement with the prosecutor."

Handicapped newborn. The case was narrated by a bioethicist at a large hospital who chaired the hospital's ethics committee and the terminal-care committee. The case involved a neonate, born at term, who had Down's syndrome. "But the problem here was that there was a block in the stomach [duodenal atresia]." The parents were apparently quite distressed: "This was a third child, and the mother kept asking how she was going to take care of this baby." The ethicist, called to speak with the parents about surgery for the child, was very specific with the parents: "I said that they did not have to approve surgery; there [were] already two problems here, and who is to know how many more would come?"

(The case is confusing at this point, because it wasn't clear to Gomez, at least from this narrative, who brought up the issue of euthanasia.) The ethicist, however, submits that "once there was a decision [not to treat], it becomes a very cruel thing to starve a baby. The mother wanted no suffering [for the child] and this I told her we could do." Again, how exactly the decision to euthanize came about is difficult to ascertain. (One should note, for example, that the case says this child died at two days, so that whatever discussion took place, it occurred within an extremely short time frame.) What is clearer is that the child was given large doses of benzodiazepines ("to make him more comfortable") and expired very quickly. The ethicist did not expressly use the word *euthanasia* to describe this later action but said that the drugs were given "just to help the child along." The prosecutor was not notified.

Crash victim. A fifty-six-year-old man was brought into a hospital emergency room with massive internal injuries following a car accident. A member of the intensive-care staff (the narrator) was called to the emergency room by the surgeon on call. "The surgeon asked what was to be done here? Should there be an operation with such damage to the chest and the brain? Soon there would be family outside. There would soon be no [brain] signals for a neurologist to see; do you put the patient on a respirator?" The physician suggested that the matter end quickly: "I said, the heart will stop in some time, but if the family comes sooner, they must wait for this; it is a terrible situation." The physician, acting unilaterally, gave an injection of potassium chloride: "I think the surgeon and the nurse knew what I was going to do, but they were not there; a few minutes later, after the patient is dead, the nurse comes to ask, Is it over? I say yes, and [the nurse] comes to fix the body."

The physician did not actually consider this a case of euthanasia but of bringing on "what was surely going to happen, but perhaps after some hours." When the family arrived, they were told the patient had expired from his wounds shortly after being brought to the hospital. "In cases such as this, it is not like other cases of euthanasia; the death was at the door, and he would soon come in no matter what we did; in other cases, you know that death is near but do not know when it will come; [this latter situation] is what is euthanasia."

These case studies, written in the terse jargon of a physician, present graphic pictures of physician-assisted suicide and euthanasia in practice. None of these patients would have recovered from their illnesses, and all would have died soon from their underlying physical conditions (including the neonate, once the parents decided not to treat the block in the stomach). Yet in each case Dutch physicians intervened to hasten death in ways that break sharply from traditional medical practices and do not even clearly fall within the narrow, formal guidelines for euthanasia in the Netherlands.

The first three cases fall within the realm of physician-assisted suicide in that the patients drank the lethal drugs, but questions about voluntariness persist in each of them. These patients appear depressed or at least lonely, and the attending physicians recommend psychiatric consultations. Yet two of these patients refuse such a consultation, and the third one appears to ignore the psychiatrist's findings. The suicides proceed. Were these patients capable of consenting to the procedure, or did their depression impede their decision-making capacity? The widow does not appear to be "incurably ill," as specified in the guidelines for euthanasia, and all three may not satisfy the requirement of "unbearable suffering." The final two cases represent classic examples of euthanasia, but neither patient could or did request the procedure as required by the Netherlands guidelines. In the final case the doctor failed to consult with the victim's family but acted according to the norms of a medical profession that accepts euthanasia as a means to "treat" terminal illness and injury. Given the crash victim's neurological condition, the only "unbearable suffering" being avoided was that of the victim's family, not the victim, who probably could not feel pain. But family members were never asked or told.

The Dutch physicians interviewed for these case studies present them as ordinary examples of physician-assisted suicide and euthanasia in the Netherlands. Cases like them, rather than ones akin to the macabre activities of Jack Kevorkian, would likely become commonplace in any modern Western society that normalized the practice of physician-assisted suicide and euthanasia. None of them would have shocked public sensibilities in ancient Greece or Rome. Greeks and Romans probably would have expressed surprise more at the care and treatment offered to these seriously ill or injured patients than at the ultimate hastening of their deaths. In a sense the ancient Roman colony located at the present site of post-Christian Holland is returning to its pre-Christian practices. Other post-Christian cultures may choose a similar course. It is the way of the world.

Conclusion

The Road Home —
Caring, Not Killing

On June 26, 1997, the U.S. Supreme Court issued its long-awaited decisions upholding the Washington and New York state laws against assisted suicide. These unanimous rulings promote traditional cultural norms regarding the sanctity of life, protect the elderly and infirm from potential pressure to die prematurely and provide an opportunity to establish caring end-of-life alternatives to euthanasia. They do not end the debate over physician-assisted suicide and euthanasia, however, but rather shift it from federal courts into legislative chambers and the public square. Although all nine justices—liberal and conservative, Republican and Democratic—agreed that states could constitutionally outlaw physician-assisted suicide, they differed somewhat in their reasoning. Those different reasons both summarize the case against euthanasia and suggest what must happen to keep it illegal.

Chief Justice William Rehnquist wrote the opinions of the court in which five of the nine justices joined. "The question presented in this case," he wrote in upholding the Washington statute, "is whether the protections of the [Constitution's] Due Process Clause include a right to commit suicide with another's assistance." To answer this question the chief justice adopted what he described as the "established method of substantive-due-process analysis," which begins with the principle "that the Due Process Clause specially protects those fundamental rights and liberties which are, objectively, 'deeply rooted in this Nation's history and tradition.'" In the course of his subsequent review of the relevant history and tradition, he concluded that to find such a right to assisted suicide, "we would have to reverse centuries of legal doctrine and practice, and strike down the considered policy choice of almost every State." That, he maintained, is not the court's role in a democratic society.[1]

In his separate opinion upholding the New York statute, the chief justice rejected the corollary argument that the constitutional guarantee of equal protection requires that because the state allows terminally ill persons on life support to die by having their physicians discontinue life-sustaining treatment, it must also allow terminally ill patients not on life support to die by having their physicians supply life-ending treatment. "This conclusion depends on the submission that ending or refusing lifesaving medical treatment 'is nothing more nor less than assisted suicide,'" Rehnquist reasoned. "Unlike the Court of Appeals, we think the distinction between assisting suicide and withdrawing life-sustaining treatment, a distinction widely recognized and endorsed in the medical profession and in our legal traditions, is both important and logical; it is certainly rational."[2]

In both opinions the chief justice described legitimate governmental interests served by outlawing physician-assisted suicide and distinguishing between what he characterized as "letting a patient die and making that patient die." As he summarized them, those interests include "prohibiting intentional killing and preserving life; preventing suicide; maintaining physicians' role as their patients' healers; protecting vulnerable people from indifference, prejudice, and psychological and financial pressure to end their lives; and avoiding a possible slide towards euthanasia."[3] Yet the court did not purport to see those interests as so compelling or certain as to bar states from legalizing physician-assisted suicide. The chief justice noted, "We need not weigh exactly the relative strengths of these various interests," and appended a concluding observation: "Throughout the Nation, Americans are engaged in an earnest and profound debate about the morality, legality, and practicality of physician-assisted suicide. Our holding permits this debate to continue, as it should in a democratic society."[4]

Concurring Opinions

Although they concurred in the judgment upholding state laws against assisted suicide, several of the justices filed separate opinions expressing further concerns and qualifications. For example, Justices Sandra Day O'Connor, Ruth Bader Ginsburg and Stephen Breyer stressed that the availability of palliative care weighed heavily in their decisions to reject the claimed right to physician-assisted suicide. "That is because, in my view, the avoidance of severe pain (connected with death) would have to comprise an essential part of any such claim and because, as Justice O'Connor points out, the laws before us do not *force* a dying person to undergo that kind of pain," Breyer wrote. "Medical technology, we are repeatedly told, makes the administration of pain-relieving drugs sufficient, except for a very few individuals for whom the ineffectiveness of pain control medicines can mean, not pain, but the need for sedation which can end in a coma."[5] Given such pain-control options, these three justices agreed "that the State's interest in protecting those who are not truly competent or facing imminent death, or those whose decisions to hasten death would not truly be voluntary, are sufficiently weighty to justify a prohibition against physician-assisted suicide." For these justices this societal interest in protecting these large classes of vulnerable patients outweighed the individual interests of the few competent, terminally ill patients who might voluntarily decide to hasten death. As O'Connor stated it, "The difficulty in defining terminal illness and the risk that a dying patient's request for assistance in ending his or her life might not be truly voluntary justifies the prohibitions on assisted suicide we uphold here."[6]

Although agreeing that the "*potential* harms [associated with the practice of physician-assisted suicide] are sufficient to support the State's general policy against assisted suicide," Justice John Paul Stevens carried the concern about unmanageable pain a step further and expanded it to include suffering generally. "Encouraging the development and ensuring the availability of adequate pain treatment is of utmost importance; palliative care, however, cannot alleviate all pain and suffering," he noted in his concurring opinion. "An individual adequately informed of the care alternatives thus might make a rational choice for assisted suicide. For such an individual, the State's interest in preventing potential abuse and mistake is only minimally implicated." Such an individual might possess a constitutionally recognizable right to assisted suicide, Stevens suggested, though not necessarily one that would overturn general state laws against assisted suicide.[7]

Justice David Souter placed even stronger qualifications on his concurrence in upholding the assisted-suicide statutes. "The patients here sought not only an end to pain (which they might have had, although perhaps at the price of stupor) but an end to their short remaining lives with a dignity that they believed would be denied them by powerful pain medication, as well as by their consciousness of dependency and helplessness as they approached death," he wrote. "In my judgment, the importance of the individual interest here . . . cannot be gainsaid." Yet he concluded that at least for now it was outweighed by the state's interest in "protecting terminally ill patients from involuntary suicide and euthanasia, both voluntary and involuntary." In Souter's opinion, "The case for the slippery slope is fairly made out here . . . because there is a plausible case that the right claimed would not be readily containable." The case is only plausible, he stressed, and opined that the evidence on this point from "the Dutch experience" was mixed. "The day may come when we can say with some assurance which side is right, but for now it is the substantiality of the factual disagreement, and the alternatives for resolving it, that matter. They are, for me, dispositive of the due process claim at this time."[8]

Such concerns and qualifications led the concurring justices to amplify the chief justice's call for state legislatures to address the issue. In an opinion joined by Ginsburg and Breyer, O'Connor wrote, "Every one of us at some point may be affected by our own or a family member's terminal illness. There is no reason to think the democratic process will not strike the proper balance between the interests of terminally ill, mentally competent individuals who would seek to end their suffering and the State's interest in protecting those who might seek to end life mistakenly or under pressure."[9] Stevens added, "There remains room for vigorous debate about the outcome of particular cases that are not necessarily resolved by the opinions announced today."[10] For his part Souter all but demanded legislative "experimentation" with "the emerging issue of assisted suicide" and cited the Oregon initiative as an example. Although conceding that the judiciary should "stay its hand to allow reasonable legislative consideration" of the issue, he warned, "I do not decide for all time that claim [of a right to physician-assisted suicide] should not be recognized."[11]

Taken together these various opinions by the justices suggest that far from resolving the issue of euthanasia, the Supreme Court opened a new and probably more intense phase of the public-policy debate. Americans will now have to grapple with the issue as a matter of legislative policy. The Dutch experience will be examined and reexamined. Some states will likely commence experiments of their own — limited at first but sufficient to open floodgates that may prove impossible to close. Upon hearing the court's decisions, even euthanasia critic Yale Kamisar conceded that within the decade several states would probably legalize the practice, most likely Oregon, Florida and California.[12] At the very least, however, the rulings prevent physician-assisted suicide from becoming immediately legal everywhere. Further, the court's unanimity in recognizing the grave risks inherent in the practice should reinforce existing bans. Yet the justices' words focus attention on the urgent need for alternatives to assisted suicide and euthanasia, alternatives that stress caring over killing at the end of life. Their words highlight three issues of critical concern: pain management, patient control over life-sustaining treatment and the recognition and treatment of depression. All of these concerns must be addressed, or the public pressure for legalized euthanasia will become irresistible. Each of them merits special attention in shaping our society's response to physician-assisted suicide and euthanasia.

Pain Management
In their written opinions upholding the Washington and New York laws against assisted suicide, every justice stressed the importance of pain management to his or her decision. Writing separately to explain her decision to join the majority opinion, for example, Justice O'Connor, who has personal experience with cancer therapy, observed, "There is no need to address the question whether suffering patients have a constitutionally cognizable interest in obtaining relief from the suffering that they may experience in the last days of their lives. There is no dispute that dying patients in Washington and New York can obtain palliative care, even when doing so would hasten their deaths."[13] In his opinion Justice Breyer, whose wife counsels terminally ill children and their families, explained the importance of this observation when he added, "Were the legal circumstances different—for example, were state law to prevent the provision of palliative care, including the administration of drugs as needed to avoid pain at the end of life—then the law's impact upon serious and otherwise unavoidable physical pain [accompanying death] would be more directly at issue. And as Justice O'Connor suggests, the Court might have to revisit its conclusions in these cases."[14]

Just as the alternative of pain management emboldened these justices to reject pleas for a constitutional right to physician-assisted suicide, the availability of pain management undoubtedly will be a major factor in public and legislative debates over the issue. This was apparent during the Oregon initiative campaign, where proponents successfully used the specter of dying in agonizing pain as justification for legalizing physician-assisted suicide. If voters and legislators in other states are to resist calls for similar legislation, they will need to learn, just as the Supreme Court learned, that physical pain can be managed in virtually every case. "This reflective association between pain and euthanasia—so strong and un-shakable in the public mind—is a fiction," explains Ezekiel J. Emanuel, a leading expert in end-of-life treatment at the Harvard Medical School. Dr. Joanne Lynn, director of George Washington University's Center to

Improve Care of the Dying, adds, "People find it hard to believe, but almost all patients can be kept conscious and out of pain. The rest can be kept sedated and out of pain."[15]

The practice of pain management is bound to affect individual decisions to hasten death. Some dying patients do suffer great physical pain, and some of these patients do commit suicide or receive euthanasia to end their pain. Much of this occurs because proper pain management is not practiced in many cases. Recent studies indicate that up to 40 percent of cancer patients and a shocking 85 percent of AIDS patients receive inadequate pain treatment. This is not because the treatment is unavailable, the director of the Northwestern University Medical School's palliative care center notes, but because "most physicians haven't been trained in assessing and managing pain."[16]

Suicidologist Herbert Hendin advises each patient "to find a doctor who can assure her that he will be with her to the end and see to it that she does not suffer unduly." The respected physician and ethicist Edmund Pellegrino is such a doctor. An article about him reports his response to a "typical" patient who asked to die:

> After the patient expressed his wish, Pellegrino sought to meet the real needs behind the wish. First he used the best methods of pain relief and increased the patient's sense of control by enabling the patient to self-administer the pain medication. This patient was also feeling guilty, clinically depressed, and concerned about being a burden to others. Pellegrino treated the depression, brought in a pastoral counselor to address the guilt, and gathered the patient's family to help them see how their response to this man's illness was aggravating his sense of unworthiness. Once these needs were met, the patient thanked Pellegrino for not responding to his earlier request to die. "The most valuable days of my life have been the last days I have spent," he said.

"Patients who request euthanasia are usually asking in the strongest possible way they know for mental and physical relief from suffering," Hendin reports. "When that request is made to a caring, sensitive, and knowledgeable physician who can assure them that he or she will remain with them to the end and relieve their suffering, most patients no longer want to die."[17]

For most patients, end-of-life palliative care is provided through hospice programs, and in the United States most hospice care is provided in the home. This provides a role for family, friends and the community. A hospice nurse oversees pain treatment provided through home hospice, but much of the responsibility for the dying patient's care falls on family and friends. "If Mrs. L [a hypothetical patient] wants to die at home, as most people do, she should discuss with friends or relatives, well in advance, whether they will be available to help with her care," Hendin warns. Community groups and churches can help by sponsoring hospice programs and providing volunteers to relieve caregivers. "My experience with churches has been fairly grim. If I call up a minister of a church a person attended for 30-40 years in the prime of her life but she's now disabled, and I ask, 'Is there anything you can do to help this person's burden?' I'd say I'm no better than 50-50 to get a favorable response," Lynn notes. "Take the last 20 members who have died in your congregation and ask their families how the church responded. I've had patients who were furious when they received cards telling them people were praying for them. 'Well, why don't they come and meet me?' they ask. 'Why won't they pray with me in person while holding my hand?'" Based on his intimate knowledge of people in pain, popular psychiatrist and theologian M. Scott Peck concludes, "I submit that the answer to the problem of assisted suicide lies not in more euthanasia but in more hospice care. The first order of business should be to establish that dying patients have a constitutional right to competent hospice care."[18]

Other Caring Alternatives

In explicitly stressing that all patients legally can obtain whatever medication is appropriate to manage their physical pain ("even to the point of [inadvertently if not unexpectedly] causing unconsciousness and hastening death" as Justice O'Connor put it),[19] as an alternative to physician-assisted suicide, the Supreme Court implicitly reaffirmed that patients may seek relief through refusing life-sustaining treatment. The court assumed the existence of such a right to refuse treatment seven years earlier in the *Cruzan* decision, in which Justice O'Connor suggested that this right empowered persons to execute advance treatment directives (such as living wills and health care proxies) instructing that life-sustaining treatment end if they were dying and no longer able to speak for themselves. "By permitting anyone to refuse unwanted medical treatment while prohibiting anyone from assisting a suicide, New York law follows a longstanding and rational distinction," Chief Justice Rehnquist noted in his decision upholding that law. He also described advance treatment directives as means "to protect and promote patients' dignity at the end of life." For many people, executing such documents—and the resulting assurance that their life will not be prolonged artificially through invasive medical technology—offers an important alternative to physician-assisted suicide.[20] For a patient concerned about death with dignity, Hendin counsels that "a practical first step would be to prepare advance directives—a living will and a health care proxy—stipulating what she would want done should she become incapable of making decisions."[21]

As a psychiatrist and an expert on suicide prevention, Hendin also stresses the need for treating depression as a vital alternative to physician-assisted suicide and euthanasia. Chief Justice Rehnquist, who suffered through his wife's long battle with terminal cancer, recognized this in his opinion. "Those who attempt suicide—terminally ill or not—often suffer from depression or other mental disorders," he wrote for the court. "Research indicates, however, that many people who request physician-assisted suicide withdraw that request if their depression and pain are treated."[22] Hendin offered the following example. "A sixty-four-year-old woman with advanced lung cancer and severe chest-wall pain requested that she be aided in death. She was tearful, felt helpless, and stated that there was no purpose or meaning to her life; she also viewed herself as a burden to her husband," Hendin explained. "Her husband viewed the request as a sign of profound depression and requested help to keep her alive." This help came in the form of effective pain management, antidepressant medication and psychiatric counseling. With treatment, Hendin reported, "her mood improved rapidly, there was a dramatic reduction in her pain, and she began to view her life more positively. She spoke openly about dying but wanted to be alive as long as her pain could be controlled. When asked whether the doctors should have 'killed' her when she requested it, she responded with a definite no, recognizing that pain has so depressed her that she could only wish for death."[23]

As this example illustrates, most depression, like most pain, can be treated. "The demoralizing triad of depression, anxiety, and the wish to die, seen as a response to serious illness, can usually be treated by a combination of empathy, psychotherapy, and medication. Such treatment most likely would alter a patient's attitude about living with illness," Hendin asserts. But when such depression is met by physicians, family and friends who reaffirm the death wish, as might happen if physician-assisted suicide became an accepted practice, then it could only increase. Perhaps worse yet, such depression often festers in the elderly who face serious illness alone. "An 88-year-old lady with bad hearing, bad eyesight, and who has outlived most of her siblings gets a bad disease, doesn't want to be Medicaid dependent, yet doesn't have enough resources and knows she'll end up in a nursing home, which she hates," Lynn hypothesized based on her professional experience with such cases. "The patient says she wants to be dead. She wouldn't be saying she wants to commit suicide if she had Rockefeller's resources. She's saying she wants to commit suicide because we have made long-term care the step-child of medical care." She is depressed and no one cares. Such a patient would not last long in a society that normalized physician-assisted suicide and euthanasia. "Who will show up when 5 percent of deaths are done this way?" Lynn asks. "We have an awful lot of 85-year-olds who literally have no one who still cares."[24]

Here again there is a role for family, friends and the community in combating depression. "Most of the surveys show strong support for physician-assisted suicide amongst the elderly who are frightened about the ends of their lives," Yale medical school oncologist Diane Komp observes. She especially urges churches to "adopt an elderly person without family in [their] area. Try bringing music and young life to nursing homes." Yet Lynn laments, "Old people getting sick can't count on the church. There is no one to validate the patient's importance. Paid care givers can only go so far. If what one faces when one reaches the end of life is being thrown on the dung heap of humanity, then a lot of people are going to choose to be killed—and not foolishly." The best evidence indicates that 95 percent of those who commit suicide suffer from major psychiatric illness at the time of death, and this includes those who kill themselves in the face of terminal illness. Psychiatric and social intervention that recognizes and treats such depression represents a critically important alternative to physician-assisted suicide and euthanasia. Dying is part of living and should be treated as such, Peck reminds us. "The loss of control, the irrationality, the mystery and the insecurity inherent in dying are also inherent to living," he writes. "It seems to me that 'true euthanasia' patients suffer not so much from a problem of death as a problem of life. I think they have a lot to learn from being assisted to face this problem rather than being assisted to kill themselves in order to avoid it."[25]

The Supreme Court decisions upholding state laws against assisted suicide offer Americans the opportunity to decide what sort of community they want to live and die in. Adequate pain management, effective procedures for patient control over life-sustaining treatment and responsive treatment for depressive are among the life-affirming alternatives to physician-assisted suicide and euthanasia that call for a new level of societal commitment to the dying. "If society continues not to make caring alternatives available," Lynn warns, "then we must not wear blinders to what is really at stake—that is, whether this society prefers to leave dying people so bereft of hope that being killed is to be preferred to living." Should this come to pass, then lawmakers inevitably will legalize physician-assisted suicide and euthanasia at least in some states. The right to die for a few would likely become a duty to die for many more. We would suffer what Hastings Center founder Daniel Callahan has called "self-determination run amok" and a society run afoul.[26]

Notes

Abbreviations

AF K. Lake, trans. *Apostolic Fathers*. Cambridge, Mass.: Harvard University Press, 1912-1913.

ANF A. Roberts and J. Donaldson, eds. *Ante-Nicene Fathers*. Various dates, various translators. 10 vols. Reprint edition. Grand Rapids, Mich.: Eerdmans, 1973-1974.

F Federal Reporter.

FC *Fathers of the Church*. Various editors and translators. Washington, D.C.: Catholic University of America Press, 1948-.

F.Supp. Federal Supplement.

NPNF-1 P. Schaff and H. Wace, eds. *Select Library of Nicene and Post-Nicene Fathers of the Christian Church*. First series. Various translators. 14 vols. Reprint edition. Grand Rapids, Mich.: Eerdmans, 1976-1979.

NPNF-2 P. Schaff and H. Wace, eds. *Select Library of Nicene and Post-Nicene Fathers of the Christian Church*. Second series. Various translators. 14 vols. Reprint edition. Grand Rapids, Mich.: Eerdmans, 1976-1979.

S.Ct. Supreme Court Reporter.

U.S. United States Reports.

Preface: Facing a New Age of Death

[1]Gail Kinsey Hill and Mark O'Keefe, "Suicide Law Stands," *Portland Oregonian*, November 5, 1997, p. 1; and Timothy Egan, "In Oregon, Opening a New Front in the World of Medicine," *New York Times*, November 6, 1997, p. A-22.

[2]Derek Humphry to editor, *The New York Times*, December 3, 1994, p. 22.

[3]John Ritter, "Right-to-Die Initiative Bitterly Contested in Ore.," *USA Today*, October 29, 1997, p. 6-A; and Mark O'Keefe, "The Suicide Watch," *Portland Oregonian*, November 2, 1997, pp. A-1, A-12, A-13.

[4]Egan, "In Oregon, Opening a New Front," p. A-22; and Hill and O'Keefe, "Suicide Law Stands," p. A-16.

[5]O'Keefe, "Suicide Watch," p. A-13.

[6]Erin Hoover et al., "Suicide Law Spawns Uncertainty," *Portland Oregonian*, November 8, 1997, pp. A-1, A-14.

[7]Egan, "In Oregon, Opening a New Front," p. A-22.

Introduction: Euthanasia & Christianity

[1]Émile Durkheim, *Suicide: A Study in Sociology*, trans. J. A. Spaulding and G. Simpson (Glencoe, Ill.: Free Press, 1951), p. 44.

[2]Ibid., p. 227; cf. p. 67.

[3]Alfred Alvarez, *The Savage God: A Study of Suicide* (New York: Random House, 1970), p. 51.

[4]Ibid., p. 68.

[5]Ibid., p. 73.

[6]Margaret Pabst Battin, *Ethical Issues in Suicide* (Englewood Cliffs, N.J.: Prentice-Hall, 1982), pp. 29, 71-73, 89.

[7]Glanville Williams, *The Sanctity of Life and the Criminal Law* (1957; reprint ed., New York: Knopf, 1970), pp. 254-55. See also Glanville Williams, "Suicide," in *The Encyclopedia of Philosophy*, ed. Paul Edwards, 8 vols. (New York: Macmillan, 1967), 8:43-46.

[8]Arthur J. Droge, "Suicide," in *The Anchor Bible Dictionary*, ed. D. N. Freedman, 6 vols. (Garden City, N.Y.: Doubleday, 1992), 6:225-31.

[9]Arthur J. Droge, "Did Paul Commit Suicide?" *Bible Review*, December 1989, p. 14.

[10]Ibid., p. 19.

[11]Ibid., p. 21.

[12]Arthur J. Droge and James D. Tabor, *A Noble Death: Suicide and Martyrdom Among Christians and Jews in Antiquity* (San Francisco: Harper, 1992).

[13]Ibid., p. 4.

[14]Ibid., p. 187.

[15]Ibid., p. 5.

[16]Ibid., p. 125.

[17]Ibid., p. 114.

[18]Ibid., p. 125.

[19]Ibid., p. 119.

[20]Ibid., pp. 124, 187.

[21]Ibid., p. 189.

[22]*United States Reports: Cases Adjudged in the Supreme Court at October Term, 1972* (Washington, D.C.: U.S. Government Printing Office, 1974), 410:116-17.

[23]Ibid., p. 171.

[24]WL 603212 (Mich. Cir. Ct.), p. 7.

[25]Ibid., p. 6.

[26]Ibid., p. 7.

[27]Ibid., pp. 7-8.

[28]Ibid., p. 10.

[29]Ibid., p. 9.

[30]Judge Kaufman's quotations are from Alfred Alvarez's "The Background," in *Suicide: The Philosophical Issues*, ed. M. P. Battin and D. J. May (New York: St. Martin's, 1980), pp. 7-32; "The Background" was originally chapter one of Alvarez's *The Savage God*.

[31]WL 603212 (Mich. Cir. Ct.), p. 9.

[32]Alvarez is misleading. Roman law held the suicide of one charged with a crime to be an admission of guilt, and hence his or her estate was confiscated.

Furthermore, Roman law interdicted suicide by soldiers.

[33]WL 603212 (Mich. Cir. Ct.), p. 9.

[34]Justice Blackmun is quoting Ludwig Edelstein, *The Hippocratic Oath: Text, Translation and Interpretation,* Supplements of the *Bulletin of the History of Medicine* 1 (Baltimore: Johns Hopkins University Press, 1943); reprinted in Ludwig Edelstein, *Ancient Medicine: Selected Papers of Ludwig Edelstein,* ed. Owsei Temkin and C. Lilian Temkin (Baltimore: Johns Hopkins University Press, 1967), pp. 3-63.

[35]1993 WL 603212 (Mich. Cir. Ct.), p. 10.

[36]Since Pythagorean beliefs and practices were so atypical of classical culture, attributing the oath to that school effectively marginalizes it.

[37]1993 WL 603212 (Mich. Cir. Ct.), p. 10.

[38]Ibid., pp. 10-11.

[39]*Compassion in Dying* v. *Washington* 79 F.3d 790 (9th cir en banc 1996) at 808.

[40]Ibid., at 824.

[41]Droge and Tabor, *Noble Death,* p. 187.

[42]William Birmingham, review of *Noble Death,* by Droge and Tabor, *Cross Currents* 42 (1992): 273.

[43]Droge and Tabor, *Noble Death,* p. 185.

[44]Joseph Bayly, *The Last Thing We Talk About,* rev. ed. (Elgin, Ill.: David C. Cook, 1973), p. 74.

[45]E.g., William Morris, ed., *The American Heritage Dictionary of the English Language* (Boston: Houghton Mifflin, 1976), p. 1287.

[46]Carlos F. Gomez, *Regulating Death: Euthanasia and the Case of the Netherlands* (New York: Free Press, 1991), p. 23.

[47]Ann Alpers and Bernard Lo, "Does It Make Clinical Sense to Equate Terminally Ill Patients Who Require Life-Sustaining Interventions with Those Who Do Not?" *Journal of the American Medical Association* 277 (1997): 1705-8.

Chapter 1: Suicide & Euthanasia When Christianity Arose

[1]Pliny, *Natural History: A Selection,* trans. John F. Healy (New York: Penguin, 1991), pp. 12-13.

[2]Ibid., p. 14.

[3]John M. Rist, *Human Value: A Study in Ancient Philosophical Ethics* (Leiden: E. J. Brill, 1982), p. 9.

[4]There is an extensive secondary literature on suicide in classical antiquity. Good starting points in English are Anton J. L. van Hooff, *From Autothanasia to Suicide: Self-Killing in Classical Antiquity* (London: Routledge, 1990); Miriam Griffin, "Philosophy, Cato and Roman Suicide," *Greece and Rome* 33 (1986): 64-77, 192-202; John M. Cooper, "Greek Philosophers on Euthanasia and Suicide," in *Suicide and Euthanasia: Historical and Contemporary Themes,* ed. Baruch A. Brody (Dordrecht, Netherlands: Kluwer, 1989), pp. 9-38; and Elise P. Garrison, "Attitudes Toward Suicide in Ancient Greece," *Transactions of the American Philological Association* 121 (1991): 1-34.

[5]*Epidemics* 1.11.

[6]See, e.g., Danielle Gourevitch, "Suicide Among the Sick in Classical Antiquity," *Bulletin of the History of Medicine* 43 (1969): 509.

[7]Pliny *Natural History* 25.7.23.

[8]See Gourevitch, "Suicide Among the Sick," p. 508.

[9]See Fridolf Kudlien, "Medical Ethics and Popular Ethics in Greece and Rome," *Clio Medica* 5 (1970): 91-121; Vivian Nutton, "Murders and Miracles: Law Attitudes Towards Medicine in Classical Antiquity," in *Patients and Practitioners: Lay Perceptions of Medicine in Pre-industrial Society*, ed. Roy Porter (Cambridge: Cambridge University Press, 1985), pp. 23-53.

[10]See J. S. Hamilton, "Scribonius Largus on the Medical Profession," *Bulletin of the History of Medicine* 60 (1986): 209-16.

[11]Ludwig Edelstein, *The Hippocratic Oath: Text, Translation and Interpretation*, Supplements of the *Bulletin of the History of Medicine* 1 (Baltimore: Johns Hopkins University Press, 1943); reprinted in Ludwig Edelstein, *Ancient Medicine: Selected Papers of Ludwig Edelstein*, ed. Owsei Temkin and C. Lilian Temkin (Baltimore: Johns Hopkins University Press, 1967), pp. 3-63.

[12]See, e.g., Karl Deichgräber, *Der hippokratische Eid* (Stuttgart: Hippokrates-Verlag, 1955); Kudlien, "Medical Ethics"; Charles Lichtenthaeler, *Der Eid des Hippokrates: Ursprung und Bedeutung* (Cologne: Deutscher Arzte-Verlag, 1984); Vivian Nutton, "Beyond the Hippocratic Oath," in *Doctors and Ethics: The Earlier Historical Setting of Professional Ethics*, ed. A. Wear, J. Geyer-Kordesch and R. French (Amsterdam: Rodopi, 1993), pp. 10-37.

[13]Kudlien's translation ("Medical Ethics," p. 118 n. 47). Heinrich von Staden (" 'In a Pure and Holy Way': Personal and Professional Conduct in the Hippocratic Oath?" *Journal of the History of Medicine and Allied Sciences* 51 [1996], p. 407), staying very close to the Greek, translates, "And I will not give a drug that is deadly to anyone if asked [for it], nor will I suggest the way to such a counsel."

[14]Darrel W. Amundsen, "The Physician's Obligation to Prolong Life: A Medical Duty Without Classical Roots," *Hastings Center Report*, August 1978, pp. 23-30; reprinted in Darrel W. Amundsen, *Medicine, Society and Faith in the Ancient and Medieval Worlds* (Baltimore: Johns Hopkins University Press, 1996), pp. 30-49.

[15]*The Art* 3.

[16]For a balanced treatment of the primary sources, see Heinrich Von Staden, "Incurability and Hopelessness: The Hippocratic Corpus," in *La maladie et les maladies dans la collection Hippocratique: Actes du VIe colloque international Hippocratique*, ed. Paul Potter, Gilles Maloney and Jacques Desautels (Quebec: Editions du Sphinx, 1990), pp. 75-112.

[17]Owsei Temkin, *Hippocrates in a World of Pagans and Christians* (Baltimore: Johns Hopkins University Press, 1991), p. 139.

[18]For a discussion of these texts, see Amundsen, "Physician's Obligation."

[19]E.g., according to the Mishnah, *Sanhedrin* 4.5, "Man was created alone, to teach you that whoever destroys a single Israelite soul is deemed by Scripture as if he had destroyed a whole world. And whoever saves a single Israelite soul is deemed by Scripture as if he had saved a whole world," in Jacob Neusner, *The*

Mishnah: A New Translation (New Haven, Conn.: Yale University Press, 1988), p. 591. This attitude is reflected in various talmudic texts where it is stipulated that the sabbath must be violated to save the life of an Israelite or a person whose ethnicity was in doubt but who was not a heathen (including a Samaritan or a Christian), as in the Babylonian Talmud, *Yoma* 84b-85b.

[20] Josephus *Against Apion* 1.60. Unless otherwise indicated, quotations from Josephus's works are from the Loeb Classical Library edition, various translators (Cambridge, Mass.: Harvard University Press, various dates).

[21] Ibid., 1.42-43. This was a reality of such importance to Josephus that he referred to it twice more in this treatise: *Against Apion* 2.218, 2.233.

[22] Babylonian Talmud, *Sanhedrin* 74a. Quotations are from *The Babylonian Talmud: Translated into English with Notes and Glossary,* ed. I. Epstein, various translators (New York: Traditional Press, 1983).

[23] Babylonian Talmud, *'Aboda Zara* 27b.

[24] Ibid., 54a.

[25] Babylonian Talmud, *Sanhedrin* 74b.

[26] Babylonian Talmud, *Pesahim* 53b.

[27] Second Maccabees 6:18-31. Quotations from 1 Maccabees and 2 Maccabees are from the New English Bible, *The First and Second Books of the Maccabees,* with commentary by John R. Bartlett (Cambridge: Cambridge University Press, 1973). A more embellished version of Eleazar's martyrdom occurs in 4 Maccabees 5—6.

[28] See H. Anderson's introduction to his translation of 4 Maccabees in *The Old Testament Pseudepigrapha,* ed. James H. Charlesworth, 2 vols. (Garden City, N.Y.: Doubleday, 1983-1985), 2:533-34. Quotations from 4 Maccabees are from this edition.

[29] Ibid., 2:539.

[30] Ibid., 2:562 n. 17a.

[31] Babylonian Talmud, *Gittin* 57b.

[32] H. H. Cohn, "On the Dichotomy of Divinity and Humanity in Jewish Law," in *Euthanasia,* ed. A. Carmi (Berlin: Springer-Verlag, 1984), pp. 48-49.

[33] *Gittin* 57b.

[34] Josephus *Antiquities of the Jews* 5.252-53.

[35] Ibid., 5.317.

[36] Ibid., 6.370-71.

[37] See A. Carmi, "Live like a King, Die like a King," in *Euthanasia,* ed. A. Carmi (Berlin: Springer-Verlag, 1984), pp. 47-50.

[38] Josephus *Antiquities of the Jews* 7.228-29.

[39] Ibid., 8.309.

[40] Ibid., 8.314. See also the account of the suicide of Herod's brother Phasael when he had been captured by the enemy in ibid., 14.367-68, and Josephus *Jewish War* 1.271-72. Quotations from the latter work are from the translation by G. A. Williamson, revised by E. Mary Smallwood (New York: Dorset, 1985).

[41] E.g., Babylonian Talmud, *Ta'anit* 29a; Josephus *Jewish War* 1.150; 3.425;

4.79-80.

[42] Josephus *Jewish War* 3.356-59.

[43] Ibid., 3.362-82.

[44] Ibid., 3.354.

[45] Ibid., 7.323-36.

[46] Ibid., 7.341-88.

[47] Ibid., 7.404-5.

[48] See the corrective analysis by David J. Ladouceur, "Josephus and Masada," in *Josephus, Judaism and Christianity*, ed. Louis H. Feldman and Gohei Hata (Detroit: Wayne State University Press, 1987), especially pp. 104-6.

[49] Josephus *Jewish War* 7.405. See, e.g., H. St. J. Thackeray's translation in the Loeb series.

[50] Ladouceur, "Josephus and Masada," p. 105. There is an ever-expanding body of scholarly analyses of Eleazar's suicide speeches. See, e.g., David J. Ladouceur, "Masada: A Consideration of the Literary Evidence," *Greek, Roman and Byzantine Studies* 21 (1980): 245-60; I. Jacobs, "Eleazar ben Yair's Sanction for Martyrdom," *Journal for the Study of Judaism* 13 (1982): 183-86; and Menahem Luz, "Eleazar's Second Speech on Masada and Its Literary Precedents," *Rheinisches Museum für Philologie* 126 (1983): 25-43.

[51] See David Daube, "Josephus on Suicide and Liability of Depositee," *Juridical Review* 76 (1964): 212-24.

[52] We have found two other examples of such suicides in the Babylonian Talmud: *Ketubot* 103b and *Ta'anit* 29a.

[53] Babylonian Talmud, *'Aboda Zara* 17a.

[54] Ibid., 18a.

[55] CCAR Responsa Committee, "On the Treatment of the Terminally Ill," *CCAR Journal: A Reform Jewish Quarterly*, Spring 1997, p. 12.

[56] Ibid., p. 13.

[57] Babylonian Talmud, *Baba Qamma* 91b.

[58] *The Tractate "Mourning,"* trans. Dov Zlotnick, Yale Judaica Series 17 (New Haven, Conn.: Yale University Press, 1966), pp. 1-9.

[59] *Semaḥot* 2.1-5, in ibid., pp. 33-34.

[60] CCAR Responsa Committee, "On the Treatment of the Terminally Ill," p. 23.

[61] Ibid., p. 13.

[62] Ibid., pp. 13-14; emphasis in the original.

[63] Ibid., p. 14.

[64] Ibid.

[65] Ibid., p. 15.

[66] Josephus *Jewish War* 1.663. The same account is given in Josephus *Antiquities of the Jews* 17.183-84.

[67] Babylonian Talmud, *Baba Qamma* 51a: *Ketubot* 37b; *Pesaḥim* 75a; *Sanhedrin* 45a, 52a, 52b; *Soṭa* 8b.

[68] *Semaḥot* 1.1, in *Tractate "Mourning,"* p. 31.

[69] Ibid., p. 9.

[70] Babylonian Talmud, *Sanhedrin* 78a.

[71] Baruch A. Brody, "A Historical Introduction to Jewish Casuistry on Suicide and Euthanasia," in *Suicide and Euthanasia: Historical and Contemporary Themes,* ed. Baruch A. Brody (Dordrecht: Kluwer, 1989), p. 63.

[72] *Tractate "Mourning,"* p. 97.

[73] *Šabbat* 23.5, in Neusner, *Mishnah,* p. 207.

[74] Babylonian Talmud, *Šabbat* 151b; cf. ibid., 30b.

[75] According to the Babylonian Talmud, *Yoma* 84b, the sick must be cared for on the sabbath, and those who were in peril must be rescued. See *Yoma* 85a-b for the rabbinic justification.

[76] Babylonian Talmud, *'Aboda Zara* 27b.

[77] Brody, "Historical Introduction to Jewish Casuistry," p. 71.

[78] Babylonian Talmud, *Ta'anit* 23a.

[79] Babylonian Talmud, *Baba Meṣi'a* 84a.

[80] Babylonian Talmud, *Ketubot* 104a.

[81] Cohn, "On the Dichotomy of Divinity and Humanity," p. 31.

[82] Brody, "Historical Introduction to Jewish Casuistry," p. 41.

[83] Ibid., p. 62; emphasis in the original.

Chapter 2: Why Early Christians Condemned Euthanasia & Suicide

[1] Exodus 21:22-25, the one possible exception, is patient of two different interpretations: the "serious injury" applies to the mother or to the baby. Regardless, the passage does not involve intentional, induced abortion.

[2] We now recognize, however, that they often confused abortion and contraception owing to their rudimentary knowledge of obstetrics and embryology.

[3] For a thorough discussion see David Daube, "The Linguistics of Suicide," *Philosophy and Public Affairs* 1 (1972): 387-437.

[4] George P. Fisher, *The Beginnings of Christianity* (New York: Scribner's, 1911), pp. 174-75.

[5] Ibid., p. 175.

[6] E.g., Matthew 13:43; Luke 10:20; John 14:2-3; 17:24; Romans 8:17; 1 Corinthians 15:12-19; 2 Corinthians 4:17; Ephesians 1:18; 1 Thessalonians 4:13-18; Titus 2:13; 1 Peter 1:3-4; Jude 21; Revelation 21:1-4.

[7] Ambrose *Death as a Good* 1.1, in *FC,* 65:70.

[8] Ibid., 2.3, *FC* 65:71.

[9] Ibid., 8.31, *FC* 65:93.

[10] Ibid., 12.57, *FC* 65:112.

[11] Peter Brown, *The Cult of the Saints: Its Rise and Function in Latin Christianity* (Chicago: University of Chicago Press, 1981), pp. 69-70.

[12] John Chrysostom *Homily 8 on Philippians,* in *NPNF-1,* 13:233.

[13] Tertullian *Patience* 9, *FC* 40:209.

[14] For the imperative to care for people's material needs, see chapter three.

[15] John 15:20; cf. Mark 10:28-30; Acts 9:16; 14:22; 1 Thessalonians 3:2-4; 2 Timothy 1:8; 2:3; 3:12; 4:5.

[16]There is an enormous literature on the subject of martyrdom and persecution in early Christianity. The most authoritative and reliable treatment is W. H. C. Frend, *Martyrdom and Persecution in the Early Church* (Oxford: Blackwell, 1965).

[17]Clement *Stromateis* 4:4, in *ANF* 2:412.

[18]Ibid., 4.10, *ANF* 2:423.

[19]Ibid., 4.4, *ANF* 2:411.

[20]Tertullian *Scorpiace* 1.11.

[21]Tertullian *Patience* 13.6.

[22]Tertullian *Ad Uxorem* 1.3.

[23]Tertullian *Flight in the Time of Persecution* 6.3, *FC* 40:287.

[24]For a discussion of this case see Timothy D. Barnes, *Tertullian: A Historical and Literary Study* (Oxford: Clarendon, 1971), pp. 168-71.

[25]Frend, *Martyrdom and Persecution,* p. 197.

[26]Eusebius *Ecclesiastical History* 4.15.

[27]Ibid.

[28]*Martyrdom of Polycarp* 4, *AF* 2:317.

[29]Tertullian *To Scapula* 5, *FC* 10:160.

[30]What may have been more common was Christians' provoking persecution and potential martyrdom by symbolic acts such as destroying pagan idols. Canon 60 of the Synod of Elvira, held around 305, condemned such acts on the grounds that the gospel does not suggest deeds of this kind and the apostles did not act in this fashion. The synod decreed that people who die as a result of doing so should not be regarded as martyrs. See C. J. Hefele, *A History of the Christian Councils* (Edinburgh: T & T Clark, 1871), p. 163.

[31]Lucian *The Death of Peregrinus* 13, in *Selected Satires of Lucian,* trans. L. Casson (New York: Norton, 1968), p. 369.

[32]Marcus Aurelius *Meditations* 11.3.

[33]Clement of Alexandria *Stromateis* 4.4, *ANF* 2:411.

[34]Boniface Ramsey, *Beginning to Read the Fathers* (New York: Paulist, 1985), p. 126.

[35]Clement of Alexandria *Stromateis* 7.11, *ANF* 2:541-42.

[36]Cyprian *Mortality* 17, *FC* 36:213.

[37]E.g., Acts 13:38; Ephesians 1:7; Colossians 1:14; Hebrews 9:14; James 4:8; 1 John 1:9; 3:3.

[38]This was a point of considerable dispute during the early centuries of Christianity, as views varied enormously on the nature of forgiveness of postbaptismal sins and the state of those who had lapsed during times of persecution and then wished to be readmitted to the Christian community.

[39]See, as a beginning point, E. R. Dodds, *Pagan and Christian in an Age of Anxiety,* reprint ed. (New York: Norton, 1970), especially pp. 26-36.

[40]E.g., Clement of Alexandria *Stromateis* 3.7; Lactantius *The Divine Institutes* 5:22; Ambrose *Epistle* 63:91.

[41]Augustine *City of God* 14.3, trans. H. Bettenson (London: Penguin, 1972), pp. 550-52. See R. M. Miles, *Augustine on the Body* (Missoula, Mont.: Scholars Press, 1979).

[42]See also chapter three.

[43]Jerome *Letter* 3.5.

[44]Ibid., 39, *NPNF-2*, 6:53. The cynical reader might suggest that Jerome condemned Paula's fasting and public grief from fear that her actions might draw attention to his own role in Blaesilla's death. Jerome appears, however, to be making a theologically categorical distinction between the asceticism of the daughter and the austerities of her mother.

[45]E.g., Romans 11:22; Hebrews 3:6, 14; Revelation 2:7, 11, 17, 26; 3:5, 12, 21; 21:7.

[46]The writer of Hebrews is here quoting Proverbs 3:11-12. The words translated "discipline," both in the Hebrew of Proverbs and in the Greek of this epistle, mean discipline in the sense of training, instruction and upbringing.

[47]For an insightful discussion see David Daube, "Death as a Release in the Bible," *Novum Testamentum* 5 (1972): 82-104.

[48]The New Testament, however, does not deal with suicide by the mentally ill, for instance, by the severely depressed or melancholic. Several centuries would elapse before any extant Christian source would consider the theological or spiritual implications of such suicides.

[49]Cyprian *The Good of Patience* 10, *FC* 36:273.

[50]Ibid., 12-14, *FC* 36:275-77.

[51]Ibid., 17, *FC* 36:279-80, quoting Ecclesiasticus 2:4-5.

[52]Ibid., 17-18, *FC* 36:279-81.

[53]Ibid., 20, *FC* 36:282-83.

[54]Ibid., 24, *FC* 36:287.

[55]Cyprian *Mortality* 8, *FC* 36:204-5.

[56]Ibid., 11, *FC* 36:207, quoting Psalm 50:19.

[57]Ibid., 12, *FC* 36:208.

[58]Ibid., 20, *FC* 36:215.

[59]Ibid., 26, *FC* 36:220-21.

Chapter 3: Euthanasia in Early Christianity

[1]E.g., the contrast between the rich man and Lazarus (Lk 16:19-31).

[2]E.g., Jerome *Epistles* 10; 39; Augustine *Tractate 30 on John* 1; Augustine *On the Good of Marriage* 9; Augustine *City of God* 9.13; 22.24; Augustine *Epistles* 130; John Cassian *Conference of Abbot Theodore* 3.

[3]For a more thorough discussion of the meaning of sickness, see Darrel W. Amundsen and Gary B. Ferngren, "The Perception of Disease and Disease Causality in the New Testament," *Aufstieg und Niedergang der römischen Welt* 2, no. 37.3 (1996): 2934-56.

[4]H. Roux, "Sickness," in *A Companion to the Bible*, ed. J.-J. von Allmen (New York: Oxford University Press, 1958), p. 402.

[5]E.g., Numbers 12; 2 Samuel 12:15-18; 2 Kings 5:21-27; 2 Chronicles 21:12-19; 26:16-21.

[6]E.g., 2 Kings 13:14, 20; 20:1-11 (cf. 2 Chron 32:24-26; Is 38); Psalm 73:14 (cf. Ps 73:4); Psalm 88; Daniel 8:27.

[7]When visiting his hometown, Nazareth, Jesus "did not do many miracles there because of their unbelief" (Mt 13:58). But Mark 6:5-6 expresses the matter somewhat differently: "And He could do no miracle there except that He laid His hands upon a few sick people and healed them. And He wondered at their unbelief." Animated discussion continues among New Testament scholars concerning the relationship between faith and healing in the New Testament in particular and the numerous interpretive problems posed by Jesus' miracles in general. See Darrel W. Amundsen and Gary B. Ferngren, "The Healing Miracles of the Gospels: Problems and Methods," *Aufstieg und Niedergang der römischen Welt*, 2, no. 26.3, forthcoming.

[8]The *astheneia* word group, used by Paul in this passage, is employed by New Testament writers more than any other to express the idea of illness, sickness or disease.

[9]Luke 13:16. This is a rather peculiar case in that although the woman is described as "having a sickness caused by a spirit" (Lk 13:11), there is no exorcism but simply a healing of the condition. Hence this appears to be the only instance in the New Testament in which a sickness is attributed to a demon extraneous to the afflicted person.

[10]Raymond E. Brown, *The Gospel According to John (i-xii)* (Garden City, N.Y.: Doubleday, 1966), ad loc.

[11]E.g., Gregory of Nyssa *De Virginitate* 21; John Chrysostom *Homily 1 on the Statues* 11; John Chrysostom *Homily 6 on the Statues* 14; John Chrysostom *Homily 22 on John* 3; John Chrysostom *Homily 16 on Acts*.

[12]See, e.g., Edwin Yamauchi, "Magic or Miracle: Diseases, Demons and Exorcisms," in *The Miracles of Jesus*, ed. David Wenham and Craig Blomberg, vol. 6 of *Gospel Perspectives: Studies of History and Tradition in the Four Gospels*, ed. R. T. France and David Wenham (Sheffield, U.K.: JSOT, 1986), pp. 89-183.

[13]Michael Green, *Evangelism in the Early Church* (Grand Rapids, Mich.: Eerdmans, 1970), p. 190; cf. F. van der Meer, *Augustine the Bishop: The Life and Work of a Father of the Church*, trans. B. Battershaw and G. R. Lamb (London: Sheed and Ward, 1961), pp. 67-75; and Peter Brown, *Augustine of Hippo* (Berkeley: University of California Press, 1967), p. 395.

[14]See Gary B. Ferngren, "Christianity and Healing in the Second Century," in *Proceedings of the Thirty-second International Congress on the History of Medicine, Antwerp, 3-7 September 1990* (Brussels: Societas Belgica Historiae Medicinae, 1991), pp. 131-37, and Gary B. Ferngren, "Early Christianity as a Religion of Healing?" *Bulletin of the History of Medicine* 66 (1992): 1-15.

[15]Peter Brown does both with sensitivity and remarkable insight. See especially *The Making of Late Antiquity* (Cambridge, Mass.: Harvard University Press, 1978); and *The Cult of the Saints: Its Rise and Function in Latin Christianity* (Chicago: University of Chicago Press, 1981).

[16]Jerome *Letters* 10.

[17]Ibid., 39.2, *NPNF-2* 6:50.

[18]Ibid., 38.2.

[19] Ambrose *Letters* 79.

[20] Ambrose *Concerning Repentance* 1.13.63.

[21] Basil of Caesarea *The Long Rules* 55.

[22] Gregory Nazianzen *On the Death of His Father* 28.

[23] John Chrysostom *Homily 1 on the Statues.*

[24] The categorizing of some individuals and groups (e.g., Marcion and the Marcionites) evokes considerable scholarly disagreement. Marcion is regularly credited with a blanket rejection of physicians and the art of medicine on the basis of his radical dualism and such flimsy evidence as his expunging from Colossians 4:14 the designation of Luke as *ho iatros ho agapētos.*

[25] *Shepherd of Hermas, Similitude* 10.4.3, *AF* 2:305.

[26] Although Peter Brown, *The Body and Society: Men, Women and Sexual Renunciation in Early Christianity* (New York: Columbia University Press, 1988), is concerned primarily with the subject described in the book's subtitle, he offers some interesting observations on the motivations for ascetics' discipline of their bodies. It was not a hatred of the body but a love of the body, because it was to be resurrected, that stimulated measures that seem to us rather harsh. See especially pp. 222-26, 235-39.

[27] Clement of Alexandria *Stromateis* 4.26, *ANF* 2:439.

[28] Ibid., 4.4, *ANF* 2:412.

[29] Tertullian *Apology* 42.4, *FC* 10:107.

[30] Some church fathers (e.g., Origen and pseudo-Macarius) taught that the most spiritually mature Christians should rely entirely on God for the healing of their physical ills but held that medicine and physicians were gifts of God for the succor of the rest of humanity, which included the vast majority of Christians.

[31] Jaroslav Pelikan, *The Shape of Death: Life, Death and Immortality in the Early Fathers* (Nashville: Abingdon, 1961), p. 5.

[32] Adolf von Harnack, *The Expansion of Christianity in the First Three Centuries*, trans. J. Moffat (1905; reprint, New York: Books for Libraries, 1972), pp. 69-70.

[33] Pseudo-Justin *Epistles* 17.

[34] E.g., Hippolytus *Apostolic Tradition* canon 20; Polycarp *Epistle* 6; Pseudo-Clement *De Virginitate;* Tertullian *Ad Uxorem* 2.4; Justin *Apology 1* 67; Jerome *Epistle* 52.15, 16.

[35] See Gary B. Ferngren, "The Organization of the Care of the Sick in Early Christianity," in *Proceedings of the Thirtieth International Congress of the History of Medicine*, ed. H. Schadewaldt and K.-H. Leven (Düsseldorf, Germany: Vicom KG, 1988), pp. 192-98.

[36] Eusebius *Ecclesiastical History* 7.22.7-8; Pontius *The Life and Passion of Cyprian* 9—10.

[37] See Gary B. Ferngren, "Lay Orders of Medical Attendants in the Early Byzantine Empire," in *Actes/Proceedings of the XXXI International Congress of the History of Medicine*, ed. R. A. Bernabeo (Bologna, Italy: Monduzzi Editore, 1990), pp. 793-99.

[38] Julian *Epistles* 22.

[39]See Timothy S. Miller, *The Birth of the Hospital in the Byzantine Empire* (Baltimore: Johns Hopkins University Press, 1985).

[40]Julian *Epistles* 49.

[41]E. R. Dodds, *Pagan and Christian in an Age of Anxiety* (1965; reprint, New York: Norton, 1970), p. 138. For a similar assessment see Rodney Stark, *The Rise of Christianity: A Sociologist Reconsiders History* (Princeton, N.J.: Princeton University Press, 1996).

[42]See Darrel W. Amundsen and Gary B. Ferngren, "Philanthropy in Medicine: Some Historical Perspectives," in *Beneficence and Health Care,* ed. Earl E. Shelp (Dordrecht, Netherlands: Reidel, 1982), pp. 1-31, especially pp. 1-12.

[43]See John M. Rist, *Human Value: A Study in Ancient Philosophical Ethics* (Leiden: E. J. Brill, 1982).

[44]See Darrel W. Amundsen, "Medicine and the Birth of Defective Children: Approaches of the Ancient World," which is chapter three of Amundsen's *Medicine, Society and Faith in the Ancient and Medieval Worlds* (Baltimore: Johns Hopkins University Press, 1996).

[45]See Gary B. Ferngren, "The *Imago Dei* and the Sanctity of Life: The Origins of an Idea," in *Euthanasia and the Newborn: Conflicts About Saving Lives,* ed. R. C. Macmillan, H. T. Engelhardt and S. F. Spicker (Dordrecht, Netherlands: Reidel, 1987), pp. 23-45.

[46]Cyprian *Mortality* 5; 18; 24; *FC* 36:202-3, 214, 219.

[47]Basil of Caesarea *The Long Rule* 55, *FC* 9:331.

[48]John Chrysostom *Homily 8 on Colossians.*

[49]Augustine *Sermon* 345.2.

[50]Ibid., 84.1, in M. M. Getty, *The Life of the North Africans As Revealed in the Sermons of Saint Augustine* (Washington, D.C.: Catholic University of America Press, 1931), pp. 24-25.

[51]Augustine *Sermon* 344.5, in ibid., p. 25.

Chapter 4: Suicide in Early Christianity

[1]*Shepherd of Hermas, Similitude* 10.4.3, *AF* 2:305.

[2]Justin Martyr *Apology 2* 4, *FC* 6:123.

[3]L. W. Barnard, *Justin Martyr: His Life and Thought* (Cambridge: Cambridge University Press, 1967), p. 154.

[4]*Epistle to Diognetus,* in J. Quasten, *Patrology,* vol. 1, *The Beginnings of Patristic Literature,* reprint ed. (Westminster, Md.: Christian Classics, 1983), p. 251.

[5]*Clementine Homilies* 12.14, *ANF* 8:295.

[6]Clement of Alexandria *Stromateis* 4.6, *ANF* 2:414.

[7]Ibid., 4.7, *ANF* 2:418.

[8]Ibid., 7.11, *ANF* 2:540-41.

[9]Ibid., 7.13, *ANF* 2:547.

[10]Ibid., 6.9, *ANF* 2:497.

[11]Ibid., 2.20, *ANF* 2:374.

[12]Ibid., 4.5, *ANF* 2:412.

[13]Tertullian *Patience* 11.2-5, *FC* 40:212.

[14]Ibid., 14.2-6, *FC* 40:218-19.

[15]Tertullian *Flight in Time of Persecution* 13.2, *FC* 40:304.

[16]Tertullian *Apology* 23.3, *FC* 10:71-72.

[17]Tertullian *To the Martyrs* 4.9, *FC* 40:24.

[18]Ibid., 9, *FC* 40:27-28.

[19]Tertullian *Apology* 46.14, *FC* 10:113.

[20]Ibid., 50.4-11, *FC* 10:123-25.

[21]Timothy Barnes, *Tertullian: A Historical and Literary Study* (Oxford: Clarendon, 1971), pp. 218-19.

[22]C. P. Williams, "Lactantius," in *The New International Dictionary of the Christian Church*, 2nd ed., ed. J. D. Douglas (Grand Rapids, Mich.: Zondervan, 1974), p. 575.

[23]P. de Labriolle, *History and Literature of Christianity from Tertullian to Boethius*, reprint ed. (New York: Barnes & Noble, 1968), p. 205.

[24]Lactantius *Divine Institutes* 3.18, *ANF* 7:88-89.

[25]Lactantius *Epitome* 39, *ANF* 7:237.

[26]Eusebius *History of the Church from Christ to Constantine* 2.7.1, trans. G. A. Williamson (New York: Penguin, 1965), p. 81.

[27]Ibid., 5.16.13, 15, p. 220.

[28]Basil of Caesarea *Letters* 188.2, *FC* 2:12-13.

[29]John Chrysostom *Commentary on Galatians* 1:4, *NPNF-1* 13:5.

[30]F. Homes Dudden, *The Life and Times of St. Ambrose* (Oxford: Clarendon, 1935), pp. 502, 551-54.

[31]Ambrose *Death as a Good* 3.7, *FC* 65:73-74.

[32]Ambrose *Concerning Virgins* 3.7.32, *NPNF-2* 10:386.

[33]Jerome *Letter* 39.3, *NPNF-2* 6:51.

[34]Jerome *Commentarius in Ionam Prophetam* 1.6, *Patrologia Cursus Completus, Series Latina*, ed. J. P. Migne, 221 vols. (Paris: J. P. Migne, 1844-1864), 1.12:390-91.

[35]Eusebius *History of the Church from Christ to Constantine* 8.12.2, p. 342.

[36]Ambrose *Concerning Virgins* 3.7.32; Jerome *Commentarius in Ionam Prophetam* 1.6.

[37]Eusebius *History of the Church from Christ to Constantine* 6.41.7, p. 276.

[38]Ibid., 8.6.6, p. 334.

[39]John Chrysostom, in his *Homilia Encomastica* on the most famous of these virgin suicides, Pelagia (who died about 313), enthusiastically approved her act. See *Patrologia Cursus Completus, Series Graeco-Latina*, ed. J. P. Migne, 166 vols. (Paris: J. P. Migne, 1857-1886), 49:579-84.

[40]Eusebius *History of the Church from Christ to Constantine* 8.12.3-4.

[41]Ibid., 8.14.14, p. 350.

[42]Ibid., 8.14.17, p. 351.

[43]Dudden, *Life and Times of St. Ambrose*, p. 157.

[44]For a much more thorough analysis of Augustine's arguments against suicide than space permits here, see Darrel W. Amundsen, *Medicine, Society and Faith in the Ancient and Medieval Worlds* (Baltimore: Johns Hopkins University Press,

1996), pp. 101-20.

[45]Margaret Pabst Battin, *Ethical Issues in Suicide* (Englewood Cliffs, N.J.: Prentice-Hall, 1982), p. 71.

[46]Augustine *City of God* 15.1.

[47]Augustine *Retractations* 2.69.

[48]For a thorough, scholarly treatment of the Donatist movement see W. H.
C. Frend, *The Donatist Church* (Oxford: Clarendon, 1952).

[49]Augustine *Epistle* 153.18.

[50]Possidius *Vita Augustini* 12.

[51]Augustine *Contra Litteras Petiliani* 2.19.43, *NPNF-1* 4:539-40.

[52]Ibid., 2.85.186, *NPNF-1* 4:574.

[53]Ibid., 2.20.46, *NPNF-1* 4:541.

[54]Augstine *Letters* 204, *FC* 32:6.

[55]Augustine *Letters* 173, *NPNF-1* 1:545.

[56]See Augustine *City of God* 1.26.

[57]The only hint that there might have been even a minor problem can be read
into the *City of God* 1.25, where Augustine said that he had included the
discussion of the question of suicide committed in order to avoid sinning, "for
the sake of these men or women who think that they must do mortal violence
to themselves in order to avoid, not another's sin, but a sin of their own." When
he returned to the subject in *City of God* 1.27, he conceded that "if any just cause
were possible for suicide, I am sure that there could not be one more just than
that." But we should not take this as anything more than an acknowledgment
of the realities of the spiritual warfare that caused even Paul, in his yearning
to be entirely free from sin, finally to cry out, "Wretched man that I am! Who
will set me free from the body of this death?" (Rom 7:24). The scenario of a
discouraged Christian, who, vitally concerned about his or her propensity to
sin, asked a spiritual counselor why he or she could not end the battle by going
to heaven immediately is more likely than one in which a person who wanted
to kill himself or herself might argue that this was a justifiable cause.

  This is not to say that there are no cases of newly converted Christians
committing suicide with the intention of going directly to heaven. But the earliest
examples that we have been able to locate come from the British Isles and survive
in documents written centuries after Augustine's time. See J. J. O'Dea, *Suicide:
Studies on Its Philosophy, Causes and Prevention* (New York: Putnam, 1882), pp. 75-76.

Chapter 5: Euthanasia & Suicide in the Middle Ages

[1]Hermann Buzembaum, *Medulla Theologiae Moralis*, quoted in Marvin M.
O'Connell, "The Roman Catholic Tradition: Since 1545," in *Caring and Curing:
Health and Medicine in the Western Religious Traditions*, ed. Ronald L. Numbers and
Darrel W. Amundsen, reprint ed. (Baltimore: Johns Hopkins University Press,
1998), p. 124.

[2]Thomas Aquinas *Summa Theologiae* 2a2ae.124.1.

[3]Ibid., 2a2ae.64.6.

[4]Augustine *City of God* 1.20.

[5]Razis's suicide is recorded in 2 Maccabees 14:37-46. See our discussion in chapter one.

[6]Margaret Pabst Battin, *Ethical Issues in Suicide* (Englewood Cliffs, N.J.: Prentice-Hall, 1982), p. 52.

[7]Augustine *De Libero Arbitrio* 3.7.20—3.8.23. For an analysis of this passage see Amundsen, "Suicide and Early Christian Values," in *Suicide and Euthanasia: Historical and Contemporary Themes*, ed. Baruch A. Brody (Dordrecht, Netherlands: Kluwer, 1989), pp. 149-51, n. 46.

[8]See J. J. O'Dea, *Suicide: Studies on Its Philosophy, Causes and Prevention* (New York: Putnam, 1882), pp. 77-78.

[9]John Cassian *Conferences* 2.5.

[10]*The Penitential of Theodore*, quoted in John T. Gamer and Helen M. Gamer, *Medieval Handbooks of Penance*, reprint ed. (New York: Octagon, 1965), p. 207.

[11]George Rosen, "History," in *A Handbook for the Study of Suicide*, ed. S. Perlin (New York: Oxford University Press, 1975), p. 13.

[12]See Robert Barry, "The Development of the Roman Catholic Teachings on Suicide," *Notre Dame Journal of Law, Ethics and Public Policy* 9 (1995): 474-75.

[13]The reference is to Albert Bayet, *Le suicide et la morale* (Paris: F. Alcan, 1922).

[14]Glanville Williams, *The Sanctity of Life and the Criminal Law*, reprint ed. (New York: Alfred A. Knopf, 1970), p. 258.

[15]Ibid., p. 256.

[16]The one significant exception is the suicide of women, especially virgins, to preserve their chastity. It is ironic that in this area Augustine and Aquinas continue to be at variance with some Roman Catholic moral theologians.

[17]See Richard Palmer, "The Church, Leprosy and Plague in Medieval and Early Modern Europe," in *The Church and Healing*, ed. W. J. Sheils, Studies in Church History 19 (Oxford: Blackwell, 1982), pp. 82-83.

[18]Saul Nathaniel Brody, *The Disease of the Soul: Leprosy in Medieval Literature* (Ithaca, N.Y.: Cornell University Press, 1974), p. 103.

[19]Gregory the Great, *Pastoral Care*, trans. Henry Davis (New York: Newman, 1950), 3.12, pp. 122, 125.

[20]Bede, *Ecclesiastical History*, trans. B. Colgrave and R. Mynors (Oxford: Clarendon, 1969), 4.9.

[21]Ibid., 1.19.

[22]Bede *Vita Beatorum Abbatum*, translation in *The Conversion of Western Europe, 350-750*, ed. J. N. Hillgarth (Englewood Cliffs, N.J.: Prentice-Hall, 1969), p. 121.

[23]For a discussion of the nature and effects of plague in the early Middle Ages, see J.-N. Biraben and Jacques LeGoff, "The Plague in the Early Middle Ages," in *Biology of Man in History: Selections from the Annales: Economies, Sociétés, Civilisations*, ed. R. Forster and O. Ranum, trans. E. Forster and P. M. Ranum (Baltimore: Johns Hopkins University Press, 1975), pp. 48-80.

[24]Ibid., p. 61.

[25]Jeffrey Richards, *Consul of God: The Life and Times of Gregory the Great* (London:

Routledge and Kegan Paul, 1980), pp. 41-42.

[26]Bede *Ecclesiastical History* 1.14.

[27]Bede *Life of St. Cuthbert* 9, in *Two Lives of Saint Cuthbert,* ed. and trans. B. Colgrave, reprint ed. (New York: Greenwood, 1969), p. 185.

[28]C. Mollat, *The Popes at Avignon, 1305-1378* (London: T. Nelson, 1963), p. 40.

[29]The Latin text of John of Saxony's treatise on plague is in Karl Sudhoff, "Pestschriften aus den ersten 150 Jahren nach der Epidemie des 'schwarzen Todes' 1348," *Sudhoffs Archiv* 16 (1924-25): 26; authors' translation.

[30]Barry writes that while "philosophical, political, and military suicide almost totally vanished in medieval Christian Europe[,] heterodox Christians, however, seemed to have committed suicide with much greater frequency than did the orthodox, for they were more isolated and were less influenced than the orthodox by the Christian teachings on suicide" (Barry, "The Development of Roman Catholic Teachings on Suicide," p. 474). He gives no examples of the "heterodox" Christians who were apparently more liable to commit suicide than the "orthodox." We are not sure whom he means. We know of no non-Catholic Christians (e.g., Waldensians and other pre-Reformation "protestants") who were "isolated" from the fundamental Christian beliefs that have always been inimical to suicide. Perhaps he is thinking of the Albigensians (also known as Cathari and Bogomiles) whose dualistic religion was derived from Manichaeanism. Albigenses who were unable to qualify for the highest order, that of the *perfecti,* could be saved only through the *endura,* a ritual death by self-starvation. See Emmanuel Le Roy Ladurie, *Montaillou: The Promised Land of Error,* trans. Barbara Bray (New York: George Braziller, 1978).

[31]Barry, "The Development of Roman Catholic Teachings on Suicide," pp. 473-74.

[32]Canon 22 of Lateran IV *(Cum* [or *Quum*] *Infirmitas).* The translation quoted is from *Decrees of the Ecumenical Councils,* ed. Norman P. Tanner, 2 vols. (Washington, D.C.: Georgetown University Press, 1990), 1:245-46. The kinds of "prescriptions" about which the moral theologians and canon lawyers were concerned included fornication, masturbation, the use of magical healing remedies and breaking the church's fast days. See Darrel W. Amundsen, *Medicine, Society and Faith in the Ancient and Medieval Worlds* (Baltimore: Johns Hopkins University Press, 1996), pp. 267-68.

[33]The Latin text is in S. DeRensi, *Collectio Salernitana,* 5 vols. (Naples: Filiatre-Sebezio, 1852-59), 2:74; authors' translation.

[34]The translation is in Henry E. Sigerist, "Bedside Manners in the Middle Ages: The Treatise *De Cautelis Medicorum* Attributed to Arnald of Villanova," *Quarterly Bulletin of the Northwestern University Medical School* 20 (1946): 141.

[35]The Latin text is in Karl Sudhoff, "Pestschriften aus den ersten 150 Jahren nach der Epidemie des 'schwarzen Todes' 1348," *Archiv für Geschichte der Medizin* 11 (1918-1919): 160; authors' translation.

[36]For a brief introduction see Brian Copenhaver, "Death: Art of Dying I: *Ars Moriendi,*" in *The Encyclopedia of Bioethics,* rev. ed., ed. Warren Reich, 5 vols. (New York: Simon & Schuster/Macmillan, 1995), 1:549-51.

[37] See Ernst Hirschfeld, "Deontologische Texte des frühen Mittelalters," *Sudhoffs Archiv für Geschichte der Medizin* 20 (1928): 368-69; Loren C. MacKinney, "Medical Ethics and Etiquette in the Early Middle Ages: The Persistence of Hippocratic Ideals," *Bulletin of the History of Medicine* 26 (1952): 19.

[38] The Latin text of Sigmund Albichs's treatise is in Karl Sudhoff, "Pestschriften aus den ersten 150 Jahren nach der Epidemie des 'schwarzen Todes' 1348," *Archiv für Geschichte der Medizin* 9 (1915-1916): 139; authors' translation.

[39] Martin Navarrus, *Manuale Sive Enchiridion Confessariorum et Poenitentium* (Lyons, 1574), 25.60.2, s.v. "De peccatis medici et chirurgi"; authors' translation.

[40] The entire English prase is a rendering of the Latin adverb *medicinaliter.*

[41] The Latin text is in Bartholomaeus de Sancto Concordia, *Summa Casuum* (c. 1338; Venice, 1473), generally cited as *Pisanella;* authors' translation.

[42] See Owsei Temkin, *Hippocrates in a World of Pagans and Christians* (Baltimore: Johns Hopkins University Press, 1991), pp. 231-36.

[43] See Amundsen, *Medicine, Society and Faith,* pp. 17-20, 291-94.

[44] Thomas Aquinas *De Regimine Principum* 2, ed. Joseph Mathis (Turin: Marietti, 1971).

[45] Antoninus of Florence, *Summa Theologica* (or *Summa Moralis;* 1477), reprint of 1740 ed. (Graz: Akademische Druck- und Verlagsanstalt, 1959), p. 281; authors' translation.

[46] Ibid., p. 288; authors' translation.

[47] Ibid., p. 289; authors' translation.

[48] Gratian *Decretum* D.83.1. *Pars;* authors' translation.

[49] Thomas Aquinas *Summa Theologiae* 2-2.71.1, various translators, 61 vols. (Westminster, Md.: Blackfriars, 1964-1984), 38:145.

[50] Astesanus de Asti, *Summa de Casibus Conscientiae* (c. 1317; Venice, 1478), usually cited as *Astesana,* 1.39.

[51] Walter Ullman, "Public Welfare and Social Legislation in the Early Medieval Councils," in *Councils and Assemblies,* ed. G. J. Cuming and Derek Baker, Studies in Church History 7 (Cambridge: Cambridge University Press, 1971), pp. 35-36.

[52] See Thomas G. Benedek, "The Image of Medicine in 1500: Theological Reactions to the *Ship of Fools,*" *Bulletin of the History of Medicine* 38 (1964): 332-33.

Chapter 6: Euthanasia & Suicide Since the Middle Ages

[1] S. E. Sprott, *The English Debate on Suicide from Donne to Hume* (LaSalle, Ill.: Open Court, 1961), p. 1.

[2] Sir Thomas More, *Utopia,* trans. H. V. S. Ogden (New York: Appleton-Century-Crofts, 1949), bk. 2, chap. 7.

[3] C. S. Lewis, *English Literature in the Sixteenth Century, Excluding Drama* (Oxford: Clarendon, 1954), p. 169.

[4] Gary B. Ferngren, "The Ethics of Suicide in the Renaissance and Reformation," in *Suicide and Euthanasia: Historical and Contemporary Themes,* ed. Baruch A. Brody (Dordrecht, Netherlands: Kluwer, 1989), p. 158.

[5] Martin Luther, *Martin Luther: Selections from His Writings,* ed. John Dillenberger

(Garden City, N.Y.: Doubleday, Anchor Books, 1961), p. 31.

[6]Charles Spurgeon was especially fond of this quotation; see, e.g., C. H. Spurgeon, *The New Park Street Pulpit*, 6 vols. (London: Alabaster and Passmore, 1859), 4:461.

[7]Martin Luther, *The Table Talk or Familiar Discourse of Martin Luther* (Philadelphia: Lutheran, 1868), p. 315; and Carter Lindberg, "The Lutheran Tradition," in *Caring and Curing: Health and Medicine in the Western Religious Traditions*, ed. Ronald L. Numbers and Darrel W. Amundsen (New York: Macmillian, 1986), pp. 178-80.

[8]William J. Bouwsma, *John Calvin: A Sixteenth-Century Portrait* (Oxford: Oxford University Press, 1988), pp. 30-31.

[9]John Calvin, *Institutes of the Christian Religion* (London: T. Tegg, 1838), 3.9.3-4, pp. 568-69; Julus Bonnet, ed., *Letters of John Calvin* (New York: Franklin, 1972), p. 334.

[10]Calvin *Institutes of the Christian Religion* 3.9.4, p. 569; John Calvin, *Institutes of the Christian Religion*, ed. John T. McNeill, trans. Ford Lewis Battles, 2 vols. (Philadelphia: Westminster Press, 1960), 3.8.4-6, 1:705-6; John Calvin, "For Afflicted Persons," in *Euthansia, or the Presbyterian Liturgies*, ed. Charles W. Baird (New York: Dodd, 1855), p. 39.

[11]Sprott, *English Debate on Suicide from Donne to Hume*, pp. 5-13.

[12]Only within the last century has the magisterium allowed burial rites in consecrated ground for those Roman Catholics who in a state of insanity committed suicide.

[13]The incident is related by Paul A. Welsby, *George Abbot, the Unwanted Archbishop, 1562-1633* (London: SPCK, 1962), pp. 23-24.

[14]Ibid., p. 164.

[15]Richard Baxter, *A Christian Directory* (1673; Ligonier, Penn.: Soli Deo Gloria, 1990), pp. 780-81.

[16]Ibid., pp. 261-67.

[17]Ibid., pp. 522-47.

[18]Ibid., pp. 771-73.

[19]See Nancy Lee Beaty, *The Craft of Dying* (New Haven, Conn.: Yale University Press, 1970).

[20]Ibid., p. 31 (quoting John Sym); John Owen, *Sin and Temptation: The Challenge to Personal Godliness*, ed. James M. Houston (Portland, Ore.: Multnomah, 1983), p. 135; James H. Smylie, "The Reformed Tradition," in *Caring and Curing: Health and Medicine in the Western Religious Traditions*, ed. Ronald L. Numbers and Darrel W. Amundsen (New York: Macmillan, 1986), pp. 211-13 (quoting Richard Baxter and the Westminster Catechism).

[21]Thomas J. Marzen et al., "Suicide: A Constitutional Right?" *Duquesne Law Review* 24 (1985): 32-33.

[22]John Bunyan, *The Pilgrim's Progress* (New York: Penguin, 1987), pp. 164-66.

[23]Brother Lawrence, *The Practice of the Presence of God* (Old Tappan, N.J.: Spire, 1985), pp. 55-56.

[24]Francis Bacon, *De Augmentis Scientiarum,* in *The Philosophical Works of Francis Bacon,* ed. J. M. Robertson, trans. R. L. Ellis and J. Spedding, reprint ed. (Freeport, N.Y.: Books for Libraries, 1970), p. 487.

[25]Gregory IX *Decretales* 1.14.7.

[26]Benedict XIV *De Synodo Diocesana Libri Tredecim* 1.13.10.

[27]Marzen et al., "Suicide," pp. 33-34.

[28]Immanuel Kant, *Fundamental Principles of the Metaphysics of Morals,* trans. T. Abbott (New York: Liberal Arts Press, 1964), pp. 39-40, 46; Immanuel Kant, *Lectures on Ethics,* trans. L. Infield (New York: Harper & Row, 1963), p. 153.

[29]Voltaire, quoted in Marzen et al., "Suicide," p. 38.

[30]David Hume, "On Suicide," in *Ethical Issues in Death and Dying,* ed. Tom L. Beauchamp and Seymour Perlins (Englewood Cliffs, N.J.: Prentice-Hall, 1978), pp. 107, 109-10.

[31]John Locke, *The Second Treatise of Government,* ed. J. W. Gough (London: Blackwell, 1946), pp. 4-5, 14.

[32]John Wesley, "Thoughts on Suicide," in *Works of John Wesley,* 14 vols. (Kansas City, Mo.: Nazarene Publishing House, 1952), 13:320.

[33]William Blackstone, *Commentaries on the Laws of England,* 4 vols. (London: Clarendon, 1765-1769), 4:189-90.

[34]Zephaniah Swift, quoted in S. F. C. Milsom, *Historical Foundations of the Common Law,* 2nd ed. (London: Butterworths, 1981), p. vi.

[35]Nathan Dane, *A General Abridgement and Digest of American Law,* 9 vols. (Boston: Cummings, Hilliard & Co., 1824), 7:208.

[36]Marzen et al., "Suicide," p. 40 (quotes from both commentator and Timothy Dwight and concludes that Dwight's view reflected the "general consensus").

[37]C. H. Spurgeon, *Autobiography,* vol. 2, *The Full Harvest, 1860-1892* (Edinburgh: Banner of Truth, 1973), pp. 410-14. See also Darrel W. Amundsen, "The Anguish and Agonies of Charles Spurgeon," *Christian History* 10 (1991): 22-25.

[38]A. A. Hodge, *Popular Lectures on Theological Themes* (Philadelphia: Presbyterian Board, 1887), p. 109.

[39]*Commonwealth* v. *Bowen,* 13 Mass. 356 (1816).

[40]*Commonwealth* v. *Hicks,* 118 Ky. 637, 642, 82 S.W. 265, 266 (1904).

[41]*Blackburn* v. *State,* 23 Ohio St. 162-63 (1872).

[42]See Marzen et al., "Suicide," p. 78.

[43]*Blackburn* v. *State,* 23 Ohio St. at 163.

[44]"Get Jury for Slayer of Child-Woman," *New York Times,* November 7, 1925, p. 3.

[45]Edward J. Larson, *Sex, Race and Science: Eugenics in the Deep South* (Baltimore: Johns Hopkins University Press, 1995), pp. 52, 146-54.

[46]Charles P. Curtis, *It's Your Law* (Cambridge: Harvard University Press, 1954), p. 95.

[47]"Something Less Than Murder," *New York Times,* November 9, 1925, p. 14.

[48]See Yale Kamisar, "Some Non-religious Views Against Proposed 'Mercy-Killing' Legislation," *Minnesota Law Review* 42 (1958): 972 n. 17.

[49]*House of Lords Debates* 169, 5th ser. (London: His Majesty's Stationery, 1950), pp. 575-76.

[50]Joseph Fletcher, *Morals and Medicine: The Moral Problems of the Patient's Right to Know the Truth, Contraception, Artificial Insemination, Sterilization, Euthanasia* (Princeton, N.J.: Princeton University Press, 1954), pp. 172-73; Joseph Fletcher, *Humanhood: Essays in Biomedical Ethics* (New York: Prometheus, 1979), pp. 16, 151-52.

[51]Karl Barth, *Church Dogmatics*, ed. and trans. G. W. Bromiley and T. F. Torrance, 5 vols. in 14 vols. (Edinburgh: T & T Clark, 1956-1977), 3/4:404-13.

[52]American Law Institute, "Model Penal Code" (tentative draft 9, 1959), pp. 56-57.

[53]Kamisar, "Some Non-religious Views," p. 970 n. 5.

[54]*Model Penal Code* sec. 201.5, cmt. 5 (1962).

[55]Kamisar, "Some Non-religious Views," pp. 974-77.

Chapter 7: The Right-to-Die Movement

[1]*In re Quinlan*, 70 N.J. 10, 355 A.2d 647 (1976), *cert. denied sub nom. Garger* v. *New Jersey*, 429 U.S. 922 (1976).

[2]Paul Ramsey, *Ethics at the Edge of Life: Medical and Legal Intersections* (New Haven, Conn.: Yale University Press, 1978), pp. 293-94.

[3]Lowell O. Erdahl, *Pro-Life/Pro-Peace: Life-Affirming Alternatives to Abortion, War, Mercy Killing and the Death Penalty* (Minneapolis: Augsburg, 1986), p. 105.

[4]Robert D. Orr, "Get It in Writing," *Christianity Today*, April 6, 1992, p. 25.

[5]Joanne Lynn, quoted in Leon Jaroff, "Knowing When to Stop," *Time*, December 4, 1995. For a further discussion of the study see Susan Gilbert, "Doctors Often Fail to Heed Wishes of the Dying Patient," *New York Times*, November 22, 1995, p. 1.

[6]Orr, "Get It in Writing," p. 25; Rob Roy MacGreagor, in Beth Spring and Ed Larson, *Euthanasia: Spiritual, Medical and Legal Issues in Terminal Health Care* (Portland, Ore.: Multnomah Press, 1988), pp. 26-27.

[7]James F. Freis, "Aging, Natural Death and the Compression of Morbidity," *New England Journal of Medicine* 303 (1980): 130-35; Bruce C. Vladeck, "End of Life Care," *Journal of the American Medical Association* 274 (1995): 449.

[8]For a discussion of the relationship between the doctrine of medical futility and patient autonomy, see Tom Tomlinson and Diane Czlonka, "Futility and Hospital Policy," *Hastings Center Report*, May-June 1995, pp. 28-36; Mary A. Crossley, "Medical Futility and Disability Discrimination," *Iowa Law Review* 81 (1995): 179-259. The quotes are from Nat Hentoff, "When a Hospital Goes to Court to End a Life," *Washington Post*, 28 Sept. 1991, p. A-21.

[9]Alexander Morgan Capron, "Abandoning a Waning Life," *Hastings Center Report*, July-August 1995, p. 24.

[10]Judith Wilson Ross and William J. Winslade, *Choosing Life or Death: A Guide for Patients, Families and Professionals* (New York: Free Press, 1986), pp. 12-13; Howard H. Hiatt, *America's Health in the Balance: Choice or Chance?* (New York:

Harper & Row, 1987), pp. 3-6; Richard Benedetto, "Medicare Needs an Injection—of Your Money," *USA Today*, November 19, 1996, p. 2A.

[11]Vladeck, "End-of Life Care," p. 449; and Jaroff, "Knowing When to Stop," p. 76.

[12]Richard A. Lamm quoted in "Gov. Lamm Asserts Elderly, if Very Ill, Have 'Duty to Die,'" *New York Times*, March 29, 1984, p. A-16.

[13]E.g., William A. Hensel, "My Living Will," *Journal of the American Medical Association* 275 (1996): 588.

[14]Ross and Winslade, *Choosing Life or Death*, pp. 20-21.

[15]C. Everett Koop, "The End Is Not the End," *Christianity Today*, March 6, 1987, p. 18.

[16]Paul Ramsey, quoted in Spring and Larson, *Euthansia*, pp. 99-101; and authors' interview of Paul Ramsey, August 14, 1987.

[17]Edith Schaeffer, *Forever Music* (Nashville: Nelson, 1968), pp. 62-63.

[18]Shirley Du Boulay, *Cicely Saunders: The Founder of the Modern Hospice Movement* (London: Hodder & Stoughton, 1984), pp. 155-71.

[19]Vladeck, "End of Life Care," p. 449; Spring and Larson, *Euthanasia*, pp. 173-93.

[20]Sidney Hook, "In Defense of Voluntary Euthanasia," *New York Times*, March 1, 1987, sec. 4, p. 25; and authors' interview of Sidney Hook, August 14, 1987.

[21]Joseph J. Piccione, *Last Rights: Treatment and Care Issues in Medical Ethics* (Washington, D.C.: Free Congress Foundation, 1985), p. 45; Nancy Gibbs, "Love and Let Die," *Time*, March 19, 1990, pp. 64, 68; John Pickering, "Don't Prolong Life Needlessly," *Fulton County (Georgia) Daily Report*, November 13, 1989, p. 14.

[22]Gibbs, "Love and Let Die," p. 65.

[23]*In re Quinlan*, 355 A.2d at 644.

[24]C. Everett Koop and Edward R. Grant, "The 'Small Beginnings' of Euthanasia: Examining the Erosion in Legal Prohibitions Against Mercy Killing," *Notre Dame Journal of Law, Ethics & Public Policy* 2 (1986): 606; Paul Ramsey, *Ethics on the Edges of Life: Medical and Legal Intersections* (New Haven, Conn.: Yale University Press, 1978), p. 329; Paul Ramsey, quoted in Spring and Larson, *Euthanasia*, pp. 70-71, 156.

[25]Koop and Grant, "'Small Beginnings' of Euthanasia," p. 602.

[26]James Bopp Jr., "The Patient's Rights Act: A Comprehensive Approach," *National Right to Life News*, March 27, 1986, p. 11.

[27]Gary A. Sachs, "Increasing the Prevalence of Advance Care Planning," *Hastings Center Report*, November-December 1994, p. S14; Joan M. Teno et al., "Advance Care Planning: Priorities for Ethical and Empirical Research," *Hastings Center Report*, November-December 1994, p. S33 (quote); Edward J. Larson and Thomas A. Eaton, "The Limits of Advance Directives: A History and Assessment of the Patient-Self Determination Act," *Wake Forest Law Review* 32 (1997): 249-93.

[28]Uniform Health-Care Decisions Act, secs. 2, 4, 5 (1993).

[29]Ibid., at sec. 5(f).

[30]*In re Storar,* 52 N.Y.2d 363, 420 N.E.2d 62, 438 N.Y.S.2d 266, *cert. denied* 454 U.S. 858 (1981).

[31]*In re Conroy,* 98 N.J. 321, 486 A.2d 1209, 1217, 1232 (1985).

[32]*Cruzan* v. *Harmon,* 760 S.W.2d 408, 425 (Mo. 1988).

[33]*Cruzan* v. *Director, Missouri Department of Health,* 497 U.S. 261, 284-86 (1990).

[34]Ibid., at 279 and 281.

[35]"Doing Justice to Life," *New York Times,* June 27, 1990, p. A18.

Chapter 8: From the Right to Die to the Right to Be Killed

[1]*Compassion in Dying* v. *Washington,* 850 F.Supp. 1454, 1456 (W.D.Wash. 1994).

[2]*Compassion in Dying* v. *Washington,* 79 F.3d 790 (9th Cir. 1996); *Quill* v. *Vacco,* 80 F.3d 716 (2d Cir. 1996).

[3]Yale Kamisar, "Against Assisted Suicide—Even a Very Limited Form," *University of Detroit Mercy Law Review* 72 (1995): 745; *People* v. *Kevorkian,* 527 N.W.2d 714, 736 (Mich. 1994), *cert. denied,* 115 S.Ct. 714 (1995).

[4]Yale Kamisar, "Physician-Assisted Suicide: The Last Bridge to Active Voluntary Euthanasia," in *Euthanasia Examined,* ed. John Keown (Cambridge: Cambridge University Press, 1995), pp. 230-31.

[5]Lawrence Gostin, "Drawing a Line Between Killing and Letting Die: The Law, and Law Reform, on Medically Assisted Dying," *Journal of Law, Medicine and Ethics* 94 (1993): 96.

[6]Kamisar, "Against Assisted Suicide," pp. 745-46; Herbert Hendin, "Selling Death and Dignity," *Hastings Center Report,* May-June 1995, p. 19.

[7]Yale Kamisar, "Some Non-religious Views Against Proposed 'Mercy-Killing' Legislation," *Minnesota Law Review* 42 (1958): 974-77.

[8]Cicely Saunders, "In Britain Fewer Conflicts of Conscience," *Hastings Center Report,* May-June 1995, p. 44.

[9]Kathleen Foley, "The Relationship of Pain and Symptom Management to Patient Requests for Physician-Assisted Suicide," *Journal of Pain and Symptom Management,* 1991, pp. 289-90.

[10]Sidney H. Wanzer et al., "The Physician's Responsibility Toward Hopelessly Ill Patients," *New England Journal of Medicine* 320 (1989): 847.

[11]Daniel Callahan, *The Troubled Dream of Life: Living with Mortality* (New York: Simon & Schuster, 1993), p. 102; Daniel Callahan and Margot White, "The Legalization of Physician-Assisted Suicide: Creating a Regulatory Potemkin Village," *University of Richmond Law Review* 30 (1996): 1-84; Hendin, "Selling Death," p. 23; Albert Jonsen, "To Help the Dying Die—A New Duty for Anesthesiologists?" *Anesthesiology* 78 (1993): 227.

[12]Yale Kamisar, "After Assisted Suicide, What Next?" *Legal Times,* May 30, 1994, p. 26.

[13]*Bouvia* v. *Superior Court,* 225 Cal.Repr. 297 (Cal. Ct. App. 1986).

[14]William A. Hensel, "My Living Will," *Journal of the American Medical Association* 275 (1996): 588.

[15]Franklin G. Miller et al., "Sounding Board: Regulating Physician-Assisted Death," *New England Journal of Medicine* 331 (1994): 119. See also Kamisar, "Physician-Assisted Suicide," pp. 231-33.

[16]Kamisar, "Physician-Assisted Suicide," p. 245.

[17]Coordinating Council of Life-Sustaining Medical Treatment Decision Making by the Courts, *Guidelines for State Court Decision Making in Life-Sustaining Medical Treatment Cases*, 2nd ed. (St. Paul, Minn.: West, 1993), p. 145.

[18]Hendin, "Selling Death," p. 19.

[19]Betty Rollin, *Last Wish* (New York: Linden, 1985), pp. 91-92, 149-50, 134-35.

[20]Beth Spring and Ed Larson, eds., *Euthanasia: Spiritual, Medical and Legal Issues in Terminal Health Care* (Portland, Ore.: Multnomah Press, 1988).

[21]Joseph J. Piccione, "You Die Your Way . . . ," *National Right to Life News*, September 26, 1985, p. 12.

[22]Quotes in this and the subsequent three paragraphs are from Lisa Belken, "There's No Simple Suicide," *New York Times Magazine*, November 14, 1993; and Hendin, "Selling Death," pp. 21-23.

[23]Quotes in this and the subsequent four paragraphs are from Derek Humphry, "The Case for Rational Suicide," *Euthanasia Review* 1 (1986): 173; Hendin, "Selling Death," p. 23; Derek Humphry, *Jean's Way: A Love Story* (Los Angeles: Hemlock, 1978); Derek Humphry, *Dying with Dignity: Understanding Euthanasia* (Secaucus, N.M.: Carol, 1992); Ann Wickett, *Double Exit: When Aging Couples Commit Suicide Together* (Los Angeles: Hemlock, 1988); Thomas W. Case, "A Requiem for the Hemlock Society," *Fidelity*, June 1990, pp. 24-32; "Hemlock Society: Built on a Myth?" *Christianity Today*, December 16, 1991, p. 51; "Group May Split over Right-to-Die," *USA Today*, June 2, 1995, p. 2.

[24]"Public Attitudes on the Legalization of Euthanasia," *Euthanasia Review* 1 (1986): 179; John A. Pridonoff, "Fear of Suffering Outweighs Death," *Insight*, August 29, 1994, p. 22; "Physician-Assisted Suicide," *USA Today*, November 19, 1996, p. 1A.

[25]James Vorenberg and Yale Kamisar, "The Limits of Mercy," *New York Times*, November 5, 1991; Edward J. Larson, "Making Washington the Los Vegas of Death," *Seattle Times*, November 1991, p. A12; Kim A. Lawton, "The Doctor as Executioner," *Christianity Today*, December 16, 1991, pp. 51-52.

[26]Hadley Arkes et al., "Always to Care, Never to Kill," *Wall Street Journal*, November 27, 1991, p. 11; Lawton, "Doctor as Executioner," p. 52.

[27]Lawton, "Doctor as Executioner," p. 50; Pridonoff, "Fear of Suffering," p. 22.

[28]Pridonoff, "Fear of Suffering," p. 22; Oregon Secretary of State, "Ballot Measure 19 with Explanatory Statements" (1994), secs. 3.01 – 3.03.

[29]Alexander Morgan Capron, "Sledding in Oregon," *Hastings Center Report*, November-December 1995: pp. 34-35; Sherwin Nuland, "The Debate over Dying," *USA Weekend*, February 3-5, 1995, p. 5.

[30]David Brown, "A Legal Exit from Terminal Illness," *Washington Post National Weekly Edition*, November 21-27, 1994, p. 32.

[31]Paul Cotton, "Medicine's Position Is Both Pivotal and Precarious in Assisted-

Suicide Debate," *Journal of the American Medical Association* 273 (1995): 363.

[32]Nuland, "Debate over Dying," p. 4; David A. Asch, "The Role of Critical Care Nurses in Euthanasia and Assisted Suicide," *New England Journal of Medicine* 334 (1996): 1374; Victor Cohn, "Is It Time for Mercy Killing?" *Washington Post*, August 15, 1989, p. 13 (Health); Brown, "Legal Exit from Terminal Illness," p. 32; Wanzer et al., "Physician's Responsibility," p. 848.

Chapter 9: Current Legal Issues in Physician-Assisted Suicide

[1]"It's Over, Debbie," *Journal of the American Medical Association* 259 (1988): 272.

[2]Isabel Wilkerson, "An Essay on Euthanasia," *Portland Oregonian*, February 29, 1988, p. A2.

[3]Yale Kamisar, "Against Assisted Suicide—Even a Very Limited Form," *University of Detroit Mercy Law Review* 72 (1995): 735.

[4]2 NY Rev. Stat. pt. 4, ch. 1, tit. 2, art. 1, sec. 7 at 661 (1829).

[5]Field Penal Code, secs. 229-32.

[6]Act of July 26, 1881, ch. 676, sec. 175, 3 1881 N.Y. Laws 42.

[7]Thomas J. Marzen et al., "Suicide: A Constitutional Right?" *Duquesne Law Review* 24 (1985): 78.

[8]Act of July 20, 1965, ch. 1030, sec. 125.15(3), 1965 N.Y. Laws at 2355.

[9]New York State Task Force on Life and the Law, *When Death Is Sought: Assisted Suicide and Euthanasia in the Medical Context* (New York: State Task Force on Life and the Law, 1994), pp. 142-46.

[10]Wash. Rev. Code sec. 9A.36.060 (1).

[11]1854 Wash. Laws p. 78, § 17.

[12]Oliver Wendell Holmes, *Collected Legal Papers* (New York: Harcourt, Brace & Howe, 1920), p. 187.

[13]1992 Wash. Laws, ch. 98, sec. 10.

[14]*Cruzan* v. *Director, Missouri Department of Health*, 495 U.S. 261, 278-79 (1991).

[15]*Compassion in Dying* v. *Washington*, 850 F.Supp. 1454, 1461 (W.D. Wash. 1994).

[16]*Compassion in Dying* v. *Washington*, 79 F.3d at 816.

[17]*Quill* v. *Vacco*, 80 F.3d at 723-24.

[18]*Griswold* v. *Connecticut*, 381 U.S. 479, 484 (1965).

[19]*Planned Parenthood* v. *Casey*, 505 U.S. at 847.

[20]Ibid., p. 851.

[21]Charles Colson, "Casey Strikes Out," *Christianity Today*, October 3, 1994, p. 104; John H. Robertson, "Physician-Assisted Suicide: Its Challenge to the Prevailing Constitutional Paradigm," *Notre Dame Journal of Law, Ethics and Public Policy* 9 (1995): 359.

[22]*Compassion in Dying* v. *Washington*, 850 F.Supp. at 1459, 1461.

[23]Ibid., p. 1459.

[24]*Compassion in Dying* v. *Washington*, 49 F.3d 586 (9th Cir. 1995).

[25]Ibid., pp. 813-14, 838.

[26]Ibid., p. 806 (quoting *Compassion in Dying* v. *Washington*, 49 F.3d 586, 591 [9th Cir. 1995]).

[27] Ibid., p. 808.

[28] Robert Barry, "The Development of the Roman Catholic Teachings on Suicide," *Notre Dame Journal of Law, Ethics and Public Policy* 9 (1995): 467.

[29] *Compassion in Dying* v. *Washington,* 79 F.3d at 808.

[30] Ibid., p. 808 n. 25.

[31] *Moore* v. *City of East Cleveland,* 431 U.S. 494, 503 (1977); see also *Griswold* v. *Connecticut,* 381 U.S. 479, 506 (1965) (White, J., concurring).

[32] *Compassion in Dying* v. *Washington,* 79 F.3d at 819.

[33] David C. Clark, " 'Rational' Suicide and People with Terminal Conditions or Disabilities," *Issues in Law and Medicine* 8 (1992): 147-53.

[34] Yeates Conwell and Eric D. Caine, "Rational Suicide and the Right to Die: Reality and Myth," *New England Journal of Medicine* 325 (1991): 1100-1102.

[35] *Compassion in Dying* v. *Washington,* 850 F.Supp. at 1464-65.

[36] *Compassion in Dying* v. *Washington,* 79 F.3d at 816.

[37] Ibid., p. 831.

[38] "Behind a Boy's Decision to Forgo Treatment," *New York Times,* June 13, 1994, p. A12.

[39] *Compassion in Dying* v. *Washington,* 79 F.3d at 831.

[40] *Griswold* v. *Connecticut,* 381 U.S. 479 (1965); *Eisenstadt* v. *Baird,* 405 U.S. 438 (1972).

[41] *Compassion in Dying* v. *Washington,* 79 F.3d at 818.

[42] A committee of leading physicians in this field suggested that there is little risk of prosecution in such cases. Sidney H. Wanzer et al., "The Physician's Responsibility Toward Hopelessly Ill Patients," *New England Journal of Medicine* 320 (1989): 847.

[43] Ibid., pp. 825-26.

[44] Yale Kamisar, "Are Laws Against Assisted Suicide Unconstitutional?" *Hastings Center Report,* May-June 1993, p. 39; George Colt, *The Enigma of Suicide* (New York: Summit, 1991), pp. 342, 394 (includes Boldt quote); and Sissela Bok, "Euthanasia and the Care of the Dying," in *The Dilemma of Euthanasia,* ed. John A. Behnke and Sissela Bok (Garden City, N.Y.: Anchor Press, 1975), pp. 8-9 (these risks may be limited to physician-assisted suicide, as Bok notes in this article, but are the same if physician-assisted suicide leads to euthanasia).

[45] Hastings Center, *Guidelines on the Termination of Life-Sustaining Treatment and the Care of the Dying* (Bloomington, Ind.: Indiana University Press, 1987), pp. 78-84, 129. See also Bok, "Euthanasia," p. 9.

[46] *Quill* v. *Vacco,* 80 F.3d at 727.

[47] Ibid., p. 729.

[48] American Medical Association Council on Ethical and Judicial Affairs, *Code of Medical Ethics Reports* 5 (1994): 269-74.

[49] "Conclusions of a British Medical Association Review of Guidelines on Euthanasia," in *Euthanasia: The Moral Issues,* ed. Robert M. Baird and Stuart E. Rosenbaum (Buffalo, N.Y.: Prometheus Books, 1989), p. 115.

[50] Hastings Center, *Guidelines,* pp. 128-29.

[51]Michael M. Uhlmann, "The Legal Logic of Euthanasia," *First Things*, June/July 1996, p. 42; and Yale Kamisar, "Physician-Assisted Suicide: The Last Bridge to Active Voluntary Euthanasia," in *Euthanasia Examined*, ed. John Keown (Cambridge: Cambridge University Press, 1996), p. 250 (emphasis in original).

[52]Willard Gaylin et al., "Doctors Must Not Kill," *Journal of the American Medical Association* 259 (1986): 2139.

[53]*Quill v. Vacco*, 80 F.3d at 729.

[54]Hastings Center, *Guidelines*, p. 6.

Chapter 10: Euthanasia Practices Today

[1]Timothy E. Quill et al., "Care of the Hopelessly Ill—Proposed Clinical Criteria for Physician-Assisted Suicide," *New England Journal of Medicine* 327 (1992): 1381; Daniel Callahan and Margot White, "The Legalization of Physician-Assisted Suicide: Creating a Regulatory Potemkin Village," *University of Richmond Law Review* 30 (1996): 1-84; Timothy Quill, *Death and Dignity: Making Choices and Taking Charge* (New York: Norton, 1994), p. 137; Franklin G. Miller et al., "Regulating Physician-Assisted Death," *New England Journal of Medicine* 331 (1994): 120.

[2]Derek Humphry, *Dying with Dignity: Understanding Euthanasia* (Secaucus, N.J.: Carol, 1992), pp. 102, 159.

[3]R. M. Dworkin, *Life's Dominion: An Argument About Abortion, Euthanasia and Individual Freedom* (New York: Knopf, 1993), p. 3.

[4]Andrew D. Firlik, "Margo's Logo," *Journal of the American Medical Association* 265 (1991): 201.

[5]Dworkin, *Life's Dominion*, pp. 201-32.

[6]Peter J. Bernardi, "Dr. Death's Dreadful Sermon," *Christianity Today*, August 15, 1994, p. 31.

[7]Robert A. Sedler, "Are Absolute Bans on Assisted Suicide Constitutional? I Say No," *University of Detroit Mercy Law Review* 4 (1995): 728.

[8]"Jack Kevorkian," *60 Minutes: Transcript for May 19, 1996* (Livingston, N.J.: Burrelle's Information Service, 1996), pp. 15, 18.

[9]Herbert Hendin, *Seduced by Death: Doctors, Patients and the Dutch Cure* (New York: Norton, 1997), pp. 31-32.

[10]"Jack Kevorkian," p. 18.

[11]Ibid.

[12]Richard Epstein and Yale Kamisar, "Pondering the Kevorkian Question," *Chicago Tribune*, May 6, 1994, p. A-15.

[13]"Jack Kevorkian," pp. 16, 21.

[14]Ibid., p. 19; Jack Lessenberry, "Kevorkian Wins Acquittal Again: 'Jury Saved Me,' " *Seattle Post-Intellegencer,* May 15, 1996, p. 2.

[15]John Hughes, "Coroner Sees No Fatal Illness in Latest Kevorkian Suicide," *Seattle Post-Intellegencer,* August 20, 1996, p. 2; "Which Is a Terminal Disease," *Newsweek,* September 2, 1996, p. 9; "Jack Kevorkian," pp. 18, 21.

[16]Epstein and Kamisar, "Pondering Kevorkian," p. A-15. See also John A.

Prindonoff, "Fear of Suffering Outweighs Death," *Insight,* August 29, 1994, p. 21, in which a Hemlock Society leader endorsed the practices in the Netherlands over those by Kevorkian.

[17] See Hendin, *Seduced by Death,* pp. 135-45 (Hendin cites various commentators).

[18] H. J. J. Leenen, "Euthanasia, Assistance to Suicide and the Law: Developments in the Netherlands," *Health Policy* 8 (1987): 200.

[19] H. R. G. Feber, "The Vicissitudes of Article 293 of the Penal Code from 1981 to the Present," trans. Walter Lagerway, *Issues in Law and Medicine* 3 (1988): 458.

[20] Gerrit van der Wal et al., "Euthanasia, Physician-Assisted Suicide and Other Medical Practices Involving the End of Life in the Netherlands," *New England Journal of Medicine* 335 (1996): 1699-1705.

[21] John Keown, "Euthanasia in the Netherlands: Sliding Down the Slippery Slope," *Notre Dame Journal of Law, Ethics and Public Policy* 9 (1995): 438; P. J. van der Maas et al., "Euthanasia and Other Medical Decisions Concerning the End of Life," *Health Policy* 22 (199): 72, 178-82 (English translation of the official survey); Carlos F. Gomez, *Regulating Death: Euthanasia and the Case of the Netherlands* (New York: Free Press, 1991), p. 53.

[22] Van der Mass et al., "Euthanasia," pp. 61-66.

[23] Ibid.; Leigh B. Middleditch Jr. and Joel H. Trotter, "The Dying Game," *Experience,* Fall 1995, p. 19; Keown, "Euthanasia," pp. 427, 440, 444; Hendin, *Seduced by Death,* p. 93; Herbert Hendin et al., "Physician-Assisted Suicide and Euthanasia in the Netherlands," *Journal of the American Medical Association* 277 (1997): 1722.

[24] Van der Mass et al., "Euthanasia," p. 45.

[25] Anastasia Toufexis, "Killing the Psychic Pain," *Time,* July 4, 1994, p. 61; and Herbert Hendin, "Seduced by Death: Doctors, Patients and the Dutch Cure," *Issues in Law and Medicine* 10 (1994): 155.

[26] Van der Maas et al., "Euthanasia," p. 40; Ilinka Haverkate and Gerrit van der Wal, "Policies of Medical Decisions Concerning the End of Life in Dutch Health Care Institutions," *Journal of the American Medical Association* 275 (1996): 437; Middleditch and Trotter, "Dying Game," p. 19.

[27] Daniel Callahan, *The Troubled Dream of Life: Living with Mortality* (New York: Simon & Schuster, 1993), p. 115; Keown, "Euthanasia," p. 444; *Physician-Assisted Suicide and Euthanasia in the Netherlands,* Report of the Chairman to Subcommittee on the Constitution, House Committee on the Judiciary, 104th Congress, 2d Session (Comm. Print 1996), p. 19; Henk A. M. J. ten Have and Jos V. M. Welie, "Euthanasia: Normal Medical Practice?" *Hastings Center Report,* March-April 1992, p. 38.

[28] Quotations in this and the subsequent three paragraphs are from Herbert Hendin, "Selling Death and Dignity," *Hastings Center Report,* May-June 1995, pp. 20-21.

[29] Gomez, *Regulating Death,* pp. 65-89 (reprinted case studes from pp. 73-75, 77-79, 83-84, 85-89).

Conclusion: The Road Home

[1] *Washington* v. *Glucksberg*, U.S. Supreme Court, 117 S.Ct. 2258, 2268-75 (1997).

[2] *Vacco* v. *Quill*, U.S. Supreme Court, 117 S.Ct. 2293, 2298 (1997).

[3] Ibid., at 2302.

[4] *Washington* v. *Glucksberg*, at 2275.

[5] *Washington* v. *Glucksberg*, 117 S.Ct. 2302, 2311-12 (Breyer, J., concurring).

[6] Ibid., at 2303 (O'Connor, J., concurring).

[7] Ibid., at 2308-09 (Stevens, J., concurring).

[8] *Washington* v. *Glucksberg*, 117 S.Ct. at 2289-92 (Souter, J., concurring).

[9] *Washington* v. *Glucksberg*, 117 S.Ct. at 2303 (O'Connor, J., concurring).

[10] Ibid., at 2310 (Stevens, J., concurring).

[11] *Washington* v. *Glucksberg*, 117 S.Ct. at 2293 (Souter, J., concurring).

[12] Janny Scott, "An Issue That Won't Die," *New York Times*, June 27, 1997, p. A1.

[13] *Washington* v. *Glucksberg*, 117 S.Ct. at 2303 (O'Connor, J., concurring).

[14] Ibid., at 2314 (Breyer, J., concurring).

[15] Ezekiel J. Emanuel, "The Painful Truth About Euthanasia," *The Wall Street Journal*, January 7, 1997, p. A-16; Joanne Lynn quoted in Gary L. Thomas, "Deadly Compassion," *Christianity Today*, June 16, 1997, p. 21.

[16] Joan Stephenson, "Experts Say AIDS Pain Dramatically Undertreated," *Journal of the American Medical Association* 276 (1996): 1369.

[17] Herbert Hendin, *Seduced by Death: Doctors, Patients and the Dutch Cure* (New York: Norton, 1997), pp. 204, 211; Thomas, "Deadly Compassion," p. 17.

[18] Hendin, *Seduced by Death*, p. 203; Thomas, "Deadly Compassion," p. 21; M. Scott Peck, "Living Is the Mystery," *Newsweek*, March 10, 1997, p. 18.

[19] *Washington* v. *Glucksberg*, 117 S.Ct. at 2303 (O'Connor, J., concurring).

[20] *Vacco* v. *Quill*, 117 S.Ct. at 2300-2302.

[21] Hendin, *Seduced by Death*, p. 199.

[22] *Washington* v. *Glucksberg*, 117 S.Ct. at 2272-73.

[23] Hendin, *Seduced by Death*, pp. 210-11.

[24] Ibid., p. 130; Thomas, "Deadly Compassion," pp. 20-21.

[25] Diane Komp, "Life Wish," *Christianity Today*, March 3, 1997, p. 21; Thomas, "Deadly Compassion," p. 21; New York State Task Force on Life and the Law, *When Death Is Sought: Assisted Suicide and Euthanasia in the Medical Context* (New York: State Task Force on Life and the Law, 1994), pp. 13-22, 126-28; Peck, "Living Is the Mystery," p. 18.

[26] Letter from Joanne Lynn to editor, *New England Journal of Medicine* 321 (1989): 119; Daniel Callahan, "When Self-Determination Runs Amok," *Hastings Center Report*, March-April 1992, pp. 52-55.

Name & Subject Index

—